# Research in Peace and Reconciliation

Edited by
Martin Leiner and Francesco Ferrari

in co-operation with
Benoît Bourgine (Louvain-la-Neuve),
François Dermange (Genève), Dennis Doyle (Dayton/Ohio),
Matthias Gockel (Jena), Makoto Mizutani (Kyoto),
Arie Nadler (Tel Aviv), Bertram Schmitz (Jena)
and David Tombs (Belfast/Dublin)

Volume 7

Francesco Ferrari / Martin Leiner / Zeina M. Barakat /
Michael Sternberg / Boaz Hameiri (eds.)

# Encountering the Suffering
# of the Other

Reconciliation Studies amid
the Israeli-Palestinian Conflict

Vandenhoeck & Ruprecht

Printed with the kind support of the Deutsche Forschungsgemeinschaft, Bonn.

Bibliographic information published by the Deutsche Nationalbibliothek
The Deutsche Nationalbibliothek lists this publication in the Deutsche Nationalbibliografie;
detailed bibliographic data available online: https://dnb.de.

© 2023 by Vandenhoeck & Ruprecht, Robert-Bosch-Breite 10, 37079 Göttingen, Germany,
an imprint of the Brill-Group (Koninklijke Brill NV, Leiden, The Netherlands; Brill USA Inc.,
Boston MA, USA; Brill Asia Pte Ltd, Singapore; Brill Deutschland GmbH, Paderborn, Germany,
Brill Österreich GmbH, Vienna, Austria)
Koninklijke Brill NV incorporates the imprints Brill, Brill Nijhoff, Brill Hotei, Brill Schöningh,
BrillFink, Brill mentis, Vandenhoeck & Ruprecht, Böhlau, Verlag Antike, V&R unipress and
Wageningen Academic.
All rights reserved. No part of this work may be reproduced or utilized in any form or by any
means, electronic or mechanical, including photocopying, recording, or any information storage
and retrieval system, without prior written permission from the publisher.

Cover image: © Auschwitz Birkenau – L'ingresso di Birkenau (2008). Source: Giomodica,
https://commons.wikimedia.org/wiki/File:Auschwitz_Birkenau_-_L%27ingresso_
di_Birken-au_-_panoramio.jpg

Cover design: SchwabScantechnik, Göttingen
Typesetting: le-tex publishing services, Leipzig
Printed and bound: ⊕ Hubert & Co. BuchPartner, Göttingen
Printed in the EU

**Vandenhoeck & Ruprecht Verlage** | www.vandenhoeck-ruprecht-verlage.com

ISSN 2198-820X
ISBN 978-3-525-56737-1

# Table of Contents

*Martin Leiner, Francesco Ferrari*
Encountering the Suffering of the Other. Introduction to the present volume .. 9

*Francesco Ferrari*
The Concept of Reconciliation after Auschwitz.
Hermeneutic Phenomenology of the Irrevocable ........................................ 27

*André Zempelburg*
Rabbinic Jewish Perspectives on Interpersonal Reconciliation and
the Reconciliation with Oneself in the Context of Yom Kippur ................... 45

*Zeina M. Barakat*
Reconciliation as Transformation from Extremism to Moderation.
The Case of Palestine-Israel ...................................................................... 59

*Martin J. O'Malley*
Narratives and Justice in Reconciliation Research. An Applied
Ethics Perspective ................................................................................... 69

*Yoav Kapshuk*
Reconciliation in Peace Agreements? The Case Study of the
Israeli-Palestinian Peace Process ............................................................. 87

*Dina Dajani Daoudi*
Transitional Justice and Reconciliation in Intractable Conflicts.................... 103

*Rahav Gabay, Boaz Hameiri, Tammy Rubel-Lifschitz, Arie Nadler*
The Tendency for Interpersonal Victimhood. Conceptualization,
Cognitive and Behavioral Consequences, and Antecedents ....................... 115

*Tammy Rubel-Lifschitz, Rahav Gabay, Boaz Hameiri, Arie Nadler*
The Victimhood Oriented Leader. Tendency for Interpersonal
Victimhood among Powerholders............................................................. 127

*Boaz Hameiri, Rahav Gabay, Tammy Rubel-Lifschitz, Arie Nadler*
Victimhood Acknowledgment as a Vehicle to Promote Intergroup
Conciliatory Attitudes in the Context of Intergroup Conflict ....................... 139

*Anat Sarid, Anan Srour, Shifra Sagy*
Sense of National Coherence and Willingness to Reconcile.
The Case of the Israeli-Palestinian Conflict ............................................... 151

*Michael Sternberg, Shifra Sagy*
When Israeli Students Encounter Palestinian Narratives ........................... 165

*Efrat Zigenlaub, Shifra Sagy*
Learning the Narrative of the Other. What Type of Encounter is
More Effective?...................................................................................... 181

*Becky Leshem, Shifra Sagy*
Legitimization of the Other Narrative as a Mediator
of the Relationships Between National Honor, Dignity Perceptions,
and the Willingness to Reconcile. The Case of the Israeli-Palestinian Conflict .. 203

*Manar Faraj*
Palestinian Students introduced to the historical narrative of the
other. The role the intragroup Dialogue Encounters [Play] in Reconciliation... 221

*Sharón Benheim*
The Impact of Encountering the Other. A Long-Term Study of
Jordanian, Palestinian, and Israeli Participants in a Multicultural
Program at the Arava Institute for Environmental Studies.......................... 241

*Yael Ben David, Orly Idan*
Talking Politics. The Delimitation of the "Political" as a Gendered
Disciplinary. Mechanism in Intragroup Dialogue among Young Israelis........ 263

*Shiri Levinas*
Women in Conflict, Narratives from the Periphery. Stories of
Women Living in the Southern Periphery of Israel .................................... 279

*Iyad Muhsen Al Dajani*
Applied Ethics in Digital Humanities for Reconciliation Processes .............. 295

About the Editors .................................................................. 309

About the Authors ................................................................ 311

Martin Leiner, Francesco Ferrari

# Encountering the Suffering of the Other

## Introduction to the present volume

*Encountering the Suffering of the Other. Reconciliation Studies amid the Israeli-Palestinian Conflict* offers a collection of essays from team members of the DFG-funded project Hearts of *Flesh–Not Stone*: Does Meeting the "Suffering of the Other" Influence Reconciliation in the Middle of Conflict? (GZ: LE 1260/3–2). Research activities of the trilateral partners from Germany, Israel, and Palestine began on March 19, 2013, and continued until 31st August 2021. Led by the Friedrich-Schiller University Jena (Germany) and directed by the theologian and reconciliation scholar Martin Leiner, "Hearts of Flesh–Not Stone" comprised four cooperating teams: Ben-Gurion University of the Negev-team (Israel, leader: Prof. Dr. Shifra Sagy); Friedrich-Schiller University Jena-team (Germany, leader: Prof. Dr. Martin Leiner); Tel Aviv University-team (Israel, leader: Prof. Dr. Arie Nadler); Wasatia team (Palestinian, leader: Prof. Dr. Mohammed Dajani).

## 1. Initial questions and objective of the project "Hearts of Flesh–Not Stone"

To our knowledge, "Hearts of Flesh–Not Stone" is the first major international project in transdisciplinary reconciliation studies. It generated innovative research and fruitful new perspectives for reconciliation studies. It was guided by the following theoretical frameworks:

- Arie Nadler's "Needs-Based Model" of inter-group relations (Shnabel and Nadler 2008)
- Shifra Sagy's narrative-oriented "Action-Research" (Sagy 2020)
- Amélie Mummendey's "Ingroup-Projection Model" (Wenzel, Mummendey and Waldzus 2007), represented by her pupil and successor Thomas Kessler, member of the Jena-team
- Martin Leiner's Hölderlin Perspective of transdisciplinary reconciliation research (Flämig and Leiner 2012)
- Mohammed Dajani Daoudi's "Wasatia" concept of moderation in a challenging political climate (Dajani Daoudi 2009)

## 1.1 Three main hypotheses

"Hearts of Flesh–Not Stone" analyzed the effects of encountering the suffering of the opposing group (out-group), by investigating three main hypotheses:

1. Encountering the suffering of the out-group "other" can effectively counter widespread marginalization or even denial of such suffering in conflicting societies.

2. Encountering the suffering of the out-group can generate empathy and contribute to willingness to reconcile. "Hearts of Flesh–Not Stone" showed both potentials and limitations of empathy generation for addressing conflict contexts. Research findings reveal the need for identifying and clarifying conditions of conflict contexts within which empathetic relations are relevant and potentially impact willingness to reconcile. Interventions of "encountering the suffering of the other" can be effective. However, they require careful identification and controlling of a) contributing and limiting intervention conditions, b) the nature of empathy generated, and c) the potential of generated empathy to impact conflict-relevant conditions. Helpful approaches for understanding empathy dynamics include, for example, Tragedy Sensitive Truthfulness (TST) and Empowerment to Human and Sensitive Communication with the Enemy (ESC).

3. Contextual factors play a very important role in encountering the suffering of the out-group, and affect the willingness of groups to reconcile. "Hearts of Flesh–Not Stone" studied contextual factors relevant to empathy and willingness to reconcile.

## 1.2 Three different approaches

"Hearts of Flesh–Not Stone" primarily focused upon groups of Palestinians and Israelis. German and South African groups were studied for the purpose of comparison and control. The research was organized following three different approaches:

– A series of nine empirical field experiments named ESOs (from "Encountering the Suffering of the Other") took place. Sequentially numbered, "Hearts of Flesh–Not Stone" is referred to them as ESO1, ESO2, etc. till, ESO9. Their object has been the encounter of mixed-gender, mixed-region, and mixed-age Palestinians with the Holocaust (in Auschwitz and Buchenwald) and Israeli students with the Nakba by visiting sites of Palestinian displacement (in Ramle and refugee camps). These experiments were treated with methods from different disciplines (participant observation; questionnaires; semi-structured interviews; content analysis of texts, specifically letters).

– A series of laboratory experiments were conducted in Jena and Tel Aviv aiming at assessing the impact of "respect" on willingness to reconcile (Jena) (Nägler,

Harth, Kessler in prep.) and identifying a new personality construct in the Tendency for Interpersonal Victimhood (Tel Aviv) (Gabay, Hameiri, Rubel-Lifschitz and Nadler 2022). In laboratory experiments, some factors favorable to reconciliation could be studied in more detail. Respectful communication was one such factor. The distinctions of victimhood, victim identity and the so-called "competitive victimhood" to understand the needs and discourses of reconciliation better, as well as to critically examining diverse forms of acknowledgment of victim identity (Hameiri, Gabay, Rubel-Lifschitz and Nadler 2022; Rubel-Lifschitz, Gabay, Hameiri and Nadler 2022). Arie Nadler also further developed his Needs-Based Model during the time of the project's inception by replacing "empowerment" with "agency" as a need in the victim position (SimanTov-Nachieli, Shnabel & Nadler 2013).

- A series of academic qualification writings took place at the Friedrich-Schiller University Jena and at the Ben-Gurion University of the Negev. They have also been partly based on the "Hearts of Flesh–Not Stone" empirical research and implemented further methodologies and approaches, such as:
  - Netnography as content analysis in social media and on websites. In his examination of social media, Aldajani 2020 was able to show that netnography can be used for deliberative processes and to promote reconciliation.
  - Biographical research. Providing an account of the lifelong journey of the Jerusalem-born educator and peace activist Mohammed Dajani Daoudi from extremism to moderation, Barakat 2017 pointed out the key agents which caused such transformation in favor of reconciliation.
  - Textbook reform. Challenging one-sided historical narratives, Dajani 2019 highlighted ways to take further steps to promote reconciliation through schoolbooks.
  - Semi-structured interviews. Faraj 2022 addressed the question of Palestinian refugee women's identity by conducting interviews in a refugee camp and a village.
  - Narrative-oriented Action-Research. Researchers from Ben-Gurion University explored in different ways the contribution of meeting narratives of the other to foster reflexive learning in the context of a binational conflict:
    a. as intragroup dialogue, i. e., within one national group (Sternberg and Sagy 2022);
    b. comparing intra- and inter-group dialogue groups (Zigenlaub and Sagy 2022);
    c. analyzing long-term full-time residential programs, with participants from social groups in conflict (Benheim 2022).
- Gender studies. Practices that discipline the political discourse from a gender perspective were analyzed, demonstrating how emotionality can serve as a tool for resistance within the hegemonic male-dominated political sphere (Ben

David and Idan 2022), as well as to which extent gender roles are charged with new meanings and significances in societies that are involved in violent conflicts (Levinas 2022).

With reference to the processes that emerged during the ESOs and to key issues of reconciliation research, further qualification writings addressed topics such as:

– Reconciliation in Judaism. Zempelburg 2019 aimed to cover the meaning and major trends of the concepts of reconciliation and atonement within the Jewish tradition, starting in the days of Ancient Israel and ending in the early twenty-first century.
– The philosophical debate on reconciliation after Auschwitz. Ferrari 2022 dealt with the most important texts of Jewish philosophy of the mid-twentieth century on the issue. Given the many layers of the topic, his research adopted a transdisciplinary approach as a hermeneutic phenomenology through which the concept of reconciliation faced that of irrevocable. He previously presented this concept in Ferrari 2019.
– Assessing the role of justice, transitional justice, and peace processes in reconciliation. O'Malley 2022 introduced three derivative priority rules (of ethics, politics, and local) in the context of a justice definition for reconciliation, offering practical guidance for understanding and dealing with conflict and post-conflict transitions. Dajani 2022 also formulated critical insights on the interrelation between transitional justice and the role of reconciliation in intractable conflicts. Challenging the widespread assumption according which reconciliation is understood as a process or an aim to be achieved after or beyond formal peace processes between political leaderships, Kapshuk 2022 found that principles of reconciliation as crucial elements may be applied in formal agreements to end conflicts.
– National pride and willingness to reconcile. The correlation between the willingness to reconcile and variables such as "national honor" (Leshem and Sagy 2022) and "sense of national coherence" (Sarid, Srour and Sagy 2022) has also thematized by scholars from Ben-Gurion University.
– Empathy research. Further development of empathy research was also brought into the discussions in the project by the doctoral dissertation of Krauß 2020, supervised by Miriam Rose and Martin Leiner.

## 2. Development of the project "Hearts of Flesh – Not Stone"

"Hearts of Flesh–Not Stone" allowed transdisciplinary and multidirectional research to thrive. International conferences and workshops, such as *Alternative Approaches in Conflict Resolution* (Zürich, November 2015) and *Transitional Justice:*

*Contemporary Theories and Practices* (Jerusalem, September 2016), investigated the relationship between reconciliation research, conflict resolution, and transitional justice. These conferences provided the best opportunity to share the obtained results and exchange and implement fruitful feedback by the "Hearts of Flesh–Not Stone" teams. Relevant topics received important impulses for their further developments, such as empathy and emotions in conflict and reconciliation, research on trauma and loyalties, narratology, and general reconciliation theory. This was also made possible thanks to workshops and conferences held by international experts, with whom intensive cooperation has been initiated thanks to "Hearts of Flesh–Not Stone", such as: Björn Krondörfer; Eran Halperin; Pumla Gobodo-Madikizela; Christo Thesnaar; Dagmar Kusa; Boyd Blundell; Richard Kearney; Fanie du Toit.

The field experiments ESO1 to ESO9 were a series of encounter experiences beginning in 2014 of approximately 30 persons for each experience. These were conducted together with empirical analyses as planned in the DFG-supported project despite delays and complications from violence-impacted tensions in the Holy Land (especially in 2014), unrest due to the relocation of the American Embassy to Jerusalem (announced 2017, completed 2018), and, at the end of the project, the COVID-19 pandemic (since late 2019). The COVID-19 pandemic required the transformation of ESO9 from a face-to-face encounter between Israeli and Palestinian participants of the preceding ESO into an exchange in epistolary form. Except for ESO9, the ESOs organized by Ben-Gurion University took place without postponements between February 2015 and July 2018.

The interim evaluation after the first three years of "Hearts of Flesh–Not Stone" already considered the changes in the trips of Palestinians that were needed. The first Auschwitz trip (ESO1) had a worldwide and very positive press echo (Haaretz, New York Times, Washington Post, CNN, Wall Street Journal, Le Monde, La Repubblica, Die Zeit, Die Welt, etc.) as the first group trip from the West Bank visited Auschwitz organized by Palestinians. A very positive article about the trip was reported in Haaretz (by Matthew Kalman, March 28, 2014), but that account was erroneously maligned in the online Al Quds News website, claiming that the trip was funded by Zionist organizations instead of by the DFG. The project leader of the Palestinian group, Mohammed Dajani Daoudi, subsequently faced threats to his life and scholarly occupation. His office at Al Quds University and his library were vandalized, and a little later, his car was torched. Some of the students as well as some organizers of the project had to cope with mixed emotions and with pressure from their respective societies. All this showed a tragic reality inherent in reconciliation research: resistance to reconciliatory processes often comes from one's own in-group. As a result of these experiences, and in coordination with DFG officials, ESO field trips with Palestinian participants were postponed for a year and redesigned to provide safe and productive experiences. The intervention was designed to emphasize in-group experiences and avoid potential contact-intervention conditions. The destination was changed from Krakow and Auschwitz to an entirely German national context with visits to Berlin and Buchenwald instead of encountering Jewish historical suffering of the Holocaust. Also, Mohammed Dajani Daoudi transferred leadership of the field experiences to the coordinator of the Palestinian team, Zeina Barakat. The goal of modifying the study design was to optimize conditions for encountering the historical suffering of the outgroup "other".

Presenting the outcomes of "Hearts of Flesh–Not Stone" at the conference *Reparation, Recognition and Reconciliation* (November 2018), hosted by Stellenbosch University (South Africa), also was not possible. The attendance of "Hearts of Flesh–Not Stone" team members had to be canceled at the last minute because the boycott movement against Israeli scholars made participating impossible (Weinthal 2020). From the beginning, "Hearts of Flesh–Not Stone" was aware that conflict events would impact its development and the results of its field experiments and was prepared to adjust.

## 3.    Achievements of the project "Hearts of Flesh–Not Stone"

### 3.1    Visiting places of suffering of the opposing group

"Hearts of Flesh–Not Stone" assessed that visiting sites of memory by traveling to places where the suffering of the out-group can be experienced is of great importance in making reality and the extent of historical events clear. This is especially relevant when the reality and extent of the out-group's suffering are denied or downplayed. "Hearts of Flesh–Not Stone" recognized the participants as partners who both want to and are able to find out the truth themselves. A significant outcome of the ESOs included acknowledging the reality and extent of the suffering of the out-group by all participants, who then also integrated it into their worldview.

### 3.2    Inputs for theorizing reconciliation research

Field experiments on encountering the suffering of the out-group are of great importance for reconciliation research on the theory level. More and more scholars understand reconciliation as a long-term process. Reconciliatory acts such as confessions of guilt or expressions of forgiveness must be charted as moments on that long-process timeline. And this raises an important question for research: How can reconciliatory processes be optimally explored and profiled in terms of distinct developmental elements and stages?

"Hearts of Flesh–Not Stone" assessed Tragedy Sensitive Truthfulness (TST) and Empowerment for Human and Sensitive Communication with the Enemy (ESC) as two specific and interrelated stages that ought to be examined in more detail in their components through further research. For both TST and ESC, visiting sites of memory by traveling to places where the suffering of the out-group can be experienced is valuable. The strongest effect of traveling to such places is the recognition of the atrocities the out-group endured as fact-reality. These visits have lasting consequences on the worldview of the participants. They modify their emotional attitude toward the suffering of the out-group and lead to a reflective departure from one-sided nationalist narratives or even denial and the emotions associated with them.

"Hearts of Flesh–Not Stone" showed that attitudes of Tragic Sensitive Truthfulness and Empowerment for Human and Sensitive Communication with the Enemy can be reinforced by initiatives such as: participating in additional classes related to the topic; encountering personal testimonies and-or members of the opposing group who are willing to reconcile; viewing and commenting on artworks, documentaries, and films; discussing within spaces that encourage each participant's own development. In the midst of the Israeli-Palestinian conflict, this is probably the maximum that can be achieved for a larger number of people under the current conditions of spatial separation and incessant violence.

## 3.3    Tragedy Sensitive Truthfulness (TST) within Action-Research approach

Theorized by the Ben-Gurion University team of the "Hearts of Flesh–Not Stone" project, Tragedy Sensitive Truthfulness describes the shift away from nationalistic stereotypes toward a personal, complex view of the conflict – one that searches for truthfulness grasps the tragedy of the present situation and is open to the opposing group (Ben David et al. 2017; Sternberg, Litvak Hirsch and Sagy 2018). Tragedy Sensitive Truthfulness can be reached by integrating the now reflected narrative of the out-group into one's narrative. For this purpose, the approach of Historical Dialogue has also been integrated into reconciliation research. The goal of such dialogues is the emergence of a common narrative that includes and respects the opposing side. The participants of "Hearts of Flesh–Not Stone" were well prepared for this step.

The Action-Research approach, also adopted by the Ben-Gurion University team, pursued the goal of creating a space for the participants' own reflection during the ESOs. In the beginning, all participants were influenced by the fact that at school, in the army, and the media, they had learned nothing or very little about the Nakba and the suffering of the Palestinians. By encountering the suffering of the Palestinians, this narrative was challenged. "Exclamation points" became "question marks"; the overly clear nationalist narrative was replaced by a more complex multi-perspective perception of history that included the narratives of Palestinians and different groups of Israelis (e. g., Israelis who immigrated from North Africa and the Middle East and felt culturally closer to Palestinians).

The change was not solely cognitive but also emotional. Participants displayed emotions typical of grieving stages, such as denial of reality, sadness, aggression, and loneliness. Expressions of aggression were directed against the group leaders (Yael Ben David and Michael Sternberg), and also against other group members, the educational system, the media, and sometimes against themselves. As stimulated by the encounter with the suffering of the Palestinians and through the diversity in one's own group, the reflexive view did not lead to withdraw loyalty to one's group but a reflected loyalty. For example, one participant commented: "Without the Nakba, there would have been no state of Israel. The state of Israel is necessary for our survival. Nevertheless, the Nakba as injustice against Palestinians (and other injustices against them) should be redressed after so many decades."

Willingness to acknowledge the narrative of the out-group and to reconcile were further analyzed as (negatively) correlated with factors such as "national honor" (Leshem and Sagy 2022) and (positively) with "human dignity" and "sense of national coherence" (Sarid, Srour and Sagy 2022). In a comparative study, Telaku, Mana, Srour, and Sagy 2021 have also assessed and confirmed the positive correlations between willingness to reconcile and a sense of national coherence among Serbs and Albanians in Kosovo.

### 3.4 Empowerment for Human and Sensitive Communication with the Enemy (ESC)

Empowerment for Human and Sensitive Communication with the Enemy (Barakat et al. 2022), i. e., new possibilities of conversation between Palestinians and Israelis based on the common emotionally-anchored rejection of the Holocaust as a terrible and heinous crime against humanity, consistently took place in the "Hearts of Flesh–Not Stone" project, from the encounter between the two groups in Auschwitz (ESO1, Spring 2014) to their exchange of letters (ESO9, Spring 2021), as well as in private and professional encounters outside the project.

In the Palestinian groups, the encounter with the suffering of the Holocaust and its recognition as real and heinous led to new behaviors. By witnessing the historical evidence of the Holocaust's six million murdered Jews, all Palestinians who participated in the ESOs realized the incomparable suffering of Jews from that tragedy. Some came forward through articles and posts on social media to affirm the reality of the Holocaust and what they had experienced. In their responses to questionnaires, they often answered that they would recommend such trips and repeat them with friends. One participant of the first trip to Buchenwald (ESO 5) visited on his own initiative Sachsenhausen Concentration Camp with some

Palestinian friends during the following vacations. Almost all participants asked for additional trips of this kind.

Palestinian doctoral students visited Buchenwald several times with friends. These sites of memory become significant places for the participants of "Hearts of Flesh–Not Stone". Their meaning unfolded individually in each participant through reflection and empathy, often only over time. Those who continued to work more intensively on these experiences regularly showed empathy with the victims.

## 3.5   Contextual factors matter

In the midst of an existing conflict, "Hearts of Flesh–Not Stone" was able to determine to which extent traveling together to the places of the suffering of the out-group can have very different effects.

Contextual factors matter. Without preparation for the visiting group and trust building, the presence of out-group members within a field experience was disruptive to the encounter of the outgroup's historical suffering. During ESO1 in Auschwitz, for instance, some Palestinians felt observed and emotionally pressured by the presence of project members who were Israeli Jews. After the reaction to Al Quds news after ESO1 travel to Auschwitz, encounters with Israelis were not possible for security reasons. However, ESOs organized by the Ben-Gurion University team showed that encounters with singular members of the other group, who were emphatically conciliatory, could produce increased willingness to reconcile.

In the mixed travel to Auschwitz, reactions such as distrust (suspicion of "brainwashing"), reactance, competitive victimhood, or shifting to current political discussions interfered quite often with the experience of encountering the suffering of the other. Members of the group whose suffering was being addressed, were often overwhelmed by the memories of their in-group suffering. They therefore, appeared to be dismissive interlocutors for the out-group. Members of the visiting group may also be reminded of their own suffering. This was described (Barakat et. al. 2022) by a Palestinian participant who was reminded of her time in an Israeli prison during her visit to Auschwitz. When participants are massively thrown back on their own suffering, opening up to the suffering of others is very difficult. Here too, "Hearts of Flesh–Not Stone" made clear that participants on educational trips to places of suffering never enter such journeys as a *tabula rasa* but are always accompanied by their previous history.

## 3.6   Empathy and-or willingness to reconcile

Empathy (in the sense of taking victims' perspective), compassion (for example, expressed through tears or shock reactions), and sympathy with the victims could be observed in numerous participants through the ESOs-visits of places of suffering. Unsettling empathy (Krondörfer) or an empathy leading to forgiveness was not observed. Some affective response was universally observed – there was no observation of indifference or lack of emotion. One interesting common response from Palestinian participants emphasized that their in-group (Palestinians) was not to blame for the suffering of the out-group (Jews) caused by the Holocaust.

The average effect of increased empathy and willingness to reconcile as measured by questionnaires was not very high among Palestinians. Disruptive contextual factors were so strong during the first trip to Auschwitz (ESO1) that the questionnaires' scores for empathy and willingness to reconcile actually decreased. An important factor was the appearance of the above-described media report in Al Quds News (online) while the ESO1 was still taking place. The following onset of critical reactions from friends and family members demanded the participants loyalty towards Palestine and disassociation from Zionism.

Encounters with the suffering of the out-group also depend strongly on the context in which they take place. If reconciliation is socially desirable in one's own group and if there is hope for peace, it can be expected that such encounters give rise to this sequence:

a) Encounter with the suffering of the other → b) Empathy → c) Willingness to Reconcile

In "Hearts of Flesh–Not Stone," this sequence was statistically verifiable only in individual participants. Conversely, it is to be expected that in more violent conflicts filled with hatred or contempt, satisfaction with the suffering of the other group would also occur to a greater extent instead of empathy. We found small hints of this in only two participants, one of whom changed her mind during the project toward compassion for the victims of the Holocaust. The other participant was ideologically very strongly tied to the view of Hamas.

## 3.7  Unexpected loyalty-increase

The most paradoxical result of the "Hearts of Flesh–Not Stone" project was the increase in loyalty to one's own national narrative found among both Israelis and Palestinians during the ESOs. This desire was expressed externally to participants during the interventions of friends and relatives on the occasion of the Al Quds News article (ESO1) but also came very clearly from participants themselves during the visits to Buchenwald. During the bus ride to Buchenwald (ESO5), some participants unfurled Palestinian flags and sang Palestinian folklore, and held a minute's silence in remembrance of the Nakba. Only after acknowledging of their own group's suffering were, they open to talking about their Buchenwald experience.

This outcome is most easily explained by the fact that the readiness to encounter the out-group aroused a strong desire to express loyalty toward one's in-group.

Loyalty effects can be triggered simply by spending time abroad. Since these effects could also be measured among the Israelis at home, it seems that in important subgroups of one's in-group, it is socially undesirable (or not strongly desired) to feel empathy and willingness to reconcile with the out-group. This fact has a major influence on reinforcing loyalties to one's own group and its view of the conflict. In the case of the Israelis, their own national narrative was changed in the sense of Tragedy Sensitive Truthfulness as described above. A next step in the dialogue was explicitly achieved only among doctoral students from Palestine, namely that the tragedy-sensitive narrative of the Israelis was also adopted into their own Palestinian narrative, and empathic dialogue was considered. In addition, the desire to express loyalty among Palestinians was reinforced by the fact that they faced accusations of "normalization" from within their group.

## 3.8 Individual variables in dealing with incomprehensible atrocities

"Hearts of Flesh–Not Stone" confirmed that individual variables played a large role in enacting participants' emotional reactions. During the ESOs, it was very clearly observed that emotionally accessing incomprehensible suffering (of others) through the memory of one's own suffering is a widespread strategy. In our ESOs, this strategy was observed not only among Palestinians and Israelis who experienced each other's suffering by visiting their sites of memory, and among South Africans who visited Buchenwald with Christo Thesnaar and Francesco Ferrari and recalled their Apartheid-experiences (Leiner 2019).

This way of dealing with incomprehensible atrocities does not preclude and rather often allows visitors of sites of memory to see the suffering of the Jews during the Holocaust (as a group, and usually as individuals too) as greater and different than that of black South Africans or Palestinians. Encounters with the suffering of the out-group led to a heightened perception of the suffering of one's in-group. In Auschwitz, each group wanted to show the other that it was suffering and hoped for listening and recognition. In many discussions, the effects of being a victim were inextricably intertwined with victimhood as identity (Gabay et al., 2020; Hameiri et al., 2017).

A recurring comment among Palestinians who visited sites of the Holocaust was: "If the Jews experienced this terrible thing once, why are they doing to us know what they are doing to us?" This question was central in the letters between Palestinian participants and Israelis (ESO9). On a broader horizon, the question was asked whether the Holocaust has universal ethical meaning ("Never again for anyone!"), or group ethical meaning ("Never again against Jewish people!"). Another issue in both groups was the connection between those who suffered the

Holocaust and the Nakba and the suffering of Israelis and Palestinians of today. These differences (today's counterparts and victims of that time) allow for different emotional attitudes toward the victims (with whom empathy and compassion were felt in both cases) and toward today's members of the group (whose behavior is experienced as threatening and unjust on both sides). Palestinian participants articulated the continuing relevance of the Holocaust in their conflict with Israeli Jews. With the Holocaust as a reference point, Palestinian-Israeli engage in human and sensitive communication and inquiry, an experience that can benefit both groups. Jewish Israelis conversations with Palestinians benefited from a shared recognition of the Holocaust as a great, perhaps the greatest, human crime in history. This was a claim made publicly by President Mahmoud Abbas shortly after our ESO1 and most likely in reference to its highly publicized travel of Palestinian students to Auschwitz.

### 3.9 Identity-related resources and the role of recognition

The project also examined religious, cultural, and identity-related resources for willingness to reconcile, such as role models, family tradition, gender, condition as a refugee, etc. In several unexpected places, the importance of these resources was revealed to be very high. One doctoral student associated with the project brought her experience of having committed to be a suicide bomber in the First Intifada (1987) but changed her mind after a conversation with an imam. Another very religious Palestinian woman, whose brother had been kidnapped and murdered by an Israeli settler in 2014 as an act of revenge for an incident near Hebron, decided to participate in the first trip to Buchenwald (ESO5) and was confirmed in her religious view that she cannot have any desire for revenge against Israelis. In this area, there are great opportunities among Israelis and Palestinians to strengthen reconciliation. The avenues of the school system and social media could also lend themselves as ways to disseminate these resources (Dajani 2019; Aldajani 2020).

Further observations were made on intergenerational transmission of trauma and \multiple forms of recognition (of suffering, achievements, humanity, rights, and personal respect for all involved). ESO1, ESO 5, ESO7 (second travel to Buchenwald), and laboratory experiments conducted by Larissa Nägler in Jena were able to show that respect is an independent factor in the success of reconciliation processes. According to Gryglewsky 2013, the recognition of the Holocaust is particularly difficult when the suffering of the Palestinians has not been acknowledged beforehand. This study conducted simultaneously with the preparatory phase of "Hearts of Flesh–Not Stone" is in line with the outcomes of our project. Beyond it, "Hearts of Flesh–Not Stone" incorporated trauma, lack of hope for peace, and conflicts of loyalty more strongly as further explanations for the scarcity of willingness to reconcile.

## 3.10 Long-term effects

In addition to contextual factors, individual variables, and identity-related resources, an essential role for empathy and for the willingness to reconcile with the out-group is played by loyalty dynamics, by the tendency to defend and maintain one's own narrative, the social desirability of empathic and reconciliatory behavior, and by the existing hope or hopelessness with regard to a just, reconciled peace with the adversary. Far-reaching positions such as cooperation and willingness to reconcile can usually only be achieved if trust and hope are reinforced. They can only emerge in tandem with favorable contextual and individual variables.

Despite the numerous political confrontations during the project (Gaza wars, relocation of the American embassy to Jerusalem, numerous local experiences of violence), long-term effects were observed: the convictions that the suffering of the opposing group was real were very stable; the empathy with the victims and the self-reflective attitude towards one's own history were lasting experiences. Together with the desire awakened in numerous participants to know and find out for themselves and share these experiences, these are significant effects for a path toward further reconciliation in the Israeli-Palestinian conflict.

For any conflict context, the goal of reconciliation takes on characteristics of the conflict history. The Holocaust and Nakba tragedies and the histories since 1948 present historically and geographically unique elements, and thus, any reconciliation would be likewise unique. In a theoretical sense, a "thick reconciliation" would require public confessions of guilt, responsibility-taking, and requests for forgiveness, which would all be followed by the acceptance of confessions and the granting of forgiveness. Given the complexity of the Israeli-Palestinian context, it is hard to imagine how such a "thick reconciliation" could emerge, and certainly, the "Hearts of Flesh–Not Stone" project activities did not strive for such a result. O'Malley 2022 attempts to deal with conceptual questions relevant to reconciliation processes, such that realistic "justice" goals of non-violence and mutually beneficial social cooperation can break impasses of the perceived inconsistency of justice versus peace. Moreover, the approach of Tragedy Sensitive Truthfulness and Empowerment to Human-Sensitive Communication offers insight to promote processes of interaction whereby opposing groups can find their own paths toward a reconciliation recognizing historical traumas, value commitments, and potentials for shared futures.

In a conflict with strong power asymmetries, it is evident that a further process will emerge when the stronger side, according to traditional power aspects such as military and economic strength (Israel) will open up to critical self-reflection via Tragedy Sensitive Truthfulness and when the weaker side, according to the same traditional power aspects (Palestinian Territories) will receive Empowerment for Human Sensitive Communication.

## 4. Final Remarks

Reconciliation research began as a scholarly field in the 1990s. It is concerned with the question of how states, societies, organizations, groups, and individuals can come together again after serious incidents (Leiner, 2018). "Hearts of Flesh–Not Stone" was the first major interdisciplinary reconciliation research project in Germany, Israel, and the Palestinian Territories on this new field of studies.

"Hearts of Flesh–Not Stone" dealt with the issue in conflicts that the suffering of the out-group is often unknown or actively minimized and denied - an issue especially challenging for Israelis and Palestinians. Most Israelis know little about, or even deny, Palestinians' displacement from the Nakba (1948). For Palestinians, recognition of the Holocaust (1941–1945) is a topic often burdened with misinformation and denial. The "Hearts of Flesh–Not Stone" approach was based on the hope of encountering the suffering of the out-group through visits to the actual sites of memory like Auschwitz and Ramle. Such encounters required preparation through courses, workshops, attentive personal support, and debriefing afterward. All such project activities aimed to develop participants' reflective awareness of in-group and out-group narratives and the ways such narratives impact the conflict.

Without exception, all participants in the ESOs organized by the "Hearts of Flesh–Not Stone" project acknowledged the reality and extent of the suffering of the out-group. The biggest additional step towards reconciliation was that many Israelis developed a reflective attitude towards their own history, which can be described as a position of Tragedy Sensitive Truthfulness (TST). It manifested itself in statements such as: "The Jews need a state in order to be safe. But the state was founded on the land of the Palestinians, and as a result, new injustice has occurred". Among the Palestinians, a recurrent reaction was: "If the Jews experienced this terrible thing once, why are they doing to us now, what they are doing to us?" This position can be called Empowerment to Human Sensitive Communication with the Enemy (ESK). Both positions leave behind one-sided nationalist narratives and acknowledge the suffering of others. Both positions play a major role in the beginning of reconciliation processes, even before apologies in each other occur.

"Hearts of Flesh–Not Stone" showed surprising characteristics in its ESOs, such as increased loyalty to one's in-group and the development of a reflexive narrative. Whereby feelings of empathy, sympathy, and decreased fear toward the opposing group were noted, however, further processes toward reconciliation are blocked by contextual factors, such as the lack of a political partner that would convey trust and of a situation that would convey hope. Emotional effects were not as large, nor did they lead as clearly toward the willingness to reconcile as hypothesized at the beginning of the project. Reflexive recognition of reality led a relatively large proportion of participants to share their findings beyond the experiment and to want to find out more themselves.

In addition to the field experiments, laboratory experiments in Jena and Tel Aviv investigated the positive influence of respect on willingness to reconcile, agency as a basic need of victims, and the distinction between victimhood and victim identity. "Hearts of Flesh–Not Stone" made further studies possible as well, which have examined: the centrality of Auschwitz for the concept of reconciliation; the importance of religious and social resources for reconciliation; the particular experience of Palestinian refugee women, and their view of reconciliation and martyrdom; the importance of textbooks in transmitting images of the enemy; the possibilities of using social media to promote reconciliation. All these studies contribute to a better understanding of the field experiments.

The "Hearts of Flesh–Not Stone" project was invaluable for the still young research direction of reconciliation studies, It has developed a very efficient transdisciplinary approach to overcome Holocaust and Nakba denial. The most important project result is the description of reconciliation as a long-term process in which trust, forgiveness, and recognition of the truth, including the guilt (culpability) of one's in-group, are often not achieved directly. As formulated by Israeli participants in the project, a tragedy-sensitive perception of the Israeli-Palestinian conflict is an essential step toward improving relations.

"Hearts of Flesh–Not Stone" interventions provide insights relevant to other reconciliation processes, especially those where contested traumatic histories are relevant. Organized site visits or trips to sites of memory and places of suffering (Holocaust, Nakba) of the out-group, perhaps considered hostile, can also benefit from project results and experiences.

The scientific reconciliation research conducted in "Hearts of Flesh–Not Stone" is also economically relevant for peace-, encounter- and history projects carried out by governmental and non-governmental institutions. This applies to projects in contexts outside the Israel-Palestine conflict and in relation to other experiences of suffering than the Holocaust and the Nakba. The relatively large sums invested in such projects are still matched by a relatively low level of scientific evaluations of the respective interventions. There is often criticism of such projects (see: Engstrom 2009), but there is also a lack of empirical studies working with an appropriate variety of methods.

Although the results of "Hearts of Flesh–Not Stone" are commercially relevant, they are made available to the public as open access by parties involved in the project. Further studies can be initiated at numerous points. The two positions of Tragedy Sensitive Truthfulness and Empowerment to Human Sensitive Communication with the Opponent should be researched more closely. They are often at the beginning of reconciliatory processes and are also specific to how people deal with war experiences.

In addition, the significance of different forms of recognition for reconciliation processes is still a broad field that needs to be investigated in a much more differentiated way. What is the significance of the recognition of facts and-or narratives? What is the recognition of persons? For what and what do people in conflicts want to be recognized? For their suffering as victims? For their humanity? As persons who have rights? Or for a combination of all of the above? These are questions we would like to explore in later research.

## References

AlDajani, I. 2020, *Internet Communication Technologies for Reconciliation: Applied Phronetic Netnography in Internet Research Methodologies*, Springer, Berlin.

Barakat, Z.M., Dajani Daoudi, M., Leiner, M., O'Malley, M., Ferrari, F. (eds) forthcoming, *Hearts of Flesh–Not Stone*, Vandenhoeck & Ruprecht, Göttingen.

Barakat, Z.M. 2017, *From Heart of Stone to Heart of Flesh. Evolutionary Journey from Extremism to Moderation*, Herbert UTZ Verlag, Munich.

Ben David, Y., Hameiri, B., Benheim, S., Leshem, B., Sarid, A, Sternberg, M., Nadler, A., Sagy, S. 2017, 'Exploring Ourselves within Intergroup Conflict. The Role of Intragroup Dialogue in Promoting Acceptance of Collective Narratives and Willingness Toward Reconciliation', *Peace and Conflict. Journal of Peace Psychology,* 23/3, pp. 269–277.

Ben David, Y., Idan, O. 2022, 'Talking Politics. The Delimitation of the "Political" as a Gendered Disciplinary Mechanism in Intragroup Dialogue among Young Israelis', *present volume.*

Benheim, S. 2022, 'The Impact of Encountering the Other. A Long-Term Study of Jordanian, Palestinian and Israeli Participants in a Multicultural Program at the Arava Institute for Environmental Studies', *present volume.*

Dajani, D. 2022, 'Transitional Justice and Reconciliation in Intractable Conflicts', *present volume.*

Dajani, D. 2019, *Reconciliation through Education. From Conflict Education to Peace Education in Palestine.* Dissertation, Friedrich-Schiller University Jena.

Dajani Daoudi, M. 2009, *Wasatia. The Spirit of Islam*, Wasatia Publishing, Jerusalem.

Engstrom, C. 2009, 'Promoting peace, yet sustaining conflict? A fantasy-theme analysis of Seeds of Peace publications', *Journal of Peace Education*, 6/1, pp. 19–35.

Faraj, M. 2022, 'Palestinian Students Encountering the Suffering of the Other: The Role the Intergroup and Intragroup Dialogue Encounters Play in Reconciliation', *present volume.*

Ferrari, F. 2022, 'The Concept of Reconciliation after Auschwitz. Hermeneutic Phenomenology of the Irrevocable', *present volume.*

Ferrari, F. 2019, 'Vladimir Jankélévitch's "Diseases of Temporality" and Their Impact on Reconciliatory Processes', in *Contemporary Perspectives on Vladimir Jankélévitch*, eds M. La Caze, M. Zolkos, Rowman & Littlefield, London 2019, pp. 95–116.

Flämig, S., Leiner, M. 2012, 'Reconciliation in the Middle of Dispute. Introduction to the Series', in *Societies in Transition. Latin America between Conflict and Reconciliation*, eds S. Flämig, M. Leiner, Vandenhoeck & Ruprecht, Göttingen, pp. 7–19.

Gabay, R., Hameiri, B., Rubel-Lifschitz, T., Nadler, A. 2022, 'The Tendency for Interpersonal Victimhood. Conceptualization, Cognitive and Behavioral Consequences, and Antecedents', *present volume*

Gabay, R., Hameiri, B., Rubel-Lifschitz, T., Nadler, A. 2020, 'The Tendency for Interpersonal Victimhood: The Personality Construct and its Consequences', *Personality and Individual Differences*, 165, pp. 110–134.

Gryglewsky, E. 2013, *Anerkennung und Erinnerung: Zugänge arabisch-palästinensischer und türkischer Berliner Jugendlicher zum* Holocaust, Metropol, Berlin.

Hameiri, B., Gabay, R., Rubel-Lifschitz, T., Nadler, A. 2022, 'Victimhood Acknowledgment as a Vehicle to Promote Intergroup Conciliatory Attitudes in the Context of Intergroup Conflict', *present volume*.

Hameiri, B., Nadler, A. 2017, 'Looking Backward to Move Forward: Effects of Acknowledgment of victimhood on Readiness to Compromise for Peace in the Protracted Israeli-Palestinian Conflict', *Personality and Social Psychology Bulletin*, 43/4, pp. 555–569.

Kapshuk, Y. 2022, 'Reconciliation in Peace Agreements? The Case Study of the Israeli-Palestinian Peace Process', *present volume*.

Krauß, K. 2020, *Ethik der Empathie: eine Grundlegung*. Dissertation, Friedrich-Schiller University Jena.

Leiner, M. 2019, 'Encountering the Suffering of the Other - Experiences from Palestinians and South Africans Visiting Places of Suffering', in *Historical Trauma and Memory. Living with the Haunting Power of the Past*, Pumla Gobodo-Madikizela et al. (eds), African Sun Media, Stellenbosch, pp. 135–140.

Leiner, M. 2018, 'From Conflict Resolution to Reconciliation', in *Alternative Approaches in Conflict Resolution*, eds M. Leiner, C. Schliesser, Palgrave Macmillan, London/New York, pp. 175–186.

Leshem, B., Sagy, S. 2022, 'Legitimization of the Other Narrative as a Mediator of the Relationships Between National Honor, Dignity Perceptions and the Willingness to Reconcile. The Case of the Israeli-Palestinian Conflict', *present volume*.

Nägler, L.A., Harth, N.S., Kessler, T. (in prep.). 'Fostering positive relations through respectful encounters: The role of respect in reconciliation processes.'

O'Malley, M.J. 2022, 'Narratives and Justice in Reconciliation Research. An Applied Ethics Perspective', *present volume*.

Rubel-Lifschitz, T., Gabay, R., Hameiri, B., Nadler A., 'The Victimhood Oriented Leader. Tendency for Interpersonal Victimhood among Powerholders', *present volume*.

Sagy, S. 2020, 'Can we Empathize with the Narrative of Our Enemy? A Personal Odyssey in Studying Peace Education', in *Israeli and Palestinian Collective Narratives in Conflict: A Tribute to Shifra Sagy and Her Work*, eds A. Mana, A. Srour, Cambridge Scholars Publishing, Newcastle upon Tyne, pp. 8–18.

Sarid, S., Srour, A., Sagy, S. 2022, 'Sense of National Coherence and Willingness to Reconcile: The Case of the Israeli-Palestinian Conflict', *present volume*.

Shnabel, N., Nadler, A. 2008, 'A Needs-Based Model of Reconciliation. Satisfying the Differential Emotional Needs of Victim and Perpetrator as a Key to Promoting Reconciliation', *Journal of Personality and Social Psychology*, 94, pp. 116–132.

SimanTov-Nachlieli, I., Shnabel, N., Nadler, A. 2013, 'Individuals' and groups' motivation to restore their impaired identity dimensions following conflicts: Evidence and implications', *Social Psychology*, 44, 129–137.

Sternberg, M., Sagy, S. 2022, 'When Israeli Students Encounter Palestinian Narratives', *present volume*.

Sternberg, M., Litvak Hirsch, T., Sagy, S. 2018, 'Nobody Ever Told Us. The Contribution of Intragroup Dialogue to Reflexive Learning about Violent Conflict', *Peace and Conflict: Journal of Peace Psychology*, 24/2, pp. 127–138.

Telaku, M., Mana, A., Srour, A., Sagy, S. 2021, 'Sense of Community Coherence and Perceptions of Collective Narratives and Intergroup Relations in Post Conflict Context', *Peace and Conflict: Journal of Peace Psychology*, 27/3, pp. 350–361.

Wenzel, M., Mummendey, A., Waldzus, S. 2007, 'Superordinate identities and intergroup conflict: The ingroup projection model', *European Review of Social Psychology*, 18, pp. 331–372.

Weinthal, B. 2020, "'Antisemitic' academic pushed for boycott of Israeli professors in 2018'. From: https://www.jpost.com/diaspora/antisemitism/antisemitic-academic-pushed-for-boycott-of-israeli-professors-in-2018–626964 [18th November 2021].

Zempelburg, A. 2019, *Versöhnung im Judentum, Eine religionswissenschaftliche Perspektive auf den jüdischen Versöhnungsbegriff in Bezug auf Gott, den Nächsten, den Anderen und sich selbst*, Tectum, Baden Baden.

Zigenlaub, E., Sagy, S. 2022, 'Learning the Narrative of the Other. What Type of Encounter is More Effective?', *present volume*.

Francesco Ferrari

# The Concept of Reconciliation after Auschwitz

## Hermeneutic Phenomenology of the Irrevocable

### Abstract

Francesco Ferrari's paper raises his research question – the concept of reconciliation after Auschwitz – primarily in the domain of philosophy. He proceeds systematically, in dialogue with authors from the mid-twentieth century, particularly with the most important texts of the Jewish philosophy of that time. Given the many layers of the topic, his research adopts a transdisciplinary approach that benefits from the contributions of reconciliation studies, Jewish studies, intellectual history, psychology, and sociology. Its methodology can be defined as a hermeneutic phenomenology in the philosophical sense formulated by Ricœur 1974 [1969]. On the one hand, his work is structured as a phenomenological exploration, through which the concept of reconciliation faces that of irrevocable. From the other one, it is shaped through a hermeneutical stance, given the existential relevance of the topic, i. e., it concerns the world of the lived human experience. This paper introduces and summarizes Ferrari's studies on the philosophical debate regarding the concept of reconciliation after Auschwitz he carried out in the course of the project "Hearts of Flesh – not Stone" and presents some of the post-doctoral research hypotheses he is currently working on.

### Introduction

#### "Reconciliation"

The concept of reconciliation is astonishingly under-researched among philosophers in the strict sense. Yet, its roots are profound, and it has been thematized by authors such as Hölderlin, Schelling, Hegel. Still today, Hegel's concept of *Versöhnung* represents an indispensable reference for any study of reconciliation in philosophical terms. In dialogue with his works, particularly with his *Phänomenologie des Geistes* (Hegel 1807), many crucial antitheses of reconciliatory processes can be articulated. Above all, the one between reconciliation as a process vs. reconciliation as an outcome: "the process [of reconciliation] may be variously defined [via Hegel] as a process of overcoming conflict, division, enmity, alienation, or estrangement; the result, as the restoration of harmony, unity, peace, friendship, or love" (Hardimon 1994, 85). Hardimon's definition considers the outcome of reconciliation as "being part of a whole". It is, however, a controversial one: Is it too demanding for the victim? What about difference and dissent? Isn't a certain "agonism" a constitutive element of human interactions? (Du Toit 2018, 167–188) This work acknowledges the immense *Wirkungsgeschichte* of Hegel's concept of reconciliation. Particularly, it engages in a dialogue with Jewish philosophers of the 20th century that have been profoundly influenced by it, even by taking, not rarely, a harsh critical stance on it, as we can learn, paradigmatically, from Emil Fackenheim and Theodor W. Adorno.

Working on reconciliation implies engaging in a dialogue with many authors, topics, and methodologies (Radzik and Murphy 2019), at the crossroads with many disciplines. In the social sciences, reconciliation studies constitute an overarching approach, which investigates diverse practices and policies (for instance: apologies, reparations, politics of memory…) (Leiner 2016, 185–186), as well as the role of emotions – for individuals and groups – as inhibitors or facilitators of sustainable peace (Halperin 2016). Particularly, the concept of reconciliation is redefined through a wide spectrum, which ranges from a "thin" reconciliation, identifying it as the ceasing of violence, to a "thick" one, identifying it as the achievement of harmony and unity (Govier 2006, 13).

The present research works through a relational conception of reconciliation, which defines reconciliation as the process of "building [or re-building] relationships between antagonists" (Lederach 1997, 34; see also Lederach 2005) that "wrongs have ruptured[,] aiming to realize a condition of right relationship" (Philpott 2012, 54). Reconciliatory processes are about repairing and-or constructing relationships after serious wrongdoing, aiming "to create 'normal,' 'trustful,' and if possible 'good' and 'peaceful' relationships" (Leiner 2018, 179). Such wrongdoing is addressed as an occurrence that has created a rift between its agent(s) ("perpetrators") and its sufferer(s) ("victims"), to such an extent that, as this paper is going to show, it may be acknowledged as an irrevocable event.

### "Auschwitz"

The term "Auschwitz" recognizes "the specificity of the Jewish genocide without isolating it, since it refers at the same time to the broader context of the world of the Nazi concentration camps" (Traverso 1999, 8), i. e., to the diverse groups of its victims. The term "Auschwitz" defines first a place, i. e., the biggest concentration and extermination camp operating under the Third Reich. Quite soon, due also to philosophers such as Max Horkheimer and Theodor W. Adorno, its reference shifted from the concrete place (Oświęcim) to its related historical events during World War II, gaining symbolic and philosophical implications. In this research, the term "Auschwitz" is chosen over other commonly used options, such as "Final Solution of the Jewish Question" (the Nazis' term as recorded in the minutes of the Wannsee Conference), "Holocaust" (from the Ancient Greek *holokaustos*, it refers to sacrifices through fire. Its theological connotation, which provides a justification, makes this term a problematic one), and "Shoah" (Hebrew word for catastrophe: it is an appropriate one, yet it addresses exclusively the Jewish victims).

Writings we owe to authors such as Hannah Arendt, Max Horkheimer, and Theodor W. Adorno recognized very soon the unprecedented character of Auschwitz, foremostly in its aim at the annihilation of the targeted groups for the mere fact of belonging to them, i. e., because of their "ipseity" (Jankélévitch 1996 [1971]). Already in the '40s, Arendt 1945 et 1946 as well as Horkheimer and Adorno 1947 perceived Auschwitz as the outcome of an anti-humanist racial ideology, that comprehended itself as science, and operated together with the dumbness of bureaucratical administration and the efficiency of technical, "industrial" devices (Bauman 1991).

Now as then, Auschwitz constitutes an enigma, which imposes to rethink the course of the history of Western civilization, as the "breakdown of [that] civilization" (*Zivilisationsbruch*) (Diner 1988). The abyssal novelty of Auschwitz has been questioned by philosophers and theologians as the irruption of evil amid history, hence as an ontological rupture, by defining it, for instance, in the terms of a "tremendum as caesura" (Cohen 1981). Therefore, this work is aware of the structural obstacles and limits of any academic endeavor that aims to understand the "extreme" of Auschwitz (Lyotard 1988 [1983]; Todorov 1999 [1991]), foremostly the incomprehensibility of the evil (Wiesel 1966), which resists any attempt to unveil its fundament.

## "Irrevocable"

French philosopher Vladimir Jankélévitch introduces the concept of irrevocable with ethical terms as he writes: "We can neutralize the fact (*factum*), but we cannot undo the fact-of-having-done (*fecisse*) as if it was not-done (*infectum*)" (Jankélévitch 1980, 28). Recognizing Auschwitz as irrevocable means to define it as an epoch-making event that in ethical – but also normative – terms cannot be undone, since it imposes such a radical transformation that no *status quo ante* can be regained, and its repetition must be avoided. Adorno's categorical imperative "never again Auschwitz" (Adorno 1967) can be interpreted as the classical and clearest formulation of such a principle. The normative character of memory, peculiar to an ethics of "never again" and inescapably rooted in Auschwitz even on a transnational level (Baer and Sznaider 2017), has its philosophical basis in the concept of the irrevocable. The irrevocable acknowledges an occurrence that shakes axes of relationships among individuals, groups, states, and finally impacts one's stance toward oneself and to the Transcendence. Therefore, it constitutes the ultimate framework of reference for reconciliatory processes.

This research considers the systematic negation of humanity, which took place in Auschwitz, as a turning point for any philosophy and ethics (Benso 1992), which, as such, ought to be assessed *despite* the "breakdown of species" (*Gattungsbruch*) (Zimmermann 2005) of Auschwitz, and also *because of* Auschwitz (Finkielkraut 2000 [1996]). It addresses Auschwitz as an irrevocable event, as a "wound" that harmed – and in many cases broke – multiple levels of relationships, often with long-term consequences, so that it might rather be comprehended as a "scar". Victims' relationships toward the out-group and the in-group, with the Transcendence, but also with themselves, appear injured, if not irreconcilable even in transgenerational terms after Auschwitz (Krondorfer 1995; Bar-On 2006). At the same time, this research does not ignore that, notwithstanding the enormous moral, psychological, and political hurdles constituted by the irrevocable-traumatic character of Auschwitz, German policies of reconciliation with Israel can be acknowledged as profoundly successful (Gardner Feldman 1999).

The concept of "irrevocable cultural trauma" is going to be introduced to comprehend to which extent the irrevocable does not merely affect the direct victims of atrocities, but rather shapes collective identities, and becomes institutionalized. It will be analyzed to which extent the "irrevocable cultural trauma" of Auschwitz can pave but also impede reconciliation, for example through the series of processes that lead to formulating the categorical imperative of the "duty of remembrance" (Margalit 2004).

### "The Concept of Reconciliation after Auschwitz" as a "Hermeneutic Phenomenology of the Irrevocable"

This work deals with the concept of reconciliation *after* Auschwitz. It raises the question of the extent to which it is possible to think and to strive toward reconciliation (i. e., repairing-rebuilding relationships) in the wake of an event, which is recognized as epoch-making and irrevocable like Auschwitz. By defining Auschwitz as an irrevocable event, this research presents it as a turning point, which imposes to rethink the concept of reconciliation in radical terms, too. Developing "The Concept of Reconciliation after Auschwitz" therefore requires – and will be articulated as – a "Hermeneutic Phenomenology of the Irrevocable".

The first section of the research, under the title *Auschwitz as Irrevocable. Hermeneutic Phenomenology of the Wrongdoing* thematizes in philosophical terms the impact of the wrongdoing – recognized as irrevocable – on reconciliatory processes. It consists of four chapters:

1.1 Vladimir Jankélévitch's 'Diseases of Temporality' and Their Impact on Reconciliatory Processes;

1.2 Memory, Identity, Forgiveness. Archaeological and Teleological Perspectives of Reconciliation from Paul Ricœur;

1.3 Auschwitz as "Epoch-Making Event" beyond any "Aufhebung" in the Writings of Emil Fackenheim;

1.4 Theodor W. Adorno: "The Realization of the Generality in the Reconciliation of Differences".

The second section of the research, under the title *Questions of Reconciliation with Oneself after Auschwitz*, focusses on reconciliation with oneself in philosophical terms, i. e., on possibilities and limits of healing an individual existence, which has been plagued by the trauma of wrongdoing recognized as irrevocable – such as Auschwitz. It consists of four chapters:

2.1 Autobiography as a Hermeneutic Practice of Reconciliation with Oneself

2.2 Between Quest for a Heimat and Alienation. Jean Améry's Journey after Auschwitz

2.3 Resistance and Reconciliation. Martin Buber's Stance towards Nazi and Post-War Germany

2.4 Empowering Agency for All. Insights for Reconciliatory Processes from Hannah Arendt's Works.

## 1. Auschwitz as Irrevocable. Hermeneutic Phenomenology of the Wrongdoing

### 1.1 Vladimir Jankélévitch's "Diseases of Temporality" and Their Impact on Reconciliatory Processes

French-born Jewish moral philosopher Vladimir Jankélévitch (1903–1985) has set a fundamental thesis for the present research so that its first chapter (published as Ferrari 2019) is entirely devoted to his thought. According to him, time has two main dimensions: 1. Ratifying nature laws, considered as the flow of constant becoming and as a forward-oriented ceaseless production of future, time is *irreversible*; 2. As the recognition of the indestructible "what-has-been" of an epoch-making event in its "having-taking-place" operated by a moral agent, time is *irrevocable*. Whereby reversing time is impossible, and regaining a past moment in the purity of its pastness is unattainable too, a moral option is offered in the resistance against irreversibility, which takes place through the recognition of a past moment as "irrevocable".

From this standpoint, it will be explored the spectrum of moral feelings (resentment, remorse, repentance, and nostalgia), which paves or obstacles reconciliatory processes, focusing on their temporal connotation. Jankélévitch 1974 calls them *malheurs de la temporalité*, i. e. "diseases of temporality", aptly focusing on their constitutive relationship with the irrevocable, and their painful, sometimes even traumatic, dimensions. Through their phenomenological examination, it becomes evident that the past does not merely pass, but rather remains as "lived time", that structures and burdens the consciousness of victims and perpetrators and is crucial for further notions such as the imprescriptible and the unforgivable. Therefore, it becomes salient to analyze how and why the diseases of temporality represent tenacious counterforces, which often lead to enduring stares of irreconcilability.

The final section of the chapter sets the thesis that the diseases of temporality cannot be successfully healed with the equivalence-logic of justice to restore a *status quo ante*. Therefore, a new beginning stemming out of the overabundance-logic of love is needed, beyond any tit-for-tat measures, which inhabits justice in its punitive-retributive paradigm as well as in its commutative-reparative one. The gift-giving relationship of forgiveness is crucial in this regard, and it gains evidence in the moral confrontation between love and justice. Amid this struggle, fundamental in reconciliatory processes, the final polarity of this chapter announces itself: namely, the one between the hyperbolical order of grace and the linear order of law.

## 1.2 Memory, Identity, Forgiveness. Archaeological and Teleological Perspectives of Reconciliation from Paul Ricœur

The second chapter (published as Ferrari 2016) reconstructs and presents the hermeneutic approach of French philosopher Paul Ricœur (1913–2005) to reconciliatory processes. It deals with three central issues in his late thought, namely: memory, identity, and forgiveness. They are presented as actual forces, working through two inseparable movements: an archaeological movement directed towards the past, and a teleological one aiming towards the future. The paper presents their intertwined action to be a constitutive dimension of reconciliation, by showing that: 1. A merely archaeological dimension of memory faces a host of contradictions and aporias and may lead to an intolerant *idem*-identity, based on "sameness" (*mêmeté*); 2. On the other side, a teleological dimension of memory is required to establish a "just memory" (*juste mémoire*), that configures our identity as an *ipse*-identity based on "selfhood" (*ipséité*).

Ricœur's distinction between *idem*-identity and *ipse*-identity reveals his temporal understanding of human existence as a central issue behind the identity question. Narrative identity is then introduced as paramount in reconciliatory processes. A "narrative" identity defines "identity" not just as the sameness of an *idem*, but as a configuring act, that operates via emplotment, i. e., by turning confused, contingent occurrences (potentially alienating or even traumatic ones) into episodes of a consistent and interwoven life-plot. Narrative identity hence provides constancy of the self and represents a massive contribution toward reconciliation with oneself (see here, 2.1).

Finally, the paper examines Ricœur's reflection on forgiveness. Although directed to the past, forgiveness is introduced as an act occurring in a real, present moment, with consequences capable of shaping a shared future for victims and perpetrators, potentially moving on a joint path toward reconciliation. Here, Ricœur's reflections address the massive wave of apologies, delivered by political and religious leaders worldwide in the '90s, but also by unprecedented institutions, such as the South African Truth and Reconciliation Commission and the International Criminal Court of The Hague. Ricœur's remarks target the extension of forgiveness to the sphere of public affairs, as a juridical and political actor, also in dialogue with Derrida 2019 et 2020's conception of "unconditional forgiveness". Forgiveness, finally, is discussed as the core of Ricœur's philosophical anthropology, which defines the human being both as fallible and as capable.

## 1.3 Auschwitz as "Epoch-Making Event" beyond any "Aufhebung" in the Writings of Emil Fackenheim

This chapter investigates the irrevocable in dialogue with philosophers of religion and authors from the "Holocaust Theology" (Rubenstein 1966; Cohen 1981; Fackenheim 1967 and 1982). It is mainly concerned with Emil Fackenheim's writings and moves from his definition of Auschwitz as an epoch-making event that, as such, imposes to rethink one's reconciliation with the Transcendence, with the *continuum* of historical time, and with the world.

Like the occurrences that are recognized as irrevocable ones, epoch-making events constitute an absolute novelty in the historical *continuum* of time, that opens an abyss between past and present, which seems to be unbridgeable. This notion implies that time-segments prior to and subsequent to these events are so radically different that the default application of an assumed historical unity is not admitted. As a response to the annihilating threat of epoch-making events, Fackenheim 1967 recurs to the key lessons earned by paradigmatic biblical narratives, he names "root experiences", by developing "a hermeneutical teaching that begins with the acceptance of historical situatedness" (Morgan 2013, 43), whose enactment will be critically reconstructed in the current chapter.

The chapter then shows to which extent Fackenheim 1967 refuses any attempt of reconciliation in the terms of traceless healing of the wounds of Spirit à la Hegel ("*Aufhebung*") and formulates a duty of memory, which goes together with the positive affirmation of Jewish existence as a 614th commandment for the Jew. Along this way, it finally reconstructs how Fackenheim 1982 rethinks reconciliation as the imperative of mending the world.

Concepts like Jankélévitch's "irrevocable" and Fackenheim's "epoch-making event" can be linked with notions such as "chosen trauma" (Volkan 2001) and "cultural trauma" (Alexander 2012). They focus on the close relationship between individual- and group-memory, by recognizing the significance of trauma in history as an "irrevocable cultural trauma", which requires, as such, a certain temporal latency to be worked through (Traverso 2000 [1997]). Addressing the mutual interaction between historians, witnesses, and the "public use of history" (Habermas 1988 [1986]) in reconciliatory processes, therefore requires to take into account the aporias of post-traumatic Holocaust testimonies (Langer 1991; Felman and Laub 1992) and also those "abuses of memory" (Todorov 1996 [1995]), which represent the dark side of the so-called "era of the witness" (Wieviorka 1998), that opened in the 1990s.

### 1.4 Theodor W. Adorno: "The Realization of the Generality in the Reconciliation of Differences"

This chapter investigates the irrevocable in the terms of a philosophy of history, by dealing with Theodor W. Adorno's logic of the non-identical, which safeguards the "particular" of Auschwitz from any attempt to insert it into the "universal" *continuum* of the Western civilization and represents, therefore, a "single catastrophe" beyond any persistent "chain of events" (Benjamin 2007 [1955], 257).

To elucidate Adorno's understanding of Auschwitz, the chapter reconstructs and discusses his universal-particular dialectics and his concept of reconciliation as they are formulated in his main works. It will be presented how and why, from Horkheimer and Adorno 1947 to Adorno 1966, Auschwitz has been recognized as the apex of thought of pure identity (i. e., universality), which cannot tolerate any otherness (i. e., particularity), and finally leads to the physical extermination of the non-identical. The chapter will also reconstruct how Adorno 1951 takes a stance in defense of particularity, through his endorsing the concept of reconciliation. By defining an emancipated society as the one that does not correspond to a "unitary state, but [one that enables] the realization of the generality in the reconciliation of differences" (Adorno 1951, 184), Adorno also challenges and overturns Hegel's dialectics. This is aptly condensed in statements, such as: "the whole is the untrue" (Adorno 1951, 81) and: "there is no right life in the wrong one" (Adorno 1951, 59), that will be analyzed during the chapter.

Adorno 1967's categorical imperative, setting "never again Auschwitz" as the prime demand of education, will be analyzed as the most urgent principle of ethics, according to which one ought not to subsume the particular and non-identical of Auschwitz by inserting it, through an *Aufhebung*, into a universal- and teleologically-oriented philosophy of history. There is, indeed, productive tension between reconciliatory processes and the recognition of the irrevocable, that requires to be further analyzed. Whereas at a first glimpse the irrevocable appears as a moral principle that impacts relationships in the opposite way of reconciliation, a closer look reveals a complementarity between them. A paradigmatical example is provided by the importance of establishing the conditions that – following Adorno's categorical imperative – will ensure that massive wrongdoings happen "Never Again".

Adorno's defense of the "non-identical" at the basis of his understanding of Auschwitz will be further compared with consonant arguments in Lévinas' writings, which constitute a polemical stance against the entire course of Western philosophy, he defines as "an ontology: a reduction of the Other to the Same" (Lévinas 2012 [1961], 43). According to Lévinas, ethics requires overturning the idolatry of the Same, i. e., to respect the constitutive exteriority, foreignness, and separation of the Other (Lévinas 2013 [1974]). Lévinas' theses, therefore, will be interpreted in parallel with the universal-particular dialectics according to Adorno's writings.

## 2. Questions of Reconciliation with Oneself after Auschwitz

### 2.1 Autobiography as a Hermeneutic Practice of Reconciliation with Oneself

This chapter (published as Ferrari 2022a) presents autobiography as the self-narrative hermeneutic practice which, put in place by a retrospective look, following a peculiar logic of "retrospective teleology" (Brockmeier 2001), that operates by localizing the irrevocable in hindsight (Freeman 2010), articulates the reconciliation of the particular of a single occurrence within the universal provided by the perception of one's own life as a "whole". In dialogue with contemporary hermeneutics and moral philosophers, this chapter deals with the writings of Shoah survivors such as Améry 1966 et 1971 and Frankl 1946; 1972; 1982. Its goal is to show how and to which extent autobiographical life-writing is a hermeneutic practice of reconciliation with oneself (Gusdorf 1980 [1956], 39).

As the emplotment of occurrences that appear in the first instance as contingent, unrelated, even alienating ones ("potentially irrevocable"), autobiography enacts a work of appropriation (Jaeggi 2014 [2005]; Bieri 1986) of one's lived experiences, through the unfolding of a "narrative identity" (Ricœur 1988 [1985]; Ricœur 1984 [1983]). This takes place as a "meaning-making" (Bruner 2001) process, through which (autobiographical) sense is made out of the irrevocable by embedding it in the whole of one's life story. The success of this process requires a framework of value orientation (Frankl 1982; Scheler 1916; Fromm 1947). Autobiography becomes, therefore, the diachronic reading of the story of oneself in terms of the narrative of the progressive actualization of one's agency. Agency (see 2.4), indispensable for the fulfillment of one's project of a good life, is linked, in turn, to the perception of one's own life as a "whole" (MacIntyre 1981).

Taylor 1989 has developed MacIntyre's theses, by defining one's identity as one's unfolding story of moving forward and back in relation to what one acknowledges as the Good. Along this way, a ("particular") occurrence or action receives its meaning by being localized in relationship to one's conception of the ("universal") "good life". Autobiography shows that a "good life" is a whole one, i. e., a meaningful unity, in which single actions and occurrences are embedded as coherent episodes. In the mediation that leads the single occurrence back to the perception of one's own life as a "whole", autobiography, therefore, traces a hermeneutic arc from the particular to the universal, whose stake is reconciliation with oneself. The "good life", therefore, finally coincides with the reconciled one. Within this research hypothesis, autobiographical recollections of Auschwitz survivors are of the highest relevance, as they paradigmatically show to which extent "witnessing is a necessary condition of agency" (LaCapra 1998, 12).

This chapter has among its sources state-of-the-art research on trauma, with particular focus on the interpretations that focus on the close connection between the recognition of trauma and that of the irrevocable, as something that challenges the sense of one's life as something coherent (Antonovksy 1987), and, as such, leads to fragmentation (Fisher 2017), dissociation (Van der Hart et al. 2006), "undoing of the self" (Van der Kolk 2014; Gobodo Madikizela and Van der Merwe 2009).

## 2.2 Between Quest for a Heimat and Alienation. Jean Améry's Journey after Auschwitz

Jean Améry's personal and intellectual journey constitutes one of the most profound and tragic testimonies of the necessity and impossibility of reconciliation with oneself after Auschwitz, which finds its paradigmatic expression in his quest for a homeland (*Heimat*). This chapter (published as Ferrari 2021) hence investigates to which extent the irrevocable shakes and shatters trust and willingness to reconcile at the same time, leading to perduring states of self-alienation.

Améry 1966 witnesses that suffering a violent wrongdoing, experienced as a traumatic one, shatters one's capacity for relationships – at the physical, psychological, and moral level – in such a pervasive way that regaining trust in the world is hard, if not impossible. Trust, defined by Govier 2006, 19 as "an attitude of confident expectation that most others will act in a moral, decent way", inherently implies a certain amount of exposure to risk and vulnerability. Losing trust in the world, we learn from Améry, stems from feeling massive alienation, and leads to a limited capacity to impact one's circumstances, i. e., to an overwhelming feeling of powerlessness. Contemporary psychologists would frame this process in terms of perceived low expectations of self-efficacy (Bandura 1982). Améry's reflections on his condition of refugee, which describe the need to "feel at home" as a prerequisite to restore agency, are paradigmatical in this regard. As we can learn also from Améry 1971, an agentic (or powerless) self depends on the quality of its relations with the world. Broken trust weakens one's capacity for healthy, agentic, "resonant" (Rosa 2016) relationships with the world, and then with oneself. Alienation describes the experience of losing power over circumstances, becoming a stranger to oneself. Its antithesis is perceiving reconciliation as the feeling of being connected (as part of a whole).

Impossibility to reconcile with oneself goes often together with an unwillingness to reconcile with the other. Resentment, as thematized by Améry 1966, constitutes the main moral feeling at the basis of the refusal to reconcile with others (see also: Gabay et al. present volume). For a long time, it had a bad reputation in philosophy and religion. Yet, as moral philosophers like Jankélévitch, Améry, and, more recently, Brudholm 2008 have shown, resentment expresses a moral protest, which needs to be taken seriously into account in the analysis of reconciliatory processes.

## 2.3 Resistance and Reconciliation. Martin Buber's Stance towards Nazi and Post-War Germany

This chapter (published as Ferrari 2022b) reconstructs the stance the Jewish philosopher of religion Martin Buber took towards Nazi and Post-War Germany, presenting it as a complex dynamic of resistance and reconciliation. During Hitler's dictatorship, Buber was exposed to an increasingly dreadful conflict, through which he suffered systematic human rights violations. Yet, he faced it with steadfast, tireless agency, without ceasing to recognize his German opponents as members of a shared moral and human community. In several conferences and public roundtables, which also involved members of the *NSDAP*, Buber did not avoid addressing issues from the contemporary historical moment. Welcoming the challenge of a conversation connoted as an open confrontation within a collapsing democracy, and also shortly after, amid a totalitarian regime, he made clear that encountering the other as a "Thou" takes place also by sustaining adversarial debate. Fostering political spaces for dissent, guided by the "courage to be an outsider" (Mendes-Flohr 2018), Buber asserted the strength of his dialogical principle by facing irreducible differences.

Buber's dynamic of resistance and reconciliation can, therefore, be properly understood as an agonistic one (Maddison 2017, 161; Du Toit 2018, 167–186). It gained further evidence during the Nazi time, as he engaged himself in a spiritual resistance, throughout manifold initiatives and publications for the sake of the German Jewry in its more desperate hour. It will be nonetheless visible in his stance towards the *Shoah* and post-war Germany. The chapter will reconstruct along which ways, few years after the end of World War II, Buber became one of the first Jewish intellectuals who actively engaged in reconciliatory processes with the German

Federal Republic. His readiness to reconcile raised controversial reactions among Jews. Paradigmatically, Rubenstein 1979 condemned Buber's "indifference to the Holocaust as a religious problem". This sentence requires reassessment, as this chapter will do, by commenting on a text like Buber 2018 [1951], in which the Jewish philosopher raised the questions *par excellence* regarding the possibility of theology after Auschwitz already in the early Fifties.

Buber's relationships with the Divine, with the German state and people, but also with oneself (as a Jew) were severely wounded. Consequently, possibilities of reconciliation did not appear readily available to him. The second half of this paper will be devoted to Buber's healing of injured relationships on multiple levels, challenging widespread alienation and pervasive mistrust, and reopening a dialogue like the German-Jewish one, so that (as we learn from Silberstein 1981) Buber aptly gained the epithets of *Gosher HaG'sharim*, "builder of bridges".

### 2.4 Empowering Agency for All. Insights for Reconciliatory Processes from Hannah Arendt's Works

This chapter aims to redefine agency as the human capacity of doing and undoing the irrevocable, i. e., of starting something anew, but also of undoing one's and others' deeds. It is developed in continuity with the theses of Ricœur's 1992 [1990], according to which the self (re)gains its agency over potentially irrevocable-traumatic occurrences by emplotting them within an intelligible story through the unfolding of a narrative identity. By integrating "appropriated" past deeds and projected future ones, narrative identity constitutes a vantage point, from which it is possible to lead one's life. From here on, the self can be analyzed as agency: the "capacity of the acting subject to make events happen" (Ricœur 2005 [2004], 96).

In dialogue with Hannah Arendt's writings, in particular with her *The Human Condition* (Arendt 1958), this chapter aims to interrogate to which extent performative acts, such as promising and forgiving, have a profound impact on reconciliatory processes. Two further fundamental facts, which attest to our agency in political terms, according to Arendt, will be reconstructed in the present chapter: "natality" and "plurality". The former constitutes the human capacity of acting as "beginning", by initiating something anew and making a distinct mark on the public dimension of the world. The latter requires to acknowledge that one is born within a public dimension, hence it is the human capacity to live with others, who are different from oneself. Agency empowers human beings as free ("natality") and responsible ("plurality") persons. It also implies having oneself at one's command and being accountable for one's deeds, so that freedom of thought, will, and action cannot be separated. No wonder the eradication of individual agency is on the agenda of all totalitarian regimes (Arendt 1951).

Social psychology teaches us that empowering agency is crucial in reconciliatory processes, for victims and perpetrators as well (Nadler and Schnabel 2008). This might appear as a supplementary stressor for victims, since they lack agency, because of the traumatic consequences of the irrevocable wrongdoing they suffered. At the same time, it requires an enormous amount of trust in perpetrators, since wrongdoings they committed can also be defined as a misuse of their agency. Nevertheless, in Arendt's terms, being empowered in one's agency will be presented as crucial for both. For victims, such empowerment means to restore their injured capacity to start something anew. For perpetrators, it means to be restored in their moral credit, as active members of a plural society. For both, being empowered in their agency positively impacts reconciliatory processes, as it heals damaged relationships with oneself, the other, and the world in the wake of a suffered or acted major wrongdoing which remains irrevocable in moral terms.

## 3. Conclusions

The present research unfolds a hermeneutic phenomenology of the concept of reconciliation after Auschwitz by articulating a key moral-philosophical issue., i. e., the recognition of wrongdoing as irrevocable. It provides foundations for the irrevocable at a philosophical level, as well as it introduces the issue of coping with the irrevocable, by addressing its traumatic consequences in processes of reconciliation with oneself.

Interestingly, many philosophers, from Adorno to Lyotard, have set the moral imperative not to reconcile with the irrevocable. On the other side, psychotherapists, such as Kohut 1984, Spence 1982, Schafer 1992, intensively esteemed by Charles Taylor and Paul Ricœur, have endorsed the healing produced by meaning-making, as it takes place by reconciling the single traumatic occurrence into the broader frame of one's life story.

We should not forget that reconciliatory processes have mostly to do with concrete scenarios, within which there is no option but togetherness, interconnectedness, even interdependence between victims and perpetrators (Du Toit 2018, 189–225). The question of relationships in reconciliation after violent wrongdoing cannot escape, hence, unsurmountable dialectics of physical proximity and metaphysical distance. By defining relatedness as an originating, unescapable, ontological a-priori, reconciliation studies hint at the web of human relationships and offer the theoretical framework for an embodied philosophy of relatedness.

## References

Adorno, T. 1951, *Minima Moralia. Reflexionen aus dem beschädigten Leben*. Suhrkamp, Berlin-Frankfurt am Main.

Adorno, T. 1966, *Negative Dialektik*. Suhrkamp, Frankfurt am Main.

Adorno, T. 1967, „Erziehung nach Auschwitz." In: *Zum Bildungsbegriff der Gegenwart*. Ed. H.J. Heydorn. Diesterweg-Verlag, Frankfurt am Main.

Alexander, J. 2012, *Trauma. A Social Theory*. Polity Press, Cambridge.

Améry, J. 1966, *Jenseits von Schuld und Sühne. Bewältigungsversuche eines Überwältigten*. Szczesny, München.

Améry, J. 1971, *Unmeisterliche Wanderjahre*. Klett-Cotta, Stuttgart.

Antonovksy, A. 1987, *Unraveling the Mystery of Health: How People Manage Stress and Stay Well*. Jossey-Bass, San Francisco.

Arendt, H. 1945, "Organized Guilt and Universal Responsibility." *Jewish Frontier*, 12, p. 19–23.

Arendt, H. 1946, "The Image of Hell." *Commentary*, 2, p. 291–295.

Arendt, H. 1951, *The Origins of Totalitarianism*. Schoken, New York.

Arendt, H. 1958, *The Human Condition*. University of Chicago Press, Chicago.

Baer, A. and Sznaider, N. 2017, *Memory and Forgetting in the Post-Holocaust Era: The Ethics of Never Again*. Routledge, New York.

Bandura, A. 1982, "Self-Efficacy Mechanism in Human Agency." *American Psychologist*, 37, p. 122–147.

Bar-On, D. 2006, *Tell Your Life Story: Creating Dialogue Among Jews and Germans, Israelis and Palestinians*. Central European University Press, Budapest.

Bauman, Z. 1991, *Modernity and the Holocaust*. Polity Press, New York.

Benjamin, W. 2007 [1955], *Illuminations*. Schoken, New York.

Benso, S. 1992. *Pensare dopo Auschwitz. Etica filosofica e teodicea ebraica*. Edizioni Scientifiche Italiane, Napoli.

Bieri, P. 1986. „Zeiterfahrung und Personalität." In: *Zeit, Natur und Mensch*. Ed. H. Burger. Berlin Verlag, Berlin, p. 261–281.

Brockmeier, J. 2001, "From the End to the Beginning: Retrospective Teleology." In: *Narrative and Identity. Studies in Autobiography, Self and Culture*. Eds. J. Brockmeier, D. Carbaugh. John Benjamins Publishing Company, Amsterdam-Philadelphia, p. 247–282.

Brudholm, T. 2008, *Resentment's Virtue: Jean Améry and the Refusal to Forgive*. Temple University Press, Philadelphia.

Bruner, J. 2001, "Self-Making and World-Making." In: *Narrative and Identity. Studies in Autobiography, Self and Culture*. Eds. J. Brockmeier, D. Carbaugh. John Benjamins Publishing Company, Amsterdam-Philadelphia, p. 25–38.

Buber, M. 2018 [1951], „Der Dialog zwischen Himmel und Erde." In: Id., *Schriften zum Judentum (MBW 20)*. Eds. P. Mendes-Flohr, M. Fishbane. Gütersloher Verlagshaus, Gütersloh, p. 345–353

Cohen, A. 1981, *The Tremendum: A Theological Interpretation of the Holocaust*. Crossroads Publishing Co, New York.

Derrida, J. 2019. *Le parjure et le pardon : Volume 1, Séminaire (1997–1998)*. Seuil, Paris.

Derrida, J. 2020. *Le parjure et le pardon : Volume 2, Séminaire (1998–1999)*. Seuil, Paris.

Diner, D. (ed.). 1988, *Zivilisationsbruch: Denken nach Auschwitz*. Fischer, Frankfurt am Main.

Du Toit, F. 2018, *When Political Transitions Work: Reconciliation as Interdependence*. Oxford University Press, New York.

Fackenheim, E. 1967. *God's Presence in History*. New York University Press, New York.

Fackenheim, E. 1982, *To Mend the World: Foundations of Post-Holocaust Jewish Thought*. Schoken Books, New York.

Felman, S. and Laub, D. 1992, *Testimony. Crises of Witnessing in Literature, Psychoanalysis and History*. Routledge, New York.

Ferrari, F. 2016, "Memory, Identity, Forgiveness. Archaeological and Teleological Perspectives of Reconciliation from Paul Ricœur." *Polylog. Forum for Intercultural Philosophy*, 34, p. 151–167.

Ferrari, F. 2019, "Vladimir Jankélévitch's 'Diseases of Temporality' and Their Impact on Reconciliatory Processes." In: *Contemporary Perspectives on Vladimir Jankélévitch*. Eds. M. La Caze, M. Zolkos. Rowman & Littlefield, London, p. 95–116.

Ferrari, F. 2021. "Between Quest for a Heimat and Alienation. Jean Améry's Journey after Auschwitz." In: *Remembering the Holocaust in Germany, Austria, Italy and Israel*. Ed. V. Pinto. Brill, Leiden, p. 89–98.

Ferrari, F. 2022a. "Autobiography as a Hermeneutic Practice of Reconciliation with Oneself." In: *Reconciliation, Heritage and Social Inclusion in the Middle East and North Africa*. Eds. M. Leiner, I. Aldajani. Springer, Cham.

Ferrari, F. 2022b. "Resistance and Reconciliation. Martin Buber's Stance towards Nazi and Post-War Germany." In: *Literarische Interventionen im deutsch-jüdischen Versöhnungs-diskurs seit 1945*. Eds. R. Forkel, B. Pick. Transcript, Bielefeld.

Finkielkraut, A. 2000 [1996], *In the Name of Humanity. Reflections on the Twentieth Century*. Columbia University Press, New York.

Fisher, J. 2017, *Healing the Fragmented Selves of Trauma Survivors: Overcoming Internal Self-Alienation*. Routledge, New York.

Frankl, V. 1946, *Trotzdem Ja zum Leben sagen. Ein Psycholog erlebt das Konzentrationslager*. Verlag für Jugend und Volk, Wien.

Frankl, V. 1972, *Der Wille zum Sinn. Ausgewählte Vorträge über Logotherapie*. Huber, Bern.

Frankl, V. 1982, *Ärztliche Seelsorge. Grundlagen der Logotherapie und Existenzanalyse. 10. Auflage*. Deuticke, Wien.

Freeman, M. 2010, *Hindsight. The Promise and Peril of Looking Backward*. Oxford University Press, New York.

Fromm, E. 1947, *Man for Himself. An Inquiry into the Psychology of Ethics*. Rinehart, New York.

Gabay, R., Hameiri, B., Rubel-Lifschitz, T., and Nadler, A. 2022, 'The Tendency for Interpersonal Victimhood. Conceptualization, Cognitive and Behavioral Consequences, and Antecedents', present volume.

Gardner Feldman, L. 1999, "The Principle and Practice of 'Reconciliation' in German Foreign Policy: Relations with France, Israel, Poland and the Czech Republic." *International Affairs,* 75/2, p. 333–356.

Gobodo Madikizela, P. and Van der Merwe, C.N. 2009, *Narrating Our Healing: Perspectives on Working Through Trauma.* Cambridge Scholars Publishing, Cambridge.

Govier, T. 2006, *Taking Wrongs Seriously: Acknowledgment, Reconciliation, And the Politics of Sustainable Peace.* Humanity Books, Amherst, NY.

Gusdorf, G. 1980 [1956], "Conditions and Limits of Autobiography." In: *Autobiography: Essays Theoretical and Critical.* Ed. J. Olney. Princeton University Press, Princeton, p. 28–48.

Habermas, J. 1988 [1986], "Concerning the Public Use of History." *New German Critique,* 44, p. 40–50.

Halperin, E. 2016, *Emotions in Conflict. Inhibitors and Facilitators of Peace Making.* Routledge, New York.

Hardimon, M.O. 1994, *Hegel's Social Philosophy: The Project of Reconciliation.* Cambridge University Press, Cambridge.

Hegel, G.W.F. 1807, *System der Wissenschaft. Erster Theil, die Phänomenologie des Geistes.* Verlag Joseph Anton Goebhardt, Bamberg/Würzburg.

Horkheimer, M. and Adorno, T. 1947, *Dialektik der Aufklärung. Philosophische Fragmente.* Querido, Amsterdam.

Jaeggi, R. 2014 [2005], *Alienation.* Columbia University Press, New York.

Jankélévitch, V. 1974, *L'Irréversible et la nostalgie.* Flammarion, Paris.

Jankélévitch, V. 1980, *Le Je-ne-sais-quoi et le Presque-rien. Vol. III.* Seuil, Paris.

Jankélévitch, V. 1996 [1965], "Should We Pardon Them?" *Critical Inquiry,* 22/3, p. 552–572.

Kohut, H. 1984, *How Does Analysis Cure?* University of Chicago Press, Chicago-London.

Krondorfer, B. 1995, *Remembrance and Reconciliation: Encounters Between Young Jews and Germans.* Yale University Press, New Haven.

LaCapra, D. 1998, *History and Memory after Auschwitz.* Cornell University, Ithaca, N.Y.

Langer, L. 1991, *Holocaust Testimonies.The Ruins of Memory.* Yale University Press, New Haven.

Lederach, J.P. 1997, *Building Peace: Sustainable Reconciliation in Divided Societies.* United States Institute of Peace, Washington D.C.

Lederach, J.P. 2005, *The Moral Imagination: The Art and Soul of Building Peace.* Oxford University Press, New York.

Leiner, M. 2016, "Thinking Differently about Identity and Harmony – The Potential of Asian Thinking for Reconciliation." In: *Asia-Pacific between Conflict and Reconciliation.* Eds. P. Tolliday, M. Palme, D.C. Kim. Vandenhoeck & Ruprecht, Göttingen, p. 183–204.

Leiner, M. 2018, "Conclusion: From Conflict Resolution to Reconciliation." In: *Alternative Approaches in Conflict Resolution*. Eds. M. Leiner, C. Schliesser. Palgrave Macmillan, Cham, p. 175–185.

Lévinas, E. 1968. *Quatre lectures talmudiques*. Minuit, Paris.

Lévinas, E. 2012 [1961], *Totality and Infinity: An Essay on Exteriority*. Springer, Dordrecht.

Lévinas, E. 2013 [1974], *Otherwise Than Being: Or Beyond Essence*. Springer, Dordrecht.

Lyotard, J.F. 1988 [1983], *The Differend: Phrases in Dispute*. University of Minnesota Press, Minneapolis.

MacIntyre, A. 1981, *After Virtue. A Study in Moral Theory*. University of Notre Dame Press, Notre Dame.

Maddison, S. 2017. "Can We Reconcile? Understanding the Multi-Level Challenges of Conflict Transformation." *International Political Science Review*, 38/2, p. 155–168.

Margalit, A. 2004, *The Ethics of Memory*. Harvard University Press, Cambridge, MA.

Mendes-Flohr. P. 2018, "The Courage to be an Outsider." In: *Dialog und Konflikt (Martin Buber-Studien 3)*. Eds. U. Frost, J. Waßmer, H.-J. Werner. AV Verlag, Bodenburg, p. 17–28.

Morgan, M.L. 2013, *Fackenheim's Jewish Philosophy. An Introduction*. University of Toronto Press, Toronto.

Nadler, A., and Shnabel, N. 2008, "A Needs-Based Model of Reconciliation: Satisfying the Differential Emotional Needs of Victim and Perpetrator as a Key to Promoting Reconciliation." *Journal of Personality and Social Psychology*, 94/1, p. 116–132.

Philpott, D. 2012, *Just and Unjust Peace: An Ethic of Political Reconciliation*. Oxford University Press, New York.

Radzik, L. and Murphy, C. 2019, "Reconciliation." *The Stanford Encyclopedia of Philosophy (Winter 2020 Edition)*. Ed. E.N. Zalta, URL = https://plato.stanford.edu/archives/win2020/entries/reconciliation/ retrieved on February 03, 2021.

Ricœur, P. 1974 [1969], *The Conflict of Interpretations*. Northwestern University Press, Evanston.

Ricœur, P. 1984 [1983], *Time and Narrative. Vol. I.* University of Chicago Press, Chicago.

Ricœur, P. 1988 [1985], *Time and Narrative. Vol. III.* University of Chicago Press, Chicago.

Ricœur, P. 1992 [1990], *Oneself as Another*. University of Chicago Press, Chicago.

Ricœur, P. 2005 [2004], *The Course of Recognition*. Harvard University Press, Cambridge, MA.

Rosa, H. 2016, *Resonanz. Eine Soziologie der Weltbeziehung*. Suhrkamp, Frankfurt am Main.

Rubenstein, R. 1966, *After Auschwitz: Radical Theology and Contemporary Judaism*. Bobbs-Merrill, Indianapolis.

Rubenstein, R. 1979, "Buber and the Holocaust. Some Reconsiderations on the 100th Anniversary of His Birth." *Michigan Quarterly Review*, 18/3, p. 382–402.

Schafer, R. 1992, *Retelling a Life: Narration and Dialogue in Psychoanalysis*. Basic Books, New York.

Scheler, M. 1916, *Der Formalismus in der Ethik und die materiale Wertethik*. Niemeyer, Halle an der Saale.

Silberstein, L.J. 1981, „Martin Buber. The Social Paradigm in Modern Jewish Thought." *Journal of the American Academy of Religion*, 49/2, p. 211–229.

Spence, D. 1982, *Narrative Truth and Historical Truth: Meaning and Interpretation in Psychoanalysis*. W.W. Norton & Company, New York.

Taylor, C. 1989, *Sources of the Self. The Making of the Modern Identity*. Harvard University Press, Cambridge, MA.

Todorov, T. 1996 [1995], "The Abuses of Memory." *Common Knowledge*, 1, p. 6–26.

Todorov, T. 1999 [1991], *Facing the Extreme: Moral Life in the Concentration Camps*. Weidenfeld and Nicolson, London.

Traverso, E. 1999, *Understanding the Nazi Genocide: Marxism After Auschwitz*. Pluto Press, London.

Traverso, E. 2000 [1997], *Auschwitz Denken. Die Intellektuellen und die Shoah*. Hamburger Edition, Hamburg.

Van der Hart, O., Nijenhuis, E.R.S., Stelle, K. 2006, *The Haunted Self: Structural Dissociation and the Treatment of Chronic Traumatization*. Norton, New York.

Van der Kolk, B. 2014, *The Body Keeps the Score: Brain, Mind, and Body in the Healing of Trauma*. Viking, New York.

Volkan, V. 2001, "Transgenerational Transmissions and Chosen Traumas: An Aspect of Large-Group Identity." *Group Analysis*, 34(1), p. 79–97.

Wiesel, E. 1966, *Le Chant des Morts*. Seuil, Paris.

Wieviorka, A. 1998, *L'Ère du témoin*. Plon, Paris.

Zimmermann, R. 2005, *Philosophie nach Auschwitz: Eine Neubestimmung von Moral in Politik und Gesellschaft*. Rowohlt, Reinbek.

André Zempelburg

# Rabbinic Jewish Perspectives on Interpersonal Reconciliation and the Reconciliation with Oneself in the Context of Yom Kippur

## Abstract

In the Jewish tradition, reconciliation with the divine was unimaginable without previous reconciliation with the other human being. Throughout the centuries, rabbis and Jewish intellectuals had to think, debate, and adapt the concept of reconciliation within the horizon of their changing reality over time. This frame introduces André Zempelburg's Rabbinic Jewish Perspectives on Interpersonal Reconciliation and the Reconciliation With Oneself in the Context of Yom Kippur. The paper is based on the author's doctoral dissertation at the Friedrich-Schiller University of Jena, which recently appeared as a book (2019), which aimed to cover the meaning and major trends of the concepts of reconciliation and atonement within the Jewish tradition, starting in the days of Ancient Israel and ending the early twenty-first century by focusing on central insights of traditional and modern understanding of reconciliation in the inter-personal level and with oneself. Although the concept of reconciliation or atonement (in Hebrew, they are just a single word) has its roots in the God-man-relation, the paper argues how and why a constant "ethizising" took place over time.

## Introduction

Intending to enterprise a religious studies' perspective on the concept of reconciliation in rabbinic Judaism, Zempelburg 2019 assumes that, according also to Adele Reinhartz (Reinhartz 2011), *Versöhnung* or reconciliation is poly-dimensional within rabbinic Judaism. Concretely, reconciliation appears in three types of relation: namely the God-man relationship, the man-man relationship, and the relation of man to oneself. Whether the Jewish rabbinic tradition distinguishes between the Jewish fellow or neighbor (חבר) and a non-Jewish other (Ibid., p. 9), it has to be examined in detail in the case of the man-man relationship.

In contrast to the first part of Zempelburg 2019, which is about reconciliation in the God-man relationship from Lev 16 through mYom to the liturgy of Yom Kippur (Day of Atonement), which is still being performed nowadays, the second part of the book focuses on reconciliation in the man-man relationship in the context of Yom Kippur in rabbinic Judaism (interpersonal reconciliation). Finally, its third part deals with man's reconciliation with oneself. By omitting the excursuses done in this study on Shnejur Zalman of Liady's (the founder of Ḥabad-Lubavitch Ḥassidism), on an understanding of interpersonal reconciliation and the problem of forgiveness in the victim's name, raised by Simon Wiesenthal, only the key results of these last two sub-studies (interpersonal reconciliation, reconciliation with oneself) are given below.

The ethical core of mYom 8:9 (see: Baneth 1986, p. 331; Weinreb 2013, p. 428) was the starting point for the entire investigation: עברות שבין אדם לחברו אין יום הכפרים מכפר עד שירצה את חברו ["Transgressions, which are between a man and his fellow, the Day of Atonement (reconciliation) is not reconciling/atoning until he appeases his fellow." (All translations are mine unless otherwise indicated.)] Considering the Hebrew verbal root *kpr* as the concept of reconciliation and Yom Kippur as the spatiotemporal 'place' of reconciliation helps to understand the meaning of reconciliation on the Day of Atonement, Yom Kippur, and the extent of reconciliation (*kpr*), existentially necessary for the (human) subject. Reconciliation is always done by God even if a mediator seems to work reconciliation even if in purely phenomenological terms, such as Aaron in Ancient Israel or the high priests following him.

The human being whose "individual […] existence is forfeited" because of his transgressions/sins, offenses, and/or insurgencies and who "stands between life and death" (Janowski 2000, p. 176) on the Day of Atonement arises based on reconciliation effected by God. This is symbolically represented in the temple cult of the Day of Atonement with the High Priest as his *agent* "as an atoned one, not as a punished one" (Ibid., p. 5). In the words of Janowski, the reconciliation requested and aimed for by man and granted by God is thus intended to result in a "salvation from fallenness to death" and the "enabling of new life" (Ibid., p. 176).

In parallel with the relationship between God and man, which was examined in detail in Part I of Zempelburg 2019 in terms of its content of reconciliation, there is also the man-man relationship, in which man, as a social being, finds himself exposed daily. This relationship, too, can be fatally disturbed due to man-made "transgressions" (עברות) – a term that summarizes the sins, offenses, and/or insurgencies – and therefore requires reconciliation. However, such a phenomenon, namely interpersonal reconciliation in the context of Yom Kippur, was not yet existent in the Priestly source (P). Testified in written form, this changes only with the abovementioned ethical core of mYom 8:9.

It is possible to speculate on the particular reasons for such a development, that is, the emphasis on the interpersonal relationship by the rabbis to be reconciled with God before the reconciliation with God. In my opinion, Galley (2003) aptly grasped the motivation of the rabbis, a practice that also existed in the early Jesus movement or was even quoted by Jesus (cf. Mt 5:23). According to Galley, Yom Kippur "should not become a cheap pretext for behaving carelessly towards his fellow human beings for the rest of the year and careless against the Torah (Galley 2003, p. 74)." Of course, the explicit connection of the interpersonal relationship with Yom Kippur cannot prevent the individual (אדם) from carrying out "transgressions" against his fellow (חבר) in a calendar year. However, it urges the restoration of an interpersonal relationship, which otherwise would remain disturbed. According to mYom 8:9, it should be unmistakably clear to the transgressor that interpersonal reconciliation is a necessary prerequisite for the reconciliation of the God-man relationship. However, this also presupposes that the one who has committed the "transgressions" hopes to be saved from the "fallenness to death" which threatens him as a consequence of divine judgement on the first of the two "Judgement Days" (i. e., Rosh ha-Shanah) and thus being "inscribed and sealed" (bT RH 16b: נכתבין ונחתמין) into the book of life on the second "Judgement Day," i. e., Yom Kippur (cf. Scherman 2008, p. 706; cf. bT RH 16b).

## 1. Interpersonal Reconciliation in the Context of Yom Kippur

> *"Hominem homini Deum esse"*
> Baruch de Spinoza

The Gemara (i. e., in the broadest sense, the amoraic-rabbinic commentary to the Mishnah) of the Palestinian or Jerusalemite Talmud (pT/yT) to the Mishnaic tractate Yoma (see yT Yom 56a (8:7))[1] offers the first tangible discussion of the ethical content of mYom 8:9 by the rabbis. It was the acknowledgment of the truth by the transgressor ("sinner") to one's fellow (חביר), namely, that the former had sinned against the latter. Thus, truthfulness is a necessary prerequisite for interpersonal reconciliation. However, the transgressed may reject the confession as an implicit request of the "sinner" for pardon. To prove his seriousness, the "sinner" only has the option of gathering a group of people of indeterminate size in order to confess while they are present to his being-a-sinner to his fellow and to pacify or appease him (מפייס). The salvation of the "sinner" by God is the consequence, according to the Gemara of yT Yom. The publicization of interpersonal reconciliation was interpreted as a pedagogical measure. However, the guilt of the "sinner" extends beyond the death of the one against whom he sinned. Therefore, the need to appease

---

1 The folio pages are counted according to the yT Yom edition of Malinowitz/Schorr/Marcus (Eds.), מסכת יומא/Tractate Yoma, in: Talmud Yerushalmi. The Schottenstein Edition, Vol. 21, New York 2011.

him beyond his death remains. Consequently, the act of appeasement takes place at the fellow's grave.

Something similar was found in the study of the Gemara of mYom 8:9 in the Babylonian Talmud (bT Yom 87a), claiming that the fellow (חביר) must be appeased by the "sinner" (צריך לפייסו), incurred material damage must be repaired and likewise pardon must be requested at the grave in the case the fellow already died. In the Gemara of the bT on the tractate Yoma, the protocol for interpersonal reconciliation is more detailed than that of the Gemara of yT Yom. Above all, the Gemara of bT Yom transcends that of yT Yom with the ethical content of the formula which is to be spoken at the grave of the fellow whom man (אדם) had transgressed: חטאתי לה' אלהי ישראל ולפלוני שחבלתי בו ["I have failed/sinned against h[a-Shem] (i. e., JHWH), God of Israel, and against a so-and-so[2] to, which I inflicted pain."] From this, it could be deduced that the transgressions (sins) against man are always to be understood as transgressions against God and, therefore, in the nature of their severity, must also be considered equal to the transgressions against God. By no means it can be said that, from a rabbinic perspective, the significance of the man-man relationship and thus, also, its reconciliation is simply to be subordinated to that of the God-man relationship and, again, its reconciliation. Consequently, the transgressions against one's fellow man are no less severe and thus no less significant – quite the contrary seems to be the case.

The discussion of the proceedings of reconciliation in the Gemara of yT Yom and bT Yom was followed by the discussion of Maimonides' (1135/38–1204) *Hilkhot Teshuvah* (HT) 2:9ff. in the *Sefer ha-Madda*, which is the first part of his halakhic (legal) masterpiece *Mishneh Torah* (completed 1177/78). In this work, he postulates that transgressions of man against his fellow (חבר) will not be "pardoned" (נמחל)[3] "forever" (לעולם.(

Of course, Maimonides' apodictic statement applies only if the "sinner" does not seek pardon from his fellow. Reconciliation or a reconciling event (מכפרין) occurs in the context of Yom Kippur only in the event of previous forgiveness/סליחה and pardon/מחילה (cf. HT 2:7.9). For Maimonides, too, the ultimately hoped-for reconciliation, but mostly the fellow's and God's pardon, is subject to certain conditions. Maimonides starts with mYom 8:9 in consultation with the corresponding Gemara (bT Yom)[4] but goes beyond the latter. Maimonides understands the group of people

---

2 Cf. Jastrow 1946, p. 1178: "a specified person or thing, such and such, name 'blank'".

3 A qualitative difference to *kpr* has been identified, because, in contrast to *mḫl*, *kpr* is constantly worked by God.

4 Material damage is to be reimbursed, even if the fellow (the victim) has already died, and it has to be asked for forgiveness. If the fellow indeed died, the material reparation shall go to the heirs of the fellow or to court, insofar as he has no offspring.

to be gathered insofar as the two parties that have been divided due to transgressions do not reunite as passive witnesses to the interpersonal act of reconciliation, but as active participants. According to Maimonides, if two people come into conflict this affects the community. Therefore, interpersonal reconciliation is also a community concern. The motivation behind HT 2:9 probably is the desire to strive for harmony and the benefit of interpersonal relationships and the community, whose members always have to be just. This aspiration for harmony must elicit the active support of the one against whom has been sinned. This person is the victim of the transgressions because he is forced to pardon "with a whole heart and soul of will (בלב שלם ובנפש חפצה)". The one against whom was sinned must not remain in his victim role. If he chooses to remain immured in this role, he acts unjustly against the person who willingly asks for pardon and ultimately not in the interests of the whole community, which is not allowed to be cruel (אסור לאדם להיות אכזרי) and (cf. HT: 2:10) "easy to pacify and difficult to anger (יהא נוח לרצות וקשה לכעס)". Interpersonal reconciliation in the context of Yom Kippur is, according to Maimonides, the desired and almost enforced goal which becomes possible insofar as each of the Jewish people involved in the proceedings of reconciliation acts and reacts according to an ideal defined by him.

Since the last written testimony of rabbinic learning discusses the concept of interpersonal reconciliation in the context of Yom Kippur, I analysed Shlomoh ben Josef Ganzfried's (1804–1886) magnum opus *Kitzur Shulchan Aruch* (QŠA), published in 1864. His original idea was not to involve several people in the process of reconciliation, as was the case in yT Yom, bT Yom and HT, but to use only a single "mediator" (אמצעי, literally: "a means"), who seems to be a kind of *Zweckgegenstand* (item of purpose), is ignored. Thus, two points, in particular, stand out because of their ethical salience:

1. Ganzfried (2001) explicitly emphasizes that dealing with one's own transgressions in the context of Yom Kippur[5] is even more urgent than dealing with the Torah. The transgressor should not waste any time in asking the person against whom he has transgressed for pardon (לבקש [...] מחילה). Thus, the task of interpersonal reconciliation precedes the human effort of reconciliation with God. In other words, Ganzfried places reconciliation of the man-man relationship over the usually most highly valued occupation with the Torah. Therefore, he prioritizes interpersonal reconciliation over the engagement with the divine and the reconciliation of the God-man relationship. This explicit decision of Ganzfried undoubtedly has its origin in the ethical content of mYom 8:9. Concerning the attainment of reconciliation in the context of Yom Kippur, already mYom prioritized the man-man

---

5  One should not wait until the evening of Yom Kippur (לא ימתין עד ערב יום הכפורים); the occupation with one's own transgressions or sins should already take place at Rosh ha-Shanah.

relationship over the one with God. However, Ganzfried explicitly expresses this by referring to the study of the Torah as the ideal of rabbinic Jewish piety and learning. At the same time, he uses it as a cipher for the God-man relationship – both interwoven and inseparable – but subordinates it to the necessity of interpersonal reconciliation.

2. Following the example[6] of the eighteenth-century rabbi Josef Juzpa Hahn, the other outstanding phenomenon of the passages examined here is the instruction for the fellow to actively promote the process of reconciliation, even if the "sinner" (החוטא) has not yet requested pardon (cf. QŠA 131:4). Therefore, the QŠA radically changed the realization of interpersonal reconciliation's fairly clear role (perpetrator: active, must appease; victim: mostly passive, eventually pardons/forgives). The victim of the transgression(s) must neither be caught up in victimhood (cf. Maimonides 1994, p. 427) nor remain passive until the "sinner" requests pardon of him. However, the active role within the act of reconciliation is not transformed into a passive one. These two roles are not simply reversed. In contrast, the active role is extended to all involved and thus replaces the passive in its entirety. According to Ganzfried, interpersonal reconciliation in the context of Yom Kippur demands to take the first step from all participants to promote reconciliation actively.

Finally, I examined Emmanuel Levinas' (1906–1995) Talmudic reading of *Envers autrui* (engl.: *Toward the Other*, Levinas 2005). Compared to the previous examples, Levinas is the only non-rabbinic but philosophical scholar I reference in this paper who dealt with mYom 8:9 (bT Yom 85b) and bT Yom 87a-b in detail. Using the terms "pardon" and "expiation makes it clear how strongly rabbinic Jewish thinking affects Levinas' philosophical mindset and how an understanding of his philosophical terminology is indispensable to appreciate the depth of his discussion of this Talmudic reading.

In the center of Levinassian thinking stands the other (*autrui*), the other human being (*l'homme autrui*). Although the Hebrew term of the other (אחר) was already embedded in the collective of others (אחרים) in Ganzfried's QŠA, no generalization of the fellow (חבֵיר) in the sense of the other human being, regardless of his ethnic and/or religious identity, could be identified. While in the QŠA, the other must only be understood as the other Jewish person, Levinas invariably means another human being by using the term *autrui*. Applying this understanding to mYom 8:9, it could mean that Yom Kippur does not reconcile transgressions against the other, i. e., the other human being, until the perpetrator has appeased him. According to

---

6 "It is custom to go to visit one's friends on the eve of Yom Kippur to beseech their forgiveness […]. Even if it is the other person who has sinned, one ought to go to that person and make peace with him" (Agnon 1995, p. 162f).

Levinas, the transgressor has to admit his guilt and must appease the other, even if the conflict has not yet been resolved. Only a judge as the third between the I (the transgressor) and the other (the victim) creates justice, which is founded by the divine. For Levinas, God is the other who remains different, who in his "epiphany" in the other pledges the I to take responsibility for the other human being (Levinas 2008, p. 107). God is "this permanent refusal of a history which would come to terms with our private tears" (Levinas 1990, p. 20).

In the consistent application of his concept of the other (*autrui*) to the Hebrew term Chaver/חביר (fellow), Levinas achieves something previously unknown. With this reinterpretation of Chaver in mYom 8:9 (bT Yom 85b), he opens the consciousness of (Jewish) recipients of the Mishnah or the Talmud in terms of reconciliation for the human being in general. The claim to appease, which the mentioned rabbinic passage directs to the Jewish individual, is no longer limited to the fellow belonging to the in-group by birth or conversion. This demand concerns a man in general, towards whom the I is obligated to take responsibility by the divine even before his birth and with whom the transgressor has to reconcile. At any rate, the ethical reception of bT Yom 85b.87a–b by Levinas represents an inner-Jewish and, at the same time, explicit rejection of the thesis of Sfard (2016). The latter argued that the rabbinic Jewish religion could not name a "tradition of public contrition" or a "culture in which one apologizes" and "confesses" guilt. Therefore, it must be foreign to implement "truth and reconciliation committees".

Consequently, reconciliation must be remote from rabbinic Judaism. Such a thesis cannot be maintained in the overall picture of this study. It is important to remember the concept of *Teshuvah* (turning back), which is often understood as a form of repentance as well as the confession of the transgressions by the perpetrator, the inclusion of parts of the public in the process of reconciliation, the use of a mediating person or institution, the material reparation, and the generally expected appeasement (*rṣh*) or pacification (*pjs*) of the fellow, who is inconceivable without "encountering the suffering of the other". Of course, it should be emphasized that not all Jewish scholars at all times thought and wrote as inclusively as Levinas did in the twentieth century despite or even because of the greatest catastrophe (Shoah/Holocaust) that has ever befallen the Jewish people in Europe and beyond.

If, as Galley says, the rabbis were intensely thinking about "making atonement for the sins of the people" in the face of human wrongdoing against their fellows, then Levinas has undoubtedly given much thought to how the transgressions against other human beings will not be forgotten or pass unnoticed.

If the God-man reconciliation on Yom Kippur is at the same time the creator of the world, it is not plausible to claim that only transgressions against the Jewish fellows will be reconciled if the prerequisites are fulfilled. From the rabbinic and Levinassian perspective, the God of the fathers is also the God of the world, who created all humans and pledged them to take responsibility for the other human being. Thus, the phrase "until he has appeased his fellow" (עד שירצה את חברו) must by no means be understood as restricted to the in-group's fellow man. Therefore, a summary of the thinking and language of Levinas, mYom 8:9 should be phrased as follows:

עברות שבין אדם למקום יום הכפרים מכפר

עברות שבין אדם לאחר (לעצמו) אין יום הכפרים מכפר עד שירצה את האחר (לעצמו)

["Transgressions which are between a man and the place (i. e., God), the Day of Atonement is reconciling. Transgressions which are between man and the other (for himself), the Day of Atonement is not reconciling until he has appeased the other (for himself".] No matter which of those interpretations of mYom 8:9 one might follow, interpersonal reconciliation in rabbinic Judaism in the context of Yom Kippur is a normative claim to the (Jewish) man. In particular, the one who transgressed against his fellow (חבר) or the other (אחר) cannot escape it insofar; the transgressor hopes for reconciliation on that very day.

As for the concept of reconciliation, expressed as such by the Hebrew root *kpr*, it can be seen from the works used here that the root *kpr* is hardly used for interpersonal reconciliation. Once the task to appease is excluded, mYom 8:9 does not list another way of reconciliation, forgiveness, or a pardon-related word (root). Instead, bT Yom (cf. parallel texts: mBQ 8:7; yT BQ 6c) frequently uses the root *mḥl* (to pardon). A particularly extreme form of the phenomenon is found in Levinas' *Envers autrui* because terms such as "*expiation*" or "*reconciliation*," do not play any role there but "*pardon*" and its verbal derivatives of "*pardonner*" do. In the context mentioned above, interpersonal reconciliation requires a previous human, sometimes divine, forgiveness. Alternatively, the *concept of reconciliation* (*kpr*) seems to be replaced by the term "*pardon*," as in the case of Maimonides HT 2:9 and Levinas' *Envers autrui,* where both terms are used synonymously (cf. Goldberg 2011, col. 51).

If the opportunity of interpersonal reconciliation has become a reality, the transgressor can hope for reconciliation with the divine. From the perspective of the Jewish *homo religious,* that is "salvation from fallenness to death" and thus for the return into an order of life or "social order that defines the Israelite individual and Israel as a corporate community" (Neusner 2002, p. XVIII) given by the divine. In the language of bT RH 16b and orthodox liturgy, this means being "inscribed and sealed" (נכתבין ונחתמין) in the Book of Life (ספר חיים). To this end, the divine judgment was given on Rosh ha-Shanah, the first "Judgement Day", which in the case of performed transgressions means to be inscribed to death immediately (נכתבין למיתה ונחתמין לאלתר). These transgressions must be altered on Yom Kippur, the second "Judgement Day" (cf. Scherman 2008, p. 706; cf. bT RH 16b). That is the reason why the individual confesses his transgressions to show his sincere will to turn (תשובה) from ‚wrong just like the people of Israel during *Widduj* (ודוי) when they repeatedly beseech the sealing in the Book of Life[7] during *Ne'ilah* (נעילה)[8]:

זכרנו לחיים מלך חפץ בחיים
וחתמנו בספר החיים למענך אלהים חיים[9]

["Remember us to life, king of zestfulness in life. And seal us into the Book of Life, in your favour, living God."]

With the sounding of the Shofar, the worshipers call "next year in Jerusalem" (לשנה הבאה בירושלים) and express their joy at the end of *Ne'ilah*, which arises from the confidence "that God has accepted our prayers, fast, and repentance and has responded with His merciful forgiveness (Scherman 2008, p. 764f.)." This exclamation is more than just joy; it also expresses the certainty that the redemption that has taken place will not last and that in the new year, the individual will again be exposed to temptations and will eventually transgress the social order mentioned above. Therefore, the phrase "next year in Jerusalem" symbolizes the hope for the dawn of messianic times, times of lasting redemption, and a better future in the here and now (cf. Scherman 2008, p. 765f.). However, until then, the existence of Yom Kippur as an institution offers the person who got through the day, as well as the Jewish people, the chance to experience another year, which may be free from transgressions. Thus, the event provides an opportunity that would not have existed without a previously achieved interpersonal reconciliation.

---

7 Cf. Trepp 2004, p. 147f.; the wish to be sealed is found especially in *'Āḇīnū Malkēnū*/אבינו מלכנו (wörtl.: "our father, our king") shortly before the end of *Nə'īlāh* (Scherman 2008, p. 758f.).

8 The beginning of *Nə'īlāh* initiates the end of the service, which goes hand in hand with the closing, that is, the sealing of the books for another year with the names given to life or death (Galley 2003, p. 67).

9 Scherman 2008, p. 712, 726; comparable formulas occur during *Nə'īlāh* also in two *'Amīdōt*/עמידות or *Šəmōnæh 'Æśreh* (Ibid., p. 720, 758).

## 2.   Reconciliation of Man with Oneself

*"Mit wem hatte ich mich zu versöhnen?"*[10]

Ignaz Goldziher

The preceding sub-study has shown that by transgressing the social order, fractures have been caused between a man and his fellow, respectively the people, and between man and the divine (social order); those fractures had necessarily to be reconciled. Otherwise, life would become impossible according to bT RH 16b. Following the sub-study, it was argued that based on certain decisions, actions, or externally added phenomena, fractures or separations within the I can be caused. At the moment of the genesis of this fracture/separation, the I sees itself confronted with the other declared as one-self, which, however, is not an ontological other.

At-one-ment, i. e., becoming-one again after the separation, would be the actual goal of internal-personal reconciliation, namely the reconciliation of the I within oneself, or as I call it: one-self. Both examples being used here assumed that reconciliation with the self could work by self-acceptance. In the case of the orthodox rabbi and psychiatrist Abraham J. Twerski's publication *Happiness and the Human Spirit*, this means for the I to accept its own inherent, but by no means fatalistically negatively connoted, "imperfection" (Twerski 2008, p. 27). Only when the I is aware of its actual state it can become one and whole by overcoming the already existing separation between the self and what it considers that belongs to itself. Only a self-reconciled person, i. e., a person that is reconciled with oneself, can strive to be the best one possible to gain "true happiness," according to Twerski (cf. Twerski 2008, p. 27f.). Only in the state of being reconciled with oneself, a person is capable of asking his fellow in "true penitence" for forgiveness if the former has transgressed against the latter (cf. Twerski 2008, p. 41f.). The latter corresponds closely to the prescribed rule in mYom 8:9 that man should appease his fellow. Otherwise, no life of maintaining reconciliation on Yom Kippur (with the divine) is to be expected. Based on the correlation of the dimension of reconciliation, the following definition could be made: No reconciliation with the other without reconciling with oneself and the one-self. If interpersonal reconciliation is directly dependent on internal-personal reconciliation, at least in the case of Twerski's work, it is inevitably to aim for reconciliation with the divine on Yom Kippur. Consequently, in a sense, the psychic (internal-personal), ethical-social (inter-personal), and transcendent (divine) spheres to which man, however, appears to have access form a causal unity.

---

10  Translation: "With whom I had to reconcile?" Haber 2006, p. 136. Haber uses the diary entries of Ignaz Goldziher (1850–1921) to illustrate how, in the context of Yom Kippur, Goldziher's inner disruption becomes evident due to the unresolved conflicts with his own Jewish and especially rabbinical tradition and identity.

When the I is reconciled with the one-self, it can potentially reconcile with the fellow or the other person in general. As soon as this became a reality, reconciliation with the divine is potentially possible.

Unlike the analysis of Twerski, rabbi Karyn D. Kedar's narrative *Tug-of-War* (published in a book of collected writings: *The Bridge to Forgiveness*, 2007) on the struggle of a terminally ill friend of hers is conceptually and contextually even closer to mYom 8:9. The process of reconciliation described by Kedar in this narrative takes place on Yom Kippur. Even if Kedar does not use the term "reconciliation," forgiveness is essential to her throughout the entire work, particularly regarding the relationship of the I with oneself or the one-self. In other words, for Kedar, forgiveness is the cure for all that creates a separation within the human being. Even though the event described by Kedar, which occurred during the Yom Kippur liturgy and was understood as a reconciliation of the I within oneself or oneself, cannot be objectified, it provides at least an idea of the immense spiritual significance that the Day of Atonement still has for the Jewish individual.

According to Kedar's description, what was happening during the liturgy shortly before the "closing" (*Ne'ilah*) of the gates – that is, moments before the end of Yom Kippur, and thus the last opportunity to turn back to the divine, standing before him dressed in white, sometimes in the burial shroud as a sign of repentance, like on Rosh ha-Shanah (cf. Galley 2003, p. 55) – is the regaining of one's own "faith," as well as the attainment of a state of "inner peace" (Kedar 2007, p. 75). The quasi-new condition befalls the terminally ill person due to an act of (one-)self-forgiveness. In this context, forgiveness means the acceptance of the one-self by the subject, the I. What was split off by the I had to be conceived and accepted as belonging to the I. Consequently, the inner separation has to be overcome. Overcoming the internal- and interpersonal "tug-of-war" (Ibid., p. 74f.),[11] which gives the narrative its name and describes the releasing or letting go of the manifold inner conflict, provided a space for reconciliation, occurring on the Day of Atonement for that particular person.

Overcoming the internal separation of the I with something that it did not regard as belonging to itself, the so-called one-self, is understood as becoming one, which semantically corresponds to the abstract atonement (at-one-ment). As a consequence of (one) self-forgiveness, a state of being reconciled with the other,

---

11 Certain separations within the I may possibly be generated by an external counterpart, that is, another person. "The day I met you, you declared, 'I am not very spiritual, you know.' From then on, we played a friendly game of thug-of-war. Sometimes gentle. Sometimes fierce. Always high stakes—eternity versus oblivion" (Kedar 2007, p. 74). Thus, Kedar herself is this other person, the opposite, which challenges the terminally ill person because of what she represents. At the same time, she is the addressee of the questions of meaning articulated by that person; the inner disruption only penetrates outward through the confrontation with the human counterpart (Ibid.).

who is actually a part of the self, follows the state of being separated. This can also be understood as a state of not-being-reconciled and does not necessarily have to be considered the result of transgressions. Something separating can also befall the I from the outside (e. g., a disease). Therefore, reconciliation with the oneself could be understood as a particular form of interpersonal reconciliation.

Following Kedar's account of how internal reconciliation in the context of Yom Kippur suddenly happened, it could also be concluded that due to the events that occurred, the terminally ill person achieves reconciliation with God, which Lev 16 at least implicitly and mYom 8:9 explicitly determine as the goal of that very day. Because of the reconciliation process, the person does not plunge into "oblivion" but has attained "eternity"[12]. According to Kedar's account, "eternity won", which must be understood as a result of reconciliation with oneself, just like the regaining of "faith" and "inner peace." Thus, if reconciliation with oneself or the one-self can be associated with interpersonal reconciliation and thus represents a subdimension of this and interpersonal reconciliation, it is again a necessary condition for the reconciliation of the God-man relationship. The process of reconciliation in Kedar's *Tug-of-War* coheres with the inherent causality of mYom 8:9, namely the causality of the dimensions of reconciliation set forth therein (reconciliation of the man-man relationship as a prerequisite of the reconciliation of the God-man relationship)[13].

### References

Agnon, S.Y. (ed.) 1995, *Days of Awe. A Treasury of Jewish Wisdom for Reflection, Repentance, and Renewal on the High Holy Days*, Schocken Books, New York.

Albertini, F. 2003, *Das Verständnis des Seins bei Hermann Cohen. Vom Neukantianismus zu einer jüdischen Religionsphilosophie*, Königshausen & Neumann, Würzburg.

Baneth, E. 1986, Ordung Mo'ed: Übersetzt und erklärt/סדר מועד: מתורגם ומפורש, in *Mischna-jot: Die sechs Ordnungen der Mischna*/ששה סדרי משנה: משניות, Victor Goldschmidt Verlag, Basel.

Cohen, H. 2008, *Religion der Vernunft aus den Quellen des Judentums. Eine jüdische Religion-sphilosophie*, Marix Verlag, Wiesbaden.

---

12 "As it turned out, eternity won" (Kedar 2007, p. 75).

13 In my opinion, Albertini 2003, p. 182 has felicitously argued in her analysis that Cohen in his philosophy of religion shows that reconciliation with oneself is an indispensable prerequisite for the reconciliation of the *I* with the divine, still only the latter grants reconciliation (Cohen 1924/2002, p. 143/517: "*Kein anderer kann die Versöhnung bewirken als nur Gott allein*"), but that reconciliation with oneself in its necessity becomes evident only as soon as man has attained "the knowledge of injustice in the relationship between men" (Cohen 2008, p. 242).

Cohen, H. 2002, ‚Der Tag der Versöhnung', in Id., *Werke. Kleinere Schriften VI.*, eds H. Holzhey, J.H. Schoeps, C. Schulte, Georg Olms Verlag, Hildesheim.

Cohen, H. 1924, *Jüdische Schriften 1. Ethische und religiöse Grundfragen*, C. A. Schwetschke & Sohn, Berlin.

Galley, S. 2003, *Das jüdische Jahr. Feste, Gedenk- und Feiertage*, C. H. Beck, München.

Ganzfried, S. 2001, קצור שלחן ערוך/Kizzur Schulchan Aruch, 2, Victor Goldschmidt Verlag, Basel.

Goldberg, Y.S. 2011, Atonement: III. Judaism. C. Medieval Judaism, in *Encyclopedia of the Bible and ist Reception*, 3, eds H.J. Klauck, V. Leppin, B. McGinn, C.L. Seow, H. Spieckermann, B.D. Walfish, E. Ziolkowski, De Gruyter, Berlin, col. 50–52.

Haber, P. 2006, *Zwischen jüdischer Tradition und Wissenschaft. Der ungarische Orientalist Ignác Goldziher (1850–1921)*, Böhlau Verlag, Köln.

Heschel, A.J. 2008, ‚Der Mensch – ein heiliges Bild', in *Weltethos aus den Quellen des Judentums*, eds H. Küng, W. Homolka, Herder, Freiburg, pp. 57–66.

Janowski, B. 2000, *Sühne als Heilsgeschehen. Traditions- und religionsgeschichtliche Studien zur Sühnetheologie der Priesterschrift*, Vandenhoeck & Ruprecht, Neukirchen-Vluyn.

Jastrow, M. 1946, *Dictionary of the Targumim, the Talmud Babli, and Yerushalmi, and the Midrashic Literature*, Hendrickson Publishers, New York.

Kedar, K.D. 2007, *The Bridge to Forgiveness. Stories and Prayers for Finding God and Restoring Wholeness*, Jewish Lights Publishing, Woodstock.

Levinas, E. 2008, *Totalität und Unendlichkeit. Versuch über die Exteriorität*, Karl Alber, Freiburg.

Levinas, E. 2005, *Envers Autrui. Texte du Traité « Yoma » (85 a – 85 b)*, in Id., *Quatre lectures talmudiques*, Les Éditions de Minuit, Paris.

Levinas, E. 1990, *Toward the Other*, in *Nine Talmudic Readings*, Indiana University Press, Bloomington.

Maimonides, M. 1994, *Das Buch der Erkenntnis*/ספר המדע, in *Jüdische Quellen*/מקורות ישראל, 2, eds E. Goodman-Thau, C. Schulte, Akademie Verlag, Berlin.

Malinowitz, C., Schorr, Y.S., Marcus, M. (eds) 2011, מסכת יומא/*Tractate Yoma*, in *Talmud Yerushalmi. The Schottenstein Edition*, 21, Mesorah Publications, New York.

Neusner, J. 2002, *Handbook of Rabbinic Theology. Language, System, Structure*, Brill Academic Publishers, Boston.

Reinhartz, A. 2011, ‘Repentance, Reconciliation and Relationship in Judaism. The Book of Jonah as Case Study', in *Reconciliation in Interfaith Perspective. Jewish, Christian and Muslim Voices*, eds R. Bieringer, J.D. Bolton, Peeters, Leuven, pp. 9–27.

Scherman, N. 2008, מחזור זכרון יוסף ליום כפור: נוסח אשכנז/*The Complete ArtScroll Machzor Yom Kippur. Nusach Ashkenaz*, Mesorah Publications, New York.

Sfard, M. 2016, ‘The Israeli Occupation Will End Suddenly'. From: http://www.haaretz.com/opinion/. premium-1.698821 [23[th] March 2018].

Spinoza, B. 2010, *Ethik in geometrischer Ordnung dargestellt*, in Id., *Sämtliche Werke*, 2, ed W. Bartuschat, Felix Meinen Verlag, Hamburg.

Trepp, L. 2004, *Der jüdische Gottesdienst. Gestalt und Entwicklung*, Kohlhammer Verlag, Stuttgart.

Twerski, A.J. 2008, *Happiness and the Human Spirit. The Spirituality of Becoming the Best You Can Be*, Jewish Lights Publishing, Woodstock.

Weinreb, T.H. (ed) 2013, *Yoma*, in *Koren Talmud Bavli: The Noé Edition*, 9, Koren Publishers, Jerusalem.

Zempelburg, A. 2019, *Versöhnung im Judentum, Eine religionswissenschaftliche Perspektive auf den jüdischen Versöhnungsbegriff in Bezug auf Gott, den Nächsten, den Anderen und sich selbst*, Tectum, Baden Baden.

Zeina M. Barakat

# Reconciliation as Transformation from Extremism to Moderation

## The Case of Palestine-Israel

### Abstract

The Arabic term *wasatia* lies at the core of the Wasatia movement, whose creation and development are analyzed in Zeina M. Barakat's *From Heart of Stone to Heart of Flesh*. The paper is based on her doctoral dissertation at the Friedrich-Schiller University of Jena, which appeared as a same-titled book in 2017. It will provide an account of the lifelong journey of the Jerusalem-born educator and peace activist Mohammed Dajani Daoudi from extremism to moderation. Barakat points out the key agents in Dajani's life that caused such transformation by examining his family background, his personal and national narrative, changing attitude by behavior and the ethical point of reference influencing his thinking. Her paper analyzes the deep-rooted ethical teaching that moved Dajani to become committed to seeking moderation, reconciliation, and democracy. Those values inspired the creation of the Wasatia Movement, aimed by Dajani as a platform to transform Palestinian public opinion positively by recognizing them as necessary educative components in a peace strategy for the next generations of Israelis and Palestinians.

\*\*\*

The book *From Heart of Stone to Heart of Flesh. Evolutionary Journey from Extremism to Moderation,* published in 2017 (Barakat 2017), borrows its title from the trilateral project "Hearts of Flesh–Not Stone." This metaphor refers to an image in the book of the Prophet Ezekiel: "And I will give you a new heart, and a new spirit I will put within you. And I will remove the heart of stone from your flesh and give you a heart of flesh" (Ezekiel XXXVI:26, ESV). This image is significant also in Muslim culture since the Holy Quran says: {"Then your hearts became hardened after that, being like stones or even harder. For indeed, there are stones from which rivers burst forth, and there are some of them that split open, and water comes out, and there are some of them that fall for fear of God. Moreover, God is not unaware of what you do."} (Quran 2:74).

ثُمَّ قَسَتْ قُلُوبُكُم مِّن بَعْدِ ذَٰلِكَ فَهِيَ كَالْحِجَارَةِ أَوْ أَشَدُّ قَسْوَةً ۚ وَإِنَّ مِنَ الْحِجَارَةِ لَمَا يَتَفَجَّرُ مِنْهُ الْأَنْهَارُ ۚ وَإِنَّ مِنْهَا لَمَا يَشَّقَّقُ فَيَخْرُجُ مِنْهُ الْمَاءُ ۚ وَإِنَّ مِنْهَا لَمَا يَهْبِطُ مِنْ خَشْيَةِ اللَّهِ ۗ وَمَا اللَّهُ بِغَافِلٍ عَمَّا تَعْمَلُونَ [البقرة: 74]

The book's central question, similar to that of the project, seeks to explain and study the transformation of individuals and groups from extremism to moderation and from lesser to a more significant willingness for reconciliation. It addresses what explains such a shift in human behavior and what role empathy plays in such transformation. The book, inspired by the project's central theme, describes an individual's journey from a closed mindset of "us or them" to an open mindset of "us and them" by taking as its case study Palestinian intellectual and peace activist Mohammed S. Dajani Daoudi. The primary focus of the publication is experiencing the "suffering of the other" as a means of understanding how and why individuals may become more open to reconciliation.

The book has five main objectives. First, it seeks to identify and examine the agents of change that contributed to the performance of the reconciliation process. Second, it explores whether such a transformation is a unique individual case or can be generalized. Third, it evaluates the role of moderation and middle ground in paving the way for reconciliation, coexistence, and peace. Fourth, it assesses how encountering "the humanity of the other" (as was the case with Dajani when his parents received critical healthcare attention from Israeli medics) can have an *independent* influence on the general reconciliation process, in particular, its impact on the likelihood of consolidating a group transition from a culture of conflict to a culture of peace. Fifth, it considers the role of the Wasatia movement[1] as a trusted Muslim religious entity capable of engaging in the midst of conflict (what Martin Leiner calls the "Hölderlin Perspective") of people-to-people public engagement to generate new forms of soft dialogue to bridge the gap between both clashing ideologies to warm attitudes towards reconciliation.[2] In combination with the needs-based model of reconciliation, developed by Tel Aviv University psychologist Arie Nadler, the Hölderlin perspective demands that the needs of people in the process of reconciliation amid conflict must be respected (Nadler

---

1 The Wasatia Movement derives its name from the term *wasatia* which appears in verse 143 in The Cow (*Al Baqarat) Surah* in the Holy Quran which says: ["And thus We have created you Ummatan Wasatan [a middle ground (moderate) nation/ a centrist ummah (community)]". The term *wasatia* in Arabic means center and middle. In the Quranic text it means justice, moderation, balance and temperance. Verse 143 of the second chapter falls exactly in the midst of the 286 verses composing the surat. The passage demonstrates that the need to be moderate and temperate is a central code of Islamic doctrine.

2 The Hölderlin Perspective (Leiner 2012, pp. 8–16) derives its name from the German poet, theologian, and philosopher Friedrich Hölderlin (1770–1843) who in the end of his novel *Hyperion* calls for reconciliation in the midst of strife: "*Versöhnung ist mitten im Streit und alles Getrennte findet sich wieder*" ["Reconciliation is in the middle of dispute and all things separated find each other again."]. The Hölderlin maxim is deeply rooted in the New Testament. The principle is inspired by Hölderlin's (1797) argument that elements of peace and reconciliation are already found in the midst of conflict (Barakat 2018).

et al. 2008). According to his pyramid of needs, Abraham Maslow, especially basic needs, require attention (Maslow 1943). The needs Maslow lists are food security, medical care, housing, and safety. For Dajani, these needs focus more on the love of the country, attachment to the land, liberty, identity, honor, dignity, respect, and self-esteem.

The book addresses questions such as: What role would knowing the other (and showing empathy for the "suffering of the other") play in acknowledging, accepting, and understanding the psyche of the other? How did the evolution of Mohammed Dajani from extremist to moderate take place? What were the moral motivations that inspired Dajani to shift from the state of dehumanization, delegitimization, demonization, non-recognition, and non-acceptance of the other to legitimization, recognition, appreciation, and humanization of the other? What moral principles guided this transformation from stone to flesh, and what role did his moral and ethical upbringing play in changing his behaviour? What role did his ethical identity play in this transformation? How does the Hölderlin Perspective relate to the *Wasatia* Perspective as a tool in the reconciliation process? Should moderation and reconciliation precede or follow the resolution of the conflict? What are the values that led Dajani to take the path of moderation? What is the right thing to do when it comes to suffering, human rights, and delivering justice and equality to the other?

The answers to how to transform human behaviour from extremism to moderation hold enormous significance not only for the communities in conflict in the region but also within any community where inter-communal conflict exists. Extremists are attempting to change the course of history to fit their vision. If extremists' triumph, the political stability, economic prosperity, and human security of people living in states dominated by extremists will be at risk. Moreover, international trade and human mobility will be at risk. Conflict will spread, and people will resort to violence, armed struggle, and terrorism to control resources. Monopolies of power would become more common, economies would deteriorate, and genocide would become more prevalent. The middle path would be a way to a meaningful life.

Hence the book *From Heart of Stone to Heart of Flesh* aims to demonstrate the significance of morality and ethics for human behavioral and intellectual transformation changes shifting from radicalism, extremism, and intransigence (the heart of stone) to balance, moderation, and reconciliation (the heart of flesh). In exploring the causes of of transformative processes, the role of family, religion, education and ethics cannot be underestimated. *From Heart of Stone to Heart of Flesh* focuses on the descriptive ethical dimension of the events that play a significant role in shaping the individual and collective consciousness and memory. The aspiration is to contribute to the ethical research on moderation of being just, doing what is right, and being balanced in motivation by taking the middle path.

Reconciliation may blossom through mutual empathy, trust-building, forgiveness, and compassion. The vision of transforming cold, stony hearts full of anger, hatred, fear, bitterness, and fury into hearts of flesh full of life, hope, courage, and optimism holds enormous potential for a happy life. The book illuminates the mysterious ways morality and ethics play a challenging role in transforming individuals from being entirely exclusive to becoming inclusive. Also, causing a person to shift their ideological orientation from one end of the spectrum to the middle through realizing the Wasatia principle of temperance, the Aristotelian golden mean, and Maimonides'concept of the *mida beinonit*, referred to as "the doctrine of the mean."

The trend would be more in line with the thesis, which argues that practitioners of conflict resolution need to focus more on reconciliation (the restoration of hope, confidence, trust, cooperation, accord, and harmony between rivals) than on temporarily resolving the issues that fuel the conflict. Here, reconciliation techniques shift the focus in two ways. First, they take more of a grassroots bottom-up approach to build peace within the civil society of rival communities and not only between its leaders. Second, reconciliation is a long process that requires an extended time to resolve disputes and end conflicts.

The book *From Heart of Stone to Heart of Flesh* employs the case study as its methodology to seek answers to questions raised. The case study examines Palestinian intellectual and peace activist Mohammed S. Dajani Daoudi and studies his shift from a mindset of radicalism and extremism to moderation, compromise, tolerance, peaceful coexistence, and normalization. Such a transformation is eagerly sought to put an end to people's suffering in a protracted conflict. It describes Dajani's upbringing in a liberal Muslim family, educational and political journeys, ethical and moral development, professional career, and efforts to enhance creativity and critical thinking in his teachings. It portrays his educational philosophy of breaking taboos by establishing the American graduate Studies program at Al-Quds University in 2002 and leading a controversial student trip in March 2014 to the Auschwitz Nazi death concentration camp to teach his students about the Holocaust. The book sheds light on the long-term effect of seeking knowledge, searching for the truth, and showing empathy for the historical suffering of his occupiers in the transformation process of his values, behaviour, and aspirations.

*From Heart of Stone to Heart of Flesh* is divided into eight chapters of different perspectives dealing with moderation concepts and philosophy. The introductory chapter lays down the historical background of the Arab-Israeli conflict. Chapter One narrates the major historical events which shaped the Middle East and contributed to the ideological, intellectual, and political transformation of Dajani. It successfully blends the historical narrative of the Israeli-Palestinian controversy and contemporary thought on theoretical and practical importance issues to illuminate the linkage between the essential concepts of moderation and reconciliation (see Hameiri et al. present volume). The historical background aims to help explain the environment in which Dajani grew up and identifies the significant events that shaped his career. It recounts history through advancing three narratives: the international, the Israeli, and the Palestinian. Chapter two describes the factors influencing the change process for Dajani, such as his family, education, religion, culture, and media. From the Friends Quaker School, Dajani adopted his views on religious tolerance and religious freedom, which later played an essential role in shaping his Wasatia philosophy. At the Friends School in the West Bank city of Ramallah, Dajani was taught not to feel any distinction between people with different faiths, colors, and ethnic backgrounds and not to differentiate between someone rich and someone poor. The Quaker philosophy coincided with the Quran that all religions and beliefs, called for similar values, and became his guiding light. Later on, he taught his students the significance of seeking mutual understanding through education. He kept a strong sense of egalitarianism within himself and the professional skills to deal with adversity, and the broad sense of self-confidence that eventually helped him to overpower his intense feelings for retaliation and retribution. Chapter Three focuses on converting the case study from a "heart of stone to a heart of flesh", i. e., from extremism to moderation. Chapter Four discusses the concept of moderation in ancient and modern times and brings a range of classic philosophers – from Plato to Aristotle to Maimonides to al-Ghazali – to bear witness on the significance of the middle path in human lives. The book illustrates that classical philosophy can still deal with crucial modern issues.

Consequently, Chapter Five outlines the factors influencing the creation in Palestine of the moderate Islamic movement named *Wasatia* and outlines its activities to spread the culture of justice, balance, middle ground, and centrism within the Palestinian society and abroad. Chapter Six analyzes Dajani's views on peace initiatives and reconciliation, stressing that the best pathway to settlement is finding solutions both parties would accept as good enough. The Seventh Chapter details the actions Dajani took and the risks to which he exposed himself as well as his professional career to enrich the knowledge of his students by taking them on a breakthrough visit to the Nazi death concentration camp at Auschwitz in Poland. The trip aimed to teach Palestinian students reconciliation through empathy and expose them to the realities of the taboo topic of the Holocaust (Dajani et al., 2016; Barakat, 2014). However, the Palestinian public was outraged, and Dajani was condemned even among his colleagues at al-Quds University as a "traitor" and "collaborator." His car was torched, and his life was threatened. Chapter Eight concludes the research by stressing the significance of the *Wasatia* moderation approach as being essential for creating an environment conducive to attaining reconciliation in the midst of conflict by building bridges of understanding, trust, empathy, and goodwill – all essential ingredients for negotiating in good faith and achieving a comprehensive sustainable settlement.

In his book *Sources of the Self,* Canadian philosopher Charles Taylor provides a thoughtful insight into moral biography (Taylor 1992, p. 15). In the first part of his book, he explains that identity always evolves within a moral landscape, where traditions bring good and evil but change through shifting environments, social processes, and individual choices. Dajani first constructed his identity within a family and school environment, where values of kindness, compassion, tolerance, and forgiveness were dominant, even though intense experiences of injustice have been significant. At the American University in Beirut, his moral landscape changed. Extremism and violence frequently gained positive connotations. Moderation and tolerance were not perceived as esteemed values anymore. Moving to the West, Dajani found his way back to the values of his childhood. Being distanced from the conflict and exposed to a liberal culture opened his eyes to see the bigger picture. Exposure to the clashing Israeli-Palestinian narratives, educational insights, personal experiences, and openness to the perspectives of the other may facilitate our journey from extremism to moderation.

Through his life journey, Dajani has developed two models of reconciliation: the first is entitled "Big Dream Small Hope" (Dajani Daoudi 2006), and the second is the Wasatia Initiative (Dajani Daoudi 2009). The model describes how the mindset of two groups in conflict decides their willingness to reconcile or continue fighting. The model raises the question: Is it our psychology, nature, culture, or our politics that prevents achieving a negotiated settlement to a conflict? According to Dajani, the "Big Dream" for one side is to wake up one morning and find that the other has disappeared. The "Small Hope" for both disagreeing groups is to find that peace prevails, and both coexist in harmony with secure borders, and good neighbourly relations, enjoying the prosperity reconciliation and democracy entails. In his model, Dajani describes the rise of a new paradigm in which people in conflict are not divided by national affiliation but by political ideology: those who support peace in one camp and those who oppose it. The model calls upon people to become aware of the immorality of exclusivity embedded in the "Big Dream" since it implies ethnic cleansing of the other. The "Small Hope" holds a positive value since it symbolizes the Wasatia cycle of moving from extremism to moderation, reconciliation, peace, and democracy in an experience of creativity, wonder, enlightenment, and inspiration.

In his famous poem *The Road Not Taken*, published in 1916, American poet Robert Frost describes the dilemma of choosing one of two forks in a road through the woods. Having settled for the less-traveled fork, with some regret, the traveler notes that regular momentum would cause him to press ahead and thus negating a return trip to try the other path. Similarly, conflict momentum pushes groups in conflict to press ahead and deny them a return trip to adopt the other path of peace.

A complex issue the book raises is whether ethics have a role in changing extremists with "hearts of stone" and "big dreams" of exclusivity to "hearts of flesh" with "small hope" of inclusivity. The first may use unilateralism, boycotts, anti-normalization, violence, terrorism, genocide, and mass-deporting the other to enjoy the right to the land by denying the human rights of others; the second are those committed to dialogue, diplomacy, normalization, compromise, and peaceful resolution of conflict. As a task of political philosophy, the book addresses how and why a leading Palestinian influential figure, who once used to be an extremist, became a moderate, overcoming dualistic thinking forms like "I am right/you are wrong; my cause is just/your cause is wrong; I am an angel/you are the devil; I am destined to enter heaven/you are going to Hell; my religion is what God desires/your religion is what God rejects," developing commitment to religious tolerance, diversity, plurality, peaceful coexistence and cooperation.

The book carefully examines the ethical indicators which determine the choice of the path to take when one faces crucial decisions. The central focus is targeting three core values: (a) *moderation* — reflecting justice and balance in dealing with daily personal and national issues, and (b) *reconciliation* — reflecting the willingness to resolve by sacrificing maximalist demands, respecting the personal and collective narrative of the other, feeling compassion for the pain and suffering of the other, and showing interest by putting oneself in the shoes of the other, (c) *democracy* — reflecting one's feeling of respect for the views and expressions of others and tolerating the faith and beliefs of others. These three concepts are linked together, each leads to the other, and one cannot flourish without the other. They form what Dajani calls the "Reconciliation Cycle," i. e., that moderation paves the way for reconciliation, which in turn contributes towards the creation of a more trustful society, influencing its attitude for a peaceful end to the conflict by ushering in peace, democracy, and prosperity.

The book concludes by stressing the urgency to follow the path of moderation to achieve peace, security, and prosperity as a treasured heritage for future generations. Though Dajani's family background, personal experience, and educational development played a crucial role in changing his way of thinking and conduct, he is not an isolated case. It is possible to replicate his transformation by creating a peaceful environment and culture. Findings of the book assert that the deep-rooted ethical and academic teachings are essential agents who facilitated his shift from the periphery to the center: "Us or them" / "I am right, you are wrong" / "It is either black or white" / "My way right or wrong" (win-lose outcome), to adopting moderation, i. e. "us and them" / "I may be wrong, you may be right" / "Between black and white there is gray" (win-win outcome).

The research identifies the new trend of benefiting from modern communication social media and technologies, such as Facebook, to reach out to the public. The Wasatia initiative benefits from websites and groups social networks by using them as a sounding board to enable direct citizen engagement with the reconciliation process and call for a deep commitment to a vision of moderation as a transformative, democratizing force. Such a medium is a powerful and vital tool to voice the aspirations of Wasatia as a movement with limited financial resources, providing fresh, unexpected insights about politics, religion, and culture.

The research emphasizes that reconciliation is not a static state but an almost never-ending dynamic process. In our world, reconciliation is an unsatisfied craving. Therefore, spirituality is necessary for sustaining continuous efforts toward reconciliation. However, the commitment to a religion, is not needed, but it can help to motivate persistent engagement and may act as a heavenly resource of inspiration for reconciliation.

*From Heart of Stone to Heart of Flesh* is a textbook to help readers understand the twin subject matter of moderation and reconciliation. With this publication, teachers, students, and anyone interested in the topic will find interesting practical insights and answers to their questions concerning reconciliation. Readers could think about the questions and then discuss the ideas with others, which would serve as a starting point for future research of the issues it debates. Reading through the book provides the reader with a deep understanding of the issues it covers and is enlightening for those concerned about whether one should do the right thing if the personal costs are high?

In conclusion, *From Heart of Stone to Heart of Flesh* is a discourse on pluralism, heterogeneity, and cultural diversity dissected and extensively illustrated for peace and reconciliation scholars. It explores critical approaches to moderation and relates them to the field of coexistence. It approaches the inter-relationships between moderation and reconciliation from two perspectives. First, is the theoretical approach that places high value and distinctive characteristics on the concept of moderation. Second, the on-ground practical implementation of the concept by the Islamic movement Wasatia within the Palestinian society to generate a national culture of temperance and acceptance. The book offers a comprehensive account of how people may shift their philosophy and identity from political extremism to a moderate philosophy in theory and practice amid conflict.

### References

Barakat, Z.M. 2008, "Islam in Our Times," *Crosscurrent,* pp. 220–223.

Barakat, Z.M. 2014, 'A Palestinian Student Defends Her Visit to Auschwitz'. Accessed 02.10.2015. http://www.theatlantic.com/international/archive/2014/04/a-palestinian-student-defends-her-visit-to-auschwitz/361311

Barakat, Z.M. 2017, *From Heart of Stone to Heart of Flesh. Evolutionary Journey from Extremism to Moderation*, Herbert UTZ Verlag, Munich.

Barakat, Z.M. 2018, 'Reconciliation in the Midst of Strife. Palestine', in *Reconciliation in Global Context. Why It Is Needed and How It Works*, ed B. Krondorfer, SUNY Press, New York, pp. 129–150.

Barakat, Z.M. and Dajani, M. 2015, "Israeli/Palestinian Narratives: Challenges and Opportunities", in Ertablierte und Aussenseiter zugleich: Selbst und Fremdbilder in den paelestinensischen Communities im Westjordanland und Israel, edited by Gabriela Rosenthal. Campus Verlag: Frankfurt am Main, pp. 295–312.

Dajani Daoudi, M. 2006, 'Big Dream/Small Hope. A Peace Vision', in *Educating Toward a Culture of Peace*, ed Y. Iram, Information Age Publishing, Greenwich, CT, pp. 39–56.

Dajani Daoudi, M. 2009, *Wasatia. The Spirit of Islam*, Wasatia Publishing, Jerusalem.

Dajani Daoudi, M. [Mohammed], Dajani Daoudi, M. [Munther], Leiner, M., Barakat, Z. (eds) 2016, *Teaching Empathy and Reconciliation in Midst of Conflict*, Wasatia Academic Institute, Jerusalem and Jena.

Hameiri, B., Gabay, R., Rubel-Lifschitz, T., Nadler, A. 2022, 'Victimhood Acknowledgment as a Vehicle to Promote Intergroup Conciliatory Attitudes in a Context of Intergroup Conflict', present volume.

Leiner, M., Flämig, S. (eds) 2012, *Latin America Between Conflict and Reconciliation*, Vandenhoeck and Ruprecht, Göttingen.

Maslow, A. 1943, 'A Theory of Human Motivation', *Psychological Review*, vol. 50, no. 4, pp. 370–396.

Nadler, A., Malloy T.E., Fisher, J.D. (eds) 2008, *The Social Psychology of Intergroup Reconciliation*, Oxford University Press, Oxford.

Taylor, C. 1992, *Sources of the Self. The Making of the Modern Identity*, Cambridge University Press, New York.

Martin J. O'Malley

# Narratives and Justice in Reconciliation Research

## An Applied Ethics Perspective

### Abstract

Martin J. O'Malley's contribution, *Narratives and Justice in Reconciliation Research: An Applied Ethics Perspective*, examines methods and principles for reconciliation research. The first part outlines Martin Leiner's keystone principle, the Hölderlin perspective, which is central to the Jena Center of Reconciliation Studies (JCRS) endeavors. The second part proposes a related justice principle, the Schiller correlative. Part three deepens the conceptual reflection on reconciliation and justice and introduces three derivative priority rules for dealing with intergroup conflicts. The ethical, political, and local (subsidiarity) priorities offer practical guidance for understanding and dealing with conflict and post-conflict transitions. Finally, part four describes how reconciliation work can promote justice through memory narratives that contribute to social flourishing. The Hölderlin perspective softens many rigid boundaries used to conceptually separate situations of war from peace, antagonism from reconciliation, and even victim(s) from perpetrator(s). It draws insight from the poet Hölderlin (1770–1843) to contemplate reconciliation existing within our modern condition's complex but inherently social nature. O'Malley argues that justice – the concept – is optimally understood as a virtue that is actualized in practical reasoning ordered to the elusive but necessary goal (telos) of social flourishing. Conversely, understanding justice in some essentialist, idealistic, or universalistic way can undermine the pursuit of practical actions with unrealizable expectations. The author's applied ethics perspective argues that both reconciliation and justice share a telos of social flourishing and are therefore necessarily mutually supportive.

### Introduction

This essay examines the methods and principles of reconciliation research. The first part outlines Martin Leiner's keystone principle, the Hölderlin perspective, which is central to the Jena Center of Reconciliation Studies (JCRS) endeavors. The second part proposes a related justice principle, the Schiller correlative. Part three deepens the conceptual reflection on reconciliation and justice, introducing three derivative priority rules for dealing with intergroup conflicts. The ethical, political, and local (subsidiarity) priorities offer practical guidance for understanding and dealing with conflict and post-conflict transitions. Part four describes how reconciliation work can promote justice through memory narratives that contribute to social flourishing. The Hölderlin perspective softens many rigid boundaries used to conceptually differentiate war situations from peace, antagonism from reconciliation, and even victim(s) from perpetrator(s). It draws insight from the poet to contemplate reconciliation existing within the complex but inherently social nature of our modern condition. The virtue justice is, like reconciliation, ordered to the elusive but necessary goal (telos) of social flourishing. Justice and reconciliation are necessarily mutually supportive because they share a telos of social flourishing. This essay represents part of a larger argument developed for an applied ethics monograph.

## 1. Hölderlin Perspective. Keystone of the Jena Approach to Reconciliation

The Hölderlin perspective is an approach to "seeing" conflict contexts that intentionally investigates reconciling dynamics that persist even during conflicts' most violent expressions. It is inspired by Friedrich Hölderlin's poetry from the early Romantic era – when the glory of the Enlightenment was dimmed by terror and tumult following the French Revolution. The perspective also represents the judgment that conflict and post-conflict interventions and research should be guided by an umbrella category of reconciliation. Reconciliation provides the teleologically-ordered framework of principles, priorities, disciplines, and goals, within which transitional justice, restorative justice, and many other fields of activities and research have important roles. Leiner uses the word "perspective" to highlight its instructive role in guiding reconciliation work. The Hölderlin perspective supports the principles, methods, and spirit of the Jena approach (Leiner 2012).

The perspective we use to "see" a conflict impacts the ways we come to understand the conflicts themselves and the potentials for dealing with them. The Hölderlin perspective softens many hard boundaries used to conceptually separate situations of war from peace, antagonism from reconciliation, and even victim(s) from perpetrator(s). Instead, it draws insight from the poet to contemplate, first, reconciliation existing within the complex but inherently social nature of our modern condition, and second, fuller reconciliation as the elusive but necessary goal towards which individuals and communities strive. Conflict and violence present situations of immense personal and social cost to be avoided and resolved, when possible, but we are indelibly marked by historical, recent, and continuing conflicts – large and small. Our lives are never free from conflict and its effects. Reductive individual and group identifications are counter-productive for promoting sustainable peace and reconciliation. And the Hölderlin perspective draws from the field of hermeneutics to bring critical attention to abstract, exclusionary, or alienating group boundaries. Even categories such as victim/perpetrator, for example, deserve close critical attention for the ways that such identifications promote or reduce openness to reconciliation. In this teleological approach, reconciliation as goal (*telos*) is stimulus and measure.

## 1.1 Three Axes of the Narrative Frame: Historical, Relational, Subsidiarity

For post-conflict societies, interventions must consider the broadly shared narrative-like interpretations of conflict-related experiences because they are potentially more or less productive for reconciliation.

The Jena approach methodologically analyses the narrative language present in conflict contexts and therefore integrates hermeneutical methods for understanding conflict and reconciliation dynamics. When using critical hermeneutic tools, one must avoid naïve narrative assumptions and be suspicious of historical rationalizations or traditions supporting or even tolerating recognized injustices such as racism, violence, sexism, etc. A well-developed reconciliation hermeneutic is a valuable instrument to study how individuals and groups understand themselves as embedded in a context deeply marked by a past that shapes a present and future.

The reconciliation hermeneutic – perspective – constructs an interpretative frame in three dimensions: historical, relational, and subsidiarity – this last dimension identifies the "geographic" context as more local (polis) or more general (cosmos). These three dimensions can be graphed along three intersecting axes. The "narrative frame" graphs a society's past, the historical axis, in relation to a present axis of social relations and values – including value traditions of critical rationality. Individuals and groups are bound together in meaningful relationships created and sustained by common historical events, historically developed values, and historically achieved laws and customs. With the historical axis intersected by the social-relational axis, the narrative landscape has further dimensions relative to the social organizations on familial and interpersonal levels (polis), extending to larger communities and further expanding to religious, city, local state, national, and cosmopolitan levels.

The reconciliation hermeneutic of the Jena approach uses these three axes (historical, relational, subsidiarity) to "understand" conflict contexts and the already-existing reconciliation dynamics within those contexts. Even on the most personal subsidiarity level, namely the individual, there are many narrative arcs used to describe and understand ourselves. We are each members of families, social groups, friendships, businesses, schools, community groups, etc. Our membership identities can be wide-ranging and complex. Associated group narratives may overlap, but there may be also narratives with little overlap beyond their relevance to the individual.

## 1.2 Hermeneutical Tools for Reconciliation

Paul Ricœur (1913–2005) developed a hermeneutical philosophy that provides rich insights and support for reconciliation. Ricœur's hermeneutical approach is pragmatic and epistemological in the sense that narrative analytic tools help make sense of how humans are simultaneously living in history and creating history. This hermeneutic approach benefits from Heidegger's work on time and focuses on the understanding of the person as a social reality. This temporally mediated understanding brought Ricœur back to Augustine's famous reflection on time in *Confessions* XI. Like Augustine, Ricœur reflects upon the essence of human temporal perception to undermine too-simple ontological-semantic dichotomies. Stated more simply, to understand the "what" of who we are in society, we must understand the "how" we are as historically and socially mediated. We understand ourselves – our "whatness" – by telling our stories about ourselves. Ricœur uses narrative analysis in a pragmatic and hermeneutic way and shows how the stories (plural) of history and fiction bear meanings (again plural) that help configure the way persons and groups make sense of their own experiences. People in history can be aware of their own stories as having been "written" or created and thus bearing the mark of those creators. Histories of migration, wars, struggles, and triumphs are imbued with meaning that communicates human values. By being aware of our own participation in the recognition, approval, and passing on of our stories, we can use careful reflection and good judgment. We can become creative and ethical co-authors of the narratives, and thereby, we can help bend those narrative arcs towards justice. Using this framework in a conflict context highlights the relevance of hermeneutics for justice. Co-authoring narratives is an ethical act requiring responsibility, principles of justice, notions of memory, history writing, and forgiveness as inherently creative moral actions ordered towards a telos that is itself only understood within the dynamics and dialectics of narrative-like epistemological ordering.

This hermeneutic approach to understanding justice presents a very different model from essentialist approaches, where justice is understood to be some "thing" that, for example, exists within (or is identical to) hierarchically ordered rights, principles, duties, and laws. The vast complexity of conflict situations demonstrates the inadequacy of essentialist building-brick models because interventions of justice are not merely the Humpty-Dumpty repair of conflict tragedies. Undeniably, human rights, ethical principles, moral duties, and laws are all relevant. And promoting justice requires institutions that embody, foster, and enforce human rights and good laws. Nevertheless, reconciliation requires deeply creative insights into interventions, legal processes, truth-finding, and society building. Functioning human relationships are not "created" but can be fostered. Reconciliation and justice conceptions must therefore foster, not hinder, creativity ordered towards social flourishing in even the most deeply traumatized conflict situations.

At best, any attempts to swim to a shore of rock-solid ontological, ethical foundations of essentialism are illusory. We cannot transcend the search for meaning in the search for meaning. Ricœur's hermeneutic framework is not a rejection of truth or dismissal of subjective and group meaning, but rather carries a conviction that truth is always situated, always understood within a matrix of meanings, and always woven in complex, overlapping, and even conflicting narrative-mediated meanings. This leaves ethical reflection in potentially deep and turbulent waters, so it is best to learn to swim with strength, technique, and endurance.

The Ricœurian method informs the Jena approach in requiring all analysis to first inquire: "*D'ou parlez vous?*" ("From where do you speak?"). This starting point (Blundell 2010, p. 562) reflects a commitment to an embodied perspective that marks this essay's reconciliation as one of local priority. Ricœur writes in 1996 (*New Ethos for Europe*) that the content of tradition is provided within an exchange of memories subject to ethical judgment. He even references the prophet Ezekiel's image of dry bones to describe how ethically ordered and mutually realized traditions give flesh to the present and future. "Indeed, the past is not only what is bygone – that which has taken place and can no longer be changed – it also lives in the memory thanks to arrows of futurity which have not been fired or whose trajectory has been interrupted. The unfulfilled future of the past forms perhaps the richest part of a tradition" (Ricœur 1996, p. 8).

Though Ricœur assigns such forgiveness models to a principle of charity and elsewhere to love, the Jena approach frames all reconciliation-relevant actions ordered to social flourishing as matters that also fall within the relevance of justice reflection. Ricœur's differentiation of social spheres (political, moral) and his oppositions of justice to charity/love reflect, perhaps his fundamentally dialogical approach and/or his unwillingness to collapse the differentiated social discourses relevant to narrative memories. Yet even this differentiation is nuanced by his integration of Aristotelian teleology and his hermeneutic phenomenology in what he calls "three moments of ethics, morality, and practical wisdom" (Ricœur 1995, p. 51). Of these three, he prioritizes the ethical. Though his semantic differentiation is not Aristotle's, Ricœur's definition of ethics shows his affinity: "Ethics … is defined as follows: the wish to live well with and for others in just institutions" (Ibidem). And while practical wisdom is considered another moment, a moment that brings attention to the complexity of concrete situation, Ricœur's treatment of narrative ideas, legal systems, and ethics in *The Just* (2000) is consistent with a principle of justice in Aristotle's *Nicomachean Ethics* as ultimately a principle that orders social relations to the good of society, which is another way of saying social flourishing.

Thus, Ricœur's exploration of narrative, memory, forgiveness, and reconciliation reflects an ethical priority to remember rightly, and he makes this argument explicitly with Aristotelian ethical terms and references. Volf 2006 makes a similar move, but in less compelling philosophical arguments. Even the burden of tragic historical injustice is affected by this ethical insight, though on this descriptive account, this approach might seem abstractly indifferent to historical situations deserving clear condemnation, such as genocide. Even foundational ethical principles are best understood as historically-contexted achievements. For example, the principle of human dignity was born amidst post-war reflection upon the human capacity for evil demonstrated in the Holocaust. Memories in the form of narratives, or stories, or whatever, can have impact on the trajectories of individual and social development towards the realization of capacities for flourishing (O'Malley 2011).

Relevant to the applied ethics perspective of this essay is the appreciation of the historical nature of our present social values. The justice virtue, discussed below, develops in history through persistent practice and reasonable reflection regarding how a group's future can be directed towards its best – not perfect – future. Our "social imaginary," as Taylor 2007 shows, represents the vast matrix of meanings by which we understand ourselves. A justice perspective views potentials and challenges regarding social well-being. The Hölderlin perspective, analogously, is both realistic and utopic in the sense that it approaches conflict with a view to already operative "reconciling" patterns of social cooperation despite tragic dynamics of violence and disruption. Reconciliation is never wholly absent, nor ever achieved fully and finally. Reconciliation as telos, and thus stimulus and measure, guides the Jena approach's processes of analysis, interventions, and reassessments with respect to social values.

## 2. Schiller Correlative: Justice is a Virtue Characterized as Prudent Political Action Ordered to Social Flourishing

Justice, as concept, is best understood as a virtue expressed in prudent political action necessary for and ordered to the best flourishing of the community. Because justice and reconciliation processes share a common purpose (telos), on the conceptual level they must be at least potentially compatible and mutually supportive. The applied level is immensely complex, of course, but nevertheless the Jena approach holds that there is no justice without reconciliation; no reconciliation without justice. Intergroup conflict that is marked by dehumanizing violence must be dealt with in ways that not only respond to the violence with justice-relevant processes, but those processes must contribute to some possible productive future for the groups involved. The "Schiller correlative" taps insights from the historical figure regarding the vastly complex tragic histories, which exclude future-oriented "justice" options.

Tragedies such as genocide, deliberate targeting of non-combatants, intentional displacement of peoples, and so on, all call for international and legal responses that seem incompatible with any mutually acceptable terms for sustainable peace.

War and peace have been topics for philosophical analysis and a famous example is Immanuel Kant's 1795 Perpetual Peace. Kant's contemporary Schiller, however, preferred to explore the topic of conflict as a playwright. He used the dramatic form to address the complexity of violent conflict; an example is the Wallenstein trilogy based on a Thirty-Years-War context. The Hölderlin perspective draws attention to reconciling realities within situations of violent conflict, the Schiller correlative sheds light on the individual and social paths of dealing with conflict despite the quagmires they may present. For example, in "Wilhelm Tell" (1805), the play's conflict situation calls forth the hero Tell to identify and condemn injustice. Yet, his heroic action best expresses justice in its transcendence of injustice – when Tell's creative action opens a potential future for his family and community. A more contemporary real-life Tell would be Nelson Mandela in post-Apartheid South Africa. Mandela understood the importance of recognizing past injustice and the need to build law-based courts and governing institutions, and he also understood that his land required creative leadership to transcend its troubled past with a compelling narrative of future flourishing. In so acting, Mandela expressed the virtue of justice.

Virtues are praiseworthy habits, and justice is a praiseworthy habit of practical reasoning or prudence. Whereas the virtuous musician expresses her virtuosity in the playing of music, justice is expressed in practical reasoning, in pragmatic action in the midst of messy social contexts. With Schiller in mind, the justice concept is defined to integrate the wisdom of philosophical traditions as well as contemporary social science approaches. The claim here is both simple and profound. As simple, defining justice as a virtue has a long tradition. Yet the profound claim is that this is not just one more justice approach among many, but a formal definition of the concept itself. Justice cannot be reduced to some abstract idea of balance, nor to some static essentialist thing like a catalog of rights. Justice, as concept, is most appropriately understood as being expressed in actions that optimally deal with conflict contexts to achieve situations most generative of social well-being.

Justice is therefore appropriately described in the philosophical tradition as a virtue. This is as true now as it was for Aristotle, Aquinas, Hume, Peirce, to the present. This tradition informs the following definition: "Justice as virtue" is a trained faculty of practical reasoning that is expressed in action and characterized by the following five elements:

1. It is expressed by a community or by a leader on behalf of the community, though it is obviously relevant to individuals.
2. It is characterized by prudence, which is another way of saying good judgment or practical reasoning.

3. It is based upon stable dispositions – that on the social level are institutionalized in systems of governance, principles of rights, ethics, social rules, and traditions.
4. It is ordered to the telos or purpose of the community's best flourishing.
5. And, it is applied in the most local context – a characteristic clarified in the principle of subsidiarity.

Ethical reflection upon the nature of justice is relevant because actions undertaken to achieve reconciliation require a telos by which those actions can be measured, and this telos is the vision of the good – the common good. Achieving consensus on a justice definition may seem like a path of more conflict, as opposed to reconciliation, given the wide divergence of political worldviews, religious commitments, and ethical beliefs existing among and within social groups dealing with conflict. However, the present attempt to provide a justice definition does not attempt to achieve unanimity on metaphysical, religious, or even deep ethical levels, but rather to establish a formal conceptual framework upon which reconciliation efforts can be guided and evaluated. The justice definition builds upon ethical theories from classical sources, especially from Aristotle's teleological approach of practical reasoning, Schiller's aesthetic pedagogy, and Dewey's pragmatism. This approach respects the rich pluralisms of our complex world. It builds on O'Malley 2016 and summarizes positions developed in a forthcoming monograph.

Having outlined the Hölderlin perspective above, the justice definition of the Schiller correlative supports the three priority principles relevant to reconciliation. The priority of the ethical and the political are direct consequences of the justice concept definition, given its teleological nature. And the subsidiarity principle provides a limiting framework for determining the reconciling community. These three sub-principles are relevant to present discussions regarding the various academic approaches to conflict and post-conflict studies such as transitional justice, restorative justice, negotiation, conflict resolution, etc…. The position argued here is that it is prudent to have a broad-umbrella reconciliation field for integrating the various practical disciplines that address particular needs relevant to the always unique local expressions of violent conflict. Moreover, the argument here is that on the level of concept, it is incoherent to consider justice as merely one approach, discipline, strategy, or whatever that could compete with another approach, discipline, strategy, or whatever.

A military doctor's son, Friedrich Schiller (1759–1805) was trained for military medical service and familiar with violent conflict's terrible trauma. Political and violent conflict provides setting for Schiller's dramatic works, which remain most revelatory of his prodigious philosophical and historical wisdom. The use of non-formal philosophical expressions such as drama and poetry is typical for many of the figures associated with Jena Romanticism. Dalia Nassar (2014) argues that Romanticism can be differentiated from idealism by looking at the questions figures were attempting to address. This seems a productive way of reading the figures in Jena. Schiller, for example, is associated with *Sturm und Drang*, Goethe's classicism, and idealism. Yet his pursuit of questions regarding personal identity vis-à-vis society, aesthetics, and morality are characteristically Romantic, in my judgement. Leaving aside the debate on philosophical schools and periods, these brilliant thinkers gathered in Jena, during the last decade of the 18th century, including Hölderlin (1770–1843), were part of a community intentionally formed by Goethe. He was directly responsible for bringing Schiller to Jena and sponsored his appointment at the university. Whether the community formed their ideas in Jena, or traveled to Jena because of already achieved commonalities, they were united in their enthusiasm for Kantian and Enlightenment ideas and their critique of overly abstract idealistic philosophy. In his *Letters on the Aesthetic Education of Man*, we have Schiller expressly describing philosophical ideas. Here, he commits himself to the practical part of the Kantian system even as he attempts to transcend its "technical formulation" (*Letters*, 1st: 24). This transcendence cannot be achieved with new abstract formulations, and he resists that temptation. "We must indeed, if we are to solve that political problem in practice, follow the path of aesthetics, since it is through Beauty that we arrive at Freedom" (*Letters*, 2nd: 27). Thus, looking at dramatic works for insights into reconciliation is principally consistent with the theoretical principles that represent Schiller and his colleagues and students who formed the core of German Romanticism.

Schiller's *The Robbers* (1781) and *Wallenstein* (1799) are similar in portraying vicious cycles of violence swelling to encompass more and more perpetrators and victims. In the dramatic literature, traumas of violence are physical and emotional, and the effects of un-healed trauma include emotional sicknesses with festering and contagious capacities no less catastrophic or mysterious than any plague. Schiller, an autodidactic reader of both Kant and Aristotle, integrated the insights of both philosophers with the early Romantic insight that subjective personal identity is an inherently social reality. This is an idea that Hegel, Schelling, and others were contemporaneously dealing with in Jena. Given the complexity of human individual and social life, justice cannot be reduced to some notion of balance or law or fairness or any other conceptual measuring stick. Like the complex characters of Schiller's plays, personal and group identities possess porous and overlapping boundaries that resist hard-edged categorization as entirely perpetrators or victims. Thus, human action is most adequately understood within the multidimensional historical matrix of active and passive participation in a "fallen" disordered world. This world has potential for hope, goodness, right action, and justice. But such potential is not actuated because of traumas, resentments, oppressions, misunderstandings, disappointments, loneliness, and misdirected longing.

Achieving good/right/just action within a disordered context requires more than, for example, Kant's universalizable moral rules or principles. Schiller does not use this language, but justice as right action is never a static thing; it is more optimally described as a virtue abiding in persons and groups acting to re-order social relationships (the polis) to be more loving, more peaceful, more equitable, and simply happier. When faced with tragedy, what does justice counsel? Justice is expressed in the creative realization of what is possible, not in some abstract idea of what is perfect or pure. Individual virtue and well-being are cherished, but justice most appropriately describes practical reasoning ordered to social flourishing. As concept, it is a social virtue.

## 3. Justice Is a Virtue – Not a Static Thing

The ethical priority distills the pragmatic Aristotelian insight that justice is always the answer to the question "What *ought* I, or we do?" Two words in that question deserve attention. "Ought" is a normative word indicating the relevance of right and wrong, better and worse. "Do" indicates that the question requires an action, a performance. Thus, it is fitting to understand justice as a virtue – because a virtue is expressed in action. The athlete expresses virtue in the activity of her sport, the pianist in her music, the artist in her creation. Virtuous activity produces artifacts and is guided by principles and ideals, but we can and should remain aware of the differences. The relevance for reconciliation is that justice is expressed in actions relevant to social conflicts. Understood in this sense that is deeply rooted in theories of western philosophy, the virtue justice is inherently relevant to reconciliation, and it is inconceivable that justice could hinder resolving conflicts because justice is always ordered to communities' flourishing.

Having established the need for clarity regarding the justice concept, the following section develops the justice definition with five elements derived from Aristotle's *Nicomachean Ethics* (NE). Though consistent with NE, the definition is a derivation constructed to address contemporary needs: *Justice is best defined as a) political action, b) characterized as prudence, c) based upon stable social systems/dispositions, d) ordered to the telos of the community's best flourishing, and e) applied most in the most local context.*

### 3.1 Political Action

Justice is primarily expressed by a community or by a leader on behalf of the community and ordered to the good of society, not the individual. "Prudent political action" describes justice in a non-essentialist way. Justice is not some "thing" like a hammer or even a balancing scale. It is the virtuous action made possible by a kind of seeing that, in a single purview, can evaluate the various resulting scenarios from relevant possible decisions. In this sense, it is like a "perspective." For an individual, practical reasoning achieves personal goods such as wealth, honor, benefits for friends and family, etc. Political action, to ensure legitimacy, should be in contexts of democracies benefiting from a vigorous press and characterized by public reasonableness.

Thus prudence, this kind of seeing, is a form of practical rationality capable of achieving action in the social sphere. This may be the action of a political actor but can include any deliberative entity or body that participates in a stable and reasonable deliberation that can be characterized as virtuous, such as a civil rights movement, a refugee assistance group, or a school-parents' association. On individual and social levels, such virtuous patterns of cooperation become embedded, reinforced, and passed on in institutions and traditions. Such decision-action is properly characterized as virtuous, not because of the value actually optimized in any specific time and context, but if that action is characteristically reasonable, such that it is the most, or at least sufficiently, reasonable action to achieve the value for the community.

## 3.2  Characterized by Prudence

Aristotle's NE begins with an epistemological argument that the method and expected results of a science are dependent upon the matter studied. Abstract sciences like mathematics are different from biology – and a wide distance from the sciences of human social relations. Thus, the abstract matter of mathematics allows precise methodologies and results. The matter of biology lends itself to more general rules and more approximate results. Human social reality is too complex to offer anything more than probable results.

For Aristotle, the goal of ethics on the personal level is to achieve the good for the person, and that good is generally the fulfillment or actualization of given capacities. On the related social level, the good – which forms the telos or purpose of social life – is the goal of social decision-making. On the personal level, the virtuous person is the one who has developed habits that support the disciplines fostering personal fulfillment. This virtue is expressed in decision-making rationality learned from long practice and described as a capacity for effective action or prudence. This personal prudence is analogous to prudence on the social level, but distinct as well.

Given the human propensity for self-interested bias, the telos of personal fulfillment is different from that of social flourishing. This is a realization-focused justice conception, one that recognizes the good of procedures establishing and valuing public deliberation. Its pragmatic focus provides a capacity for epistemological tolerance regarding the reasons people choose to support their visions of the good and the actions, which are justified in terms of that vision of the good.

Justice describes social relations that are experienced at the personal/individual level. So, it is not unusual or necessarily wrong to speak about injustice as experienced *personally*. But for Aristotle, justice is essentially action ordering *social* relations to achieve optimal flourishing for the society, the polis. Action that is "just" is well-served by good laws and social principles. Ultimately, however, it depends upon political decision-makers who have developed habits of reasoning and action proportionate to the difficulty of political leadership. Because such decision-making requires not only intellectual powers, but also experience and composure over emotions, it is best to speak about justice as a virtue. This notion is embedded in many contemporary images of judicial practice symbolized by the figure Justitia, or Lady Justice, dressed in Roman style and holding a scale in one hand and in the other either a book symbolling positive law or a sword symbolizing enforcing power. Justitia herself is the symbol of justice, not the balancing scales, book of law, or force of the state. Those tools are at hand, but the action of justice is fully embodied in the virtuous human actor herself.

### 3.3 Based Upon Stable Political Systems/Disposition

The insights of Lederach, Zehr, and Schiesser are integrated into the Jena approach that takes for granted that justice, as virtue, involves the creation and sustaining of institutions that embody "organized routines of meaningful living; they are constituted by shared beliefs, convictions, values, and assumptions; they specify roles according to shared views of common projects, and these roles [become part of the] identity of persons" (Melchin 1998, p. 10). A virtue is a habit reflecting long-practiced actions and is not a random thing. By accident, a maliciously intended action may do good, but it is not justice if it does not reflect a stable disposition as instituted in governing bodies, civil society institutions, or religious and cultural practices.

### 3.4 Ordered to Community's Best-Possible Flourishing

This fourth element of the definition deals with the teleological dimension discussed above. The common good is a formal description of social telos that describes all characteristics of a fully flourishing society. Social groups exist in great degrees of size and form, and the justice of these levels will be dealt with by the integrated fifth element below, subsidiarity. Included among characteristics are ethical-legal conventions such as human dignity, human rights, state & local law, etc. Contrary to essentialist justice conceptions, these rights and principles are context-rooted entities. In addition to legal ethical-legal conventions, other elements of a flourishing society are relevant to justice, such as the actualization of capabilities. The capabilities include physical\economic\social conditions that should be potentially measurable in some quantitative or qualitative ways. Sen and Nussbaum take an anthropological and empirical approach to differentiate a catalog of key capabilities to be actualized in a flourishing society. Their exemplary approach is one of many, though its reference to an Aristotelian approach makes it particularly fitting to the present system. Social flourishing includes psychological elements relevant to intra/inter-group realities such as: a) secure identities, b) trust, c) egalitarian values, and d) coherence. The best-possible flourishing will never be a perfect society. Just actions may be those that reduce injustice better than all other options. That may not feel like justice when compromises are achieved that do not end much suffering. However, all other options may have been worse, and according to this approach, that is potentially a virtuous and thus just action.

## 3.5 Applied in the Most Local Context – Subsidiarity Logic

Finally, subsidiarity is an internal element of the justice conception, and not just an application of justice in certain circumstances. The subsidiarity conception used here is developed in O'Malley 2008. Justice action involves claims, demands, institutions, processes, and responsibilities. These justice-actions, as just, reflect and are based upon stable dispositions of rationality ordered to social flourishing. Justice is thus always context dependent. A local-context dependency establishes dispositions and embedded rationalities ordered to a local-context social flourishing. For example, as a father, I have a context-relationship with my wife and children that entails specific responsibilities.

Further, my responsibility on the local level has a priority over more general social levels. This argument could follow a number of legitimate paths, such as within Aristotelian, Ciceronian, or Hegelian frameworks of embedded social spheres. And here I think Sen's reflection on possible pluralities of competing principles is relevant. On the one hand, only rational argumentation relevant to all those impacted by the decision at hand needs to be considered. Metaphysical commitments are sometimes, in fact, relevant to the ethical question. But as pragmatists like Pierce and Dewey argue, if they need not be invoked, then better to let them aside. On the other hand, conclusions may concur despite various reasoning put forward to support those conclusions. Here too, the practical consensus can be happily embraced without further concern. Finally, justice issues with wide or even global relevance require broad deliberation and action. If the question exceeds the competence and scope of the local, then the justice discussions must expand to encompass that question. Just as a choice-of-court judicial process first decides which court can decide a case, the justice logic here argues that the subsidiarity principle is internal to the justice principle itself. Thus, the local priority supports robust "bottom-up" reconciliation endeavors when possible, and it is open to reasons to widen its scope.

## 4. "Just Memory" Approach to Analysis and Interventions

Jena's teleological approach is analogous to the multi-staged medical model with capacities for trauma triage when necessary to deal with immediate crises, followed by intervention protocols to achieve sustainable injury/disease management, and motivated by the broad goal (telos) of achieving health outcomes to the degree that they are possible. As in medicine, reconciliation requires many disciplines providing crucial research relevant for effective interventions. An example of Jena's research is "Hearts of Flesh–Not Stone," sponsored by the German Research Foundation (DFG). The project had Israeli, Palestinian, and German-based scholars working in a transdisciplinary way on a common question: Where the "other" is the adversary out-group, does encountering the suffering of the other influence willingness to reconcile?

Scholars use the tools of different disciplines collaboratively. Disciplines include social psychology, political science, religious studies, theology, and philosophy. Studies undertaken provide insight into the central question about encountering the suffering of the other. One intervention involved an academic course for students at an Israeli university on the topic of reconciliation that included field trips to locations relevant to Palestinian history and the hardships and suffering associated with the Palestinian experience from the time of the Nakba (1948) to the present. A related intervention involved students from Palestinian universities learning about Jewish history and the Holocaust in an academic setting before traveling to Europe on a five-day field trip. The field trip included experiencing the actual sites of historical injustice, memorialized in the museums preserving what is left of the concentration camps where the Holocaust was perpetrated. Many other social psychological studies and theoretical sub-projects probed the phenomenological dynamics of encountering the suffering of the other.

A theme emerging is a reinforcement of the importance of groups experiencing the suffering of the other through a lens of their own in-group suffering. This is true for both Israeli students and for Palestinian students. When conflict groups are mixed, each group can react to perceived threats by becoming defensive. Social psychologists best address these dynamics and advise how to avoid triggering responses and how to reinforce identity security. By adopting recommended measures, participants in field trips were more willing to learn about and recognize the out-group's historical tragedies. Yet even with care to avoid defensive reactions, participants' recognition of their enemies' (out-group) trauma was interpreted within a framework and moral compass of their own in-group tragedy narratives. Thus, Israelis viewed Palestinian hardships without suspending their own family historical Holocaust suffering.

Moreover, Palestinians viewed concentration-camp sites while also thinking about their own hardships of continuing Israeli occupation installations such as checkpoints and Israeli prisons. Speaking tentatively and only for myself at this stage in interpreting these experiences, the interventions show that reconciliation interventions require careful and value-transparent framing with the aim of bringing participants to situations of greater reconciliation. Interventions must be recognized as limited but perhaps helpful tools.

Sagy 2016 describes an analogous dynamic in her social-psychological approach of salutogenesis, which advocates a context-relevant teleological methodology analogous to a medical model of aiding persons or groups to achieve their own health or well-being. By working interdisciplinarily, Sagy is inspiring her field to engage other disciplines regarding how well-being can be described and fostered, and she is advocating research that engages social-context questions about peace, openness to the other, and justice, all with a view to understand how these concepts correlate with personal and social health; which are analogous to this essay's telos of human flourishing.

Using a medical model as analogy, the Jena approach seeks to develop interventions as potential resources for specific goals within a larger goal of social health/flourishing. Like an individual patient whose medical history and context must be considered by a medical professional, each conflict presents a unique narrative. Thus, narrative interpretation (hermeneutics) helps critically interpret conflict and post-conflict situations to offer practical recommendations for promoting reconciliation.

Mohamed Dajani Daoudi's work in the project with Palestinian experiences of historical Jewish suffering also helps shed light on the Jena approach. Dajani Daoudi's teaching and research on the Wasatia concept deals with a central ethical pillar of many Palestinians' Muslim religious convictions. He recommends focusing on the concrete, the local, the achievable "middle way" of Wasatia, rather than getting lost in abstractions of maximalist concepts or demands. To strike the correct balance requires understanding and framing traditions, practices, and memories within narratives ordered most optimally toward the local community's best flourishing.

Dajani Daoudi's approach is consistent with the approach of Miroslav Volf, who discusses the role of post-conflict memory in *The End of Memory* (Volf 2006). Remembering the suffering of historical injustice is a moral duty, Volf claims, but the question is, *how* should violent injustice be remembered? He answers that the potential content for memory is immense in matter and nature, and thus ought to be tied to a beneficial purpose with meaning for the future. This is not relativism, as acknowledging historical data as truthful is essential, but requires active interpretation for realizing beneficial memory. Dajani Daoudi seeks to remember the historical suffering of Palestinians, including that of his own family, while at the same time not excluding the history of Jewish suffering.

Ricœur makes similar arguments.

Trauma-focused memory can fixate on wrongdoing and suffering, whereas "exemplary memory" moves beyond passive experience and re-trauma, beyond self-destructive re-action in potential forms of violence and vengeance. Though difficult, intentionally proactive memory constitution frames memory in perhaps abstract terms as exemplary for moral meaning, in whatever form that could take (Volf 2006, pp. 87–89).

Such framing requires, of course, an ethical structure. Volf builds upon Christian traditions and scriptures. Ricœur builds upon supererogative spheres of alterity and love. Dajani Daoudi frames Palestinian suffering with Wasatia principles analogous to Aristotle's teleological teaching. For Volf, new potentially traumatic memories can be framed in Christian mysteries of suffering and redemption, which function as meaning-providing resources that are (potentially) ordered towards future action unbound from violent retributive cycles. Remembering subsidiarity, the fifth element of the justice definition, the local priority would guide our understanding of potential narrative resources for the Israeli-Palestinian context. Sagy, working in Israel among religious and secular Jews and Muslims, would draw on local traditions for that context, but the structure of the approach is analogous, using religious and cultural resources to address, heal, and focus memory. Dajani Daoudi's ethical and religious principles are relevant because of his connection to Palestinians' local context.

Building upon Ricœur, Kearney 2003 uses an analogous approach to memory, a work that has special relevance for reconciliation due to its treatment of the alienating nature of historical injustice in the construction of the narratives that give meaning and orientation to social groups. Violence is alienating in social conflicts because it is a means that is inherently destructive of future cooperative flourishing. Violence-hardened alienation finds its way into narratives in both clear and complex ways. Kearney's philosophical/hermeneutical approach helps one a) to "read" the violence of narratives, b) to analyze the narratives in terms of ethical principles, and c) to then form narratives more worthy of productive futures. It is not enough, Kearney argues, to use post-modern approaches that analyze and deconstruct power relations existing in the complexities and antinomies of separate group narratives of past injustice or trauma. This perhaps respects the different perspectives of victim groups' historical suffering but remains mired in that complexity and leaves present and future intergroup interaction without narrative openness or commonalities.

A second "false path" is characterized by the lugubrious melancholy of ruminations and depressive fixations on past trauma and present powerlessness because of historical injury. Kearney argues that using memory exclusively to ruminate on the feelings associated with trauma could keep the victim continually returning to debilitating memories, reliving them, and interpreting present realities and future possibilities in terms of loss, subjection, and hopelessness.

When conflicts stories are studied like the texts of literature or scripture, we use the methods of analysis that have been developed for such study, namely hermeneutics. As a discipline itself, hermeneutics deals with issues of meaning, bias, history, values, and much more. It is no coincidence that Ricœur and Kearney are key figures in the field. In his Hölderlin perspective, Leiner also uses hermeneutic methods to interpret conflict as already possessing reconciling elements. Likewise, the Schiller correlative is an impetus to interpret conflict from the perspective of justice. Kearney's recommended third strategy, "just memory," is consistent with and informs the Jena approach to reconciliation with its emphasis on studying existing and potential narratives relevant to conflict. "Just memory" offers a fundamentally social imagination and ethical vision of participating in processes that form narratives of justice focused upon encountering the "other" with hospitality and humility. Hospitality and humility are value-laden dispositions that implicitly embrace the principle of human dignity; it is an ethical act to be "with the other," discovering and thus writing narratives open to future flourishing. This "ethical priorities" approach is consistent with Sagy and Dajani Daoudi. Kearney's account reveals the phenomenological processes by which humans can participate in creating life-giving narratives for personal and social identity constructions ordered towards self- and community flourishing.

## References

Blundell, B. 2010, 'Unavailability. When Neighbors Become Strangers', *Religion and the Arts*, vol. 14, pp. 561–572.

Flämig, S., Leiner, M. 2012, 'Reconciliation in the Middle of Dispute. Introduction to the Series', in *Societies in Transition. Latin America between Conflict and Reconciliation*, eds S. Flämig, M. Leiner, Vandenhoeck & Ruprecht, Göttingen, pp. 7–19.

Kearney, R. 2003, *Strangers, Gods, and Monsters. Interpreting Otherness*, Routledge, London and New York.

Melchin, K.R. 1998, *Living with Other People. An Introduction to Christian Ethics Based on Bernard Lonergan*, Liturgical Press, Collegeville, MN.

Nassar, D. 2014, *The Romantic Absolute. Being and Knowing in Early German Romantic Philosophy, 1795–1804*, University of Chicago Press, London.

O'Malley, M. 2017, 'Jena Approach. Principles and Priorities for Reconciliation Studies', in *Thüringen. Braucht das Land Versöhnung?* eds M. O'Malley, M. Leiner, D. Summe, N. Knoepffler, Königshausen & Neumann, Würzburg, pp. 113–154.

O'Malley, M. 2016, 'Justice Is a Virtue, Not Some Static Thing', in *Public Theology and the Global Common Good. The Contribution of David Hollenbach*, eds K. Ahern, M. Clark, K. Heyer, L. Johnston, Orbis Books, New York.

O'Malley, M. 2011, 'A Performative Definition of Human Dignity', in *Facetten der Menschewürde*, eds N. Knoepffler, P. Kunzmann, M. O'Malley, Karl Alber Verlag, Freiburg am Breisgau, pp. 75–101.

O'Malley M. 2008, 'Currents in Nineteenth-Century German Law, and Subsidiarity's Emergence as a Social Principle in the Writings of William Ketteler', *Journal of Law, Philosophy and Culture*, vol. 2, no. 1, pp. 22–52.

Ricœur, P. 1996, 'Reflections on a New Ethos for Europe', in Id., *The Hermeneutics of Action*, Sage, London, pp. 3–15.

Ricœur, P. 1995, 'Intellectual Autobiography', in *The Philosophy of Paul Ricœur*, ed L.E. Hahn, Open Court, Chicago, IL.

Sagy, S. 2016, 'Relevance of Salutogenesis to Social Issues Besides Health. Case of Sense of Coherence and Intergroup Relations', in *The Handbook of Salutogenesis*, eds M.B. Mittelmark, S. Sagy, M. Eriksson, G.F. Bauer, J.M. Pelikan, B. Lindström, G. Arild Espnes, Springer, Cham, pp. 77–83.

Taylor, C. 2007, *A Secular Age*, Belknap Press of Harvard University Press, Cambridge, MA.

Volf, M. 2006, *The End of Memory. Remembering Rightly in a Violent World*, Eerdmans, Cambridge, UK.

Yoav Kapshuk

# Reconciliation in Peace Agreements?

## The Case Study of the Israeli-Palestinian Peace Process

### Abstract

Challenging the widespread assumption according to which reconciliation is understood as a process or an aim to be achieved in the post-conflict period, i. e., after or beyond formal peace processes between political leaderships, Yoav Kapshuk's paper on Reconciliation in Peace Agreements? The Case Study of the Israeli-Palestinian Peace Process presents principles of reconciliation as crucial elements that could be applied in formal agreements to end conflicts. They include transitional justice, historical truth, historical acknowledgement, and dealing with past injustices' socioeconomic and structural aspects. In its first part, the paper discusses these reconciliation principles in the context of formal peace processes, recommending ways of incorporating them into agreements. The second section applies them in a model for solving the Palestinian refugee issue based on the Oslo peace process. The paper argues that formal peace agreements must not be exclusively identified as the objective of the conflict settlement or resolution techniques. Integrating reconciliation principles in formal agreements can benefit attempts to end protracted conflicts such as the Israeli-Palestinian case.

### Introduction

The Israeli-Palestinian conflict is considered intractable and unresolvable. In the course of its hundred and more years, and certainly, since the establishment of the State of Israel in 1948, the Oslo Process is widely considered the most serious attempt to bring the conflict to an end. The peace process between Israel and the Palestinians began in earnest in Oslo in 1993 and ended with the outbreak of the Second Intifada, also known as Al-Aksa Intifada, in 2000. One of the most controversial issues on which no agreement could be reached is that of the Palestinian refugees from 1948. This issue was not a part of the discussion that led to the interim agreements as part of the Oslo process. US President Bill Clinton presented the proposed model for resolving this issue to both sides in December 2000. The Clinton Parameters were discussed in the 2001 Taba Summit but led to no agreement. Israeli and Palestinian veterans of the Oslo process proposed a similar model in the 2003 Geneva Accord.

In the following sections, I use this model for a permanent solution to the Palestinian refugee issue as a test case to expand the critical literature dealing with conflict resolution. Three major techniques for dealing with conflicts are settlement, resolution, and reconciliation. There is a significant difference between conflict settlement and resolution on the one hand and reconciliation on the other. Reconciliation involves the consideration of a conflict's complex root causes by exposing the truth about injustices related to the conflict as well as acknowledgement and assumption of historical responsibility by the perpetrators (Rouhana 2011; Kelman 2008). Reconciliation is also unique in that it is suitable for dealing with prolonged and intractable conflicts, which are central to collective identities shaped over generations of conflicts in the context of asymmetrical relations of power, domination, oppression, and collective exploitation (Rouhana 2004, 174). The Israeli-Palestinian conflict meets this definition, claiming reconciliation is the most appropriate technique for dealing with conflicts (Peled and Rouhana 2004).

In this paper, I use the Oslo model for a permanent settlement of the refugee issue to suggest a novel interpretation of the reconciliation technique. In the first section, I discuss four reconciliation principles. The second section demonstrates why the Palestinian refugee issue is a crucial element of the Israeli-Palestinian conflict. In a third section, I then analyze the model for resolving the refugee issue proposed at the end of the Oslo process by considering reconciliation principles as they ought to be articulated in formal agreements. In the last section, I explain how the conclusions drawn from this article could challenge civil society and the international community regarding the Israeli-Palestinian conflict.

## 1. Principles of Reconciliation in Formal Peace Negotiations

This article considers reconciliation as an umbrella concept and as an "overall perspective englobing conflict resolution and other topics" (Leiner, 2018, 178), which includes historical truth, historical acknowledgement, and coping with structural aspects of past injustices, and transitional justice.

The first reconciliation principle is revealing the historical truth about the conflict. The narrative adopted by each party to the conflict is one of the key factors that perpetuate the dispute. Usually, the perpetrators conceal the truth about their wrongdoing, and the informational gap between victimizer and victimized deepens the latter's grudge. Moreover, the victims' often silenced and marginalized voices are central to their collective identity. Accordingly, any reconciliation needs to involve public agreement on the historical truth (Bashir 2011; Crocker 1999; Dwyer 1999; Lambourne 2009; Rouhana 2011). It is also essential for the peace agreements to include a detailed description of the history of the conflict emphasizing wrongdoings.

If no consensus can be reached regarding historical truth, the agreement should at least include a statement of each party's position.

The second principle, related to historical truth, is acknowledging and assuming historical responsibility for past injustices. In the peace agreement, both parties – but mainly the more powerful ones – must admit to their wrongdoings, accept the historical responsibility, and face the consequences. This process is challenging because such recognition "undermines the internal sense of justice" and moral integrity of the perpetrating party (Jamal 2001).

Restoration and compensation for the victims are related to the third principle: dealing with the structural aspects of the conflict. The critical literature on conflict resolution has mostly ignored this aspect, which is also missing in most reconciliation mechanisms, such as truth and reconciliation commissions (Killen 2010, 315; Carranza 2008) but has recently attracted growing scholarly attention (Schmid and Nolan 2014). These studies suggest that reconciliation should reduce the structural and material inequalities of parties to a former conflict since those inequalities belong to the results of the conflict and are integral to its injustices (Hecht and Michalowski 2012). It is therefore desirable for peace agreements to include provisions for compensation, reparation and restitution of property, the return and naturalization of refugees and plans for the rehabilitation of victims. Moreover, they should include concrete steps and a schedule for socioeconomic restructuring to achieve "distributive reconciliation" (Aiken 2010, 171; Lambourne 2009; Muvingi 2009).

The last principle is transitional justice. I consider transitional justice the most appropriate approach to dealing with intractable conflicts. This approach emphasizes the process of coping with past injustices related to the conflict (Teitel 2003; Teitel 2000). The starting point is to acknowledge the parties' asymmetrical power relations, facilitating the transition from oppression or exploitation to a situation where the victims' moral dignity is restored, or at least, the transition from a "barbaric" to a "minimally decent society" (Bhargava 2000; Rouhana 2011; Rouhana 2004). Transitional justice is transformative since the reassessment of the past is designed to improve future relations and achieve a practical solution. It means the asymmetrically powerful party must be willing to implement the solution without being punished or brought to its knees (Peled and Rouhana 2004).

The concept of transitional justice is often defined as the full range of processes and mechanisms associated with a society's attempts to come to terms with a legacy of large-scale past abuses in order to ensure accountability, serve justice, and achieve reconciliation" (UN, 2010, p. 4). The transitional justice literature and practical initially focused on the legal responses of postcolonial regimes to injustices perpetrated by previous oppressive regimes (Teitel 2003). However, as the literature developed, its concept of TJ expanded beyond the legal area to include a variety of ways to deal with past injustices while integrating values such as history, truth, memory, and identity (IJTJ, 3 (2007)). Alongside the field of academic research, the title "transitional justice" is also used to describe the action, and policy and activity in the practical political sphere, including the establishment and activities of institutions such as international courts, truth, and reconciliation committees, reparation programs, as well as human rights organizations, victim organizations, and so on (McEvoy & Mallinder, 2016).

## 2. The Palestinian Refugee Issue: The Crucial Element of the Conflict

The Palestinian refugee problem is a result of the 1948 war in which hundreds of thousands of Palestinians were displaced and subsequently denied permission to return. In this catastrophe, the so-called "Nakba," the Palestinians lost their homeland, and their society and culture were destroyed (Khalidi 1992). The year 1948 is the primary date in recent Palestinian history: "That year, a country and its people disappeared from both maps and dictionaries (Sanbar 2001, 87)." Thus, many Palestinians consider the Nakba as the formative event for the Palestinian people, whose identity revolves around displacement and exile – "the disintegration of society [and] the frustration of national aspirations (Sa'di 2002, 175)."

According to the Palestinians, the historical responsibility for the Nakba lies with the Zionist enterprise. However, the Palestinian position on the issue of return is complex. On the one hand, the refugee problem constitutes the core of the Israeli-Palestinian conflict even though more than six decades have passed, and only Israeli recognition of the refugees' right of return will bring it to an end (Abu-Sitta 2009). On the other hand, the Palestinians realize the anxiety raised by the very mention of such a solution. Therefore, it is often claimed that Israel must recognize the right of return in principle, while how this is to be accomplished should be subject to negotiation (Khalidi 1992).

According to the Israeli narrative, the return of refugees to territories within the 1948 borders would threaten the state's Jewish character and lead to a significant change in society. Most Israeli Jews are terrified of this idea since the addition of millions of Palestinians to the country's population would transform Israel from a Jewish state into a "state of all its citizens." The Jewish public's strong position on the right of return was documented in a survey conducted in 2002. The survey findings indicated that the very mention of the "right of return" was a cause for anxiety, while the implementation of that right was seen as the potential cause of tragedies, such as "destruction of the state," "massacre of Jews," and even "holocaust" (Zakay, Klar and Sharvit 2002).

Since both Jews and Palestinians consider the refugee issue crucial to their future national existence (Ju'beh 2002; Peled and Rouhana 2004; Barkan 2005), it is perfectly suitable for illustrating the principles of reconciliation in a formal peace agreement. Since the refugee issue is the core of the conflict for both parties and is largely responsible for shaping their collective identity and memory, the reconciliation technique is ideally suited for dealing with it. Moreover, the formula according to which the conflict must be settled first and the reconciliation phase initiated only afterward has failed to achieve much progress in the case of the Israeli-Palestinian conflict. The refugee issue was the main reason which prevented the parties from signing a comprehensive peace agreement at the 2000 Camp David Summit (Peled and Rouhana 2004). The conclusion is to aim for reconciliation during the formal negotiation process for a peace agreement that would end all mutual claims. The importance of reconciliation during the peacemaking process is also part of the "Hölderlin Perspective," which is an antithesis to the perception of reconciliation as an event that occurs only after a peace-building process. According to this perspective, a reconciliation process should be applied in the middle of a conflict (Flämig and Leiner 2012, 16–17; Barakat, Z.M., 2018).

## 3. Model for a Permanent Agreement on the Refugee Issue

US President Bill Clinton proposed a model for resolving the refugee issue in December 2000 (Clinton 2000). The Clinton Parameters were subsequently discussed during the Taba Summit in January 2001, but no agreement could be reached. A reliable summary of the Taba discussions related to the refugee issues may be found in Article 3 of the 'EU Non-Paper' prepared by Miguel Moratinos, EU Special Envoy to the Middle East Peace Process (hereafter, Taba Document). In 2003, this model was presented with some modifications as part of the unofficial Geneva Accord (Geneva Accord 2003 [GA]), signed by Israeli and Palestinian representatives who had led the Oslo process. The following discussion focuses on the Taba Document, the Geneva Accord, the Clinton Parameters and their differences.

The model for a permanent agreement on the refugee issue is presented the Geneva Accord and the Taba Document as crucial to the peace process. Israel and Palestine recognize that "an agreed resolution of the refugee problem is necessary for achieving a just, comprehensive and lasting peace (GA, Article 7.1i)." This development demonstrates that the parties understand the importance of an agreement on this issue to facilitate a "lasting" peace. The second part of the article acknowledges that the solution "will also be pivotal in the stability and development in the region (GA, Article 7.1ii)," i. e., the parties recognize the importance of the solution to the refugee issue for the future of their relations and the entire region.

## 3.1 Justice and Acknowledgement: The Right of Return

GA Article 7.2 refers to the United Nations Resolutions 194 and 242 and the Arab Peace Initiative. The Parties recognize that UN General Assembly Resolution [UNGAR] 194, UNSC Resolution 242, and the Arab Peace Initiative (Article 2. ii) concerning the rights of the Palestinian refugees represent the basis for resolving the refugee issue. They also agree that these rights are fulfilled according to Article 7 of this agreement (GA, Article 7.2).

On the one hand, the reference to these documents, particularly Resolution 194, which provides the right of return, is a significant development compared to the interim agreements signed during the Oslo Process. On the other hand, its wording is ambiguous and avoids direct reference to the actual contents of these documents. There is no reference to the key statement in Resolution 194: "Refugees wishing to return to their homes and live at peace with their neighbors should be permitted to do so at the earliest practicable date" (UNGAR 1948, no. 194). The combination of referring to UNGAR 194 without referencing its content and the determination that only Article 7 of the current agreement would be relevant to the refugee issue represents the absolute denial of the right of return of the Palestinian refugees.

The absence of this statement becomes clear in Article 3.2 of the Taba Document, which points out that each party interprets Resolution 194 differently. "The Palestinian side reiterated that the Palestinian refugees should have the right to return to their homes," while "(t)he Israeli side expressed its understanding that the wish to return as per wording of UNGAR 194 shall be implemented within the framework" of several possibilities within which only a small number of refugees will be allowed to return to Israel (Taba Document, Article 3.2). These possibilities are also listed in the Clinton Parameters and Article 7.4 of the Geneva Accord.

This article rejects the refugees' right to return to their places of residence before 1948 unless they lived in territories to be transferred from Israeli sovereignty to that of the future Palestinian State. Thus, although GA opens by stating that refugees will exercise "a conscious choice," only the choice to return to the area under the Palestinian State's sovereignty can be fully realized. Other options, such as third countries, Israel, or current host countries, will be at these countries' discretion. This situation enables Israel to absorb a small number of refugees, particularly as "Israel will consider the average of the total numbers submitted by the different third countries to the International Commission (GA, Article 7.4)." The significance of this statement lies in that it removes all historical responsibility from Israel, equating it with that of neutral third countries.

The overall approach of this article (as well as Article 7.2) is that of a zero-sum game: the choice is between rejecting and accepting the right of return. However, the controversy surrounding the right of return may be treated in a more complex and comprehensive approach, which may turn it into a win-win situation. With this approach, the positions of both sides may be resolved by referring to two different strategies: (a) acknowledgement by Israel of the right of return to its sovereign territory and thus assuming historical responsibility for the Nakba; (b) implementing this right to an extent to be determined in negotiations between the parties, where the fears of Jewish Israeli society will be considered. This approach is consistent with the transitional justice principle (Peled and Rouhana 2004; Dudai 2007).

The Clinton Parameters are more consistent with this approach. According to Clinton, it would be difficult for the Palestinian leadership to renounce the right of return, but it is also a threat to Israel's Jewish character. Clinton began by expressing his feeling "that the differences are more related to formulation and less to what will happen on a practical level (Clinton 2000)." This statement reflects the proposed approach according to which the controversy may be resolved by distinguishing between acknowledgement and implementation. On the acknowledgement level, Clinton claimed "I believe that Israel is prepared to acknowledge the moral and material suffering caused to the Palestinian people as a result of the 1948 war" (Ibidem). Clinton then proposed two possible formulations. First, both sides should acknowledge the right to return to "historical Palestine." Second, both parties should recognize the Palestinians' right to return to their homeland. On the level of implementation, Clinton stated that "there is no specific right of return to Israel itself (Ibidem)."

The Palestinians accepted this proposal with several reservations regarding the level of acknowledgement. One of the various reservations included the reference to UNGAR 194, which states that the refugees will return to their homes, wherever they may be, rather than to their "homeland" or to "historical Palestine." The Palestinians also wrote that "recognizing the right of return and providing the refugees with a choice is a pre-requisite for terminating the conflict" (Ju'beh 2002, 10).

The proposed approach of distinguishing between acknowledgement and implementation can be seen in the Palestinian formulation proposal in the Taba Document, which included explicit acknowledgement of Israel's "moral and legal responsibility for the forced displacement and dispossession of the Palestinian civilian population during the 1948 war and for preventing the refugees from returning to their homes (Palestinian Position Paper 2001)." Nabil Sha'ath, head of the Palestinian negotiating team in the Taba Summit, stated that Israel had to take historical responsibility for the right of return, a right to be granted to every refugee and their descendants. However, its implementation depends on negotiations with Israel. He states "You cannot deprive the Palestinians of the right to return. We have to center on the issue of the implementation of that right as an agreed solution to end the conflict between us. There has to be a win-win situation." (Eldar 2002, 18) Sha'ath suggests thinking about the right of return "in a much broader context because it is return within a peace process" (Ibidem). According to Sha'ath, Palestinian refugees are entitled to return to Haifa and Jaffa. However, when the issue is addressed in the framework of the negotiations, it is not certain that the Palestinian refugees will choose this option (Ibid., 22).

The approach of the Geneva Accord to the refugee issue is anticipated in the Israeli response to the Palestinian paper in which it "expresses its sorrow for the tragedy of the Palestinian refugees" (Israeli Response RE Refugees 2001). However, they do not mention their moral responsibility throughout the document. According to Yossi Beilin, who headed the Israeli team on the issue of the right of return, "there will be no right of return to Israel. This is the most important thing for Israelis, and they cannot accept any solution which does not include this (Eldar 2002, 15)". The Israeli refusal to take any historical responsibility for the outcomes of the 1948 war is also expressed by Ehud Barak, who was Israel's Prime Minister at the time: "I approached Arafat and found out that he did not wish to solve the problem of 1967 but rather the problem of 1947" (Shavit 2008).

### 3.2 Acknowledgement and Socioeconomic Aspects: Compensation for Refugeehood

Beyond the declarative aspect, recognition and assumption of responsibility for past injustices has an important material aspect in the form of financial compensations and reparations, and in some cases also restitution of property. As seen in the first section of this paper, this aspect entails admission of responsibility, and accordingly, the compensator's identity is of symbolic importance (Barkan 2002; Barkan 2005). The Clinton Parameters include a brief reference to this issue, aiming for an international committee to compensate and rehabilitate the refugees, among other objectives. The issue is discussed to a greater extent in Articles 3.3 and 3.7 of the Taba Document, and even more extensively in Articles 7.3, 7.9 and 7.10 of the Geneva Accord.

Article 3.3 of the Taba Document states that "both sides agreed to the establishment of an International Commission and an International Fund as a mechanism for dealing with compensation in all its aspects." This sentence, as well as the single sentence devoted to the issue in the Clinton Parameters, indicate that both parties agree to compensate the refugees and consequently recognize their tragedy. The model incorporates, at least partially, one of the principles of reconciliation mentioned above. However, to strengthen the link between compensation and recognition, the perpetrator would ideally take responsibility for providing compensation, at least symbolically (Barkan 2005).

Article 3.3 of the Taba Document reports "progress on Israeli compensation for material losses, land, and assets expropriated, including the agreement on a payment from an Israeli lump sum or proper amount to be agreed upon that would feed into the International Fund." Similarly, but in greater detail, Article 7.9iii of the

Geneva Accord deals with compensation for Palestinian property abandoned and confiscated in the 1948 war. The article states that the International Commission is responsible for implementing all aspects of the agreement. The signatories should agree upon a total amount as compensation that "shall constitute the Israeli 'lump sum' contribution to the International Fund."

To adequately address the principle of recognizing past injustices, these articles would have had to clearly state that Israel bears the brunt of the responsibility for compensating the refugees, given that it has reaped the benefits from confiscated Palestinian property. The importance of Israeli compensation is further supported by the fact that in the aftermath of the 1948 war, Israel already agreed to compensate the Palestinians for this property in the 1949 Lausanne Conference convened by the UN Conciliation Commission for Palestine (UNCCP). The Arab delegations rejected this proposal (Fried 2002; Tuvy 2008), among other things, because the Palestinians demanded the restitution of the confiscated property, a demand rejected by Israel. The same claim and rejection are echoed in Article 3.3 of the Taba Document: "The Palestinian side raised the issue of restitution of refugee property. The Israeli side rejected this."

As already indicated in the quote from Article 7.3i of the Geneva Accord above, the parties also discussed compensations for the decades-long condition of refugeehood. Article 7.10 is explicitly devoted to this issue and emphasizes that Israel will not play a significant role in the proposed Refugeehood Fund but remain a "contributing party." This example testifies again to Israel's partial acknowledgement of its responsibility for the creation of the Palestinian refugee issue.

Compensation and restitution are not only symbolically important as they indicate recognition of past injustices, but they also meet a new principle of reconciliation in peace agreements, such as dealing with the socioeconomic and structural aspects of these injustices. My analysis of the relevant articles in the Geneva Accord and Taba Document indicates that this principle is proposed as part of the agreement but only partially. On the one hand, as indicated in Article 3.7 of the Taba Document, Israel opposed the restitution of refugee property. Moreover, there is no mention of the need for distributive justice or redistribution of resources. On the other hand, compensation for property and refugeehood are extensively discussed in the Geneva Accord, including a detailed action plan and timetable (see particular Articles 7.9 and 7.11). Besides, the development and rehabilitation of the refugees gained more attention with particular emphasis on "programs and plans to provide the former refugees with opportunities for personal and communal development, housing, education, healthcare, re-training and other needs (GA, Article 7.11)."

## 3.3 Historical Truth: The 1948 Narratives

The last reconciliation principle discussed in the latter phases of the Oslo negotiations is a historical truth. Article 3.1 of the Taba Document is entitled "Narrative" and reports that "the Israeli side put forward a suggested joint narrative for the tragedy of the Palestinian refugees. The Palestinian side discussed the proposed narrative, and there was much progress, although no agreement was reached [...]." Entitled "Reconciliation Programs," Article 7.14 of the Geneva Accord reads:

i.   The Parties will encourage and promote the development of cooperation between their relevant institutions and civil societies in creating forums for exchanging historical narratives and enhancing mutual understanding regarding the past.

ii.  The Parties shall encourage and facilitate exchanges to disseminate a richer appreciation of these respective narratives, in formal and informal education, by providing conditions for direct contact between schools, educational institutions, and civil society.

iii. The Parties may consider cross-community cultural programs to promote the goals of conciliation in relation to their respective histories.

iv.  These programs may include developing appropriate ways of commemorating those villages and communities that existed prior to 1949.

As discussed in the first section of this paper, each party's narrative about the conflict is a key factor in its perpetuation. In a reconciliation process, the parties would have to agree on the historical truth and express this agreement publicly (Crocker 1999; Dwyer 1999). Therefore, the fact that the parties referred to the narrative issue in the Taba Document is indicative of their awareness of the importance of incorporating one of the essential reconciliation principles in the agreement. However, no joint historical narrative was formulated in the Taba negotiations, and the parties subsequently settled for the future establishment of "forums for exchanging historical narratives (GA, Article 7.14i)." This provision is vital because it refers to the principle of historical truth but is unsatisfactory since it refers to future plans involving "cooperation between their relevant institutions and civil societies," opposing an explicit description of historical truth in the peace agreement itself.

Even in the absence of an agreement on a shared narrative, the peace agreement may include both parties' narratives to expose each side to the other's narrative. This step is critically important in the reconciliation process. According to Beilin, this procedure was part of the Taba Summit:

"The wisdom of Taba was that we could refer to the two narratives in the evolving Palestinian refugee problem without accepting either of them. The mere fact that we could refer to them and respect both narratives was enough to satisfy both sides that their story is not being ignored." (Quoted in Eldar 2002, 12)

Despite this modest progress, the two narratives were not presented in the remaining three paragraphs of Article 7.14 of the Geneva Accord, not to mention an agreement on a joint narrative. Although all refer to the principle of historical truth, they focus on plans for dealing with this truth in the future after a formal peace agreement. Although Article 7.14 does refer to principles of reconciliation, it pertains to a future reconciliation rather than tackling the issue directly. The postponement of the actual discussion on reconciliation opposes the Israeli requirement that the Palestinians declare an end to the conflict and their claims as stipulated in Article 7.7 of the Geneva Accord and Article 3.7 of the Taba Document.

Nevertheless, the final paragraph of Article 7.14 describes, albeit very briefly and indirectly, the historical truth in the actual agreement by "developing appropriate ways of commemorating those villages and communities that existed prior to 1949." Although the article also refers to future developments, the words "existed prior to 1949" constitute the only substantial reference in the Accord to the events of the 1948 war and the refugee issue as well, as a very rare acknowledgement by any Israeli official of that catastrophe.

On the other hand, these few words may be criticized for being carefully selected to skirt the events of 1947/48 and their consequences. Firstly, the villages and communities in question are Palestinian are not mentioned on purpose. Secondly, the words "existed prior" do not carry the same negative connotation as the words "destruction," "devastation," or "Nakba." If added to the agreement, such words, would have pointed to the fact that "a country and its people disappeared from both maps and dictionaries (Sanbar 2001, 87)."

Despite this criticism, it seems that the reference to the historical narrative aspect of the refugee issue in Article 3.3 of the Taba Document, as well as the reference to future reconciliation in Article 7.14 of the Geneva Accord and particularly the last paragraph, which alludes to the history of the refugee issue is commendable as it constitutes partial incorporation of reconciliation principles in the actual peace agreement. It would, therefore, be appropriate to develop these articles or include similar ones in a future peace agreement.

## Conclusion

This analysis of the model for solving the Palestinian refugee issue in the three documents – the Clinton Parameters, the Taba Document, and the Geneva Accord – partially incorporates the principles of reconciliation in formal peace agreements. Concerning the principle of transitional justice, according to which the parties would recognize the right of return but negotiate its implementation with due consideration for Israel's demographic fears so that it could remain a Jewish state, it would seem that the Clinton Parameters have incorporated it most thoroughly, albeit not completely. The Geneva Accord, on the other hand, lacks Israeli acknowledgement of the Nakba, whereas the Taba Document and the parties' Position Papers only present the controversy. Secondly, the principle of historical truth is partly incorporated. On the one hand, the Taba Document refers to the importance of agreeing on a joint historical narrative, and the Geneva Accord devotes space to future reconciliation plans where the parties would promote mutual understanding of past events.

Concerning the principle of historical responsibility, the parties recognize the importance of compensating the Palestinian refugees and thus offering certain recognition of the injustice perpetrated against them. However, Israel's avoidance of taking the brunt of the responsibility for the compensation mechanism weakens the link between compensation and recognition. Finally, the principle of dealing with the conflict's socioeconomic aspect is also only partly incorporated since, on the one hand, Israel is opposed to property restitution. At the same time, none of the three documents refers to the need for distributive justice or redistribution of resources. On the other hand, compensations are discussed in detail, particularly in the Geneva Accord, including an action plan and a clear schedule.

The proposal of incorporating principles of reconciliation in the Israeli-Palestinian formal peace negotiation can facilitate attempts to end the Israeli-Palestinian conflict (as well as other conflicts). However, in the middle of 2019, this task still seems like an insurmountable hurdle when no significant negotiations are held between Israel and the Palestinians.

## References

Abu-Sitta, S. 2009, 'The Implementation of the Right of Return', *Palestine-Israel Journal*, vol. 15, no. 4; vol. 16, no. 1.

Aiken, N.T. 2010, 'Learning to Live Together. Transitional Justice and Intergroup Reconciliation in Northern Ireland', *International Journal of Transitional Justice*, vol. 4, pp. 166–188.

Barkan, E. 2002, *The Guilt of Nations. Restitution and Negotiating Historical Injustices*, Johns Hopkins University Press, Baltimore and London.

Barkan, E. 2005, 'Considerations toward Accepting Historical Responsibility', in *Exile and Return. Predicaments of Palestinians and Jews*, eds A. M. Lesch, I. Lustick, University of Pennsylvania Press, Philadelphia, PA, pp. 85–105.

Barakat, Z.M. 2018, 'Reconciliation in the Midst of Strife. Palestine', in *Reconciliation in Global Context. Why It Is Needed and How It Works*, ed B. Krondorfer, SUNY Press, New York, pp. 129–150.

Bashir, B. 2011, 'Reconciling Historical Injustices. Deliberative Democracy and the Politics of Reconciliation', *Res Publica*, vol. 18, pp. 127–143.

Bhargava, R. 2000, 'Restoring decency to barbaric societies', in *Truth Versus Justice. The Morality of Truth Commissions*, eds R. Rotberg, D.F. Thompson, Princeton University Press, Princeton, New Jersey, pp. 45–67.

Carranza, R. 2008, 'Plunder and Pain. Should Transitional Justice Engage with Corruption and Economic Crimes?', *International Journal of Transitional Justice*, vol. 2, pp. 310–330.

Clinton, B. 2000, The Clinton Parameters. Clinton Proposal on Israeli-Palestinian Peace. Retrieved from http://www.peacelobby.org/clinton_parameters.html.

Crocker, D. 1999, 'Reckoning with Past Wrongs. A Normative Framework', *Ethics & International Affairs*, vol. 13, pp. 43–64.

Dudai, R. 2007, 'A Model for Dealing with the Past in the Israeli–Palestinian Context', *International Journal of Transitional Justice*, vol. 1, no. 2, pp. 249–267.

Dwyer, S. 1999, 'Reconciliation for Realists', *Ethics & International Affairs*, vol. 13, pp. 81–98.

Eldar, A. 2002, 'The Refugee Problem at Taba. Akiva Eldar Interviews Yossi Beilin and Nabil Sha'ath', *Palestine-Israel Journal*, vol. 9, no. 2, pp. 12–23.

Flämig, S., Leiner, M. 2012, 'Reconciliation in the Middle of Dispute. Introduction to the Series', in *Societies in Transition. Latin America between Conflict and Reconciliation*, eds S. Flämig, M. Leiner, Vandenhoeck & Ruprecht, Göttingen, pp. 7–19.

Fried, S. 2002, 'The Refugee Issue at the Peace Conferences, 1949–2000', *Palestine-Israel Journal*, vol. 9, no. 2, pp. 24–34.

General Assembly Resolution 194, December 11, 1948. 194(III). Palestine-Progress Report of the United Nations Mediator. Retrieved from http://unispal.un.org/UNISPAL.NSF/0/C758572B78D1CD0085256BCF0077E51A

Geneva Accord 2003, The Geneva Accord: A Full Text. Retrieved from http://www.geneva-accord.org/mainmenu/english.

Hecht, L., Michalowski, S. 2012, 'The Economic and Social Dimensions of Transitional Justice'. Retrieved https://www1.essex.ac.uk/tjn/documents/Theeconomicandsocialdimensionsof TJ.pdf

IJTJ. (2007). Editorial Note. International Journal of Transitional Justice, 1(1), 1–5. https://doi.org/10.1093/ijtj/ijm012

Israeli Response RE Refugees. 2001. The Taba proposals and the refugee problem. Retrieved from http://www.mideastweb.org/taba.htm

Jamal, A. 2001, 'Mutual Recognition and Transformation of Conflicts', *Isr. Sociol.*, vol. 3, pp. 313–341.

Ju'beh, N. 2002, 'The Palestinian Refugee Problem and the Final Status Negotiations', *Palestine-Israel Journal*, vol. 9, no. 2, pp. 5–11.

Kelman, H.C. 2008, 'Reconciliation from a social-psychological perspective', in *The Social Psychology of Intergroup Reconciliation*, eds A. Nadler, T.E. Malloy T.E., J.D. Fisher, Oxford University Press, Oxford, pp. 15–32.

Khalidi, R.I. 1992, 'Observations on the Right of Return', *Journal of Palestine Studies*, vol. 21, pp. 29–40.

Killen, K.Y. 2010, *Transitional Justice and the Marginalisation of Socioeconomic Issues*, Dissertation, Faculty of Social Sciences, University of Ulster, Londonderry.

Lambourne, W. 2009, 'Transitional Justice and Peacebuilding After Mass Violence', *International Journal of Transitional Justice*, vol. 3, pp. 28–48.

Leiner, M. 2018, 'From Conflict Resolution to Reconciliation', in *Alternative Approaches in Conflict Resolution*, eds M. Leiner, C. Schliesser, Palgrave Macmillan, London/New York, pp. 175–186.

McEvoy, K., & Mallinder, L. (2016). Transitional Justice. Routledge. https://pure.ulster.ac.uk/en/publications/transitional-justice-3.

Muvingi, I. 2009, 'Sitting on Powder Kegs. Socioeconomic Rights in Transitional Societies', *International Journal of Transitional Justice*, vol. 3, pp. 163–182.

Palestinian Position Paper 2001, The Taba Proposals and the Refugee Problem. Retrieved from http://www.mideastweb.org/taba.htm.

Peled, Y., Rouhana, N. 2004, 'Transitional Justice and the Right of Return of the Palestinian Refugees', *Theoretical Inquiries in Law*, vol. 5, pp. 317–332.

Rouhana, N. 2004, 'Identity and Power in the Reconciliation of National Conflict', in *The Social Psychology of Group Identity and Social Conflict. Theory, Application, and Practice*, eds A.H. Eagly, R.M. Baron, V.L. Hamilton, American Psychological Association, Washington, DC, pp. 173–187.

Rouhana, N. 2011, 'Key Issues in Reconciliation. Challenging Traditional Assumptions on Conflict Resolution and Power Dynamics', in D. Bar-Tal (ed), *Intergroup Conflicts and Their Resolution. A Social Psychological Perspective*, Taylor and Francis, New York, pp. 291–314.

Sa'di, A.H. 2002, 'Catastrophe, Memory and Identity. Al-Nakbah as a Component of Palestinian Identity', *Israel Studies*, vol. 7, no. 2, pp. 175–198.

Sanbar, E. 2001, 'Out of Place, Out of Time', *Mediterranean Historical Review*, vol. 16, no. 1, pp. 87–94.

Schmid, E., Nolan, A. 2014, "Do No Harm'? Exploring the Scope of Economic and Social Rights in Transitional Justice', *International Journal of Transitional Justice*, vol. 8, pp. 362–382.

Shavit, A. 2008, 'Ehud Barak Once Again Considers Himself Candidate for Prime Minister', retrieved from http://www.haaretz.co.il/hasite/spages/1047831.html.

Teitel, R.G. 2000, *Transitional Justice*, Oxford University Press, Oxford.

Teitel, R.G. 2003, 'Transitional Justice Genealogy', *Harvard Human Rights Journal*, vol. 16, pp. 69–94.

Tuvy, J. 2008, *On Its Own Threshold. The Formulation of Israel's Policy on the Palestinian Refugee Issues, 1948–1956*, Ben-Gurion Institute (Hebrew), Beer-Sheva.

UN. (2010). Guidance Note of the Secretary-General: United Nations Approach to Transitional Justice - United Nations and the Rule of Law. Unspeakable Truths: Transitional Justice and the Challenge of Truth Commissions.

Zakay, D., Klar, Y., Sharvit, K. 2002, 'Jewish Israelis on the 'Right of Return'', *Palestine Israel Journal of Politics, Economics, and Culture*, vol. 9, no. 2, pp. 58–66.

Dina Dajani Daoudi

# Transitional Justice and Reconciliation in Intractable Conflicts

## Abstract

According to Dina Dajani Daoudi's paper on *Transitional Justice and Reconciliation in Intractable Conflicts*, the relationship between reconciliation and transitional justice is so complex as the practices have been adopted as substitutes rather than complementarities. Her paper explores the interdependent relationship of both defining transitional justice and reconciliation through their mechanisms that at times overlap, proving their converging nature and interdependence and diverge, requiring an over-compassing approach to reconciliation that can nurture the process of changing relationships without solid institutional structures and expectations. In her conclusions, the author argues that it is futile to pursue transitional justice without addressing the psychological needs of a given society. In order to build sustainable peace, they cannot be ignored, and they can only be addressed through a comprehensive process of reconciliation, incorporating institutional mechanisms of transitional justice.

## Introduction

This paper aims to explore and explain the interdependent relationship between transitional justice and reconciliation in the case of intractable conflicts. It provides a simple but clear understanding of both concepts and their relationship to each other. In the DFG-funded project "Hearts of Flesh–Not Stone," a reconciliation-oriented project that aims to study the effects of encountering the suffering of the other on one's level of empathy in the Israeli-Palestinian context, the question of transitional justice has also been addressed at a conference, in Jerusalem in 2016, on Transitional Justice Conference: Contemporary Theories and Practices. Therefore, this paper demonstrates both the overlap and independency of the concepts that result in their interdependent nature in intractable conflicts.

Transitional justice and reconciliation are two oceans of disciplines that have evolved from conflict resolution theories and practices in recent history. Transitional justice and reconciliation emerged from the practices of peace-keeping, peace-building, nation-building, state-building, conflict management, conflict transformation, and conflict resolution and studies of political science, law, development studies, sociology, anthropology, and psychology. Such fields aim to achieve effective strategies and their successful implementation in the post-settlement phase of the conflict.

Definitions of reconciliation and transitional justice vary as both disciplines engage in a wide range of theories and practices depending on one's adopted approach toward conflict resolution. However, I argue that it is ineffective to adopt transitional justice or reconciliation without including the other in the case of intractable conflicts. To demonstrate my claim, I first explain what intractable conflicts are and how they differ from other conflicts. In attempts to develop a structure for studying social conflicts, many schemes have been developed to classify and categorize conflicts. Christopher Moore presents such a structure based on a "five-fold classification scheme involving structural, interest, value, relationship and data conflicts (Mitchell 2014, 48)." Other categorizations classify conflicts based on the "level" in society to which they occurred or on the scope of who is involved. He distinguishes between "inter-personal", "inter-group", "intra-national," and "international." These different categorizations tackle ideal key points of the conflict but, as Mitchel explains, are unfocused. To bring further clarity to the conversation, Mitchel provides five considerations of how one can categorize intractable conflicts: the nature of the issues involved, the structure and nature of the parties involved, the nature of relationships between the parties, the complexity of the conflict system involved, and the dynamics involved in the conflict (Mitchell 2014, 49).

Intractable conflicts are conflicts that last for long periods, at least for one generation, and develop a cyclical nature. As a consequence of their longevity, intractable conflicts infiltrate the societal and psychological infrastructure. They involve deep-seated identity-related topics that become existential and are perceived to be irresolvable and to have a zero-sum end (Mitchell 2014; Bar-Tal 2000). "They are demanding, stressful, painful, exhausting, and costly both in human and material terms" (Bar-Tal 2000, 353). Violence in intractable conflict "occurs over time, with fluctuating frequency and intensity" and is not restricted to military confrontations and hostility but to civilians as well (Bar-Tal 2000, 1432). As a result of their nature, "parties engaged in an intractable conflict make vast material (i. e., military, technological, and economic) and psychological investments to cope successfully with the situation" (Bar-Tal 2000, 1432).

The resolution of such conflicts would not be addressed by implementing one mechanism of transitional justice, such as retribution or reconciliation, such as truth commissions. In contrast, Bar-Tal expresses that only a comprehensive approach that caters to the psychological needs of the people involved in the conflict can alleviate the situation and ensure results. This desired outcome would result from building robust psychological infrastructures that allow the evolution of society from adopting an ethos of conflict to one of peace (Bar-Tal 2000; Bar-Tal and Rosen 2009; Bar-Tal et al. 2014).

## 1. A Comprehensive Approach?

When dealing with societies in conflict or post-conflict societies, different kinds of challenges occur, including the deterioration of trust among parties or between people and institutions, the collapse of state institutions and the inability to enforce the rule of law, the loss of legitimacy to a central unifying entity, the dominant sense of injustice, the asymmetrical balance of power and the asymmetry between victim and perpetrator or even the cyclical role of victim and perpetrator, the distortion of reality, and the absence of "truth," among others. The nature of intractable conflicts combines these challenges and demands the implementation of a combination of mechanisms from transitional justice and reconciliation.

## 2. Transitional Justice

The attempt to address all these challenges by transitional justice is evident in the discipline's effort to develop a clear understanding of them. Among the numerous definitions available, the scholar who coined the phrase, Ruti Teitel, defines *transitional justice* as "the conception of justice associated with periods of political change, characterized by legal responses to confront the wrongdoings of respective predecessor regimes (Teitel 2003, 69)." She emphasizes the relationship between political change and justice in the process of transition. Later on, the former UN Secretary-General Report *The Rule of Law and Transitional Justice in Conflict and Post-Conflict Societies*, defines it as "the full range of processes and mechanisms associated with a society's attempts to come to terms with a legacy of large-scale past abuses, in order to ensure accountability, serve justice and achieve reconciliation (UNSC 2004, 4)." In this context, transitional justice concerns situations where a state or a people tries to move from a conflict situation to a post-conflict one.

Moreover, ICTJ[1] explains transitional justice as a process that seeks to recognize the rights of the victims, promote civic trust and strengthen the democratic rule of law (ICTJ 2015). The process can vary from the mere acknowledgment of responsibility by the perpetrator to the establishment of formal judicial bodies, such as

---

1 Founded in 2001 in New York, the International Center for Transitional Justice (ICTJ) aims to pursue accountability for massive human rights violations and restore confidence and rule of law through transitional justice mechanisms. https://www.ictj.org.

criminal tribunals. ICTJ's definition highlights the victim's rights and their responsibility towards them. In addition to stating these definitions, one must expand on the layers involved, including what kind of justice is to be implemented? And where is it derived from?

Whatever kind of justice is realized, there is a consensus that these mechanisms aim "to reduce the sense of injustice felt by victims in order to reduce communal antagonisms in the post-conflict environment of divided societies (Aiken 2014, 50)." Sandford and Lincoln address the source of justice from which society can derive its methods, such as "local" and "community justice" (Sanford and Lincoln 2010), in which justice is experienced, perceived, conceptualized, transacted, and produced in various localities, ranging from village-level interactions between former victims and perpetrators to offices of nongovernmental organization and the courtrooms of international tribunals (Hinton 2010). Drexler warns against the dangers of localizing transitional justice since conflict is rarely independent of the involvement of international actors. Therefore, "[t]ransitional justice mechanisms that legalize conflicts tend to horizontalize them – that is, to posit conflicts between different groups in society rather than between the state and its citizens (Drexler 2010, 50)." Practices so far have included retribution and reparation as well as restorative, civic, socioeconomic, social, administrative, and constitutional justice.

## 3.    Mechanisms of Transitional Justice

Retributive justice is one form of institutional justice that is practiced on both levels of the international and national community. It is based on establishing tribunals to hold perpetrators accountable for their crimes. They serve a vital function of reactivating social solidarity and reaffirming moral values. However, retributive justice is criticized for providing little healing power to the victims (Andrieu 2014; Hinton 2010; Teitel 2000). Therefore, it is an attempt to rebuild relations between individuals, institutions, and rule of law enforcement. Criminal prosecution in retributive justice operates at a national and international level. Examples of international tribunals include the Nuremberg Trials and the Tokyo Trials. More recent examples are the International Criminal Tribunal for the former Yugoslavia (ICTY) and the International Criminal Tribunal for Rwanda (ICTR). Hybrid tribunals include the Extraordinary Chambers in the Courts of Cambodia (aka Khmer Rouge Tribunal), and examples of national tribunals include the cases in Greece in 1974, Argentina in 1985 and, Ethiopia in 1994 (Huyse 2003).

Restorative justice is the mechanism most associated with reconciliation. It describes the process where all parties involved in the conflict come together to resolve the conflict collectively. It addresses the asymmetrical power between victims and perpetrators and attempts to restore dignity to victims and help them process their experiences of violation and abuse towards healing (Andrieu 2014; Laplante 2014). It "relies on the concept and virtue of forgiveness, with truth commissions often accompanied by a measure of amnesty, a sacrifice justified in the name of abstract goals, such as truth or reconciliation (Andrieu 2014, 94)."

Reparation is the economic compensation for committed injustices. It is not limited to monetary compensation but includes redistribution of wealth in an inclusive manner where previously excluded, or marginalized groups would be able to enjoy an equitable share of resources (Andrieu 2014; Laplante 2014; Greiff 2006).

Civic justice specifically tackles relationships between "the government and the governed" (Laplante 2014, 74). It focuses on the ideas of citizenship and participation in public life. Civic justice also aims at establishing societies with democratic values of political participation, free speech, freedom of association, and equal and fair treatment. In return, it reinforces the rule of law and ensures the government's legitimacy. Moreover, it intends to remedy political disparities in societies.

Socio-economic justice is closely linked to the field of development as it "seeks to remedy historical social and economic inequalities" (Laplante 2014, 77). Complementary to civic justice, socio-economic justice addresses structural violence that has institutionally victimized members of society repeatedly.

Social justice is equivalent to restorative justice as it concerns victims' dignity through truth-telling and punitive measures. It seeks to protect victims from limited reparative justice without attempting institutional reform or accountability (Andrieu 2014). Administrative justice or lustration is the process of cleansing and purging a system goes through to separate itself from the remnants of the past (Teitel 2000). Constitutional justice embodies the ideal form of justice by ensuring the rule of law expressed in the constitution (Allan 2001).

This wide range of transitional justice mechanisms seems inclusive and comprehensive. However, in practice, it is limited. The limitations, which must be addressed, include the difficulty of initiating a process without the halt of conflict and political will to ensure the delivery of reparations, the sincerity of apologies and acknowledgment of guilt to restore relations, holding perpetrators accountable, and a lack of measurement techniques to determine the effects of implemented transitional justice mechanisms. These limitations lead to the question of how reconciliation can complement the process of transitional justice to resolve intractable conflicts.

## 4. Reconciliation

Most authors agree that reconciliation describes a process rather than an outcome. Martin Leiner defines *reconciliation* as "the overarching approach to conflicts with [a] focus on processes of rebuilding relationships. Its goal is to create 'normal', 'trustful', and if possible 'good' and 'peaceful' relationships (Leiner 2018, 179)." John

Paul Lederach defines reconciliation as a process of relationship-building as part of conflict transformation as well as an outcome that is part of the experience of sustainable peace (Lederach 1997). Although historically presented and practiced, Bar-Tal and H. Bennink explain that reconciliation has only "emerged as a defined area of interest in political science and political psychology" since 1994 (see Leiner 2018, 176). Therefore, reconciliation does not only acknowledge political arrangements toward conflict resolution but addresses the psychological process of changing the culture of conflict and enmity towards a culture of peace and tolerance (Leiner 2018; Whittaker 1999). Since a comprehensive approach to reconciliation is both theory and practice-based, it also means that, like transitional justice, it encompasses mechanisms and processes of healing, attaining a form of justice, truth-telling, and reparations (Fischer 2011; Huyse 2003).

The healing process in intractable conflicts is not confined to physical injury but deeply psychological and emotional. The traumatic incidents experienced during a conflict impact an individual's sense of the self and the sense of belonging to the collective. Therefore, reconciliation requires eliminating the source of the injury by tackling structural forms of violence that lead to deprivation, repression, and re-victimization, whether on a prolonged period of exposure to multiple traumas at the same time. As a result, space for individual and communal healing must be available. Strategies include psychological programs, counselling and intervention, training local capabilities, support groups, and symbolic forms of healing. The process is highly contextual and should be inspired by local rituals and culture within more comprehensive reconstruction efforts. In the absence of truth, acknowledgement, and justice, the healing process is incomplete, as demonstrated by the cases of South Africa, Chile, Argentina and Brazil (Hamber 2003).

As previously mentioned, justice has many forms. It is a normative concept that depends on local context and understanding. The neglect of this crucial point might lead to the implementation of counter-productive structures that estrange society even further from justice and thus from reconciliation.

Some scholars support retributive justice because it can diffuse tension and complement reconciliation. In the absence of retribution, Huyse argues that victims might embark on a journey of "self-help justice." Without an apparent undermining of perpetrators, the system remains vulnerable to submitting to their influence once again. Retributive justice is one form of public acknowledgment needed by victims to restore their self-confidence and trust in the system; it individualizes guilt to steer away from collective demonizing, strengthens legitimacy, and democratization processes and breaks the cycle of impunity.

On the other hand, seeking retribution may have dire effects on accomplishing a peace settlement, reconsolidating democracy, and strengthening governance and development. For example, the argument of Uruguayan President Sanguinetti for consolidating peace and human rights for the future was more important than seeking retroactive justice in the present. President Sanguinetti feared provoking retaliation against the incumbent system and the risk of returning to a military dictatorship (Huyse 2003, 103). Moreover, retributive justice has a limited impact in addressing victims' psychological needs for long-term healing and undermines the truth. It is a western-oriented approach that might not cater to the local understandings of justice in certain societies (Huyse 2003). As an alternative, societies may adopt restorative justice, the establishment of truth and reconciliation commissions, and/or reparative justice. Restorative justice focuses on the harm done to people and what the victims' needs are. Unlike retributive justice, where perpetrators must be punished, restorative justice holds perpetrators accountable by their obligation to comprehend their wrongdoing and take responsibility to make things as right as possible for their victims. As a result, restorative justice enables engagement and participation in the reconciliatory process (Zehr and Gohar 2003). For example, William Ury provides insight from traditional African jurisprudence of the San/Bushman that focus on reconciling rather than pursuing vengeance (Ury 2000).

Truth-telling is one of the essential steps in the pursuit of reconciliation. Truth commissions are established for the sole purpose of dealing with the past through truth-seeking. There are several projects that governments and regional organizations could embark on, such as historical commissions and inquiries. Historical commissions aim to clarify historical truths and acknowledge practices that have affected victims of ethnic or racial groups and their descendants, such as the US Commission on Wartime Relocation and Internment of Civilian and the Canadian Royal Commission on Aboriginal Peoples. Official and semi-official inquiries overlap with truth commissions, implying that they are more powerful but less independent than truth commissions. Governments establish them to investigate and report on severe cases of repression. Examples include the International Panel of Eminent Personalities to Investigate the 1994 Genocide in Rwanda (Freeman and Hayner 2003).

Truth commissions are non-judicial, temporary bodies that focus on the past and "are officially sanctioned, authorized or empowered by the state and, in some cases, by the armed opposition (Freeman and Hayner 2003, p. 125)" to investigate patterns of abuses and specific violations of human rights over a period of time. Truth commissions are established in periods of political transition, either from conflict to peace or from an authoritarian regime to a democratic one. Like restorative justice, commissions provide a platform for victims and establish a detailed record of the past. Besides, they enable an informed public debate that promotes a democratic transition and social reconciliation (Freeman and Hayner 2003). However, commissions may have biases and unrealistic expectations. Therefore, in the absence of a comprehensive process with political interest and accountability measures, commissions would be insufficient to produce any significant results.

Reparations are compensations to redress past wrongs. Vandeginste explains the variety of terminology embedded within reparations, such as restitution, which describes the restoration of a situation to its original before committing injustice. Compensation, in contrast, is the recognition of a committed injustice and the payment of money to compensate for suffered losses. Rehabilitation, in turn, focuses on the "restoration of victim's physical and psychological health." Satisfaction derives from redress by actions and gestures by the perpetrator towards the victim, such as acknowledgment, apologies, sanctions, and commemorations (Vandeginste, 2003).

## 5.    Complementary Nature?

As demonstrated by these mechanisms, there exists a significant overlap between transitional justice and reconciliation. Both aim for justice to prevail and function in a social and political transition. However, transitional justice is a top-down institutional approach whose implementation relies on a final status agreement. Its mechanisms are procedural. Hence fail to consider the psychological readiness of individuals to heal from the past and move towards the future. In contrast, reconciliation mechanisms are not bound to an agreement for implementation but are applicable in the midst of strife. Leiner brings forth the Hölderlin approach, supported by the quote of German poet Friedrich Hölderlin in his novel *Hyperion*, *Versöhnung ist mitten im Streit und alles Getrennte findet sich wieder* (Leiner 2018; Barakat 2017). This seemingly open-ended nature of the process of reconciliation questions its applicability and sustainability.

Intractable conflicts run deep into the psyche of its participants. While both transitional justice and reconciliation attempt to address the different needs for sustainable transition through acknowledgment, restorative justice, and reparations, it is unlikely that a successful process can take place without an inclusive, bottom-up movement to pave the way for sustainable political and social structures. Reconciliation offers the opportunity for individuals' social and political transformation in the middle of a conflict, as demonstrated by Zeina Barakat, who traces the evolution of Mohammed Dajani Daoudi from extremism to moderation in the context of the Israeli-Palestinian intractable conflict (Barakat, present volume). Also, transitional justice offers a top-down process that ensures future accountability and structural sustainability, an explicit, systematic practice that validates a form of closure. This symbiotic comprehension of transitional justice and reconciliation addresses the question of justice in a framework of reconciliation that was a recurring theme in the "Hearts of Flesh–Not Stone" project.

In conclusion, Leiner advocates that reconciliation does not mean merging all societies into one mold. In contrast, it "means creating a space where former enemies can become political opponents within the bounds of the rule of law

(Verdeja 2009, 13)." Instead, it is a process than an achievable objective (Freeman and Hayner, 2003) that can take place in circles and events during the period of conflict to prepare society for a conflict transformation. Adopting an early approach toward peace and reconciliation prepares the bases for a sturdy structure where transitional justice mechanisms can be implemented. Many cases of regression and disappointment have been recorded through attempts to implement selective mechanisms of either transitional justice or reconciliation. A successful case for transitional justice and reconciliation is West Germany in the aftermath of WW II. Although separately, both transitional justice and reconciliation practices were implemented to help society reintegrate into the community of nations. This successful case, among many failed attempts, proves that it is futile to pursue transitional justice without addressing the psychological needs of society. Thus, these psychological and social needs can only be addressed through a comprehensive reconciliation process, incorporating institutional mechanisms of transitional justice.

## References

Aiken, N.T. 2014, 'Rethinking Reconciliation in Divided Societies. A Social Learning Theory of Transitional Justice', in *Transitional Justice Theories*, eds S. Buckley-Zistel, T.K. Beck, C. Braun, F. Mieth, Routledge, New York, pp. 40–65.

Allan, T. 2001, *Constitutional Justice. A Liberal Theory of the Rule of Law*, Oxford University Press, Oxford.

Andrieu, K. 2014, 'Political Liberalism after Mass Violence', in *Transitional Justice Theories*, eds S. Buckley-Zistel, T.K. Beck, C. Braun, F. Mieth, Routledge, New York, pp. 85–104.

Barakat, Z.M. 2017, *From Heart of Stone to Heart of Flesh. Evolutionary Journey from Extremism to Moderation*, Herbert Utz Verlag, Munich.

Barakat, Z.M. 2022, 'Reconciliation as Transformation from Extremism to Moderation. The case of Palestine-Israel', present volume.

Bar-Tal, D. 2000, 'From Intractable Conflict through Conflict Resolution to Reconciliation. Psychological Analysis', *Political Psychology*, vol. 21, no. 2, pp. 351–365.

Bar-Tal, D. 2000, 'Sociopsychological Foundations of Intractable Conflicts', *American Behavioral Scientist*, vol. 50, no. 11, pp. 1430–1453.

Bar-Tal, D., Rosen, Y. 2009, 'Peace Education in Societies Involved in Intractable Conflicts. Direct and Indirect Models', *Review of Educational Research*, vol. 79, no. 2, pp. 557–575.

Bar-Tal, D., Rosen, Y., Nets-Zehngut, R. 2014, 'Peace Education in Societies Involved in Intractable Conflicts. Goals, Conditions, and Directions', in *Handbook on Peace Education*, eds G. Salomon, E. Cairns, Psychology Press, New York, pp. 21–43.

Drexler, E.F. 2010, 'The Failure of International Justice in East Timor and Indonesia', in *Transitional Justice. Global Mechanisms and Local Realities after Genocide and Mass Violence*, ed A.L. Hinton, Rutgers Univeristy Press, New Jersey, pp. 49–66.

Fischer, M. 2011, 'Transitional Justice and Reconciliation. Theory and Practice', in *Advancing Conflict Transformation. The Berghof Handbook II*, eds B. Austin, M. Fischer, H.J. Giessmann, Barbara Budrich Publishers, Opladen and Farmington Hills, pp. 405–430.

Freeman, M., Hayner, P.B. 2003, 'Truth-Telling', in *Reconciliation After Violent Conflict. A Handbook*, eds D. Bloomfield, T. Barnes, L. Huyse, International Institute for Democracy and Electoral Assistance, Stockholm, pp. 122–139.

Greiff, P.D. 2006, 'Justice and Reparations', in *The Handbook of Reparations*, ed P.D. Greiff, Oxford University Press, Oxford, pp. 451–477.

Hamber, B. 2003, 'Healing', in *Reconciliation After Violent Conflict. A Handbook*, eds D. Bloomfield, T. Barnes, L. Huyse, International Institute for Democracy and Electoral Assistance, Stockholm, pp. 77–89.

Hinton, A.L. 2010, 'Introdutction. Toward and Anthropology of Transitional Justice', in *Transitional Justice. Global Mechanisms and Local Realities after Genocide and Mass Violence*, ed A.L. Hinton, Rutgers Univeristy Press, New Jersey, pp. 1–24.

Huyse, L. 2003, 'Justice', in *Reconciliation After Violent Conflict. A Handbook*, eds D. Bloomfield, T. Barnes, L. Huyse, International Institute for Democracy and Electoral Assistance, Stockholm, pp. 97–121.

Huyse, L. 2003, 'The Process of Reconciliation', in *Reconciliation After Violent Conflict. A Handbook*, eds D. Bloomfield, T. Barnes, L. Huyse, International Institute for Democracy and Electoral Assistance, Stockholm, pp. 19–39.

International Center for Transitional Justice (ICTJ), 2015, 'What is Transitional Justice?'. Retrieved from: https://www.ictj.org/about/transitional-justice [16 June 2015].

Laplante, L.J. 2014, 'The Plural Justice Aims of Reparations', in *Transitional Justice Theories*, eds S. Buckley-Zistel, T.K. Beck, C. Braun, F. Mieth, Routledge, New York, pp. 66–84.

Lederach, J.P. 1997, *Building Peace. Sustainable Reconciliation in Divided Societies*, United States Institute of Peace, Washington DC.

Leiner, M. 2018, 'From Conflict Resolution to Reconciliation', in *Alternative Approaches in Conflict Resolution*, eds M. Leiner, C. Schliesser, Palgrave Macmillan, London/New York, pp. 175–186.

Mitchell, C. 2014, *The Nature of Intractable Conflict. Resolution in the Twenty-First Century*, Palgrave Macmillan, New York.

Sanford, V., Lincoln, M. 2010, 'Body of Evidence. Feminicide, Local Justice, and Rule of Law in 'Peacetime' Guatemala', in *Transitional Justice. Global Mechanisms and Local Realities after Genocide and Mass Violence*, ed A.L. Hinton, Rutgers University Press, New Jersey, pp. 67–94.

Teitel, R. 2000, *Transitional Justice*, Oxford University Press, Oxford.

Teitel, R. 2003, 'Transitional Justice Genealogy', *Harvard Human Rights Journal*, vol. 16, pp. 69–94.

UNSC 2004, *The Rule of Law and Transitional Justice in Conflict and Post-Conflict Socities*. Retrieved from: http://www.refworld.org/docid/45069c434.html [June 20, 2015].

Ury, W. 2000, *The Third Side*, Penguin Books, New York.

Vandeginste, S. 2003, 'Reparation', in *Reconciliation After Violent Conflict. A Handbook*, eds
D. Bloomfield, T. Barnes, L. Huyse, International Institute for Democracy and Electoral
Assistance, Stockholm, pp. 145–162.

Verdeja, E. 2009, *Unchopping a Tree. Reconciliation in the Aftermath of Political Violence*,
Temple University Press, Philadelphia.

Whittaker, D.J. 1999, *Conflict and Reconciliation in the Contemporary World*, Routledge,
London.

Zehr, H., Gohar, A. 2003, *The Little Book of Restorative Justice*, Good Books, Intercourse PA.

Rahav Gabay, Boaz Hameiri, Tammy Rubel-Lifschitz, Arie Nadler

# The Tendency for Interpersonal Victimhood

## Conceptualization, Cognitive and Behavioral Consequences, and Antecedents

### Abstract

The urgency of taking psychological needs seriously becomes dramatically evident when victimhood is assumed as identity. Rahav Gabay, Boaz Hameiri, Tammy Rubel-Lifschitz, and Arie Nadler's paper on *The Tendency for Interpersonal Victimhood: Conceptualization, Cognitive and Behavioral Consequences, and Antecedents* addresses the issue of the subjective experience of victimhood in interpersonal relations as an enduring personality disposition. According to the authors, the Tendency for Interpersonal Victimhood (TIV) is an individual-level characteristic in the general population affecting how individuals feel, think, and behave in hurtful situations. Through a phenomenology of victimhood in interpersonal relations, the paper proposes a conceptualization of TIV as made up of four dimensions: the need for recognition of the suffering, the tendency for moral elitism, the lack of empathy for others' sufferings, and a tendency for rumination about past or future interpersonal offenses. Showing how cognitive processes of interpretation, attribution, and memory reinforce feelings of victimhood and retaliation, the findings demonstrate that people high on TIV experience daily interpersonal victimization more often, more intensely, and for more extended periods.

***

Numerous studies in social psychology have characterized victimhood as a fundamental component of human conflicts. Victimhood has been widely studied as a possible result of hurtful events in interpersonal relations (Vangelisti 2009) and in the context of intergroup conflicts (Bar-Tal 2007; Bar-Tal et al., 2009; Hameiri and Nadler 2017; Noor et al., 2012; Shnabel and Nadler 2008). These studies suggest that the experience of victimhood emerges when individuals or groups feel offended, disappointed, exploited, insulted, rejected, or betrayed, which leads to the perception (see Leary et al., 1998; Schori-Eyal et al., 2017; Vangelisti et al., 2005) of victimhood as a central part of their identity. While some individuals overcome such unpleasant episodes with relative ease and move on, others continue to feel wronged and victimized. Consequently, they experience themselves as victims more often, more intensely, and for longer periods of time (Ulric, Berger, and Berman 2010).

Despite the vast interest in victimhood as a fundamental part of human conflict, surprisingly little is known about the personal dispositional tendency for victimhood after experiencing hurtful interpersonal interactions. The current research addresses this gap, reviewing and integrating the literature on victimhood in intergroup and interpersonal relations to develop a comprehensive definition of the Tendency for Interpersonal Victimhood (TIV) composed of four psychological dimensions. This analysis is followed by an empirical examination of the affective, cognitive and behavioral consequences of TIV and its antecedents.

## 1. Clinical-Based Theory on the Victimhood-Centered Personality

Works in clinical psychology have suggested that victimhood can be a factor in interpersonal relations. Whereas some individuals can move on relatively quickly after interpersonal conflicts, others dwell on feelings of hurt and victimhood (Feeney 2005; Leahy 2012; Shaver et al. Cassidy 2009). The clinical theory claims that individuals characterized by dispositional victimhood tend to be preoccupied with feelings of belligerence and display anger and aggression (Berman 2014).

Aggressiveness among individuals with dispositional victimhood may be part of a defense mechanism against painful emotions, such as shame, uncertainty, humiliation, or guilt. It seems to displace anger against a past perpetrator towards the person's current relationships. When behaving aggressively, these individuals use their suffering as a justification for causing suffering to others while perceiving themselves as highly moral and ethical. Individuals exhibiting dispositional victimhood also often attempt to control others by accusing them of immoral, unfair, or selfish behavior (Berman and Mendelson 2005).

The current study reveals that the dispositional tendency to adopt the identity of a victim in interpersonal relations (TIV) comprises four related dimensions: (a) the demand for recognition of one's suffering and victimization (from the perpetrators and others), (b) feelings of moral superiority, (c) a lack of empathy and attentiveness to the suffering of others, and (d) rumination about interpersonal conflicts. These four dimensions of victimhood have also been documented in intergroup relationships (Noor et al. 2012) and are described below.

### 1.1 Need for Recognition

The need for the recognition of the suffering incurred through victimization. The victims felt an intense need for the acknowledgement of their victimization and demanded empathy from the perpetrator and others (Hameiri et al. present volume). Experiencing trauma undermines victims' previous perceptions, schemas, and understandings about themselves, others, and the world (Janoff-Bulman 2010).

These perceptions include personal safety and morality, the ability to trust others, and the world as a just and moral place. Recognition helps to reaffirm positive assumptions about the self, other people, and the world. Recognition re-establishes the victims' confidence in their evaluation of reality. It requires that the offenders regard themselves responsible for the unjustified harm caused to the victim. In other words, this corresponds to the victims' need for the perpetrators to take responsibility for their wrongdoing and express feelings of guilt (Baumeister, Stillwell and, Heatherton 1994). For example, Herman (1992) reviewed studies and testimonies of patients and therapists and found that validation of the victimization event and its acknowledgment was a key component in therapeutic recovery from trauma and victimization.

## 1.2 Moral Elitism

Moral elitism refers to the perception of the immaculate morality of the self and the immorality of the other side. Victimhood has been associated with a sense of differentiation and moral superiority in both individual- (e. g., Leahy 2012) and group-level conflicts (Bar-Tal et al. 2009; Noor et al. 2012). The notion of moral elitism as it relates to TIV is characterized by a psychological stance in which people perceive themselves as morally and ethically superior to other people, especially those who hurt them. Moral elitism is also related to feelings of disappointment over the lack of responsiveness of the adversary to efforts made by oneself or one's side to show care and consideration. Moral elitism is expected to be directed towards perceived perpetrators among people high on TIV.

Moral elitism can also be seen as a mental reaction to distress. According to some clinical theories (e. g., Klein 1937), individuals who feel threatened by others often use a defense mechanism known as splitting. In the context of reduced mental complexity, the split is expressed in a black-and-white world view of the "absolute good" and "absolute evil". This way of thinking contrasts the ability to see the world in all its complexities or the self and others as complex entities. Klein (1937) also claims that when in distress, individuals tend to deny their aggressiveness and destructive impulses and therefore project them on others.

Consequently, one side experiences the other as threatening, accusing, and persecuting, while they perceive themselves as persecuted and weak but morally pure. This dichotomy helps the individual preserve a positive moral image of the self. Although using different terminology, Gray and Wegner (2009) suggest that people automatically contrast (and thus split) the characteristics of the perpetrator and the victim in situations of interpersonal offense. The *Moral Agent* (the transgressor) is characterized as the one who is less capable of feeling pain or distress, as opposed to the *Moral Patient* (the victim), who has a low pain threshold and is less capable of planning, and taking responsibility, and being agentic. This moral typecasting helps to defend the self's moral values and reduce negative feelings, such as guilt.

## 1.3 Lack of Empathy

The psychological state of splitting and the feeling of moral elitism are closely linked to the third dimension of TIV, a lack of empathy towards others. The victim, preoccupied with their suffering, lacks the willingness to divert attention, care about the suffering they caused to others, and take responsibility for their action. Empirical studies that manipulated feelings of victimhood revealed an increase in the individuals' sense of entitlement to behave aggressively and selfishly. This circumstance, for instance, is achieved by ignoring the sufferings of others and taking more for themselves while leaving less to others (Zitek et al., 2012). Zitek et al. (2012) emphasize that wronged individuals might feel that they have already suffered enough and thus do not have to be attentive and empathic to the needs of others.

## 1.4 Rumination

The definition of rumination focuses on the symptoms of one's distress, possible causes, and consequences instead of possible solutions (Nolen-Hoeksema, Wisco, and Lyubomirsky 2008). Within the framework of TIV, rumination is defined as a deep and lengthy emotional engagement in interpersonal offenses. Moreover, rumination may refer to expected crimes in the future or past offenses. It includes thoughts, images, and emotions related to an interpersonal offense and its offender. Studies have shown that victims tend to ruminate over their interpersonal offenses (McCullough et al. 1998) and that this rumination perpetuates psychological distress long after the experience of interpersonal stressors (Greenberg 1995), promoting aggression after insults and threats to self-esteem (Collins and Bell 1997). By increasing the drive to seek revenge (but not to avoid the offender) (McCullough et al. 1998), rumination also decreases the desire for forgiveness.

## 2. Cognitive and Emotional Consequences of TIV

In interpersonal conflict, sustaining a positive moral image is a significant motivation, which explains why the two parties of conflict are likely to construct two different subjective realities (Baumeister 1996; Baumeister et al. 1990; Baumeister, Exline and Sommer 1998). Thus, the role one assumes, whether victim or perpetrator, has a vital effect on the way the situation is perceived and remembered. Offenders tend to attribute lower severity and illegitimacy to the transgression than their victims, who often perceive the offenders' motivations as arbitrary, incoherent, senseless, and immoral. Moreover, victims are likely to perceive the offender's act as having more severe consequences than the perpetrators do (e. g., Baumeister 1996; Baumeister et al. 1990). Our studies show that these cognitive biases increase in individuals scoring high on the above described four dimensions of victimhood. In other words, interpretation, attribution, and memory biases result from both an actual offense that occurred in the course of interpersonal relations and the victim's personality disposition (TIV).

## 2.1   Interpretation Bias

In the context of TIV, interpretation biases contain two meanings. The first is the perceived offensiveness of an interpersonal situation. We pointed out that people high on TIV perceive both low-severity offenses (e. g., lack of help) and high-severity offenses (e. g., an offensive statement regarding their integrity and personality) as more severe than those who scored low on TIV. The second type of interpretation bias refers to increased anticipation of suffering in relatively innocuous interpersonal situations, i. e., in ambiguous situations. In other words, high levels of TIV are associated with an increased perceived probability of negative behaviors by others towards the self in ambiguous situations. For example, people high on TIV were assumed that a new manager in their department would show less consideration and willingness to help them even before they met. These biases also exist in close relationships, e. g., expectations that a good friend will be reluctant to assist the others in times of need.

## 2.2   Attribution of Hurtful Behaviors

TIV leads to attributing offenses to the offender's negative stable characteristics (e. g., personality) and unstable harmful properties, such as negative moods or unrealistic expectations. This finding, which shows that high TIV is associated with blaming others in offensive situations when it is unclear who is accountable, is related to theories that associate victimhood with an external locus of control (Bar-Tal et al. 2009; Zur 2005). Other related research shows that the extent to which individuals find an interaction hurtful is directly related to the perception that the harmful behavior was intentional (McLaren & Solomon, 2008; Vangelisti et al., 2005; Vangelisti & Young, 2000).

## 2.3   Memory Bias

We have shown that people high on TIV have more negative memory bias, i. e., they recalled more words representing offensive behaviors and feelings of hurt, such as betrayal, anger, disappointment, and wretchedness, compared to the participants low on TIV. This memory bias is related to the fact that people high on TIV tend to ruminate and be more preoccupied and emotionally involved in issues of offense and hurt. Related research on the effect of rumination on memory bias has found that rumination perpetuates increased negative recall (e. g., Lyubomirsky, Caldwell and Nolen-Hoeksema 1998) and recognition (e. g., Edwards, Rapee, and Franklin 2003) in different psychological situations.

## 2.4 Behavioral Consequences of TIV: Forgiveness

Individuals are described as forgiving if they inhibit retaliatory or destructive responses and respond with conciliatory or constructive behaviors, affect, and cognition (McCullough 2000). According to Baumeister et al. (1998), cognitive processes, which include perspective-taking, i. e., understanding the offender's point of view mediate forgiveness. The findings of our study indicate that TIV is related to a lack of willingness to forgive. The difficulty in adopting the perpetrator's point of view, experienced by people high on TIV is one possible cause of the decreased tendency to forgive. Moreover, rumination over interpersonal offenses, the fourth dimension of TIV, is also likely to decrease the willingness to forgive and increase the intent to retaliate against the offender (Collins & Bell, 1997; McCullough et al., 1998).

In parallel to the lesser willingness to forgive, we found that TIV is related to an increased desire for revenge. The cognitive implications of TIV seem to underlie its behavioral outcomes since the effect of TIV on the desire for revenge was mediated by negative attributions to the offender. In the experiment that yielded these results, participants imagined that they were lawyers who had received negative feedback from their senior partner in the firm. The higher a participant's TIV, the more they tended to attribute the criticism of the senior partner to the negative properties of the senior partner himself, which led to greater desires for revenge.

## 2.5 Antecedents of TIV: Attachment

According to Attachment Theory, a person's early relationships with caregiver's shape adult working models of interpersonal relations (Bowlby 1973). Mikulincer and Shaver (2016) argue that working models are generalized across recurrent interactions with others via transference processes and strongly influence attitudes, emotions, emotional regulation, and behavioral strategies in relationships throughout adult life. The literature on attachment suggests that there are at least three distinct attachment styles which are termed *secure, avoidant, and anxious.*

Anxiously-attached people tend to be dependent on others' approval and continual validation. They feel good about themselves when a partner offers praise and affection, but they often feel less worthy when others are critical or rejecting. They intensively seek reassurance, which stems from negative self-representations and doubts about their social value (e. g., Mikulincer and Shaver 2016). In their interpersonal relations, they are likely to perceive others as ambivalent. On the one hand, they anticipate rejection or abandonment and thus negatively perceive others. On the other hand, they perceive their partners as a vital source of value and esteem. Thus, they depend on others to maintain their self-esteem and self-worth (Knee et al. 2008). Hence, characterizations of anxiously attached individuals are a combination of being very sensitive to the responses of others and being unable to regulate their own hurt feelings and recover self-esteem (Mikulincer and Shaver, 2016). This combination makes anxious attachment an essential antecedent of TIV and its four related dimensions.

Our data revealed that anxious attachment is an antecedent of TIV. The relationships between TIV and anxious attachment vary across the four dimensions of victimhood. As a result, anxiously attached individuals felt a more significant need for recognition when offended than secure and avoidantly attached individuals ("*it is important to me that people who hurt me acknowledge that an injustice has been done to me*"). They also tend to experience more moral elitism ("*I give others much more than I receive from them*") and a lack of empathy ("*People claim that I have hurt them because they cannot see that they are the ones hurting me*") and rumination ("*I am flooded by more anger than I would like, every time I remember people who hurt me*") than secure and avoidantly attached individuals.

From a motivational point of view, TIV seems to offer anxiously-attached individuals an effective framework for constructing their insecure relations with others. The first dimension of TIV, the need for recognition, allows anxiously-attached individuals to express their disappointment, while the recognition of hurt feelings provides attentiveness and empathy. Thus, being acknowledged enables anxiously-attached individuals to sustain their hope for better future relationships with others, while moral elitism facilitates their confidence that good deeds will be reciprocated. The third dimension of TIV, a lack of empathy, stems from the desire of anxiously attached individuals that their victimhood will take center stage while they are unable to acknowledge the suffering of others. Finally, the fourth dimension of TIV, rumination, also relates to the preoccupations of the anxiously attached to their interpersonal relations and their hope of achieving recognition of their victimhood.

## 3.  Implications, Future Research and Limitations

The present research has important implications for both clinical and social psychology. It provides a better understanding of the cognitive processes of interpretation, attribution, and memory. It also reinforces feelings of victimhood and behaviors of retaliation, which can be applied in different types of therapy (e. g., Cognitive-Behavioral Therapy, Schema Therapy) to decrease these negative cognitive biases. Hopefully, a reduction of these cognitive mechanisms can, in turn, diminish negative feelings and forms of retaliation. The relationship between anxious attachment and TIV can also be assessed in therapy to understand the core needs of people with TIV.

Future research could directly explore whether the role of TIV increases in ambiguous situations compared to severe offenses. There could be less of a difference between high and low TIV individuals regarding the emotional, cognitive and behavioral implications of an offense in severe cases because even individuals low on TIV would experience high emotional intensity. In contrast ambiguous situations leave more room for subjective interpretation.

Finally, the development of TIV allows for an empirically thorough investigation of the interplay between individual and collective victimhood. Future research could directly investigate how individual levels of TIV are related to concepts that reflect victimhood at the group level, such as Perpetual Ingroup Victimhood Orientation (PIVO), Competitive Victimhood (Noor et al. 2012), and the notion of siege mentality (Bar-Tal and Antebi 1992). The development of TIV should enable researchers to empirically examine how victimhood at the group level influences the individuals within the group and their relationships. For example, people whose intergroup orientation is based on historical group trauma, the fear of being a victim again, and the belief that one's group remains a constant victim persecuted by different enemies (high PIVO) (Schori-Eyalet al. 2017) tend to express greater orientation toward victimhood at the interpersonal level. This relation contrasts with individuals raised in a culture that embraces other national myths.

One potentially substantial route for future research is the interplay between individual and collective levels of victimhood. We are convinced that people exhibit an increased tendency for victimhood at the interpersonal level when their intergroup orientation is based on historical group trauma when they fear becoming a victim again, or when they believe that one's group is a constant victim persecuted continually by different enemies (high PIVO; Schori-Eyal et al. 2017). The TIV scale was developed and tested on Jewish-Israelis in Israel, who tend to harbor a "perpetual victimhood" representation of their history (e. g., Bar-Tal and Antebi 1992). We expect that Jewish-Israelis show higher levels of TIV than people whose group narrative does not base on victimhood.

Another intriguing direction for future research that investigates the interaction between collective and individual victimhood is the use of social networks and new media to promote power-building and change. Various groups who struggle with inequality and oppression, such as women, homosexuals, and small ethnic groups, use social networks as a platform for individual and collective expression. These activities often include victimhood-oriented practices, such as expressions of moral elitism and demands for recognition. It has been argued that many political and cultural groups and individuals emphasize their victimhood identity in today's world. Charles Sykes, who has published extensively on the topic of victimhood in the United States during the second part of the twentieth century, noted (1992) that victimhood stems from the entitlement of groups and individuals for psychological gratification, self-actualization, self-realization, and happiness. When these feelings of entitlement are combined with a high individual-level tendency for interpersonal victimhood, social change struggles are more likely to take an aggressive, disparaging, and condescending form. For instance, the Facebook group "I got married to an idiot" was invented by women whose entire interest is the mockery of masculinity and men. Thus, the combination of social power and high TIV may transform the oppressed into the oppressor. Future research could further investigate the combination of individual and collective victimhood in current social change processes.

## References

Bar-Tal, D. 2007, 'Sociopsychological Foundations of Intractable Conflicts', *American Behavioral Scientist,* vol. 50, pp. 1430–1453.

Bar-Tal, D., Antebi, D. 1992, 'Siege Mentality in Israel', *International Journal of Intercultural Relations,* vol. 16, pp. 251–275.

Bar-Tal, D., Chernyak-Hai, L., Schori, N., Gundar, A. 2009, 'A Sense of Self-Perceived Collective Victimhood in Intractable Conflicts', *International Review of the Red Cross,* vol. 91, pp. 229–258.

Baumeister, R.F. 1996, *Evil. Inside Human Cruelty and Violence,* New York, NY, Henry Holt and Co.

Baumeister, R.F., Exline, J.J., Sommer, K.L. 1998, 'The Victim Role, Grudge Theory, and Two Dimensions of Forgiveness', in *Dimensions of Forgiveness. Psychological Research and Theological Principles,* ed E.L. Worthington Jr, Templeton Foundation Press Philadelphia, pp. 79–106.

Baumeister, R.F., Stillwell, A.M., and Heatherton, T.F. 1994, 'Guilt. An Interpersonal Approach', *Psychological Bulletin,* vol. 115, pp. 243–267.

Baumeister, R.F., Stillwell, A, Wotman, S.R. 1990, 'Victim and Perpetrator Accounts of Interpersonal Conflict. Autobiographical Narratives About Anger', *Journal of Personality and Social Psychology,* vol. 59, p. 994.

Berman, A. 2014, 'Post-Traumatic Victimhood. About the Aggressiveness of Those Who Suffers', *Sihot,* vol. 28, pp. 1–9. [In Hebrew]

Berman, A., Mendelson, Y. 2005, 'Victimization as a Personal, Social and Organizational Syndrome', *Analiza Irgunit,* vol. 9, pp. 7–17. [In Hebrew]

Bowlby, J.1973, *Attachment and Loss. Separation,* vol. 2, Basic Books, New York.

Collins, K., Bell, R. 1997, 'Personality and Aggression. The Dissipation-Rumination Scale', *Personality and Individual Differences*, vol. 22, pp. 751–755.

Edwards, S.L., Rapee, R.M., Franklin, J. 2003, 'Postevent Rumination and Recall Bias for a Social Performance Event in High and Low Socially Anxious Individuals', *Cognitive Therapy and Research*, vol. 27, pp. 603–617.

Feeney, J.A. 2005, 'Hurt Feelings in Couple Relationships. Exploring the Role of Attachment and Perceptions of Personal Injury', *Personal Relationships*, vol. 12, pp. 253–271.

Gray, K., Wegner, D.M. 2009, 'Moral Typecasting. Divergent Perceptions of Moral Agents and Moral Patients', *Journal of Personality and Social Psychology*, vol. 96, pp. 505–520.

Greenberg, M.A. 1995, 'Cognitive Processing of Traumas. The Role of Intrusive Thoughts and Reappraisals', *Journal of Applied Social Psychology*, vol. 25, pp. 1262–1296.

Hameiri, B., Gabay, R., Rubel-Lifschitz, T., Nadler, A. 2022, 'Victimhood Acknowledgment as a Vehicle to Promote Intergroup Conciliatory Attitudes in a Context of Intergroup Conflict', present volume.

Hameiri, B., Nadler, A. 2017, 'Looking Backward to Move Forward. Effects of Acknowledgment of Victimhood on Readiness to Compromise for Peace in the Protracted Israeli–Palestinian Conflict', *Personality and Social Psychology Bulletin*, vol. 43, pp. 555–569.

Herman, J.L. 1992, *Trauma and Recovery. The Aftermath of Violence*, Basic Books, New York.

Janoff-Bulman, R. 2010, *Shattered Assumptions*, Simon and Schuster, New York.

Klein, M. 1937, 'Love, Guilt and Reparation', in *Love, Guilt and Reparation and Other Works 1921–1945*, ed M. Klein, The Free Press, New York, pp. 306–343.

Knee, C.R., Canevello, A., Bush, A.L., Cook, A. 2008, 'Relationship-Contingent Self-Esteem and the Ups and Downs of Romantic Relationships", *Journal of Personality and Social Psychology*, vol. 95, pp. 608–627.

Leahy, R.L. 2012, *Overcoming Resistance in Cognitive Therapy*, Guilford Press, New York.

Leary, M.R., Springer, C., Negel, L., Ansell, E., Evans, K. 1998, 'The Causes, Phenomenology, and Consequences of Hurt Feelings', *Journal of Personality and Social Psychology*, vol. 74, pp. 1225–1237.

Lyubomirsky, S, Caldwell, N.D., Nolen-Hoeksema, S. 1998, 'Effects of Ruminative and Distracting Responses to Depressed Mood on Retrieval of Autobiographical Memories', *Journal of Personality and Social Psychology*, 75, pp. 166–177.

McCullough, M.E. 2000, 'Forgiveness as Human Strength. Theory, Measurement, and Links to Well-Being', *Journal of Social and Clinical Psychology*, vol. 19, pp. 43–55.

McCullough, M.E., Rachal, K.C., Sandage, S.J., Worthington Jr, E.L., Brown, S.W., Hight, T.L. 1998, 'Interpersonal Forgiving in Close Relationships: II. Theoretical Elaboration and Measurement', *Journal of Personality and Social Psychology*, vol. 75, pp. 1586–1603.

McLaren, R.M., Solomon, D.H. 2008, 'Appraisals and Distancing Responses to Hurtful Messages', *Communication Research*, vol. 35, pp. 339–357.

Mikulincer, M., and Shaver, PR 2016, *Attachment in adulthood: Structure, dynamics, and change*, second edition, New York, NY, Guilford Press.

Nolen-Hoeksema, S., Wisco, B.E., Lyubomirsky, S 2008, 'Rethinking Rumination', *Perspectives on Psychological Science*, vol. 3, pp. 400–424.

Noor, M., Shnabel, N., Halabi, S., Nadler, A. 2012, 'When Suffering Begets Suffering. The Psychology of Competitive Victimhood Between Adversarial Groups in Violent Conflicts', *Personality and Social Psychology Review*, vol. 16, pp. 351–374.

Schori-Eyal, N., Klar, Y., Roccas, S., McNeill, A. 2017, 'The Shadows of the Past. Effects of Historical Group Trauma on Current Intergroup Conflicts', *Personality and Social Psychology Bulletin*, vol. 43, pp. 538–554.

Shaver, P.R., Mikulincer, M., Lavy, S., Cassidy, J. 2009, 'Understanding and Altering Hurt Feelings. An Attachment-Theoretical Perspective on the Generation and Regulation of Emotions', in *Feeling hurt in close relationships*, ed A.L. Vangelisti, Cambridge University Press, New York, pp. 92–119.

Shnabel, N., Nadler, A. 2008, 'A Needs-Based Model of Reconciliation. Satisfying the Differential Emotional Needs of Victim and Perpetrator as a Key to Promoting Reconciliation', *Journal of Personality and Social Psychology*, vol. 94, pp. 116–132.

Sykes, C.J. 1992, *A Nation of Victims. The Decay of the American Character*, Macmillan, Basingstoke.

Urlic, I., Berger, M.E., Berman, A. 2010, *Victimhood, Vengefulness, and the Culture of Forgiveness*, Nova Science Publishers, New York, NY.

Vangelisti, A.L. (ed) 2009, *Feeling Hurt in Close Relationships*, Cambridge University Press, Cambridge.

Vangelisti, A.L., Young, S.L. 2000, 'When Words Hurt. The Effects of Perceived Intentionality on Interpersonal Relationships', *Journal of Social and Personal Relationships*, vol. 17, pp. 393–424.

Vangelisti, A.L., Young, S.L., Carpenter-Theune, K.E., Alexander, A.L. 2005, 'Why Does It Hurt? The Perceived Causes of Hurt Feelings", *Communication Research*, vol. 32, pp. 443–477.

Vollhardt, J.R. 2012, 'Collective Victimization', in *The Oxford Handbook of Intergroup Conflict*, ed L.R. Tropp, Oxford University Press, New York pp. 136–157.

Zitek, E.M., Jordan, A.H., Monin, B., Leach, F.R. 2010, 'Victim Entitlement to Behave Selfishlyì, *Journal of Personality and Social Psychology*, vol. 98, pp. 245–255.

Zur, O. 2005, 'The Psychology of Victimhood', in *Destructive Trends in Mental Health. The Well-Intentioned Path to Harm*, eds R.H. Wright, N.A. Cummings, Routledge, New York, pp. 45–64.

Tammy Rubel-Lifschitz, Rahav Gabay, Boaz Hameiri, Arie Nadler

# The Victimhood Oriented Leader

## Tendency for Interpersonal Victimhood among Powerholders

### Abstract

Well-established research on the psychological experience of social power and leadership joins the novel concept of TIV in Tammy Rubel-Lifschitz, Rahav Gabay, Boaz Hameiri, and Arie Nadler's essay on *The Victimhood Oriented Leader. The Tendency for Interpersonal Victimhood among Powerholder*. Given the assumption that individuals with a high-TIV are more likely to interpret conflicts as hurtful episodes in which they are the ongoing victims, the paper shows how they attribute the hurtful behavior to the malicious intentions of the offender and develop a desire for revenge that will compensate them for their suffering. Power is a crucial factor in this regard. When high-TIV individuals are in low-power positions, their ability to translate these thoughts and desires into action is limited by various constraints. On the contrary, when high-TIV individuals obtain positions of power and leadership, they have access to various resources, and limitations for action are reduced. The paper presents what happens – in cognitive and behavioral terms – when high-TIV individuals reach leadership positions by suggesting that victimhood-related cognitions and behaviors can potentially have disastrous effects when leaders possess them.

***

Power, often defined as asymmetric control over valued resources, is considered a fundamental aspect of social relations (e. g., Dépret and Fiske 1993; Thibaut & Kelley, 1959). Power is primarily relevant to the social psychology of leadership, which incorporates control over various financial, social, and symbolic resources. In this paper, we focus on powerholders with a high tendency for interpersonal victimhood (TIV) (Gabay et al. 2020; Gabay et al. present volume), meaning that they have an ongoing perception of themselves as victims, which fundamentally affects the way they perceive themselves and their relationships with others.

Exploring TIV among powerholders is particularly crucial because the decisions made by leaders have a significant effect on their personal relationships, and also, the lives of many others depend on their judgment. Thus, victimhood-related cognitions, emotions, and behaviors, which adversely affect interpersonal relations (Gabay et al. 2020), can potentially have disastrous effects when leaders possess them. Moreover, because control over valued resources reduces practical and mental limitations, power itself has a dis-inhibiting effect (Keltner, Gruenfeld, and Anderson 2003). Consequently, leaders with power are expected to exhibit victimhood-related cognitions, emotions, and behaviors more strongly than individuals with high-trait victimhood in low-power positions.

The current paper reviews and integrates social psychological literature on power and victimhood. First, we briefly examine two distinct lines of research in social psychology: from one side, the recently-developed concept of a personal tendency for victimhood (TIV) (Gabay et al. 2020), and from the other one, the research on the psychological experience of social power. Then, we integrate these two lines of research, focusing on the reinforcing effects of power and victimhood on the perceptions and behaviors of social leaders. We present our experimental findings and suggest directions for future research on TIV, power, and leadership.

## 1.     The Tendency for Interpersonal Victimhood (TIV): Perceiving Oneself as a Victim

Social life is replete with situations of interpersonal conflict that are open to interpretation. We wait for people who are late for meetings, are surprised by people who cut us off when we speak, annoyed when co-workers tackle our initiatives and insulted by those who disregard our ideas and suggestions. Some people overcome such incidents with relative ease, interpreting them as an unpleasant but natural, unavoidable part of social interactions. Others tend to interpret interpersonal conflicts as hurtful events, perceiving themselves as victims who suffer from the malicious behavior of others. We have conceptualized the latter predisposition as a tendency for interpersonal victimhood (TIV), or a personal propensity to perceive oneself as a victim in social and interpersonal relationships (Gabay et al. 2020).

TIV includes an ongoing experience of the self as a victim, a feeling that is then generalized to many types of situations over time. In their interpersonal relationships, individuals with high-TIV feel victimized more often, more intensely, and for a longer time than other people. Four psychological dimensions are part of TIV: (a) the need to have one's suffering recognized; (b) moral elitism, i. e., the feeling that the victimized self is more moral than other individuals; (c) a lack of empathy and attentiveness to the suffering of other individuals; and (d) rumination over negative feelings and thoughts related to interpersonal offenses (Gabay et al. 2020).

In hurtful events, high-TIV fundamentally affects individual emotions, cognitions, and actions. When recalling a hurtful event, high-TIV individuals use more words representing hostile behaviors and negative feelings (e. g., betrayal, anger, disappointment, wretchedness) than participants with low-TIV. Negative recall may stem from the tendency of high-TIV individuals to ruminate about incidents of interpersonal conflict since rumination has been found to increase both negative recall (Lyubomirsky, Cladwell and Nolen-Hoeksema 1998) and recognition (Edwards, Rapee and Franklin 2003). Moreover, rumination over interpersonal offenses was found to motivate the intention to retaliate against the offender (Collins and Bell 1997; McCullough et al. 1998).

Cognitively, high-TIV individuals are more likely to anticipate that others will hurt them. When offended, they tend to (a) interpret the episode as more severe and (b) attribute the offensive behavior to the malicious intentions of the offender (Rahav et al. 2018). Since indignities are deepened when hurtful behavior is perceived as intentional (Vangelisti et al. 2005), high-TIV individuals may experience offenses more intensively if they attribute higher malicious intent to the offender. Interestingly, collective-level victimhood seems to have similar cognitive effects: Perpetual In-group Victimhood Orientation (PIVO) is the belief that a person's in-group is constantly being victimized and persecuted by different enemies. High-PIVO individuals are more likely to attribute hostile intentions to members of the outgroup, particularly after being primed with reminders of historical trauma experienced by their in-group (Schori-Eyal et al., 2017).

Behaviorally, high-TIV decreases an individual's willingness to forgive an interpersonal offense and increases their desire for revenge (Gabay et al., 2020). Interestingly, negative attributions of the offender mediate the effect of TIV on the desire for revenge. Thus, the cognitive implications of TIV seem to underlie its behavioral outcomes: High-TIV increases attributions of hurtful behavior to the negative properties of the offender, which in turn leads to greater desires for revenge. Similar patterns were found on the collective level: Having a strong sense of collective victimhood was associated with low levels of willingness to forgive and increased motivation to seek revenge (Wohl and Branscombe 2008; Noor et al. 2008; Schori-Eyal et al. 2017).

In sum, high-TIV individuals are more likely to interpret conflicts as hurtful episodes in which they are the victims, attribute the hurtful behavior to the malicious intentions of the offender, and have a desire for revenge that will compensate them for their suffering. When high-TIV individuals are in low-power positions, their ability to translate these thoughts and desires into action is limited by various social and material constraints. However, when high-TIV individuals obtain positions of power and leadership, they have access to various resources. These resources are sources of power that reduce both mental and behavioral limitations for action. How does a person's characteristic tendency for victimhood (i. e., high TIV) impact their perceptions, decisions, and behaviors when in a leadership role? Do the psychological effects of power and victimhood (i. e., TIV) reinforce each other?

## 2. The Study of Power in Social Psychology. Basic Concepts and Main Findings

In social psychology, power is often defined as an asymmetric control over valued resources in social relationships. In recent decades ample social psychological research has investigated the emotional, cognitive, and behavioral effects of social power (for reviews, see Keltner, Gruenfeld, and Anderson 2003; Magee and Smith 2013; Guinote 2017). Overall, social psychological studies of power consistently indicate that because powerful individuals act in a more resource-rich environment, they experience fewer mental or behavioral constraints. Consequently, the powerful are more likely to express their thoughts, values, and goals in their actual behaviors than those with low power (Bargh et al. 1995; Chen, Lee-Chai and Bargh 2001; Galinsky et al. 2008). Powerless individuals, in contrast, experience social constraints and feel dependent on others; as a consequence, their behavior is more inhibited (Keltner, Gruenfeld, and Anderson 2003).

A large body of research shows that individuals in positions of high power direct their attention toward their own thoughts, feelings, and goals, often at the expense of devoting attention to others. Thus, power seems to increase self-focus, goal orientation, and also psychological distance, and the use of stereotypes (De Dreu and Van Kleef 2004; Fiske 1993; Goodwin et al. 2000; Keltner, Gruenfeld and Anderson 2003; Keltner and Robinson 1997; Rodriguez-Bailon, Moya and Yzerbyt 2000). For example, during negotiations, powerholders felt more confident about revealing their interests (Anderson and Galinsky 2006) and reported that they expressed their actual attitudes more often than individuals with less power (Anderson and Berdahl 2002).

At the same time, powerful negotiators were also less accurate in perceiving the emotions of their counterparts (Galinsky et al. 2006; Keltner and Robinson, 1997) and less influenced by them (Van Kleef et al. 2006). High-power participants were less likely to consider the perspective of others and the possibility that they might lack the knowledge to which the participants had private access (Galinsky et al. 2006).

Emotionally, powerholders experience overconfidence in their skills and believe that chance events are subject to personal control (Sivanathan and Galinsky 2007). At the same time, high power decreases empathy and compassion for others' suffering (Van Kleef et al. 2008) and increases objectification: a process in which people are treated as objects, a means to an end, regardless of the value of their other human qualities (Gruenfeld et al. 2008).

Galinsky et al. argue that "power reveals the person" because power decreases social and material inhibitions; powerholders can express their values and traits more freely (Galinsky et al. 2015). Indeed, experimental studies suggest that power increases generosity among individuals with a communal orientation but decreases it among individuals with an exchange orientation (Chen, Lee-Chai, and Bargh 2001). Similarly, social-value orientation significantly predicted the extent to which high-power negotiators trusted their opponent, but it did not predict the trust levels of participants in a baseline condition (Galinsky et al. 2008). Finally, findings of an organizational field study suggest that firms with liberal CEOs invest more in corporate social responsibility than firms with conservative CEOs and that this difference is significant among more powerful CEOs (Chin, Hambrick, and Treviño, 2013). Imagine that these powerholders have a high tendency for victimhood in interpersonal relations. Which thoughts would be revealed by high-power? What actions would become possible?

## 3. Reinforcing Effects of Power and TIV

This paper contributes to the literature on leadership by discussing the potential reinforcing effects of power and TIV. We reason that the disinhibiting and revealing effects of power mean that powerholders will manifest their mental and behavioral characteristics more strongly than low-power individuals. Moreover, we suggest that power and TIV may have a mutually reinforcing effect, which could significantly bias their perceptions, decisions, and actions. Since powerholders are often in leadership positions and can influence other people's lives, these biases may have disastrous effects on the high-TIV individuals themselves and all other individuals who depend on their judgment.

First, we would like to consider how high power should affect three of the basic psychological components of TIV: lack of empathy, rumination, and moral elitism. Past research indicates that high power has a detrimental effect on social attention: reducing perspective-taking, empathy, and care. Among high-TIV powerholders, these effects are likely to reinforce their lack of empathy for others. Consequently, high-TIV powerholders might be more likely to objectify and use others without much awareness of or concern about others' well-being, suffering, or pain. For example, leaders of this type are more likely to promote policies without sufficient awareness of their implications for low-power populations, such as financial policies that harm the poor, security acts that endanger entire populations, or immigration policies that put marginalized groups at risk. Studies of power further suggest that it increases self-focus and directs the powerholder's attention to their thoughts, feelings, and internal experiences. This increased self-attention should intensify rumination among high-TIV powerholders, who tend to be preoccupied with hurtful events and lead to deeper, lengthier emotional engagement with offensive situations. Similarly, the over-confidence related to high power may reinforce the moral elitism associated with TIV. Consequently, high-TIV powerholders may be particularly likely to exhibit moral overconfidence by depicting themselves and their group as good, just, and flawless while conceiving of others as evil, unfair, and unreliable.

High power may further reinforce the cognitive and behavioral consequences associated with TIV. Cognitively, high-TIV powerholders are likely to perceive and construe offences more severely and interpret ambiguous situations as offensive. There is a higher chance that they will attribute hurtful behaviors to the malicious intentions of the offender. Here, we should consider, for example, the complexities associated with supporting refugees who seek asylum in western countries. The motivation to accept and support them due to their unfortunate circumstances often comes with concerns for the financial, social, and cultural investment that may be needed. Our findings suggest that high-TIV individuals are less likely to experience such internal complexity but probably develop extreme, one-sided opinions (Rubel-Lifschitz et al., 2018).

We (Rubel-Lifschitz et al., 2018) examined the attitudes toward refugees (Esses, Hamilton, and Gaucher, 2017) among individuals with low-TIV versus high-TIV by comparing those who voted for right-wing parties to those who voted for left-wing parties. We found that among participants with low-TIV, less concern for refugees was expressed by right-wing than left-wing voters. However, the difference in their attitudes was small and insignificant ($M$=3.91 versus $M$=4.53). Among high-TIV participants, on the other hand, the gap was larger: Right-wing participants with high-TIV expressed extremely little empathy towards refugees and objected to any policies that might assist them ($M$=3.18), while left-wing participants with high-TIV articulated high concern for the refugees and willingness to invest resources in their safety and well-being ($M$=5.16). Thus, high-TIV seems to be associated with more extreme political opinions on both sides of the political spectrum. We replicated this result pattern using an experimental design in which the psychological experience of victimhood was manipulated through a recall task. Again, victimhood increased the difference between right and left-wing in their attitudes towards refugees compared to the control group. Overall, these findings suggest that the psychological experience of victimhood enhances extremity in political attitudes. When high-TIV individuals are in high-power, such extreme positions can be translated into actual policies that influence the lives of both residents and refugees.

Leadership roles include responsibility for handling numerous ambiguous situations. Organizational politics and manipulations could be interpreted as an unfortunate but natural part of professional life or a hurtful, unforgivable betrayal. Crime among poor populations can be perceived as a problematic yet understandable aspect of their economic survival or an inexcusable phenomenon that should be severely punished. Eating meat can be seen as a natural behavior supported by an unthinking industry or as an unhuman behavior that should be abolished. Large-scale international relations are also subject to interpretation: a military exercise in a neighboring country can be seen as a diplomatic challenge or as a threat of war, demonstrations can be perceived as a sign of distress and frustration that should be addressed, or as a provocation that must be eliminated and controlled.

We reason that leaders with high levels of TIV will be more likely to interpret equivocal incidents as injurious, offensive, and malicious. Behaviourally, we expect that those with high-TIV will have less motivation to forgive an offender and an increased desire for revenge (Gabay et al., 2020). Because of the disinhibiting effect of power, the likelihood that powerholders' goals and desires will develop into actual action increases (Galinsky et al. 2006). Thus, a desire for aggression and revenge can quickly transform into aggressive retaliatory actions among individuals who possess social power.

We (Gabay et al. 2020) investigated the effect of power and TIV on actual revenge behaviours in a laboratory experiment. Revenge was displayed by allowing participants to inflict monetary damage to an alleged partner who offended them. To create the offence, we used the Dictator Game (Kahneman et al. 1986), in which the alleged partner was the allocator. The participants were told that their partners did not equally divide a valuable resource (10 NIS), i. e., they took more money for themselves. The participants, who were all the recipients in this game, had to accept the unfair offer passively and were thus perceived as victims (see Selten 1978; Siman Tov-Nachlieli and Shnabel 2014). Then, participants received the opportunity for actual revenge: they could decide how much of the alleged partner's monetary gain they would keep. Thus, all participants were placed in a position of high-power in which they had control over valued resources in social relations (Keltner, Gruenfeld, and Anderson 2003). Since the funds taken from the partner were not returned to the participants, pure revenge was possible. Our findings revealed that high-TIV powerholders were more likely to use the power vested in their hands vindictively. Specifically, high-TIV powerholders were more likely to reduce the profits of a person who has hurt them compared to low-TIV powerholders. The findings further indicate that the association between TIV and revenge was mediated by increased negative emotions (anger, humiliation, and hopelessness) and the entitlement to immoral behavior. According to the critical literature on power, this mediation effect may stem from a reinforcing consequence of high-TIV and high-power: high-TIV individuals experience negative emotions and moral entitlement in a harmful event. Because high-power draws attention to the powerholders' inner world, these negative psychological experiences are amplified. Moreover, because high-power reduces mental and behavioural limitations, high-TIV powerholders were able to translate their desire for revenge into actual vindictive behaviour.

## 4.  Implications, Limitations and Future Research

This paper focused on leadership's psychological and behavioral implications with a high tendency for interpersonal victimhood (TIV). It contributed to the existing literature by (a) reviewing the social psychological literature on power and victimhood; (b) discussing and investigating potential reinforcing effects of power and victimhood on the perceptions and behaviors of social leaders. Overall, our analysis suggested that when high-TIV individuals are in power, the mental and behavioral limitations that usually inhibit their behavior are reduced. Consequently, power allows high-TIV persons the capacity to turn negative emotions and cognitions into extreme attitudes and behaviors. We, therefore, surmise that high-TIV leaders are more likely to be fear-oriented leaders (Nadler 2018), who focus on simplistic solutions in light of past collective traumas, and who are less likely to become hope-oriented leaders focussing on a complex, positive vision of a collective future.

One limitation of the current research design is that it did not compare high-TIV and low-TIV individuals in low-power positions. Future research on TIV could thus advance this investigation by directly comparing the cognition and behavior of high-TIV and low-TIV individuals in high and low-power positions. Such research could, for instance, empirically examine whether high-TIV individuals in high-power positions are indeed more likely to perceive ambiguous situations as more hurtful and respond to them in a more aggressive and vindictive manner than high-TIV individuals in low-power positions. Future research could also include a more field-oriented approach and investigate the behavior of high-TIV versus low-TIV leaders in real-life situations.

The reinforcing effects of power and TIV may be particularly relevant in situations of inter-group conflict, in which the leader's perceptions, decisions, and behaviors might have detrimental effects. We infer that high-TIV leaders will be more prone to interpret such conflicts as stemming from the destructive, malevolent intentions of the other side and, therefore, promoting more aggressive, violent responses. Moreover, they are less likely to acknowledge the victimhood of their adversary, which has positive effects on intergroup relations (Hameiri et al. present volume). These policies are likely to result in conflict escalation, rather than diplomatic negotiations, which require acts of forgiveness and reconciliation.

New media is another factor that may intensify the reinforcing effects of power and TIV. Social networks, such as Twitter and Facebook, are fast, rarely regulated, and highly accessible. Consequently, they can efficiently serve as a platform for unsophisticated and impulsive communication. High-TIV leaders who perceive the world in dichotomist and emotional terms should be more likely to use new media to share extreme, emotional, and simplistic messages.

Long before experimental studies of social power were conducted, Abraham Lincoln said that "nearly all men can stand adversity, but if you want to test a man's character, give him power." This paper reviews how the revealing effect of power interacts with a high tendency for interpersonal victimhood. Our discussion opens a theoretical and empirical path for future examination, which may shed new light on the psychology of those individuals who might lead our nations and shape the conditions of our lives.

## References

Anderson, C., Berdahl, J.L. 2002, 'The Experience of Power. Examining the Effects of Power on Approach and Inhibition Tendencies', *Journal of Personality and Social Psychology,* vol. 83, pp. 1362–1377.

Anderson, C., Galinsky, A.D. 2006, 'Power, Optimism, and Risk-Taking', *European Journal of Social Psychology*, vol. 36, no. 4, pp. 511–536.

Bargh, J.A., Raymond, P., Pryor, J.B., Strack, F. 1995, 'Attractiveness of the Underling. An Automatic Power→Sex Association and Its Consequences for Sexual Harassment and Aggression', *Journal of Personality and Social Psychology,* vol. 68, pp. 768–781.

Chen, S., Lee-Chai, A.Y., Bargh, J.A. 2001, 'Relationship Orientation as a Moderator of the Effects of Social Power', *Journal of Personality and Social Psychology,* vol. 80, pp. 173–187.

Chin, M.K., Hambrick, D.C., Treviño, L.K. 2013, 'Political Ideologies of CEOs. The Influence of Executives' Values on Corporate Social Eesponsibility', *Administrative Science Quarterly,* vol. 58, pp. 197–232.

Collins, K., and Bell, R. 1997, 'Personality and Aggression. The Dissipation-Rumination Scale', *Personality and Individual Differences,* vol. 22, pp. 751–755.

De Dreu, C.K.W., Van Kleef, G.A. 2004, 'The Influence of Power on the Information Search, Impression Formation, and Demands in Negotiation', *Journal of Experimental Social Psychology,* vol. 40, pp. 303–319.

Dépret, E.F., Fiske, S.T. 1993, 'Social Cognition and Power. Some Cognitive Consequences of Social Structure as a Source of Control Deprivation', in *Control Motivation and Social Cognition,* eds G. Weary, F. Gleicher, K. Marsh, Springer, New York.

Edwards, S.L., Rapee, R.M., Franklin, J. 2003, 'Post-Event Rumination and Recall Bias for a Social Performance Event in High and Low Socially Anxious Individuals', *Cognitive Therapy and Research*, vol. 27, pp. 603–617.

Esses, V.M., Hamilton, L.K., Gaucher, D. 2017, 'The Global Refugee Crisis. Empirical Evidence and Policy Implications for Improving Public Attitudes and Facilitating Refugee Resettlement', *Social Issues and Policy Review,* vol. 11, pp. 78–123.

Fiske, S.T. 1993, 'Controlling Other People. The Impact of Power on Stereotyping', *American Psychologist,* vol. 48, pp. 621–628.

Gabay, R., Hameiri, B., Rubel-Lifschitz, T., and Nadler, A 2022. 'The Tendency for Interpersonal Victimhood. Conceptualization, Cognitive and Behavioral Consequences, and Antecedents', present volume.

Gabay, R., Hameiri, B., Rubel-Lifschitz, T., and Nadler, A. 2020, 'Who Wants to Be a Victim? The Tendency for Interpersonal Victimhood', *Personality and Individual Differences*, 165, 110–134.

Galinsky A.D., Magee, J.C., Gruenfeld, D.H., Whitson J.A., Liljenquist K.A., 2008, 'Power Reduces the Press of the Situation. Implications for Creativity, Conformity, and Dissonance', *Journal of Personality and Social Psychology*, vol. 95, pp. 1450–1466.

Galinsky, A.D., Magee, J.C., Inesi, M.E., Gruenfeld, D.H., 2006, 'Power and Perspectives not Taken', *Psychological Science*, vol. 17, pp. 1068–1074.

Galinsky, A.D., Rucker, D.D., Magee, J.C. 2015, 'Power. Past Findings, Present Considerations, and Future Directions', in *APA Handbook of Personality and Social Psychology, Volume 3: Interpersonal Relations*, eds M. Mikulincer, P.R. Shaver, J.A. Simpson, J.F. Dovidio, American Psychological Association Washington, DC.

Goodwin, S.A., Gubin, A., Fiske, S.T., Yzerbyt, V.Y. 2000, 'Power Can Bias Impression Processes. Stereotyping Subordinates by Default and by Design', *Group Processes and Intergroup Relations*, vol. 3, pp. 227–256.

Gruenfeld, D.H., Inesi, M.E., Magee J.C., Galinsky A.D. 2008, 'Power and the Objectification of Social Targets', *Journal of Personality and Social Psychology*, vol. 95, pp. 111–127.

Guinote, A. 2017, 'How Power Affects People. Activating, Wanting, and Goal Seeking, *Annual Review of Psychology*, vol. 68, pp. 353–381.

Hameiri, B., Gabay, R., Rubel-Lifschitz, T., Nadler, A. 2022, 'Victimhood Acknowledgment as a Vehicle to Promote Intergroup Conciliatory Attitudes in a Context of Intergroup Conflict', present volume.

Keltner, D., Gruenfeld, D.H., Anderson, C. 2003, 'Power, Approach, and Inhibition', *Psychological Review*, vol. 110, pp. 265–284.

Keltner, D., Robinson, R.J. 1997, 'Defending the Status Quo. Power and Bias in Social Conflict', *Personality and Social Psychology Bulletin*, vol. 23, pp. 1066–1077.

Lyubomirsky, S., Caldwell, N.D., Nolen-Hoeksema, S. 1998, 'Effects of Ruminative and Distracting Responses to Depressed Mood on Retrieval of Autobiographical Memories', *Journal of Personality and Social Psychology*, vol. 75, pp. 166–177.

Magee, J.C., Smith, P.K. 2013, 'The Social Distance Theory of Power', *Personality and Social Psychology Review*, vol. 17, pp. 158–186.

McCullough, M.E., Rachal, K.C., Sandage, S.J., Worthington Jr, E.L., Brown, S.W., Hight, T.L. 1998, 'Interpersonal Forgiving in Close Relationships: II. Theoretical Elaboration and Measurement', *Journal of Personality and Social Psychology*, vol. 75, pp. 1586–1603.

Noor, M., Brown, R., Gonzalez, R., Manzi, J., Lewis, C.A. 2008, 'On Positive Psychological Outcomes. What Helps Groups with a History of Conflict to Forgive and Reconcile with Each Other?', *Personality and Social Psychology Bulletin*, vol. 34, pp. 819–832.

Rodriguez-Bailon, R., Moya, M. Yzerbyt, V. 2000, 'Why Do Superiors Attend to Negative Stereotypic Information about Their Subordinates? Effects of Power Legitimacy on Social Perception', *European Journal of Social Psychology*, vol. 30, pp. 651–671.

Rubel-Lifschitz, T., Hameiri, B., Gabay R., Nadler A. 2018, 'Victimhood and Political Extremism', Manuscript under preparation.

Schori-Eyal, N., Klar, Y., Roccas, S., McNeill, A. 2017, 'The Shadows of the Past. Effects of Historical Group Trauma on current Intergroup Conflicts', *Personality and Social Psychology Bulletin,* vol. 43, pp. 538–554.

Selten, R. 1978, 'The Chain Store Paradox', *Theory and Decision*, vol. 9, no. 2, pp. 127–159.

Siman Tov-Nachlieli, I., Shnabel, N. 2014, 'Feeling Both Victim and Perpetrator. Investigating Duality within the Needs-Based Model', *Personality and Social Psychology Bulletin*, vol. 40, no. 3, pp. 301–314.

Sivanathan, N., Galinsky, Adam D., 'Power and Overconfidence'. Available at http://dx.doi.org/10.2139/ssrn.1100725 or at SSRN: https://ssrn.com/abstract=1100725.

Thibaut, J.W., Kelley, H.H. 1959, *The Social Psychology of Groups*, John Wiley, New York.

Van Kleef, G.A., De Dreu, C.K., Pietroni, D., Manstead, A.S. 2006, 'Power and Emotion in Negotiation. Power Moderates the Interpersonal Effects of Anger and Happiness on Concession Making', *European Journal of Social Psychology,* vol. 36, pp. 557–581.

Van Kleef, G.A., Oveis, C., Van Der Löwe, I., LuoKogan, A., Goetz, J., Keltner, D. 2008, 'Power, Distress, and Compassion. Turning a Blind Eye to the Suffering of Others', *Psychological Science,* vol. 19, pp. 1315–1322.

Vangelisti, A.L., Young, S.L., Carpenter-Theune, K.E., Alexander, A.L. 2005, 'Why Does It Hurt? The Perceived Causes of Hurt Feelings', *Communication Research,* vol. 32, pp. 443–477.

Wohl, M.J.A., Branscombe, N.R. 2008, 'Remembering Historical Victimization. Collective Guilt for Current Ingroup Transgressions', *Journal of Personality and Social Psychology,* vol. 94, pp. 988–1006.

Boaz Hameiri, Rahav Gabay, Tammy Rubel-Lifschitz, Arie Nadler

# Victimhood Acknowledgment as a Vehicle to Promote Intergroup Conciliatory Attitudes in the Context of Intergroup Conflict

## Abstract

Boaz Hameiri, Rahav Gabay, Tammy Rubel-Lifschitz, and Arie Nadler's paper on *Victimhood Acknowledgment as a Vehicle to Promote Intergroup Conciliatory Attitudes in a Context of Intergroup Conflict* focuses on the consequences of denying and acknowledging victimhood. Although acknowledging victimhood in contexts of historical mass victimization may trigger positive effects on victims' well-being and willingness to reconcile with their former tormentors, its denial can be experienced, conversely, as a revictimization. The chapter is based on research conducted in Israel and the Palestinian Authority. Two large-scale surveys and three field experiments examine the effects of the belief by group members that their adversary acknowledges their victimhood (Holocaust and Nakba for Jews and Palestinians, respectively). This belief is associated with Israeli-Jews' readiness to accept responsibility for Palestinian sufferings and offer apologies. For Palestinians, it is also linked to a perceived higher likelihood of a reconciled future with Israelis.

## 1. Introduction

Members of groups immersed in intractable conflicts perceive them as existential and insoluble (Bar-Tal 2013). Such conflicts often resist resolution because of psychological barriers that block the path to achieving a compromise on issues that separate the two parties (e. g., division of disputed land). Among these emotional barriers are a lack of trust, the fear of being blamed as the author of immoral acts, and the victims' desire to avenge past victimization (Nadler 2012). Furthermore, in intractable conflicts, a sense of collective victimhood is an inseparable part of the shared collective memory of the conflict and the ethos of conflict (Bar-Tal 2013). The study we conducted as part of the "Hearts of Flesh–Not Stone" project focuses on how the acknowledgement of the in-group's victimhood by the adversary ameliorates the negative consequences of competitive victimhood (Noor et al. 2012). We examined this issue within the context of the Israeli-Palestinian conflict, one of the most intractable conflicts. Despite the enormous cost to human life, economic resources, and psychological traumas for both sides, it has defied resolution for more than a century.

Being a victim of violence is a negative psychological experience. It results in an increased sense of humiliation, fear, anger, hopelessness, and a desire for revenge (Skitka, Bauman, and Mullen 2004). Being a victim is a source of identity threat, as it portrays victims as powerless with no control over their fate (Shnabel and Nadler 2008). This conglomerate of affective, cognitive, and motivational reactions associated with victimhood constitutes a significant psychological barrier to ending the conflict (Noor et al., 2012). Despite the detrimental consequences of victimhood for intergroup relations, being a victim is associated with psychological benefits, such as garnering support from third parties. Indeed, groups compete with each other over which is the "true victim" (Noor et al. 2012). This competitive victimhood is documented in several conflictual contexts. It has dominated relations between Catholics and Protestants in Northern Ireland (Noor, Brown and Prentice 2008), Serbs and Croats in former Yugoslavia (Andrighetto et al. 2012), and Israelis and Palestinians in the Middle East (Shnabel, Halabi and Noor 2013). Besides, competitive victimhood is associated with belligerent attitudes towards the adversary, such as the lack of trust or the unwillingness to forgive (Noor et al. 2012). Considering the motivation of the adversarial groups to "win" the competition for victimhood, a proclamation by a reputable third party, such as the UN, that one group has suffered more than its adversary increases the readiness to reconcile (Siman-Tov Nachlieli, Shnabel, and Halabi 2015).

The group's victimization is a central element of the narrative about the causes of the conflict and its progression that serves as a major building block of the group's collective identity (Paez and Liu 2011). Frequently, an instance of past victimization is the nucleus of the story that the group tells its members about the roots of the conflict and the conditions for its resolution. Moreover, past victimization becomes the group's "chosen trauma" that affects the course of the conflict and the likelihood of its resolution (Volkan 2006). The Jewish Holocaust and the Palestinian Nakba, i. e., the Palestinians' belief that the establishment of Israel turned them into refugees, are two of these "chosen traumas" that play a central role in the Israeli-Palestinian conflict. Israelis' preoccupation with security concerns and fears of annihilation can be traced to centuries of discrimination, persecution, and pogroms, culminating in the Holocaust (e. g., Klar, Schori-Eyal, and Klar 2013). The Palestinians' desire to redeem their people from the status of stateless refugees refers to the establishment of Israel in 1948 (Auerbach 2009). Although the group's adherence to its victim identity can have positive consequences for the group, such as a sense of entitlement, it is detrimental to intergroup relations (Noor et al., 2012). For example, reminding Canadian Jews of the suffering of Jews during the Holocaust reduced their concern for the moral implications of actions committed by Israelis against Palestinians (Wohl and Branscombe 2008).

Social psychological research and theory suggest three mechanisms that may reduce the negative impact of group adherence to their victim identity on intergroup relations. The first mechanism rests on the assumption of the needs-based model of reconciliation (Nadler and Shnabel 2008) and consists of restoring the victim's sense of power. This process has been shown to increase trust in the adversary by members of victimized groups (Shnabel, Nadler, and Dovidio 2014) and readiness to reconcile with the opponent (Shnabel et al. 2009). The second mechanism focuses on inducing group members to view both the in-group and the adversarial out-group as victims (Shnabel et al., 2013). This inclusive common victim identity results in more positive intergroup perceptions and less competitive victimhood (Vollhardt and Bilali 2015). The third mechanism emphasizes the acknowledgement of the in-group's victimhood. We assessed this mechanism in our conducted study as part of the "Hearts of Flesh–Not Stone" project.

Works on the effects of acknowledgment of victimhood in intergroup relations support the claim of its ameliorative effects on the well-being of victims. Acknowledgment of the sufferings of victims in Chechnya had positive effects on their psychological well-being (Maercker et al. 2009), and acknowledgment of the suffering of political prisoners was positively related to their reduced desire to take revenge on their tormentors (David and Choi 2009). In an experiment conducted in Belgium, attitudes towards the French-Speaking community improved when they acknowledged the Dutch-speaking community's past sufferings (Alarcón-Henríquez et al. 2010). Similarly, individuals of Armenian descent who were exposed to the recognition of the Armenian genocide by Turkish groups and Jewish students who experienced the acknowledgment of violence against Jews by Poles and Germans evidenced more conciliatory attitudes towards their former tormentors (Vollhardt, Mazur, and Lemahieu 2014). The denial of an in-group's victimhood, especially when it reflects on the group's "chosen trauma," is tantamount to questioning its collective identity and is experienced as a re-victimization. Thus, the denial of the Armenian genocide elicits feelings of resentment, hatred, and anger among Armenian survivors (Kalayjian et al. 1996).

Our study examines whether the positive effects of acknowledgment of an in-group's victimhood by the adversarial group would impact people's readiness to make compromises on central issues that have been on the negotiating table between Israelis and Palestinians, such as the final status of Jerusalem or the evacuation of settlements in the West Bank. This idea departs from previous studies investigating the links between acknowledgment of victimhood and intergroup relations in at least three respects. First, the examination focuses on the effects of acknowledgment within the context of a "hot" conflict that has defied resolution for decades. Second, the studies analyze the effects of acknowledgment on the willingness to compromise on specific conflict-related issues rather than on the victims' well-being or general positive attitudes towards the adversary. Third, intense feelings of competitive victimhood characterize the Israeli-Palestinian conflict (Nadler 2002). This instance is not the case for the Jewish-German or Armenian-Turkish relations, where a relative consensus on the identity of the victims exists. This point is particularly important because competitive victimhood not only leads each party to pay exclusive attention to their own sufferings but also to minimize, or even deny, the adversary's victimhood (Vollhardt 2009). This development can be seen in the recurring attempts by Palestinians to belittle or deny the Jewish Holocaust and by Israelis to minimize or doubt the sufferings of Palestinians since 1948. This reality has contributed to the distrust and animosity that have characterized the relations between these two peoples. Moreover, the tensions have also been expressed in parties' unwillingness to make concessions to each other on critical issues, which could have facilitated a movement forward.

Current research indicates that a strong sense of collective victimhood is negatively associated with intergroup trust (Andrighetto et al., 2012; Noor, Brown and Prentice, 2008) and a decreased readiness for intergroup forgiveness (Noor, Brown and Prentice, 2008). Distrust in one's adversary also decreases the willingness to compromise to promote an end to the conflict. In situations in which the adversary cannot be trusted, making political compromises may seem to be a risk to the in-group's safety. In a study conducted in the context of the Israeli-Palestinian conflict, Jewish-Israelis who showed a stronger sense of collective victimhood were less willing to support compromises to end the conflict (Schori-Eyal, Halperin, and Bar-Tal 2014). Our study examines whether these negative trends can be reversed through the reciprocal acknowledgement by Israelis and Palestinians of the other's "chosen traumas," such as acknowledging the Jewish Holocaust by Palestinians and the Nakba-related sufferings by Israeli-Jews. Besides, we analyze whether this recognition affects the readiness to make compromises on key divisive issues.

## 2. Empirical Findings

In order to examine the link between the perceived acknowledgment by the adversarial out-group of the in-group's trauma and the readiness to reconcile with them, Hameiri and Nadler 2017 first conducted two surveys among Jewish-Israelis and Palestinians who live in the West Bank. Within a representative sample of Jewish-Israelis, the extent to which participants perceived that Palestinians acknowledge the Jewish Holocaust was associated with a greater readiness to recognize the Palestinians' suffering and an increasing willingness to take responsibility and apologize for it. These relationships between the main variables were similar for Israeli-Jews and Palestinians, particularly in a large sample of Palestinians living in the West Bank. The perceived acknowledgment of the in-group's victimhood was positively related to the in-group's readiness to acknowledge the adversary's victimhood and a conciliatory attitude towards them.

The correlational nature of these findings does not reveal that the perceived acknowledgement of the in-group's trauma by the "enemy" in a protracted conflict facilitates the end of the conflict. Group members who had conciliatory attitudes may be more willing to recognize the victimhood of the enemy and believe that the enemy acknowledged theirs in turn. Thus, to examine the hypothesis that acknowledging the in-group's victimhood by the enemy *causes* greater willingness to make compromises on key divisive issues and take a conciliatory orientation towards one's adversary, we conducted three field experiments: two with Jewish-Israeli participants and one with Palestinian citizens of Israel. These experiments also allowed us to examine the psychological mechanisms that drive these effects.

In the first field study, we found that manipulated acknowledgment of victimhood led Jewish-Israelis to express more trust toward Palestinians and, most importantly, more willingness to take responsibility, apologize and make political concessions to promote a peaceful resolution of the conflict. The mediation analysis suggests that the manipulated high levels of acknowledgment (vs. low acknowledgment) led to more trust in Palestinians, which in turn led to more positive conciliatory attitudes. In the second field study, the results generally replicated the pattern of the first one. High levels of acknowledgment (vs. low acknowledgment) by Israeli-Jews of Palestinians' sufferings led the Palestinian participants to express more trust in Israeli-Jews, adopt more positive conciliatory attitudes towards them and led to a higher willingness to endorse political concessions to promote peaceful conflict resolution. The mediation analyses also indicate that trust only played a mediating role when the dependent variable focused on the conciliatory attitudes toward Jewish-Israelis but not when it was associated with the participants' willingness to make compromises.

The final study aimed to replicate the previous findings and shed light on the psychological mechanisms potentially accounting for the link between acknowledging victimhood, the readiness to compromise, and adopting conciliatory attitudes in "hot" conflicts. Because this study was conducted in early 2016, when violence peaked in Israeli-Palestinian relations, we were only able to recruit Israeli-Jews. This study also included a control group that read a story that focused on the Holocaust but did not imply anything about the level of its recognition by Palestinians. This process allowed us to assess the effects of high vs. low acknowledgment against a comparable baseline. Finally, the study assessed the role of four conceptually relevant variables as psychological mechanisms, namely *trust, collective victim identity, need for acceptance of the in-group,* and *reciprocity,* to explain the effects of acknowledgment on concession-making, taking responsibility for the adversary's sufferings, and the act of an apology.

The results replicated the main findings of the two previous studies. Compared to the low acknowledgment and the control group, Israeli-Jews who had been exposed to a high level of victimhood acknowledgment by Palestinians evidenced greater willingness to compromise, take responsibility for causing suffering to the Palestinians, and apologize for it. This effect was mediated by decreased adherence to collective victim identity, a lower need for acceptance, and a higher need to reciprocate. Unlike the previous studies, there were no effects on trust in the Palestinian group, potentially caused by a floor effect. With regard to the second mediator, i. e., the degree to which group members regard their group's past victimization as a central element in their *collective victim identity* (Klar, Schori-Eyal and Klar 2013), protracted and violent conflicts, such as the Israeli-Palestinian conflict, are dominated by feelings and perceptions of competitive victimhood, which emphasize the state of being a victim and become a central element in the group's identity (Noor et al. 2012). This centrality of victimhood leads to perceiving the adversary as a source of potential re-victimization and results in the adopting of a cautious and unyielding stance in relations with them. The opponent's acknowledgement of the group's victimhood implied that competitive victimhood no longer dominated. Lowering the centrality of the in-group's victimhood also led to a more conciliatory orientation and greater willingness to make concessions on divisive issues.

The third mediator, i. e., the participants' *need for acceptance,* was vital in the present study with Israeli-Jews, participants, who, like many other Israeli-Jew frequently experience threats concerning their moral image since Israel is often perceived as the perpetrator of immoral behavior towards the Palestinians (Shnabel et al. 2009). According to the needs-based model and related research, the threat to moral image results in the group's need to be accepted by out-groups, which discourages reconciliation until the need is met (Shnabel and Nadler 2015). The acknowledgment of the Jewish Holocaust by the Palestinians implied that the participants understood, however conditionally and tentatively, that Jewish history compels Israelis to be overly vigilant, which may lead them to implement immoral policies. This process reduced the threat to Israelis' moral image and, concomitantly, the need for acceptance from other groups, i. e., the world community. Studies have shown that satisfaction with the need for acceptance of the perpetrator increases the readiness to reconcile (Nadler and Shnabel 2015).

Similarly, for Israelis lower need for acceptance mediated their willingness to make concessions in the present study. The fourth mediator, i. e., the participants' *need to reciprocate* the acknowledgment of their collective victimhood by adopting a conciliatory orientation. Since we could not directly ask the participants whether the acknowledging of their victimhood should be reciprocated by making concessions, we assessed variations in the need for exchange. Specifically, we asked them if they thought that an acknowledgment of their group's victimhood needed to be reciprocated by the acknowledgment of the Palestinian suffering and found that this was indeed the case.

## 3.  Discussion and Conclusion

Overall, these findings suggest that acknowledgment of the in-group's victimhood by the adversary has positive effects on intergroup relations. The two surveys conducted in Israel and the Palestinian Authority indicate that the perception by Israeli-Jews of Palestinians who acknowledge the Holocaust as a major victimizing event for the Jewish people was related to their acknowledgement of Palestinian suffering and the willingness to take responsibility and apologize for it. In the same vein, the Palestinian perception of Israeli-Jews who acknowledge Palestinian Nakba-related sufferings was related to their readiness to recognize the Jewish Holocaust and their belief in the possibility of a reconciled future with the Israelis. Three subsequent field experiments substantiated the causal link between the acknowledgement of the in-group's victimhood, the readiness to compromise on divisive issues, and the adoption of conciliatory attitudes towards the adversary. These experiments also examined the mediators of these links.

The mediational analysis in the final study suggested that the effects of acknowledgment of victimhood on concession-making and conciliatory orientation reflect the workings of (a) identity-related and (b) relationship-related psychological mechanisms. A threat to moral identity is likely to have led the Israeli-Jewish participants to embrace collective victimhood with its associated feelings of entitlement, whereas the acknowledgement of victimhood diminished this threat and the associated need for acceptance by others. This progress lessened the need to embrace a collective victim identity. Consistent with the needs-based model of reconciliation (Nadler and Shnabel 2015) and work on collective victimhood (Noor et al. 2012), these identity-related changes increased the readiness to reconcile by taking the "first step" forward, i. e., offering concessions and adopting a conciliatory orientation. Apart from acknowledging victimhood, the participants perceived that the adversary made a positive gesture towards the in-group, which impacted their readiness to reciprocate and increased their trust in the other side. These relationship-related variables mediated the effects of acknowledging the Jewish Holocaust on concession-making and conciliatory orientation. However, due to deficient intergroup trust stemming from violence on the ground, this effect did not play a similar role in the final study.

These dual identity-related and relationship-related mediational paths are likely to be operative in protracted and violent conflicts. Such conflicts generate threats to group identities and are associated with much intergroup distrust and animosity (cf. Nadler 2012 for a similar distinction between socio-emotional and instrumental processes of reconciliation). The relative salience of each of these paths in mediating the effects of acknowledgment is likely to be determined situationally. Compared to protracted and violent conflicts and therefore associated with threats to collective identities, the mediating role of identity-related aspects is expected to be smaller than in shorter and less violent conflicts. Additionally, when the source of acknowledgment is a third party (e. g., when the UN recognizes Israeli or Palestinian victimhood), the mediating role of relationship-related aspects in explaining the effects of acknowledgment is anticipated to be lower than when the source is one's adversary. These and related questions await the scrutiny of further research.

The research we conducted as part of the "Hearts of Flesh–Not Stone" project is unique on several levels. First, it examines the effects of acknowledgment of victimhood on the victimized group instead of the perpetrating group's willingness to acknowledge their adversary's victimhood, the associated collective guilt, and conciliatory orientations (as did Čehajić and Brown 2010) within the context of an ongoing, protracted and violent conflict. Second, this method extends the examination of the effects of acknowledgment beyond the commonly used attitudinal and perceptual measures employed in previous research, which has focused on conflicts that have long ended, to examine the readiness to make actual concessions that can break the cycle of violence in an ongoing protracted conflict. This focus highlights the applied implications of the current research. In conflicts where the belittling or denial of the other's victimhood may be prevalent, their recognition by the adversary, even if not caused by them, may be an essential step forward. Gubler, Halperin, and Hirschberger (2015) study, which found that Israelis who read a message written by a Palestinian who acknowledged the Holocaust evidenced empathy towards their Palestinian adversary, supports this argument. As studies on competitive victimhood (Noor et al. 2012) and moral disengagement (Bandura 1999) have shown, feelings of empathy toward one's adversary are vital steps toward ending the conflict. Finally, research on victimhood acknowledgment is in its initial stage, and the interwoven psychological process still needs to be identified.

Although victimhood acknowledgment by adversaries seems a promising and even necessary route to promote positive relations, conflict resolution, and reconciliation, it rarely happens (e. g., Kapshuk, present volume). Such acknowledgment, for example, may be perceived as hindering the in-group's campaign to garner support from third parties (Noor et al., 2012). In cases in which an out-group was victimized by one's in-group, the reluctance to acknowledge the other's victimhood may stem from the need to maintain a positive social identity, whether by belittling the other's victimhood or minimizing one's culpability for it (Leiner et al. 2010). One promising approach for addressing this low willingness to acknowledge the adversary's victimhood is intergroup and particularly *intra*group dialogue. Such dialogue was found to lead to positive effects on various conflict-related outcomes, including, expression of empathy toward the Palestinian narrative among Jewish-Israelis (Ben David et al., 2017; Sternberg, present volume; Zigenlaub, present volume).

A relevant field for future research should examine the effects of acknowledging victimhood by a third party. If the effects of acknowledgment are due to an increase in the victim's conception of feeling morally superior to the adversary, acknowledgment by a third party (e. g., the UN) should have similar, if not stronger, ameliorative effects as acknowledgment by the adversary. However, if the positive effects of acceptance are attributable to the implication that the enemy legitimizes the in-group's identity, an acknowledgment from a third party should have lesser, if any, ameliorative effects. Another branch for future research concerns the different meanings acknowledgment of victimhood has for the more and less powerful in the conflict. Consistent with the logic of the needs-based model (Shnabel and Nadler 2008), acknowledgement means that the injustice done to the weaker party is recognized and needs to be rectified, whereas, for the more powerful party, acknowledgment means that since they are perceived as victims, they are exonerated from being portrayed as evil perpetrators. The finding that Israelis' need for acceptance of Israel by the world community was weaker in high acknowledgment conditions than in low acknowledgment conditions supports this reasoning (Hameiri and Nadler 2017).

Hence, the most important implication of this study is that the first step to intergroup reconciliation is the acknowledgment of the adversary's victimhood. Adversarial groups not only deny their responsibility for the out-group's sufferings, but forces of competitive victimhood led them to deny or belittle the significance of these sufferings. When collective victimhood is a crucial component of the group's self-perception and relations with out-groups (i. e., the "chosen trauma"), denial equals invalidating the group's identity. This denial of victimhood negatively influences intergroup relations, even after the conflict has ended, and is particularly destructive in ongoing conflicts. As the present findings indicate, under these circumstances, the denial of the in-group's victimhood leads to intransigent positions on divisive issues that threaten to turn the conflict into a protracted one. Acknowledging the adversary's "chosen trauma" lowers in-group members' defenses against future re-victimization and encourages compromises on divisive issues and a more conciliatory and hopeful view of their relations with the adversary than if such an acknowledgment is withheld. By studying the effects of acknowledgment of victimhood in the context of the protracted Israeli-Palestinian conflict, the present study illustrated these processes. The question as to whether these findings are unique to such contexts where parties deny each other's "chosen trauma" or are also manifested in other kinds of intergroup conflicts should be further examined in future research.

## References

Alarcón-Henríquez, A., Licata, L., Leys, C., Van der Linden, N., Klein, O., Mercy, A. 2010, 'Recognition of Shared Past Sufferings, Trust and Improving Intergroup Attitudes in Belgium', *Revista de Psicología,* vol. 28, no. 1, pp. 81–110.

Andrighetto, L., Mari, S., Volpato, C., Behluli, B. 2012, 'Reducing Competitive Victimhood in Kosovo. The Role of Extended Contact and Common Ingroup Identity', *Political Psychology,* vol. 33, no. 4, pp. 513–529.

Auerbach Y. 2009, 'The Reconciliation Pyramid. A Narrative-Based Framework for Analyzing Identity Conflicts', *Political Psychology,* vol. 30, no. 2, pp. 291–318.

Bandura, A.1999, 'Moral Disengagement in the Perpetration of Inhumanities", *Personality and Social Psychology Review,* vol. 3, no. 3, pp. 193–209.

Bar-Tal, D. 2013, *Intractable Conflicts. Socio-Psychological Foundations and Dynamics,* Cambridge University Press, Cambridge UK.

Ben David, Y., Hameiri, B., Benheim, S., Leshem, B., Sarid, A, Sternberg, M., Nadler, A., Sagy, S. 2017, 'Exploring Ourselves within Intergroup Conflict. The Role of Intragroup Dialogue in Promoting Acceptance of Collective Narratives and Willingness Toward Reconciliation', *Peace and Conflict. Journal of Peace Psychology,* vol. 23, no. 3, pp. 269–277.

Čehajić, S., Brown, R. 2010, 'Silencing the Past. Effects of Intergroup Contact on Acknowledgment of In-Group Responsibility', *Social Psychological and Personality Science,* vol. 1, no. 2, pp. 190–196.

David, R., Choi, S.Y.P. 2009, 'Getting Even or Getting Equal? Retributive Desires and Transnational Justice', *Political Psychology,* vol. 30, no. 2, pp. 161–192.

Gubler, J.R., Halperin, E., Hirschberger, G. 2015, 'Humanizing the Outgroup in Contexts of Protracted Intergroup Conflict', *Journal of Experimental Political Science,* vol. 2, no. 1, pp. 36–46.

Hameiri, B., Nadler, A. 2017, 'Looking Backward to Move Forward. Effects of Acknowledgment of Victimhood on Readiness to Compromise for Peace in the Protracted Israeli-Palestinian Conflict', *Personality and Social Psychology Bulletin,* vol. 43, no. 4, pp. 555–569.

Kalayjian, A.S., Shahinian, S.P., Gergerian, E.L., Saraydarian, L. 1996, 'Coping with Ottoman Turkish Genocide. An Exploration of the Experience of Armenian Survivors', *Journal of Traumatic Stress,* vol. 9, no. 1, pp. 87–97.

Kapshuk, Y. 2022, 'Reconciliation in Peace Agreements? The Case Study of the Israeli-Palestinian Peace Process', present volume.

Klar, Y., Schori-Eyal, N., and Klar, Y. 2013, 'The 'Never Again' State of Israel. The Emergence of the Holocaust as a Core Feature of Israeli Identity and its Four Incongruent Voices', *Journal of Social Issues,* vol. 69, no. 1, pp. 125–143.

Leidner, B., Castano, E., Zaiser, E., Giner-Sorolla, R. 2010, 'Ingroup Glorification, Moral Disengagement, and Justice in the Context of Collective Violence", *Personality and Social Psychology Bulletin,* vol. 36, no. 8, pp. 1115–1129.

Maercker, A., Povilonyte, M., Lianova, R., Pöhlmann, K. 2009, "Is Acknowledgement of Trauma a Protective Factor? The Sample Case of Refugees from Chechnya", *European Psychologist,* vol. 14, no. 3, pp. 249–254.

Nadler, A. 2012, 'Intergroup Reconciliation. Definitions, Processes, and Future Directions', in *The Oxford Handbook of Intergroup Conflict*, ed L.R. Tropp, Oxford University Press, New York, pp. 291–309.

Nadler, A. 2002, 'Post-Resolution Processes. Instrumental and Socioemotional Routes to Reconciliation', in *Peace Education. The Concept, Principles, and Practices Around the World*, eds G. Salomon, B. Nevo, Lawrence Erlbaum, Mahwah (NJ), pp. 127–144.

Nadler, A., Shnabel, N. 2015, 'Intergroup Reconciliation. Definitions, Instrumental and Socio-Emotional Processes, and the Needs-Based Model', *European Review of Social Psychology,* vol. 26, no. 1, pp. 93–125.

Nadler, A., Shnabel, N. 2008, 'Instrumental and Socioemotional Paths to Intergroup Reconciliation and the Needs-Based Model of Socioemotional Reconciliation', in *Social Psychology of Inter-Group Reconciliation*, eds A. Nadler, T. Maloy, J.D. Fisher, Oxford University Press, New York, pp. 37–56.

Noor, M., Shnabel, N., Halabi, S., Nadler, A. 2012, 'When Suffering Begets Suffering. The Psychology of Competitive Victimhood between Adversarial Groups in Violent Conflicts', *Personality and Social Psychology Review,* vol. 16, no. 4, pp. 351–374.

Noor, M., Brown, R., Prentice, G. 2008, 'Precursors and Mediators of Inter-Group Reconciliation in Northern Ireland. A New Model', *British Journal of Social Psychology,* vol. 47, no. 3, pp. 481–495.

Paez, D., Liu, J.H. 2011, 'Collective Memory of Conflicts', in *Intergroup Conflicts and Their Resolution. A Social Psychological Perspective*, ed D. Bar-Tal, Psychology Press, New York, pp. 105–124.

Schori-Eyal, N., Halperin, E., Bar-Tal, D. 2014, 'Three Layers of Collective Victimhood: Effects of Multileveled Victimhood on Intergroup Conflicts in the Israeli-Arab Context", *Journal of Applied Social Psychology,* vol. 44, no. 12, pp. 778–794.

Shnabel, N., Halabi, S., Noor, M. 2013, 'Overcoming Competitive Victimhood and Facilitating Forgiveness through Re-Categorization into a Common Victim or Perpetrator Identity', *Journal of Experimental Social Psychology,* vol. 49, no. 5, pp. 867–877.

Shnabel, N., Nadler, A. 2015, 'The Role of Agency and Morality in Reconciliation Processes. The Perspective of the Needs-Based Model', *Current Directions in Psychological Science,* vol. 24, no. 6, pp. 477–483.

Shnabel, N., Nadler, A. 2008, 'A Needs-Based Model of Reconciliation. Satisfying the Differential Emotional Needs of Victim and Perpetrator as a Key to Promoting Reconciliation', *Journal of Personality and Social Psychology,* vol. 94, no. 1, pp. 116–132.

Shnabel, N., Nadler, A., Ullrich, J., Dovidio, J.F., Carmi, D. 2009, 'Promoting Reconciliation through the Satisfaction of the Emotional Needs of Victimized and Perpetrating Group Members. The Needs-Based Model of Reconciliation', *Personality and Social Psychology Bulletin,* vol. 35, no. 8, pp. 1021–1030.

Shnabel, N., Nadler, A., Dovidio, J.F. 2014, 'Beyond Need Satisfaction. Empowering and Accepting Messages from Third Parties Ineffectively Restore Trust and Consequent Reconciliation', *European Journal of Social Psychology*, vol. 44, no. 2, pp. 126–140.

Siman-Tov Nachlieli, I., Shnabel, N., Halabi, S. 2015, 'Winning the Victim Status Can Open Conflicting Groups to Reconciliation. Evidence from the Israeli-Palestinian Conflict', *European Journal of Social Psychology,* vol. 45, no. 2, pp. 139–145.

Skitka, L.J., Bauman, C.W., Mullen, E. 2004, 'Political Tolerance and Coming to Psychological Closure Following the September 11, 2001, Terrorist Attacks. An Integrative Approach', *Personality and Social Psychology Bulletin,* vol. 30, no. 6, pp. 743–756.

Sternberg, M. 2022, 'When Israeli Students Encounter Palestinian Narratives', present volume.

Volkan, V. 2006, *Killing in the Name of Identity. A Study of Bloody Conflicts*, Pitchstone, Charlottesville (VA).

Vollhardt, J.R. 2009, 'The Role of Victim Beliefs in the Israeli-Palestinian Conflict. Risk or Potential for Peace?", *Peace and Conflict. Journal of Peace Psychology,* vol. 15, no. 2, pp. 135–159.

Vollhardt, J.R., Bilali, R. 2015, 'The Role of Inclusive and Exclusive Victim Consciousness in Predicting Intergroup Attitudes. Findings from Rwanda, Burundi, and DRC', *Political Psychology,* vol. 36, no. 5, pp. 489–506.

Vollhardt, J.R., Mazur, L.B., Lemahieu, M. 2014, "Acknowledgment After Mass Violence: Effects on Psychological Well-Being and Intergroup Relations', *Group Processes and Intergroup Relations,* vol. 17, no. 3, pp. 306–323.

Wohl, M.J.A, Branscombe, N.R. 2008, 'Remembering Historical Victimization. Collective Guilt for Current In-Group Transgression', *Journal of Personality and Social Psychology,* vol. 94, no. 6, pp. 988–1006.

Zigenlaub, E. 'Learning the Narrative of the Other. What Type of Encounter is More Effective?' 2022, present volume.

Anat Sarid, Anan Srour, Shifra Sagy

# Sense of National Coherence and Willingness to Reconcile

## The Case of the Israeli-Palestinian Conflict

### Abstract

Anat Sarid, Anan Srour, and Shifra Sagy's paper *Sense of National Coherence and Willingness to Reconcile: The Case of the Israeli-Palestinian Conflict* examines a new concept – sense of national coherence (SONC) – and its relationship with willingness to reconcile. Based on Antonovsky's concept of sense of coherence, SONC is defined as an enduring tendency to perceive one's national group as comprehensible, manageable, and meaningful. Previous studies found SONC and other similar concepts to be a barrier to openness to the other. The authors hypothesized that after a violent and stressful event (the Gaza war in 2014), SONC would be stronger, and willingness to reconcile would be lower than before the war. Moreover, they expected that the relationship between SONC and willingness to reconcile would be negative and even stronger after the war. The research questions were examined among Israeli-Jewish students. Questionnaires were administered to a sample of 140 students before the military action and 90 students after it. The results support research hypotheses regarding the negative relationship between SONC and willingness to reconcile. This relationship was found to be stronger after the military action. The discussion focuses on the dual role of SONC as a resilience resource in hard times on one hand and at the same time as a potential barrier to a peace process in areas at war or in serious conflict.

## 1. Introduction

Research in conflict areas indicates that nations with a stressful social reality tend to develop a socio-psychological infrastructure that provides a coherent, predictable, and meaningful worldview (Bar Tal 2013). These infrastructures serve as a prism through which society members absorb information about the social reality and interpret their experiences (Moscovici 1988). The current study examines a new concept – sense of national coherence (SONC) – and suggests that it is a significant part of this infrastructure (Sagy 2014; Mana, Srour and Sagy 2019). Moreover, we examined the link between one's perceptions of his/her own nation and his/her willingness to reconcile with the other side in the conflict.

Antonovsky's salutogenic model, and its core concept of "sense of coherence" (SOC), focuses on the ability of individuals to cope with stressors in life and stay healthy. SOC is defined as a global orientation of the individual, an enduring tendency to perceive the world as comprehensive, meaningful, and manageable (Antonovsky 1987). Accordingly, the relationship between SOC and health, stress, and coping has received much attention and quite consistent results in research (Eriksson and Mittelmark 2016). Research reviews for more than 40 years have confirmed the main salutogenic hypothesis: A person with a strong SOC will be able to cope better with life stressors than someone with a weak SOC (Eriksson and Mittelmark 2016; Eriksson and Lindström 2005) and stay healthy. However, Antonovsky claimed that "in the face of collective stressors, the strength of the group, rather than of the individual sense of coherence, is often decisive in tension management" (Antonovsky 1987, p. 178–179).

Sagy and Antonovsky (1992) suggested expanding the original definition of sense of coherence from a "global orientation of the world" into a defined collective like the family. Later on, Sagy (1998) continued to develop the concept of sense of community coherence (SOCC) which related to a specific community group. The three dimensions measured in SOCC are the same as the original concept of SOC: Community comprehensibility relates to the perception that life in one's community is perceived as predictable, safe, secure, known, and understood. Manageability relates to the perception that one's community can assist its members, is available to them, and meets their demands and needs. Lastly, meaningfulness relates to the perception that belonging to the community gives meaning to its members, provides challenges, and is worthy of investment and engagement.

Like the SOC of the individual, SOCC has been studied in relation to better coping with stressful events like bomb attacks, fire disasters, and deportation (e. g., Braun-Lewensohn and Sagy 2011; Sabato and Galili 2013; Peled, Sagy and Braun-Lewensohn 2013).

Recently, Sagy (2014) proposed new salutogenic questions which no longer concerned only the relationships between SOC, stress, and health. These new questions have been studied in a few research projects: How does a collective with a strong sense of coherence perceive, feel, or behave towards the "other" group members in a conflict? Does a group's tendency to perceive its world as comprehensible, meaningful, and manageable related to greater openness to the other narratives, or does it involve clinging to the rigid in-group narratives? Is an individual, a group, a collective, or a system with a stronger sense of coherence more likely to live in peaceful relations with their surroundings? (Sagy and Mana 2017; Sagy 2014).

This new approach sought to explore the relationships between levels of SOCC and openness to the other. Findings from different social contexts revealed similar patterns: Palestinian Muslims and Christians (Mana, Sagy and Srour 2016); ultra-

Orthodox and national-religious Jews in Israel (Somech and Sagy 2019) and Serbs and Albanians in Kosovo (Telaku and Sagy 2019) – stronger SOCC was found as related to a lower level of legitimization, higher anger, and lower empathy towards the out-group collective narratives. Strong SOCC was also related to a stronger tendency to reject the other group members and to adopt a separation strategy (Mana et al. 2012; Somech and Sagy 2019). In the context of intergroup conflict, perceptions of one's community as comprehensible, manageable, and meaningful reinforce the individual group members and promote their own well-being and health (Braun-Lewensohn and Sagy 2011; Mana and Sagy 2020). At the same time, however, it strengthens their feelings and attitudes towards separation, differentiation, and superiority over the other group. Thus, it could lead to attitudes of discrimination against the other group (Mana et al. 2015; Sagy and Mana 2017).

Based on these findings, a few recent studies suggest expanding the SOC concept to the national level (Mana et al. 2019). The unique contribution of the new concept sense of national coherence (SONC) to the wide range of literature related to the national "imagined kinship" (Anderson 2006) is the salutogenic perspective and the integration of the three components of SOC: comprehensibility (the cognitive element), meaningfulness (the emotional-motivational element), and manageability (the behavioral element).

1. *Comprehensibility*. This component mainly relates to the cognitive need to perceive the national group and its action as comprehensible and logical. Several concepts have been developed in psychology, sociology, and anthropology literature in order to describe the constructs which help national group members to gain comprehensibility, for example, ethos (Bar-Tal, Oren and Nets-Zehngut 2014), collective narratives (Liu and Hilton 2005; Hanson 1989; Hein and Selden 2000) and social representations (Duveen 2007; Moscovici 1988). These constructs serve as the main prism through which the national group members understand collective phenomena as coherent and comprehensive. It helps them legitimize and justify the national group actions and the social order (Liu and Hilton 2005; Sunshine and Tyler 2003). In hegemonic societies, the sense of comprehensibility is generally high, and the shared social representations, narratives, and ethos are perceived as "common sense" and as the only legitimate way to interpret and understand the social reality. However, in more diverse societies, when members of the nation are differentially exposed to new information, their level of comprehensibility could be lower (Moscovici 1988).

2. *Manageability*. Manageability mainly relates to the behavioral level of SONC, the "doing" parts, meaning the perceptions that the nation could assist its members, is available to them, and meets their personal and collective demands and needs. National manageability is related to the levels of confidence and trust in, and satisfaction with the national institutes and systems, like the army and the justice, political, educational, welfare, and security systems (Christensen and Lægreid 2003).

It also relates to group members' perception of national institutes' and systems' capacity, efficacy, and readiness to cope in times of stress and danger (Chaskin et al. 2007; Stith et al. 2006).

3. *Meaningfulness.* Meaningfulness is related to the emotional-cognitive elements of SONC. It mainly refers to the feelings that the nation has a meaning to its members by providing challenges, goals, vision, and a shared destination. Additionally, it expresses the feeling that living in one's own nation is worthy of investment and engagement (Anderson 2006). Meaningfulness could also be related to patriotism - the set of attitudes and beliefs that refers to individuals' attachment and loyalty to their nation and country (Bar-Tal and Staub 1997). These feelings of belonging to a meaningful national group serve as the main component in the social identity or collective identity and in the way people describe and perceive themselves (Tajfel 1981). Political psychologists (e. g., Bar-Tal 2013) have described how such feelings of meaningfulness are promoted and encouraged by national interests. The nation, as an entity, speaks and acts (Anderson 2006; Hanson 1989) via its social systems (e. g., media, education) and in this way promotes ideology, ethos, collective narratives, and social representations which strengthen feelings of meaningfulness, patriotism, and solidarity (Bar-Tal, Halperin and Oren 2010; Liu and Hilton 2005).

Is SONC a barrier to reconciliation, or could it advance a willingness to reconcile? When people feel that they can rely on their nation's resources, does it promote openness towards the other group in a conflict, or does the opposite happen, and they are less open towards that group? A recent study by Mana and colleagues (2019) found that people with strong SONC tend to give less legitimization to the other group's collective narratives. Based on these findings, we hypothesized that SONC might be an obstacle on the way to reconciliation.

## 1.1 Willingness to reconcile

Social psychologists suggested different definitions for the term "reconciliation." Most of the definitions reflect the importance of the socio-psychological aspects in conflict resolution. For example, Nadler and Saguy (2004) defined reconciliation as a process in which the emotional barriers between the groups are being removed. Staub and Bar-Tal (2003) claimed that reconciliation means a psychological change in the relationship toward the enemy group and a willingness to accept the people in the other group as human (Staub 2006). Kelman (2008) also suggested that reconciliation is a process of psychological change – change in the group's collective identity, mainly concerning their perception of the enemy group and ceasing to deny the enemy group members.

Some of the research regarding reconciliation focused on identifying the factors promoting the process and enabling its feasibility. Aspects related to the group include mutual recognition of each group as part of humanity, recognition of the nationality of the other group, and of the different (and sometimes contradictory) narratives each group has regarding the history (Kelman 2004), knowledge about the narrative of the other group and legitimization to that narrative (Auerbach 2010), the willingness of each group to take responsibility for the suffering they caused to the enemy group in the conflict (Herman 2004), and willingness to apologize for its deeds (Auerbach 2004; Cohen 2004). Aspects related to the individual include demographic variables (such as age, gender, and religiosity), political tendency (Shamir and Shikaki 2002), and hope (Sagy and Adwan 2006).

Willingness to reconcile in the context of the Israeli-Palestinian conflict has been widely studied. Nadler and Liviatan (2006) found that Israeli students showed greater willingness to reconcile after receiving a message expressing empathy from a Palestinian. Shamir and Shikaki (2002) found that the political context is also an important factor. Higher expectations regarding the success of peace talks were related to a higher willingness to reconcile.

Sagy and colleagues (2002) compared the willingness to reconcile between Israeli-Jews and Palestinians and found that each group interprets the meaning of the end of conflict and making peace between groups differently. The Israeli-Jews youth tended to prefer solutions based on compromise as a way to end the conflict, whereas Palestinian youth were less willing to reconcile and had a more pessimistic view of the situation. They thought that the conflict between groups would continue.

Another research path is about barriers to reconciliation and factors that prevent or withhold ending the conflict in peaceful ways. Among the barriers to reconciliation that were studied, we can find perception of justice (Bar Siman Tov 2014), fear (Rosler 2013), and religious values (Reiter 2010).

Bar-Tal and Halperin (2011) suggested a framework to explain the affect of socio-psychological barriers. Their model refers to the cognitive, emotional, and motivational processes that lead to biased and selective information processing in subjects related to the conflict. That framework is based on the idea that group members have shared beliefs about the conflict and shared emotions regarding the conflict.

The shared beliefs compose the "conflict ethos" and include legitimization of the conflict goals and justification of the in-group instead of a negative perception of the enemy. The result of those beliefs is distrust and hostility towards the enemy group and feeling threatened. All those feelings may serve as barriers to reconciliation. In addition, because of cognitive and perception bias, this system of shared beliefs is resistant to change and prevents the acquisition of information that contradicts the existing beliefs (Maoz 2004).

Bar-Tal and colleagues (2010) suggested an analysis of the socio-psychological barriers relevant to the Israeli-Jewish society in relation to the Israeli-Palestinian conflict. The shared beliefs composing the conflict ethos include negative perceptions of the Palestinians, perceiving Jews as the victims in the conflict who are trying to act for peace but are forced to use military actions because of the acts of Palestinians, and perceiving the Jews as morally superior. In the emotional aspect, the Israeli-Jewish society is characterized by fear of wars and terror, and hate toward the Palestinians. Those characteristics are related to lower willingness to compromise and to lower openness toward new information about the conflict (Halperin and Bar-Tal 2011).

Previous studies found a negative relationship between a sense of community coherence and perceptions of others' group collective narratives in the context of religious conflicts (Mana et al. 2012; Somech and Sagy 2019), and regarding the connection between SONC and legitimization to the other group's collective narratives in the context of the Israeli-Palestinian conflict (Mana et al. 2019).

The current study suggests that SONC could be a barrier to reconciliation, and therefore, people with strong SONC will show lower levels of willingness to reconcile. In other words, the more participants perceived their nation as manageable, understandable, and providing meaning to its challenging surroundings in a conflictual context, the less they would be willing to reconcile with the other group.

## 2. The Context of the Conflict – Before and After Gaza War

We examined the research questions in the context of the Israeli-Palestinian conflict and compared two situations – before and after a violent event, the Gaza war in 2014. The Israeli-Palestinian conflict is defined as an intractable conflict (Kriesberg 1993) since it is violent, long-lasting, perceived as irresolvable, and affects many aspects of life. Over the years, the conflict expanded and is characterized by violent actions – war, military confrontations, and terror attacks.

During the last decade, one of the main areas of the conflict has been along the Gaza border. The political situation and the tension along the border between Gaza and Israel have been the cause of several military operations in Gaza. The war in 2014 lasted more than one month. During that time, thousands of rockets and missiles were fired from Gaza to Israel, and major damage and destruction were caused to buildings and infrastructure inside Gaza.

Compared to previous military operations in Gaza, the 2014 operation (to which we refer in the current study) was longer and had more severe results. It directly affected the lives of many Israelis, especially those living in the southern area of Israel (Elran and Altshuler 2014). Surveys conducted after that war showed that the Israeli-Jewish populations had moved to the right on the political map (Elran, Ben-Meir and Sher 2015). The researchers explain the prevalence of right political views after the event in the growing feelings that military force is the only way to keep security in Israel. It is also relevant in the context of willingness to reconcile – if you believe that military force is necessary, it affects how you perceive the end of the conflict (Elran, Ben-Meir and Sher 2015).

As mentioned previously SONC could be considered as an important coping resource for people in the context of national stressful events. The Gaza war in 2014 was such a stressful event. Therefore, we expected that after that event SONC would be stronger and willingness to reconcile would decrease. Moreover, we expected that strengthened SONC will be also related to lower level of willingness to reconcile.

## 3. Hypotheses

1. We expected to find a negative correlation between SONC and willingness to reconcile.
2. We expected that the violent event (the Gaza war) would have a different influence on SONC and willingness to reconcile: After the violent event, SONC will be stronger, and willingness to reconcile will be lower than before the event.
3. We expected that the negative correlation between SONC and readiness to reconcile would be stronger after the violent event (the Gaza war) than it was before that event.

## 4. Method

### 4.1 Participants

Participants were 336 Israeli-Jewish students studying at the Ben-Gurion University of the Negev. The participants were divided into 2 samples – before and after the Gaza war. Sample 1 (before the war) consists of 137 participants, 71% of them were women, with a mean age of 25. Sample 2 (after the war) consisted of 199 participants, of them, 67% women, with a mean age of 24. No age differences were found between the two samples (t=1.85, P<.05) nor gender differences ($\chi^2$=.45, P>.05).

### 4.2 Instruments

*Sense of National Coherence questionnaire* – a 7-item questionnaire using a Likert scale. The items reflect the three components of SONC: comprehensibility (two items, e. g., "To what extent does the future of your nation is clear?" 1= Not clear at all, 7= Very clear), manageability (two items, e. g., "To what extent is your nation capable of coping with the challenges of the future?" 1= Completely incapable, 7= Fairly capable), and meaningfulness (three items, one in a negative form. e. g.,

"Belonging to your nation gives meaning and purpose to life, which someone outside of your nation cannot feel" 1= Completely untrue, 7= Totally true). Alpha Cronbach for the whole questionnaire was found to be satisfying ($\alpha$=.73).

## 4.3 Willingness to reconcile

A 4-item questionnaire using a Likert scale. The items refer to the main issues in the Israeli-Palestinian conflict (settlements, Jerusalem, and the Palestinian refugees), and the participants are asked about possible solutions to those issues. The response scale in that questionnaire is from 1=strongly disagree to 7=strongly agree. Factor analysis revealed one factor explaining 61.21% of the variance. The alpha Cronbach of that questionnaire is 0.79

## 5. Results

Table 1 The means found regarding the two variables in this research – SONC and willingness to reconcile

|  | Men | Women |
|---|---|---|
| N | 90 | 213 |
| SONC | 3.7 (1.0) | 3.8 (0.9) |
| Willingness to reconcile | 4.1 (1.4) | 3.8 (1.6) |

No significant differences between males and females were found regarding SONC (t=-.90, p>.05) or willingness to reconcile (t=1.42, p>.05). Pearson analysis revealed correlation between levels of willingness to reconcile and age (r=.21, p<.01) and a negative relationship between levels of SONC and age (r= -.18, p<.05).

Our first hypothesis refers to the relationship between SONC and willingness to reconcile. We hypothesized that the relationship between those 2 variables would be negative. Indeed, we found a strong negative correlation between those two variables : r=-.49, p>.01, n=301.

We also hypothesized that the violent event (Gaza war) would have a different influence on the two variables – SONC will be stronger, and willingness to reconcile will be lower after the war. As expected, SONC was found to be weaker before the military action (M=3.42, Sd=1.02) than after it (M=3.97, Sd=0.84), and willingness to reconcile was found to be stronger before the military action (M=4.23, Sd=1.60) than after it (M=3.66, Sd=1.48). Both differences were significant (SONC: t=-4.95, p<.01; Willingness to reconcile: t=3.27, p<.01).

Our last hypothesis was that the violent event (Gaza war) would also influence the negative correlation between those 2 variables, and after the war, we would find a stronger negative correlation between SONC and willingness to reconcile. Before the war: r=-.38, p<.01, n=168 and after the war r=-.55, p<.01, n=133. Indeed, we found a significant difference between the correlations Z=1.86, p<.05.

## 6.    Discussion

This research employs a new concept – sense of national coherence (SONC) – which represents the perception of a nation's infrastructure in intractable conflict. SONC means the perception of one's nation serves as a coping resource for the individual (Mana and Sagy 2020) but, at the same time, could be a barrier to reconciliation. Our hypotheses were confirmed, and a negative relationship was found between SONC and willingness to reconcile. This suggests that the more people tend to perceive their nation as manageable and meaningful for them as individuals, the less they will be willing to end the conflict in peaceful ways and reconcile with the other side. Further research is needed to explain the mechanism that makes SONC a barrier to reconciliation.

One possible explanation is based on a recent study (Mana et al., 2019) that found strong SONC to be negatively correlated with low levels of openness toward the other group in the conflict. It may be that when people tend to feel they can rely on their nation, they are less open to the other group and less willing to reconcile.

Similar results were found in studies of a similar collective concept – SOCC– which relates to the community instead of to the nation: strong levels of SOCC were correlated with low levels of openness toward the other group (Mana et al. 2012, 2015; Telaku and Sagy 2019).

One of the realities of living in an area of intractable conflict is that episodes of violent outbreak are not rare. Our data were collected before and after a violent event in the conflict, the war in Gaza that took place in the summer of 2014. Having data from two time points enables us to compare the results before and after the violent event and thus try to understand the effect that such violent events have on people living in a conflict area.

Indeed, after the violent breakout, SONC was stronger, willingness to reconcile was lower, and the negative relationship between SONC and willingness to reconcile was stronger. These results suggest that one of the effects that episodes of the violent outbreak have on people is moving them to even greater reliance on their nation as a coping resource. In times of war or crisis, people need to perceive their nation as just and they need to feel that their lives are manageable and meaningful. In terms of SONC, we can say that violent episodes make people perceive their nation as more manageable, meaningful, and comprehensible. Mana and Sagy (2020) suggested that SONC can be considered a salutogenic resilience factor, which helps people cope well in times of violent and stressful collective episodes. Since the

Israeli-Palestinian conflict is perceived as intractable (Bar-Tal 2013), the SONC enables individuals to cope well despite the prolonged situation.

Our results suggest that SONC might be a barrier to reconciliation and, as such, it might obstruct the possibility of ending the conflict in peaceful ways. Despite this negative link, we still suggest that SONC is a meaningful concept relating to the process of reconciliation in intractable conflict. SONC may serve as a barrier to reconciliation due to its unique characteristics as a resilient factor in the continuing conflict.

Can we change this circular pattern?

We believe that educational interventions could make a change. Zigenlaub and Sagy (2020), for example, found that Israeli participants of dialogue groups, after one year of intervention, still presented strong SONC and strong identity with their collective narratives, and also expressed more acceptance of the narrative of the "other" group (the Palestinians). This effect was found whether the group was an intra-group (only Israelis) or an inter-group (Israelis and Palestinians).

Further research is needed concerning levels of SONC among people who live in relatively peaceful areas such as asking about the relationship between this national concept and openness to other groups like immigrants and minorities. These questions appear to be relevant to many Western countries these days.

## References

Anderson, B. 2006, *Imagined Communities: Reflections on the Origin and Spread of Nationalism*. London and New York, Verso Books.

Antonovsky, A. 1987, *Unraveling the Mystery of Health: How People Manage Stress and Stay Well*. Jossey-Bass, San Francisco.

Auerbach, Y. 2004, 'The Role of Forgiveness in Reconciliation', in *From Conflict Resolution to Reconciliation*, ed Y. Bar-Siman Tov, Oxford UP, New York, pp. 149–176.

Auerbach, Y. 2010, 'National Narratives in a Conflict of Identity', *Barriers to Peace in the Israeli-Palestinian conflict*, pp. 99–134.

Bar-Siman Tov, Y. 2014, *Justice and Peace in the Israeli-Palestinian Conflict,* Routledge, New York.

Bar-Tal, D. 2013, *Intractable Conflicts: Socio-Psychological Foundations and Dynamics,* Cambridge, Cambridge University Press.

Bar-Tal, D., Halperin, E. 2011, 'Socio-Psychological Barriers to Conflict Resolution', in *Intergroup Conflicts and Their Resolution: Social Psychological Perspective*, New York, Psychology Press, pp. 217–240.

Bar-Tal, D. Staub, E. 1997, 'Patriotism: Its Scope and Meaning', in *Patriotism in the Lives of Individuals and Nations*, eds D. Bar-Tal, E. Staub, Chicago, Nelson-Hill, pp. 1–19.

Bar-Tal, D., Halperin, E., Oren, N. 2010, 'Socio–Psychological Barriers to Peace Making: The Case of the Israeli Jewish Society', *Social Issues and Policy Review*, 4/1, pp. 63–109.

Bar-Tal, D., Oren, N., Nets-Zehngut, R. 2014, 'Sociopsychological Analysis of Conflict Supporting Narratives: A General Framework', *Journal of Peace Research*, 51/5, pp. 662–675.

Braun-Lewensohn, A., Sagy, S. 2011, 'Salutogenesis and Culture: Personal and Community Sense of Coherence among Adolescents Belonging to Different Cultural Groups', *International Review of Psychiatry*, 23/6, pp. 533–541.

Chaskin, R.J., Brown, V., Venkatesh. S., Vidal, A. 2007, *Building Community Capacity*, New York, Aldine Transaction.

Christensen, T., Lægreid, P. 2003, *Trust in Government–the Significance of Attitudes Towards Democracy, the Public Sector and Public Sector Reforms*, Bergen, Rokkansenteret, Stein Rokkan senter for flerfaglige samfunnsstudier.

Cohen, R. 2004, 'Apology and Reconciliation in International Relations', in *From Conflict Resolution to Reconciliation*, ed Y. Bar-Siman Tov, Oxford UP, New York, pp. 177–196.

Duveen, G. 2007, 'Culture and Social Representations', in *The Cambridge Handbook of Sociocultural Psychology*, eds J.Valsiner, A. Rosa, Cambridge University Press, Cambridge, UK, pp. 543–559.

Elran, M., Altshuler, A. 2014, 'The Civilian Frontlines in Operation Protective Edge', in *The Lessons of Operation Protective Edge*, eds A. Kurz, S Brom, INSS, Tel Aviv (In Hebrew), pp. 107–112.

Elran, M., Ben-Meir, Y., Sher, G. 2015, 'The Influences of Operation Protective Edge on Political and Social Trends in Israel', in *The Lessons of Operation Protective Edge*, eds A. Kurz, S Brom, INSS, Tel Aviv (In Hebrew), pp. 125–136.

Eriksson, M., Mittelmark, M.B. 2016, 'The Sense of Coherence and its Measurement', in *The Handbook of Salutogenesis,* eds M.B. Mittelmark, S. Sagy, M. Eriksson, G.F. Bauer, J.M. Pelikan, B. Lindström, G.A. Espnes, Springer, Cham, pp. 97–106.

Eriksson, M., Lindström, B. 2005, 'Validity of Antonovsky's Sense of Coherence Scale - A Systematic Review', *Journal of Epidemiology & Community Health,* 59/6, pp. 460–466.

Halperin, E. Bar-Tal, D. 2011, 'Socio-Psychological Barriers to Peace Making: An Empirical Examination within the Israeli Jewish Society', *Journal of Peace Research,* 48/5, pp. 637–651.

Hanson, A. 1989, 'The Making of the Maori: Culture Invention and its Logic', *American Anthropologist*, 91/4, pp. 890–902.

Hayes, F. 2013, *Introduction to Mediation, Moderation, and Conditional Process Analysis*, The Guilford Press, New York.

Hein, L.E., Selden, M. (eds) 2000, *Censoring History: Citizenship and Memory in Japan, Germany, and the United States*, M.E. Sharpe, Armonk. New York.

Herman, T. 2004, 'Reconciliation: Reflections on the Theoretical and Practical Utility of the Term', in *From Conflict Resolution to Reconciliation*, ed Y. Bar-Siman Tov, Oxford UP, New York, pp. 39–60.

Kelman, H.C. 2008, 'Reconciliation from a Social-Psychological Perspective', in *The Social Psychology of Intergroup Reconciliation*, eds A. Nadler, T.E. Malloy, J.D. Fisher, Oxford UP, New York, pp. 15–32.

Kelman, H.C. 2004, 'Reconciliation as Identity Change: A Social-Psychological Perspective', in *From Conflict Resolution to Reconciliation*, ed Y. Bar-Siman Tov, Oxford UP, New York, pp. 111–124.

Kriesberg, L. 1993, 'Intractable Conflict', *Peace Review*, 5, pp. 417–421.

Liu, J.H., Hilton, D.J. 2005, 'How the Past Weighs on the Present: Social Representations of History and Their Role in Identity Politics', *British Journal of Social Psychology*, 44, pp. 1–21.

Mana, A., Sagy, S. 2020, 'Brief Report: Can Political Orientation Explain Mental Health in the Time of a Global Pandemic? Voting Patterns, Personal and National Coping Resources, and Mental Health During the Coronavirus Crisis', *Journal of Social and Clinical Psychology*, 39/3, pp. 187–193.

Mana, A., Sagy, S., Srour, A. 2016, 'Sense of Community Coherence and Inter-Religious Relations', *The Journal of Social Psychology*, 156/5, pp. 469–482.

Mana, A., Sagy, S., Srour, A., Mjally-Knani, S. 2015, 'On Both Sides of the Fence: Perceptions of Collective Narratives and Identity Strategies among Palestinians in Israel and in the West Bank', *Mind and Society*, 14, pp. 57–83.

Mana, A., Sagy, A., Srour, S., Mjally-Knani, S. 2012, 'Perceptions of Collective Narratives and Identity Strategies: The Case of Palestinian Muslims and Christians in Israel'. *Mind and Society*, 11/2, pp. 165–182.

Mana, S., Srour, A, Sagy, S. 2019, 'A Sense of National Coherence and Openness to the "Other's" Collective Narrative: The Case of the Israeli–Palestinian Conflict', *Peace and Conflict: Journal of Peace Psychology*, 25/3, pp. 226–233.

Maoz, I. 2004, 'Social-Cognitive Mechanisms in Reconciliation', in *From Conflict Resolution to Reconciliation*, ed Y. Bar-Siman Tov, Oxford UP, New York, pp. 225–237.

Moscovici, S. 1988, 'Notes towards a Description of Social Representation', *European Journal on Social Psychology*, 18, pp. 211–250.

Nadler, A. Liviatan, I. 2006, 'Intergroup Reconciliation: Effects of Adversary's Expressions of Empathy, Responsibility and Recipients', *Trust. Personality and Social Psychology Bulletin*, 32/4, pp. 459–470.

Nadler, A. Saguy, T, 2004, 'Reconciliation Between Nations: Overcoming Emotional Deterrents to Ending Conflicts Between Groups', in *The Psychology of Diplomacy*, eds H. Langholtz, C.E. Stout, Praeger Publishers, Connecticut, pp. 29–58.

Peled, D., Sagy, S., Braun-Lewensohn, O. 2013, 'Community Perception as Coping Resource among Adolescents Living under Rockets Fire: A Salutogenic Approach', *Journal of Community Positive Practices*, 4, pp. 681–702.

Reiter, Y. 2010, 'Religion as a Barrier to Compromise in the Israeli-Palestinian Conflict', *Barriers to Peace in the Israeli-Palestinian Conflict*, 228 (in Hebrew).

Rosler, N. 2013, 'Fear and Conflict Resolution: Theoretical Discussion and a Case Study from Israel', *Research Paper*, 10. The Joseph and Alma Gildenborn Institute for Israel Studies, University of Maryland.

Sabato, H., Galili, R. 2013, 'Sense of Coherence and Sense of Community as Coping Resources of Religious Adolescents before and after the Disengagement from the Gaza Strip', *The Israel Journal of Psychiatry and Related Sciences*, 50/2, pp. 110/117.

Sagy, S. 2014, 'From the Diary of a Conflict Researcher: The Salutogenic Paradigm', *Mifgash*, 40 (in Hebrew), pp. 9–26.

Sagy, S. 1998, 'Effects of Personal, Family and Community Characteristics on Emotional Reactions in a Stress Situation: The Golan Heights Negotiation', *Youth and Society*, 29/3, pp. 311–329.

Sagy, S., Adwan, S. 2006, 'Hope in Times of Threat: The Case of Israeli and Palestinian Youth', *American Journal of Orthopsychiatry*, 76/1, pp. 128–133.

Sagy, S., Adwan, S., Kaplan, A. 2002, 'Interpretations of the Past and Expectations for the Future among Israeli and Palestinian Youth', *American Journal of Orthopsychiatry*, 72/1, pp. 26–38.

Sagy, S., Antonovsky, A. 1992, 'The Family Sense of Coherence and the Retirement Transition', *Journal of Marriage and the Family*, 54/4, pp. 983–993.

Sagy, S., Mana, A. 2017, 'The Relevance of Salutogenesis to Social Issues besides Health: The Case of Sense of Coherence and Intergroup Relations', in *The Handbook of Salutogenesis,* eds M.B. Mittelmark, S. Sagy, M. Eriksson, G.F. Bauer, J.M. Pelikan, B. Lindström, G.A. Espnes, Springer, Cham, pp. 77–81.

Shamir, J. Shikaki, K. 2002, 'Determinants of Reconciliation and Compromise among Israelis and Palestinians', *Journal of Peace Research*, 39/2, pp. 185–202.

Shnabel, N., Nadler, A., Ullrich, J., Dovidio, J.F., Carmi, D. 2009, 'Promoting Reconciliation through the Satisfaction of the Emotional Needs of Victimized and Perpetrating Group Members: The Needs-Based Model of Reconciliation', *Personality and Social Psychology Bulletin*, 35/8, pp. 1021–1030.

Somech, L.Y., Sagy, S. 2019, 'Perceptions of Collective Narratives and Identity Strategies as Indicators of Intergroup Relations', *International Journal of Conflict Management,* 30/3, pp. 290–308.

Staub, E. 2006, 'Reconciliation after Genocide, Mass Killing, or Intractable Conflict: Understanding the Roots of Violence, Psychological Recovery, and Steps toward a General Theory', *Political Psychology*, 27/6, pp. 867–894.

Staub, E., Bar-Tal, D. 2003, 'Genocide, Mass Killing and Intractable Conflict: Roots, Evolution, Prevention and Reconciliation', in *Handbook of Political Psychology*, eds D. Sears, L. Huddy, R. Jarvis, Oxford UP, New York, pp. 710–755.

Stith, S., Pruitt, I., Dees, J., Fronce, M., Green, N., Som, A., Linkh, D. 2006, 'Implementing Community-Based Prevention Programming: A Review of the Literature', *Journal of Primary Prevention*, 27/6, pp. 599–617.

Sunshine, J., Tyler, T. 2003, 'Moral Solidarity, Identification with the Community, and the Importance of Procedural Justice: The Police as Prototypical Representatives of a Group's Moral Values', *Social Psychology Quarterly*, 66/2, pp. 153–165.

Tajfel, H. 1981, *Human Groups and Social Categories*, Cambridge University Press, Cambridge.

Telaku, M., Sagy, S. 2019, 'Perceptions of Collective Narratives and Acculturation Attitudes: The Case of Serbs and Albanians in Kosovo', in *The Former Soviet Union and East Central Europe between Conflict and Reconciliation,* eds L.G. Feldman, R. Barash, S. Goda, A. Zempelburg, Vandenhoeck & Ruprecht, Göttingen, pp. 211–224.

Zigenlaub, E., Sagy, S. 2020, 'Encountering the Narrative of the "Other": Comparing Two Types of Dialogue Groups of Jews and Arabs in Israel', *Peace and Conflict: Journal of Peace Psychology*, 26/1, pp. 88–91.

Michael Sternberg, Shifra Sagy

# When Israeli Students Encounter Palestinian Narratives

## Abstract

Encountering the suffering of the others cannot be separated from acknowledging their narratives. Michael Sternberg and Shifra Sagy's paper on the question of *When Israeli Students encounter Palestinian Narratives* explores the contribution to reflexive learning about conflict reality, which takes place by meeting narratives of the other in intragroup dialogue. Their paper presents dynamics triggered by dialogue within one national group (in this case, a group of Jewish-Israeli undergraduate students) in the context of a binational conflict. Their study explores the contribution of dialogue to the capacity to relate to ongoing conflict relations from perspectives that go beyond binary and oppositional assumptions and positions ("us" and "them"). The paper shows that intragroup dialogue contributes to a reflexive exploration of participants' involvement in the conflict through an increased readiness to challenge hegemonic perceptions of conflict reality, i. e., to consider and examine alternatives to existing types of conflict engagement as valuable, and to cope with the challenges of becoming an active bystander towards the abuse of power relations.

***

This paper outlines a study of an encounter between Jewish Israeli students with Palestinian narratives (Sternberg 2017; Sternberg, Litvak Hirsch and Sagy 2018). The encounter is based on intragroup dialogue, and the research explores the cognitive and emotional contribution of such an encounter to an understanding of the other. The primary research goal is to explore the contribution of encountering narratives of the other in a setting of intragroup dialogue to reflexive learning about conflict reality and potential shifts in perceptions of conflict relations.

## 1.  Sources of Violence and Challenges for Transforming Violent Conflict

In this section, we relate to theoretical approaches that address the understanding of challenges for conflict transformation in violent conflict, adding possible roles of dialogue in this context.

Conflict transformation approaches define violence by the degree to which basic human needs are violated (Miall 2004). According to Galtung (2009), there are three fundamental forms of violence. First, violence occurs as the outcome of actions (direct violence); second, as the result of polarized social structures which cause violation of basic human needs of underprivileged populations (structural violence); third, as what occurs when cultural systems legitimize the violation of the basic human needs of selected populations (cultural violence). Within such a framework of conflict analysis, the sources of violence which need to be resolved are primarily related to a power asymmetry that permeates the violations of rights and needs of underprivileged sides (Darweish 2010). However, such asymmetric structures cannot be transformed without addressing cultural premises that legitimize or obscure violence (Bar-Tal 2013). When violence is perceived as a given element of societal reality, we can expect the evolvement of cultures within which power is considered a resource that must be monopolized. Such cultures of domination based upon power over relations and orientations not only guide attitudes towards sides in an ongoing violent conflict but also become an inherent dimension in group relations within conflict sides (Francis 2011).

Collective narratives of groups are a central aspect in the construction of group identity (Liu and Hilton 2005). Societies involved in conflicts form conflict-supporting narratives that play an essential role in satisfying the identity-based needs of the individuals and the collective. These narratives tend to focus on the themes of threats and delegitimization of the opponent, glorification and victimhood of the ingroup, the need for patriotism and unity, and the ingroup's aspiration for peace (Bar-Tal 2013).

Therefore, the students involved in this research were, challenged by the encounter with Palestinian narratives that challenge perceptions of the self, the other, and the conflict relations. A shift towards favorable positions to resolve conflict in a non-violent manner would involve emotional and cognitive challenges. Conflict reality has to be addressed from a complexity perspective, i. e., a reality in which the roles of victim and perpetrator are blurred. In contrast, Israelis must accept the loss of privileges for a while from a structural-political perspective since severe power asymmetry is an obstacle to reconciliation (Darweish 2010). The premise of these approaches is that through the belief system which underlies them, narratives play a crucial role in sustaining conflict and related intergroup relations (Sagy, Ayalon and Diab 2011). Collective representations of historical narratives based on the acknowledgement of the other can promote effective communication and behavior congruity, whereas contradicting representations are related to miscommunication and mistrust (Bar-On and Kassem 2004). These incidents lead to the proposition that the ability to acknowledge the other's narrative and recognize the inherent complexity of conflict relations can promote the readiness to reconcile (Sagy, Ayalon and Diab, 2011).

Such a shift in the context of violent conflict might ultimately contribute to the transition from passive to active bystander (Staub 2013). Passivity by witnesses or bystanders contributes massively to the evolution of violence and harm by groups (Ibidem). Contributing to the transformation of cultures of violence requires active bystandership (Lederach 2005). The shift toward active bystandership involves the ability to disengage from ethnocentric perceptions, contain the emotional challenges of acknowledging narratives that contradict collective assumptions about the conflict, and accept the moral obligation to address our contribution to violence even when this demands readiness to face psychological and material danger (Staub 2013). Addressing conflict without the defensive character of ethnocentric narratives creates the potential for the recognition of deeds that are morally "irrevocable" (Ferrari, present volume). Such acknowledgment may involve the painful experiences of remorse for wrongdoing, but at the same time, it may contribute to the potential for reconciliation. Efforts that are invested in denying memories of wrongdoing may be transformed into efforts to reconcile with deeds of the past, and attempts for actions that may contribute to a future guided by a commitment to moral obligations.

## 2.    Dialogue as a Generator of Change

Contact theory is the basis of most forms of dialogue encounters in general and particularly in Israel (Maoz 2012). Gordon Allport first formulated the theory in 1954 with his fundamental assumption that a direct encounter with the other creates opportunities to overcome negative stereotypes and humanize the other (Allport 1979). However, effective intergroup contact relies on conditions such as equal status of both groups in the contact situation, ongoing personal interaction between individuals from both groups, cooperation in a situation of mutual dependence, and institutional support attuned to norms related to equality (Pettigrew 1998). The critique of dialogue based on contact theory points out that it tends to disregard the political reality of asymmetric power relations. In this context, dialogue may prove counterproductive as the exposure to ongoing external power relations and the hostile environment may cancel the initial positive effect of the small group process (Maoz 2012).

Even though the inherent challenges of intergroup dialogue in the context of an asymmetric conflict are well-documented, less attention has been drawn to the use of intragroup dialogue as a principal setting. It is usually addressed as a supportive framework within an intergroup process and not as a principal framework in its own right (Rothman 2014). However, in the case of protracted conflict, distinct intragroup work might be necessary because we can expect conflicts towards the outgroup on the conflict sides. That is, conflicts within the sides that need attention to create the ability for constructive conflict engagement with the outgroup (Rambsbotham 2010).

The tradition of peace education and recent initiatives guided by conflict transformation perspectives focus on intragroup dialogue as a reflexive process (Broome and Collier 2012). In such dialogue programs, in-group members explore their multiple identities and different perspectives about possible ways to resolve the conflict on the intergroup level. Rothman (2014) argues that an intragroup dialogue that encourages critical reflexivity can contribute to complex thinking about the other by first fostering it within the ingroup.

This study aims to add propositions about the significance of intragroup dialogue by exploring how the intragroup setting might contribute to students' readiness to deeply explore in-intergroup conflict. Furthermore, this study examines the potential contribution to participants' readiness to address diverse perceptions of identities, power relations, and narratives, to adopt positions of critical reflexivity, challenge hegemonic perceptions of conflict reality, and explore alternative types of conflict engagement.

## 3a.  Method. Background: Field Site And Group Description

This research is part of the project "Hearts of Flesh–Not Stone," trilateral cooperation between German, Palestinian and Israeli researchers. The Israeli team conducted the study presented in this paper.

A major element in the Israeli research design is an academic year course in 2013–14 and 2014–15, each time with the participation of twenty-four Jewish Israeli B.A. students from the Department of Education at Ben-Gurion University. In the first course, approximately two-thirds of the students were women, whereas a third were men. In the second course, the majority of students were women, while only three participants were men. All students were in their mid-twenties (25–29 years, SD 1.16).

The course started with twelve weekly meetings, which combined learning about the nature of conflicts and engaging in a reflexive exploration of the participants' emotions and thoughts provoked by the topics. This was followed by encounters with Palestinian narratives involving two-day trips to sites connected to historical narratives about the Nakba and current everyday difficulties Palestinians face due to ongoing conflict. On these trips, participants met with Palestinians who shared their personal stories. In addition, dialogue sessions took place in which participants processed their experiences. In the last part of the course, several meetings were arranged in which participants processed the course experience. Two members of the Israeli research team facilitated the course, and the facilitation team was gender-balanced. The first author of this article was one of the facilitators.

The site tours aimed to provide opportunities for direct encounters with the other, which might have assisted in challenging prejudices and stereotypes. The introduction of theory-based knowledge on conflict challenged one-sided perceptions and assumptions. The encounter with and responses to Palestinian narratives served as an invitation to explore social constructions of conflict experiences and positions. The context of an Israeli ingroup exploring conflict with the Palestinian other aimed to address differences within the group.

## 3b. Method: Research Tools and Data Analysis

The study combined three qualitative components. First, phenomenological components, i. e., the student's understanding of what was happening, are expressed in their reflections about their learning experiences (Snape and Spencer 2003). Second, participative action research components are based on the joint exploration of evolving positions and group shifts towards the group's knowledge base (Kemmis and McTaggart 2000). Third, ethnographic elements are related to the contextualization of the group contents within a specific social reality, using participant observation by the researcher (Denzin and Lincoln 2000).

The data sources include recordings and verbatim transcriptions of the class sessions and discussions during the site visits, which were thematically analyzed (Ritchie, Spencer and O'Connor 2003). Another data source is a set of eight semi-structured individual interviews with randomly selected participants, conducted in the middle and at the end of each course. The interviews were recorded, transcribed, and analyzed by topic (Legard, Keegan and Ward 2003). A third source was a field diary in which the first author described his subjective experiences and observations of the evolving group processes (Denzin and Lincoln 2000). Major themes were derived from all three components. The findings were organized to provide the framework for an exploration of meanings that students ascribed to their learning experiences on conflict and students' insights about their involvement in the socially patterned context of conflict.

The research data was used to compare between findings of the academic year 2013–14 and 2014–15. These results enabled a comparison of the potential significance of shifting social reality foremost related to conflict escalation. In the summer of 2014, before the start of the academic year, the Israeli-Gaza conflict escalated. Israel launched a military operation in the Gaza strip while the Israeli public experienced rocket attacks from the Gaza strip. During the course, additional occurrences preoccupied students, such as the escalation of violence involving civilians in what is at times referred to as the Silent Intifada of summer 2014. This was also the case throughout the fall and winter of 2014–15.

## 4. Ethical Considerations

Students were informed about the research character of the course. To participate in the course was a voluntary decision. We coordinated the research together with the ethics committee of the Department of Education, which approved the combined set of academic courses and related research.

## 5. Findings

In this chapter, we present findings concerning the study goal, which was to explore the contribution of encountering narratives of the other in the setting of intragroup dialogue to reflexive learning about conflict reality. Furthermore, we explore the significance of escalating violence in group-based learning. We first summarize the major findings, then propose a conceptualization of the mechanisms that contribute to the social construction of conflict reality, which was implied throughout the evolving group conversations. The following sections focus on the main findings on the perceptions of "them and us" within the conflict and the evolving changes in these perceptions throughout the course process.

### 5.1 Encountering the Intergroup Other and the Other within the Group

The dynamic interrelations between encountering the intergroup other and the other within the group are striking discoveries. As participants discovered, the encounter with the Palestinian other triggered preoccupations with the other within the group. Both encounters reflected binary, competitive, and antagonistic premises about them-and-us relations. The intergroup division was based upon premises of the primacy of national identity as opposed to additional identity concepts, such as social class or gender. The major within-group division, particularly in the context of the escalation of conflict in the second year of 2014–2015, was defined by the political categories of right and left, which served as a defining label of all participants and their input to the dialogue.

### 5.2 Political Categories and Perceptions of Power Relations

The dialogue-based format of the course encouraged participants to explore the significance they ascribed to the political categories of right and left. This process led to reflexive observations about the power relations between social groups inherent to the categories of right and left. As students observed, these categories related to differences and related power relations in terms of ethnicity and social class, which were significant both within society and in the group.

### 5.3 Transitions from Binary Political Discourse to the Exploration of the Individual Experiences of Conflict Reality

Participants realized that the given ground rules of political discourse prioritize the presentation of competitive arguments and positions and the acting out of antagonistic group relations. The more participants disengaged from this form of discourse, the more they were able to pursue explorations of their individual experiences of conflict reality. Particularly in the aftermath of the Gaza war, participants explored the emotional challenges they experienced in escalating violence. Participants acknowledged their experiences of fear, anger, frustration, and even despair. Besides, the gradual deconstruction of a binary divide within the group contributed to the participants' ability to address the cognitive and emotional challenges they experienced in the encounter with the Palestinian other and explore the complexity of conflict relations between Israelis and Palestinians.

### 5.4 Coping with the Contradictions between the Political Discourse in Society and the Political Explorations in the Group

Participants struggled to contain the challenges inherent to the contradictions between the political discourse they experienced in society and the evolving political explorations they pursued in the course. They acknowledged the value of finding their distinct political voice, informed by their individual emotional experiences of conflict reality, value orientations, and active engagement with diverse facets of conflict reality. At the same time, participants were deeply aware that this involves active engagement with the contradictions between their effort at critical reflexivity and the hegemonic discourse based upon premises of competitive collective divides.

### 6. Students Discoveries about the Social Construction of Conflict Reality

Above, we presented the significant findings on perceptions of conflict reality and the evolving changes in these perceptions throughout the course. In the following sections, we elaborate on the major findings and propose a conceptualization of interrelated mechanisms that contribute to the social construction of conflict reality that was discerned throughout the course. Moreover, we outline the obstacles and opportunities for a change in the construction of conflict reality that could be determined. By using quotations from the documentation of the course meetings, we exemplify the social construction mechanisms and changes in the participants' involvement in these mechanisms as a result of the intragroup dialogue.

### 6.1 From Resistance to Engagement with the Other: Coping with Binary Perceptions of Inter- and Intragroup Relations

The first course in 2013–14 took place in a period of a relatively calm military situation, whereas the intragroup dialogue during the academic year of 2014–15 took place during a period of conflict escalation. The context of escalating violence contributed massively to the group's profound and antagonistic preoccupation with the intragroup other. Participants noted that the encounter with the Palestinian other drew their attention to the encounter with the intragroup political other. Dina, a female participant:

> Maybe before we talk about the Palestinian other, we have a problem here between ourselves; we do not see the other. We should stop telling each other that because I am a leftist or rightist, I am like this or like that, all those very definite labels. I feel that there is no openness towards me, which is very insulting.

As Dina expressed, the ingroup divide appeared of greater urgency and emotional challenge than the encounter with the Palestinian other. Participants also observed that whenever the group managed to move from the structures of binary and competitive confrontations, conversations gained depth and contributed to learning, as can be seen in the following example by Yasmin, a female participant:

> I think that we just had a real conversation. I don't know even how this actually happened. When I asked others about their thoughts, it was not in order to categorize them. It was really personal; I really wanted to know. Instead of defending my own positions, I wanted to know what you really think. I feel that our discourse in society is full of hate, and this is why I want to know the personal opinions; I want to know which thoughts people here in the room have. But please, let's not turn this again into categories.

The types of discovery that participants gained when they disengaged from binary confrontations indicate that the intragroup divide served as an unwitting defense against significant learning about the complexities of conflict reality, the emotional complexities inherent to the experiences of violent conflict, and the participants' involvement in both intergroup and intragroup power relations. The transition from acting out intragroup divisions to exploring these divisions implied the acknowledgement of participants' involvement in power relations between identity groups related to categories, such as ethnicity and social class. Although these categories underlie political concepts, they remained largely unaddressed as long as contradictions were limited to the categories of right and left.

## 6.2 We Are Fundamentally Different from Them: from Dichotomy to Complexity

Students initially assumed that their sense of self contrasts with that of the other entirely; in other words: "We are unlike them, they are unlike us." During the course, this way of thinking underwent a significant transformation. The course introduced complex perspectives about diverse collective identities, narratives, and power relations within Palestinian society. The resulting intragroup dialogue triggered a reflexive exploration of diversity and contradictions within Israeli society. The subsequent conversation serves as an example.

> Merav, a female participant: "In my opinion, our narrative is that we came to this land because we went through a disaster in Europe, and that is why we came here (to Israel)."
> Tamara, a female participant: "I agree with you. I took a course in which the narrative of the Holocaust was discussed, and there was the question – where is the narrative of the Mizrahi population [Oriental Jews, immigrants to Israel from North African and Middle Eastern countries] – and not just in the context of the Holocaust. Maybe here in this room, we are dealing with the conflict in opposition to somebody else [the Palestinians], and it is stronger [than the internal conflict], so we are more united in this room..."
> Merav, a female participant: "The question is whether you identify with the narrative of the Holocaust or it's not part of your narrative."
> Meital, a female participant: "But why does it contradict the collective narrative?"
> Oren, a male participant: "Because it is not the narrative of the Holocaust. Culture can dictate what [people] remember more or less, and that is how the conflict [between Ashkenazi and Mizrahi Jews] is being pushed aside [by the majority], just like they try to do with the Palestinians..."

At times, the emotional experience of complexity in perceptions of collectives and narratives was challenging. The group had to find ways to deal with the identity-based conflict between participants, mainly regarding ethnicity and religiosity/secularity. Dealing with identity-based conflicts increasingly enabled the group to succeed in relating to the other in the Israeli-Palestinian conflict from a perspective of diversity.

## 6.3 Beware of Knowledge. The Gains and Pains of Challenging Our Narratives

Throughout the course, students commented on how little knowledge they have about the complexity of the conflict and their partners in the conflict, the Palestinians. As they noted, learning about the other by encountering the other's narratives is generally deemed misleading and even illegitimate. Of interest is the observation made by some students at meetings towards the end of the course. They emphasized that a lack of knowledge about the other cannot be attributed only to a lack of opportunities. Dan, a male participant:

> You choose what to see. In the Student House on campus, "Breaking the Silence" [an NGO presenting a critical perspective about IDF actions towards the civilian population in the occupied territories] is always present; I always see them there. So, there are many ways to get to wherever you are ready to go to if you choose what to see.

The engagement with information that challenges perceptions of "us" and the "other" apparently involved difficult questions about justice and perceptions of the self within the conflict. During the course, students attributed great value to their encounters with new types of knowledge. For instance, Dana, a female participant, reflected at the last course meeting:

> The other day I was traveling by bus; all over the bus, I saw plugged-in phone chargers. It was a scary sight; I felt as if all people were being fed the same stuff. During the course, I thought about the narrative I was brought up to believe, about how much I believe in the narrative or whether it is an outcome of my upbringing, about my position on issues of politics, that I do not want to have things prescribed, I want to make up my mind on my own.

As exemplified in this quote, many participants realized that their knowledge and perceptions are rooted in one-sided narratives and perceived this as an important wake-up call. While this learning experience involved personal challenges, it proved to be liberating in the sense of increased individual autonomy as an outcome of exploring and assessing diverse types of knowledge and perceptions of conflict reality.

### 6.4 We Must Fear the Other. Complex Emotions That Await Acknowledgment

The fear of Palestinian students on the other side of the conflict was deeply rooted and powerful. Fear of Palestinians was a predisposition that was deemed self-evident apparently due to experiencing violence, such as suicide bombers and rocket attacks. From a narrative perspective, fear of the other appeared to be linked to the assumption that violence is mostly, or at least initially, directed against "us." Significant turning points were testimonies by students who served in the army and who shared their experiences of violence against the Palestinians.

Uri, a male participant, recalled: "It is obvious to me that if I were on their side, I would
be a member of the Hamas. I think everybody here or most of us went to the army, and it
isn't different from what they are doing."
Female participant [interrupts]: "But they conduct terror attacks!"
Male participant [interrupts]: "And what do we do?! We arrest them in the middle of the
night! You know how many people [detainees] I took [out of their beds] in the nighttime?
It could be that this person is ok; we do terrible things!"

In such intense debates, the group addressed the possibility that Israelis are not
the only ones who experience fear in the ongoing conflict. Notably when students
processed the encounters with Palestinians who shared their experiences of the
conflict, they explored the emotional impact of realizing that the fear of the other,
as an outcome of experiencing violence, is inherent in being Palestinian.

In these explorations, students faced several emotional challenges; some of them
related to justice. Could we possibly acknowledge the experiences of the other
and yet retain our sense of collective self, anchored in our narratives? At the same
time, students had to cope with the emotional impact of acknowledging the painful
emotions of the other in conflict. In a reflection meeting after a site visit, Yael, a
female participant, recalled: *"If I speak about the tour, I felt anger and sadness, I felt
like on 'Yom Hazikaron'* [Memorial Day for victims of war]. *The anger was for both
sides and sadness for them."*

These explorations did not necessarily result in losing the fear of the other. As
expressed by some, fear of the other is deep-seated, but learning about the pain and
fears of the other contributes to the ability to differentiate between fear intrinsic to
our experience of conflict and the ability to relate to the other beyond the one-sided
attribution of violence.

## 6.5 There is Nothing I Can Do to Solve the Conflict: From the Deconstruction of Binary Political Relations to the Position of Active Bystander

The more the group challenged the mechanisms described so far, the more we could
discern an additional mechanism related to agency, specifically the belief that "I as
an individual" cannot contribute to change in the ongoing conflict.

Following meetings in which the participants explored their involvement in
the mechanisms of intractable conflict with growing reflexivity, the feasibility of
agency became a concern. Eventually, doubts were raised about the value of the
group's learning: What is the value of the unsettling learning experience since we
cannot use the knowledge gained to solve the conflict? If the starting point was
the assumption that the conflict cannot be resolved because of the other's refusal,

the group later related to the possibility that we, too, as a society, contribute to the ongoing conflict. However, the assumption that this conflict is beyond the scope of our influence remained given. In that sense, the mechanism of accepting violence as unavoidable remained intact. The conversations and reflections towards the end of the course indicate students' attempts to challenge this mechanism.

> Yair, a male participant: "You see a certain reality, and you have to deal with what you have seen".
> Ruth, a female participant: "I do feel that I have a responsibility to say that there is another side. I don't intend to do an awareness campaign about it, but on the personal level, I did see the others' narrative."

As can be seen, the drive to act upon reflexive-gained knowledge is strong. In the last meetings, when students discussed the impact of the course, many shared their desire to take more responsibility to gain knowledge about the conflict, to be critical of the assumptions that guide public discourse and challenge the positions and opinions of their friends and families.

We suggest that this shift indicates disengagement from positions of passive acceptance of a given conflict reality. Participants acknowledged the option to address the conflict from a position of critical reflexivity and act according to their perceptions, even if this will create challenges and conflicts with others in one's society. Students acknowledged that, as individuals, they could not transform the conflict. However, in their personal context, they recognized their ability to gain more autonomy in positioning themselves concerning the premises of conflict discourse in Israeli society.

## 7. Discussion

This study aimed to explore the contribution of encountering narratives of the other in the setting of intragroup dialogue to reflexive learning about conflict reality. The university course aimed to create a learning environment that encouraged reflexivity in exploring the participants' involvement in collective narratives, related identities, and power relations. This dialogue-based exploration involved the cognitive and emotional dimensions of learning as a process of change.

We have presented the major findings on perceptions of conflict reality and the potential significance of conflict escalation to the intragroup dialogue. In addition, we have presented collective assumptions that are evident throughout the evolving conversations in the group and that are of significance to students' involvement in the social construction of conflict reality. We suggest that premises related to

Israeli deep culture, a culture that is embedded in the given structure of the conflict, influence these assumptions (Galtung 2009). These mechanisms serve to adjust students' perceptions of ongoing conflict and the violence involved (Bar-Tal 2013). The findings support previous studies, which indicate that in the context of violent conflict, specifically in the context of escalation, there is the potential for the evolution of corresponding societal structures and cultures that represent power over relations and assumptions (Francis 2011).

Moreover, the findings also support prior studies which relate to the role of narratives in supporting mechanisms that contribute to a moral disengagement from violence towards the other and indicate the potential contribution of encountering narratives of the other to reconciliation (Sagy, Ayalon and Diab 2011). Furthermore, the results add evidence to propositions about the potential contribution of intragroup work to constructive conflict engagement in the context of deep-seated intergroup conflict (Rothman 2014). We also propose that these findings indicate the contribution of specific cultural premises to the position of a passive bystander in relation to violence towards the other, the challenges and opportunities for the transformation of these premises in the context of intragroup work, and the contribution of such transformations towards transitioning into the position of an active bystander (Staub 2013).

The participative inquiry approach that guided the facilitation of the learning and the research process aimed to create opportunities for discovery. Participants in such a process attempt to explore the complexities and challenges of a given societal reality, the types of change they want to promote, and opportunities and obstacles towards change (Gergen and Gergen 2001). It is a deeply political process, a process of emancipation, since it aims to empower participants to contribute towards change; change attuned to challenges of justice and equality (Lederach 2005).

The learning process discussed in this paper reflects this orientation. This participative inquiry-inspired learning process dealt chiefly with shared involvement in the deep structure and deep culture of ongoing violence related to the Israeli-Palestinian conflict. However, the conflict-related structure and culture could not be separated from diverse power relations within Israeli society (Francis 2011). As we discovered, the focus of encountering narratives of the other runs counter to premises that guide thoughts, emotions, and actions within Israeli conflict discourse (Adwan, Bar-Tal and Wexler 2014). The exploration of cognitive and emotional responses to this learning focus led to the discovery of mechanisms that obscure, contextualize, and justify involvement in violence. Such learning provided an opportunity to experience an environment that contradicts many of the premises of the deep culture of violence. Power relations, their significance, and our involvement and contribution to them, have been critically assessed throughout the paper. Collective identities have been addressed in terms of diversity and complexity, and the political history of the conflict has been explored from different perspectives. Within such a learning environment, the individual is encouraged to explore emotional and cognitive challenges inherent to the attempt to overcome the given political discourse; encountering the narratives of the other becomes an opportunity to address conflict relations from perspectives attuned to reconciliation, such as the acknowledgement of diverse narratives, empathy for the suffering of the other, and the potential to address violence as an element that is inherent in the conflict and not necessarily attributed only to the other (Lederach 2010, Nadler, Malloy and Fisher 2008).

The research findings discussed in this paper raise questions that demand further attention. To what extent can a specific case study contribute to understanding processes in societies in violent conflict (generally) and within Israeli society (particularly)? The case study provides insights into the significance of evolving structural and cultural mechanisms in the context of violent conflict and escalation. However, further research on the findings presented in this paper could address their significance on a societal level. Similarly, regarding the processes of change that were discerned in this research, the question arises of how significant they are on a societal level, most importantly concerning transitions from positions of a passive to an active bystander?

Moreover, what is the potential role of education institutions in promoting critical learning in the context of ongoing conflict? Under what conditions and to what degree can the academic environment encourage learning that challenges major premises of hegemonic political discourse? Finally, this research focused on the processes of learning and change that could be observed during the course. However, the potential contribution of the course to the perception and position of the participants over time demands further study.

The findings of this study contributed to understanding the mechanisms that nurture the acceptance and even support for addressing the conflict by mainly violent means. We hope that further research on critical reflexivity in the midst of violent conflict will indicate how a transformation of the culture of violence can become feasible.

### References

Adwan, S., Bar-Tal, D., Wexler, B.E. 2014, 'Portrayal of the Other in Palestinian and Israeli Schoolbooks. A Comparative Study', *Political Psychology*, vol. 37, no. 2, pp. 201–217.

Allport, G. 1979, *The Nature of Prejudice*, Addison-Wesley, Reading, PA.

Bar-On, D., Kassem, F. 2004, 'Storytelling as a Way to Work Through Intractable Conflicts. The German-Jewish Experience and its Relevance to the Palestinian-Israeli Context', *Journal of Social Issues*, vol. 60, no. 2, pp. 289–306.

Bar-Tal, D. 2013, *Intractable Conflicts. Socio-Psychological Foundations and Dynamics*, Cambridge University Press, Cambridge, UK.

Broome, B.J., Collier, M.J. 2012, 'Culture, Communication, and Peacebuilding. A Reflexive Multi-Dimensional Contextual Framework', *Journal of International and Intercultural Communication*, vol. 5, no. 4, pp. 245–269.

Darweish, M. 2010, 'Human Rights and the Imbalance of Power. The Palestinian-Israeli conflict', in *Human Rights and Conflict Transformation. The Challenges of Just Peace. Berghof Handbook for Conflict Transformation Dialogue*, eds V. Dudouet, B. Schmelzle, Berghof Conflict Research, Berlin, pp. 85–94.

Denzin, N.K., Lincoln, Y.S. 2000, 'The Discipline and Practice of Qualitative Research', in *Handbook of Qualitative Research*, eds N.K. Denzin, Y.S. Lincoln, Sage, London, pp. 1–28.

Ferrari, F. 2022, 'The Concept of Reconciliation after Auschwitz. Hermeneutic Phenomenology of the Irrevocable', present volume.

Francis, D. 2011, 'New Thoughts on Power. Closing the Gaps Between Theory and Action', in *Advancing Conflict Transformation. The Berghof Handbook II*, eds B. Austin, M. Fischer, H.J. Giessmann, Barbara Budrich Publishers, Opladen, pp. 505–525.

Galtung, J. 2009, *A Theory of Conflict, a Theory of Development, a Theory of Civilization, a Theory of Peace*, Transcend University Press, Oslo.

Gergen, K.J., Gergen, M.M. 2001, "Social Construction and Research as Action", in *Handbook of Action Research. Participative Inquiry and Practice*, eds P. Reason, H. Bradbury, Sage, London, pp. 159–170.

Kemmis, S., McTaggart, R. 2000, 'Participatory Action Research', in *Handbook of Qualitative Research*, in *Handbook of Qualitative Research*, eds N.K. Denzin, Y.S. Lincoln, Sage, London, pp. 567–605.

Lederach, J.P. 2010, *The Moral Imagination. The Art and Soul of Building Peace*, Oxford University Press, Oxford.

Lederach, J.P. 1996, *Preparing for Peace. Conflict Transformation across Cultures*, Syracuse University Press, Syracuse, NY.

Legard, R., Keegan, J., Ward, K. 2003, 'In-Depth Interviews', in *Qualitative Research Practice*, eds L. Ritchie, J. Lewis, Sage, London, pp. 138–169.

Liu, J., Hilton, D. 2005, 'How the Past Weighs on the Present. Social Representations of History and Their Rule in Identity Politics', British Journal of Social Psychology, vol. 44, pp. 1–21.

Maoz, I. 2012, 'Contact and Social Change in an Ongoing Asymmetrical Conflict. Four Social-Psychological Models of Reconciliation-Aimed Planned Encounters Between Israeli Jews and Palestinians', in *Beyond Prejudice. Extending the Social Psychology of Conflict, Inequality and Social Change*, eds J. Dixon, M. Levine, Cambridge University Press, Cambridge, UK, pp. 269–285.

Miall, H. 2004, 'Conflict Transformation. A Multi-Dimensional Task', in *Transforming Ethnopolitical Conflict. The Berghof Handbook*, eds A. Austin, M. Fischer, N. Ropers, VS Verlag, Berlin.

Nadler, A., Malloy, T., Fisher, J.D. 2008, 'Intergroup Reconciliation. Dimensions and Themes', in *Social Psychology of Intergroup Reconciliation*, eds A. Nadler, T. Malloy, J.D. Fisher, Oxford University Press, New York, pp. 3–12.

Pettigrew, T.F. 1998, 'Inter-Group Contact Theory', *Annual Review of Psychology*, vol. 49, pp. 65–85.

Rambsbotham, O. 2010, *Transforming Violent Conflict,* Routledge, London.

Ritchie, J., Spencer, L., O'Connor, W. 2003, 'Carrying Out Qualitative Analysis', in *Qualitative Research Practice,* eds L. Ritchie, J. Lewis, Sage, London, pp. 219–262.

Rothman, J. 2014, 'From Intragroup Conflict to Intergroup Cooperation', in *Intersectionality and Social Change,* ed L.M. Woehrle, Emerald Group Publishing, Bingley, UK, pp. 107–123.

Sagy, S., Ayalon, A., Diab, K. 2011, 'Perceptions of the Narrative of the 'Other' among Arab and Jewish Adolescents in Israel. Between Peace Talks and Violent Events', *Intercultural Education,* vol. 22, no. 2, pp. 191–206.

Snape, D., Spencer, L. 2003, 'The Foundations of Qualitative Research', in *Qualitative Research Practice*, eds J. Ritchie, J. Lewis, Sage, London, pp. 2–23.

Staub, E. 2013, 'A World Without Genocide. Prevention, Reconciliation, and the Creation of Peaceful Societies', *Journal of Social Issues*, vol. 69, no. 1, pp. 180–199.

Sternberg, M. 2017, *Jewish Israeli Students Encounter Palestinian Conflict Related narratives*, Ph.D dissertation, Ben-Gurion University of the Negev.

Sternberg, M., Litvak Hirsch, T., Sagy, S. 2018, 'Nobody Ever Told Us. The Contribution of Intragroup Dialogue to Reflexive Learning about Violent Conflict', *Peace and Conflict: Journal of Peace Psychology*, vol. 24, no. 2, pp. 127–138.

Efrat Zigenlaub, Shifra Sagy

# Learning the Narrative of the Other

## What Type of Encounter is More Effective?

### Abstract

Efrat Zigenlaub and Shifra Sagy's contribution: *Learning the Narrative of the Other. What Type of Encounter is More Effective?* compares two types of dialogue groups (intra- and intergroup), among students at the Ben-Gurion University of the Negev in the academic year of 2016–2017. The intra-group included only Jewish students, whereby the inter-group included Jewish and Bedouin students. Aiming to measure the increase of willingness to reconcile, the authors tested whether interpersonal contact constitutes an advantage or might inhibit the processes of acknowledging the other and their narratives. The findings indicate that the legitimacy of the Palestinian narrative and trust towards Palestinians increased in both groups, while hatred, fear, and anger toward Palestinians decreased. Moreover, feelings of shame among Jewish participants towards Palestinians increased in the intra-group and decreased in the inter-group. Correlations between the different variables strengthened in the intra-group and not in the inter-group, indicating the possibility of developing a more coherent and less confused stance regarding the conflict in the intra-group but not in the inter-group.

### 1. Intergroup Relations in Conflict Situations

Research in the field of intergroup relations has developed considerably during the last decades (Sternberg, Litvack-Hirsch and Sagy 2017) in an attempt to reduce stress and prejudices between groups in conflict. The most common and accepted approach, known as the contact approach, was developed by Allport (1954), who claimed that the best way to reduce stress between members of groups in conflict is to bring people from two rival groups in contact with one another. Many social programs were developed based on the contact approach, such as ethnically integrative schools, racially mixed neighborhoods, and others (Nadler 2000). A meta-analytical study (Pettigrew and Tropp 2011) analyzed 713 independent samples from 515 research studies, which examined contact-based programs in 38 countries. Pettigrew and Tropp's study supported the approach's effectiveness by reducing prejudice between groups of different background, age, and other characteristics.

Other recent studies indicate the limitations of this approach. One limitation is that interpersonal experiences do not necessarily affect attitudes towards the whole group (Hewstone and Brown 1986). Another limitation is the difference between the majority and the minority group regarding the needs and expectations of group communication. While the majority group wants to preserve the status quo, the minority group aims for a change (Sidanius and Pratto 1999). Studies have shown that in joint meetings, members of the minority group preferred to talk about the inequality of power between the groups, while the majority group tried to blur inequalities by drawing attention to similarities between the groups and to encouraging a more personal discourse (Saguy, Dovidio and Pratto 2008; Suleiman 2000). Regardless of these limitations, the contact approach is still the primary approach on which dialogue groups are based.

Dialogue groups serve to reduce prejudice and hostility between groups in conflict (Bar Tal 2002; Salomon 2002; Stephan and Stephan 2001). In the form of meetings, dialogue groups are designed to help the participants understand the conflict and suggest ways to deal with it. This process includes the development of the participants' awareness of the complexity of the conflict and their role in it as well as the investigation and construction of their identity (Sagy, Steinberg and Fahiraladin 2002). Dialogue groups are a particular type of discourse that produces dialogues and differs from the usual meaning of a discourse between two people and from a discussion:

> "Discussion is almost like a Ping-Pong game, where people are batting the ideas back and forth, and the object of the game is to win or to get points for yourself […]. In a dialogue, however, nobody is trying to win. Everybody wins if anybody wins. There is a different sort of spirit to it. In a dialogue, there is no attempt to gain points or to make your particular view prevail. Rather, whenever any mistake is discovered on the part of anybody, everybody gains. It's a situation called win-win, in which we are not playing a game against each other but with each other. In a dialogue, everybody wins." (Bohm 1990, p. 2)

Bohm views dialogue as an essence rather than a discourse between two people: "a dialogue can be among any number of people, not necessarily two. Even one person can have a sense of dialogue within himself if the spirit of the dialogue is present" (Ibid., p. 2). This in-depth approach is most relevant to the present research, which refers to an intra-group as a dialogue group.

## 1.1 Dialogue Groups in the Israeli-Palestinian Conflict

The present study was conducted in the context of the Israeli-Palestinian intractable conflict. The intractability of this conflict is partly rooted in the adversaries' construction of collective identities resulting in de-legitimization of the narratives of the other (Bar Tal 2007).

Dialogue groups between Jews and Arabs in Israel began to develop in the 1980s to create a dialogue between the parties. They have been inter-group mainly based on the contact approach (Bar and Bar Gal 1995; Kelman 1998; Maoz 2011; Salomon 2002). Studies that evaluated the effect of such interventions found that dialogue groups led to greater acceptance of the Palestinian other by Israelis (e. g., Maoz and Ellis 2008) but simultaneously threatened the core elements of their own identity (Ron and Maoz 2013).

## 1.2 The Intra-Group

The intra-group approach of learning about the other group without interpersonal contact between the groups in conflict is less accepted in the professional literature than inter-group contact and has only recently appeared in the publication of several articles (Ben David et al. 2017; Ford 2012; Sternberg, Litvak Hirsch and Sagy 2017). This approach offers an alternative path to developing familiarities with the collective narrative of the other by reading literature, listening to lectures, participating in relevant tours, etc. Among other reasons, this approach developed as a result of the constraints of reality that prevented contact between representatives of Israeli and Palestinian groups in the conflict (Sagy 2017). The theoretical framework for these groups is not based on the contact approach but the acknowledgment of the other's narrative as a way to promote reconciliation and reduce hostility and violence among groups in conflict (Bar Tal 2013). Evaluation studies that recently investigated several intra-group programs found that working in the intra-group encouraged dynamic exposure of variance within the group, linked to collective identities, narratives, and power relations. During the program, the participants developed the ability to reflexively criticize the Israeli-Palestinian conflict reflexively and to understand the complexities inherent in these identities. The perspective of understanding complexity contributed to the participant's ability to be more empathic to the suffering of the other and to address the emotional and cognitive challenges of critical reflexivity in the context of the conflict (Sternberg, Litvak Hirsch and Sagy 2017). Moreover, the exposure of Israeli Jewish students to the Palestinian narrative produced an increased level of acceptance of both Israeli and Palestinian narratives as well as a greater willingness to reconcile, assume responsibility, and apologize for the wrongdoings of the past (Ben David et al. 2017).

In another comparative research conducted in an American school, Ford (2012) compared the formation of white identity among white people who participated in this intra-group to that of white people who participated in an inter-group that included both white and non-white students. The researcher found that both groups achieved their goal of creating a more complex personal and theoretical understanding of white identity and its development.

Several studies describe intra-groups that are part of a broader set of inter-group dialogue. For example, Sonnenschein and Hijazi (2000) describe a program for Jewish and Arab Israelis that included separate intra-group meetings called "house groups," which then met for three joint inter-group meetings. A facilitator guided each intra-group from the same identity group, who spoke the same mother tongue as the participants. Those groups were arranged based on the understanding that each national group has its own dilemmas and different questions requiring a separate discussion framework. The intra-group meetings were described as more relaxed than the joint meetings and were more efficient and significant. Moreover, some issues arose only in the separate forum, such as investigating sub-identities within each group.

Falach-Galil, Kawshinsky, and Bargal (2002) described a program where Israelis and new immigrants from Russia to Israel met for six separate intra-group meetings to prepare for joint meetings between the two groups. The intra-group meetings were designed to allow participants to explore their attitudes towards the other authentically before the joint meetings. The researchers reported that working on identity questions in separate groups enabled significant processes within the joint meetings.

To summarize, the development of intra-group meetings without joint meetings in dialogue groups is a new tool with only a few studies in the critical literature. While there are several studies where intra-group meetings were part of a broader inter-group framework, in recent years, pioneering studies have been conducted examining intra-groups that have been exposed to the narrative of the other as stand-alone interventions. The main advantages of dialogue in the intra-group include accessibility, for example, when political tensions complicate the process of bringing Palestinian and Israeli groups together. Another advantage is the opportunity of a safe space in which the variety of identities within the group and subconscious attitudes towards the other can be thoroughly explored (Sagy 2017). This investigation, which is essential for accepting the other (Lev-Weisel and Kassen 2002), is not always possible in inter-groups (Falach-Galil, Kawshinsky and Bar Gal 2002; Sonnenschein and Hajazi 2000).

## 2. Inter versus Intra-Group: Comparative Research

The review above presents two approaches to interventions (inter- and intragroup) reduce prejudice and hostility between groups in conflict. The current study compared these two approaches in the context of the Israeli-Palestinian conflict within the framework of courses at the Ben-Gurion University of the Negev. We examined the results of the two approaches, measured by levels of acknowledgment of the collective narrative of the other and the willingness to reconcile.

As far as we know, no similar studies that compare inter-and intragroup approaches have been conducted. In an in-depth review, we found the aforementioned qualitative study by Ford (2012) that compared an intra-group of white students and an inter-group of white and non-white students and found that both groups achieved their goal of creating a more complex personal and theoretical understanding of white identity and its development.

The current study is thus innovative in comparing two kinds of dialogue groups: an inter- and an intra-group. The initiators defined the purpose of the respective group meetings as acknowledging the collective narrative of the other and increasing group members' willingness to reconcile (Sagy 2017). The study examined how and to what extent each group contributed to this goal. Was there an advantage to the interpersonal contact, or did the contact block processes of recognizing the other?

In the study of relations between groups in conflict, several common and accepted variables were selected for comparison: the perception of collective narratives, feelings towards the other, trust in the other, and the willingness to reconcile. Those variables represent the goals of the initiators of the dialogue group.

### 2.1 Perception of Collective Narratives

Collective narratives of group history construct the group's identity and help the group members understand who they are and who the others are (Liu and Hilton 2005). Within groups in conflict, social beliefs are usually characterized by claims of exclusive legitimization, victimization, and the justification of in-group goals (Bar Tal 2007).

Since collective narratives play a crucial role in the formation and perpetuation of conflicts between groups, the acceptance of the collective narratives of the other is necessary for reducing these conflicts in the process of conflict resolution (Bar Tal and Halperin 2009). A study conducted among Israelis and Palestinians from the West Bank found that Israelis who believed that Palestinians recognized their narrative, the Holocaust, were more willing to take responsibility for Palestinian suffering and offer an apology for Israeli wrongdoings. The same applied to Palestinians who believed that the Israelis recognized their narrative, the Nakba (Hameiri and Nadler 2017).

Sagy, Adwan, and Kaplan (2002) developed a tool for exploring the cognitive and emotional elements of perceptions attributed to the collective narratives of what they termed the "in-group," the group to whom one belongs, and the "out-group," the group to whom the other belongs. The cognitive element is the legitimization of collective narratives, and the emotional elements are empathy and anger towards those narratives. Their study used these indices to understand the relationship between Israelis and Palestinians by presenting different collective narratives of historical and political events, such as the Holocaust, the 1948 War, and the assassination of Prime Minister Yitzhak Rabin. A longitudinal study conducted between 1999 and 2007 found that perceptions of collective narratives are a sensitive tool for measuring relationships between groups over time and reflecting changes in attitudes towards the other in the context of different socio-political situations (Sagy, Ayalon and Diab 2011). Until now, this index has been used in research to compare a variety of Israeli and Palestinian groups (Mana et al. 2015; Sagy, Adwan and Kaplan, 2002; Srour et al. 2013; Srour, Mana and Sagy 2016).

A recent longitudinal study examined the collective narratives of the in-group and out-group of young Jewish and Arab citizens of Israel over four periods: 1999–2000, 2002, 2004, and 2009. The study showed an increase in adhering to the narrative of the in-group and the denial of the legitimacy of the out-group's narratives over time, both in cognitive and emotional elements. In addition to examining the increasing or decreasing legitimacy of the narratives, Sagy et al. (2002) also analyzed the connections between the various narrative indices and the relationships between these indicators and attitudes towards ending the conflict. They examined the correlations between attitudes towards the narrative of the other and attitudes towards ending the conflict and the possibility of settling it. The researchers found that the higher the legitimization and empathy for the other narrative and the lower the level of anger directed at the other narrative, the higher the belief that the conflict could be resolved through positive processes, such as education, socialization, and trust-building. In another study, Srour, Mana, and Sagy (2016) examined the relationship between the cognitive index of legitimization of narratives, the emotional measures of empathy for narratives, and anger about those narratives throughout various periods of the Israeli-Palestinian conflict. The findings of this study revealed that the correlations were stronger during periods of violence than during calm times. For example, during the Oslo Accords, which provided hope for peace, the correlation was the weakest. The researchers explained the findings by the need for each group to feel coherent during stressful periods.

## 2.2 Emotions Felt about the Other

Emotions felt about the other play a significant role in conflict situations between groups (Bar Tal and Halperin 2009; Halperin and Gross 2011). Negative emotions lead to the rejection of positive information about the opponent (Cohen Chen et al. 2014) and opposition to negotiations, compromise, and reconciliation (Halperin 2011). Moreover, such emotions can influence political attitudes and attitudes during war (Horovitz 1985; Petersen 2002) and motivate people to participate actively in or support passive acts of violence (Halperin and Gross 2011). The emotions studied were empathy, fear, hatred, anger, and shame.

## 2.3 Trust in the Other

Trust is the confidence in the words and actions of the other and the willingness to act on and accept them. Trust is crucial for conflict resolution and successful decision-making (Maoz and Ellis 2008). Studies have shown that trust in the other is associated with a greater willingness to settle conflicts through compromise and the expansion of identity (Gaertner and Dovidio 2000). Moreover, trust is a condition for the influence of other variables, such as empathy (Nadler and Livitan 2006).

## 2.4 Willingness to Reconcile

Nadler and Shnabel (2006) noted a difference between instrumental reconciliation, which includes the cooperation between adversaries to achieve instrumental goals, and socio-emotional reconciliation, which emphasizes the realization of the emotional needs of the members of each side in the reconciliation process. In this study, we used a measure of socio-emotional reconciliation including emotional parameters, such as the expression of goodwill towards the other, the wish to be close to each other, the perception of the other as human, and the desire to learn about the other's culture (Shnabel et al. 2009).

## 2.5 Hypotheses

This study attempts to examine two types of encounters in intractable conflict via intra- and inter-group meetings. The main question addressed whether inter- or intra-group contact was more successful in enhancing the legitimacy of the other and readiness to reconcile. Based on previously reviewed critical literature, and according to the potential of the intra-group, as shown above, we expected that despite its "newness," the intra-group would yield results similar to those of the inter-group. The following section provides an overview of the detailed hypotheses:
1. Both groups would show an increase in the measures of legitimacy and empathy for the Palestinian narratives and the degree of knowledge about it, whereas the anger over the Palestinian narratives would decline. Moreover, feelings of fear, hatred, and anger would decrease in both groups, while the level of shame would rise. Trust and readiness to reconcile would increase in both groups. At

the same time, according to the results of previous studies mentioned above, we expected an advantage for the intra-group in accepting the narrative of the in-group (the Israeli narrative). Thus, the legitimacy of the Israeli narrative would increase in the intra-group and decrease in the inter-group. Beyond the hypothesis that the intra-group will produce similar results as the inter-group in the various measures, we expected the intra-group to have an advantage in formulating a more coherent position regarding the Israeli-Palestinian conflict because the limitations described above had less influence on the safe space in which we explored the attitude towards the other (Sagy 2017). Therefore, the limitations had less impact on the different needs of the majority and minority groups, which draw the discourse in different directions (Saguy, Dovidio and Pratto 2008; Suleiman 2000).

2. Only in the intra-group would there be an increase in correlations between the variables of perceptions of collective narratives, emotions felt towards the other, trust in the other, and the willingness to reconcile. Strengthening the correlations between the various variables means a more coherent conception of the conflict, which attests to a more consolidated approach. The weakening of the variables, on the other hand, would lead to a more confused perception, which indicates a lack of clarity and understanding of the positions regarding the conflict.

## 3. Method

### 3.1 The Research Setting

Two dialogue groups were carried out as semester-long courses in the Department of Education at the Ben-Gurion University of the Negev during the academic year of 2016–17. Each course consisted of thirteen weekly sessions and a study tour. The course included two sessions at the start of the course and five lectures (four on the subject of the Palestinian narrative and one on the Jewish Israeli narrative), followed by a group processing session and a closing session. The lecturers were academics and social activists, some Jewish Israeli and some Palestinian, who presented various aspects of the collective Palestinian narratives and the Jewish Israeli collective narrative in the one lecture dedicated to it.

The first dialogue group was an intra-group of Jewish Israeli students. The group included seventeen students in the second and third years of their undergraduate degree in education, of whom fourteen were women, and three were men. Two Jewish Israeli facilitators guided the group, a man, and a woman. One of them also co-facilitated the inter-group described below.

The second dialogue group was an inter-group of Israeli Jews and Israeli Arab students. Israeli Arabs (also referred to as Palestinian citizens of the State of Israel) constitute 21% of the population of Israel (Central Bureau of Statistics, Israel, December 2018). They are comprised of a Muslim majority group (85%) and Christian, Druze, and Circassian minorities. In addition to having majority-minority relations with Jewish Israeli society, this group of Israeli Arabs perceives itself and is also perceived by the Jewish majority through the prism of their connection to the Israeli-Palestinian conflict. They are exposed to various forms of discrimination which create significant barriers to successful socio-economic integration in Israeli society (Smooha 2001). In the last two decades, however, there has been a significant advancement in the field of education among Israeli Arabs, and the gaps in educational attainment relative to the Jewish population have been reduced (Foulkes 2017). Over the past decade, a large increase in Israeli Arabs in higher education has been recorded (Council for Higher Education, January 2018). The most significant increase in educational attainment is among Israeli Arab women, positively affecting their employment rate (Foulkes 2017).

The group participating in this inter-group study included fifteen females, nine Jewish students in the second or third years of their undergraduate degree in education, and six Arab students studying for an undergraduate degree, including four students of education and psychology, and two students of social work. The group was co-facilitated by a male Jewish facilitator (who had also guided the intra-group) and an Arab female facilitator.

## 3.2 The Research Strategy

The method of study is quantitative. The study was designed to examine the intervention results, i. e., whether there was a change in the variables as a result of the intervention. The research tools were questionnaires administered to all participants at two points in time. The first questionnaire was distributed at the beginning and the second at the end of the course using a computerized system (Qualtrics) via email.

## 3.3 Measures

1. *Collective narratives of the in-group and the out-group*. We based our questionnaires on those developed by Sagy and colleagues (Sagy, Steinberg and Fahiraladin 2002), which examine legitimacy, empathy, knowledge, and anger towards different collective narratives of the in-group and the out-group. The collective narratives deal with historical events and significant issues related to the Israeli-Palestinian conflict: The Holocaust, the 1948 War, the Palestinian refugee issue, the Rabin assassination, the settlements, and the Intifada. For each narrative, the participants

were first confronted with the representative Jewish-Israeli narrative. For example: "Many Israelis see the Holocaust as the most terrible tragedy that any nation has ever experienced, which justifies the establishment of a Jewish state for the Jews". Then, the participants faced the representative Palestinian narrative. For example: "Many Palestinians see the Holocaust as a tragedy that happened to the Jewish people, which nevertheless does not justify causing suffering to the Palestinian people". For each of these narratives, the participants were asked to express their position on four levels: legitimization ("I think that the attitude of the Israelis/Palestinians is legitimate"), empathy ("I feel empathy for the attitude of the Israelis/Palestinians"), anger ("I am angry at the position of the Israelis/Palestinians"), as well as the degree of knowledge about the subject ("I know too little about the subject to relate to the question"). The answers were given on the Likert scale of 1 to 5 (1 = very wrong, 5 = very true). Cronbach's alpha ranged from .72 to .80 for the legitimacy measure, from .42 to .82 for the empathy measure, from .57 to .84 for the anger measure, and from .79 to .81 for the knowledge measure.

2. *Emotions felt towards the other.* This index is based on the Halperin and Gross (2011) questionnaire, which measured the Israeli's emotions of fear and anger towards Palestinians. We assessed the emotions of hatred and shame. The index questioned the Israeli respondents to describe their feelings towards Palestinians and vice versa in the inter-group on a scale of 1 to 6 (1 = not at all, 6 = very much). Each of these emotions is a measure in itself.

3. *Trust in the other.* This index was developed by Nadler and Liviatan (2006) and includes three statements in relation to the degree of trust Israelis have in Palestinians and vice versa in the inter-group. The respondents were asked to answer on a Likert scale of 1 to 7 (1 = do not agree at all, 7 = definitely agree.) The statements were: "I do not believe in the peaceful intentions of the Palestinians/ Israelis" (scale reversal), "In general, you can't trust Palestinians/Israelis," "I believe that if a peace agreement is signed, the Palestinians/Israelis will do their share in the agreement." The Cronbach Alpha index for the trust index changed from .80 before the intervention to .74 after the intervention.

4. Willingness to Reconcile. This index is based on the questionnaire by Shnabel et al. (2009), which includes ten questions and asks the respondents to express their opinions on eleven statements, which examine the willingness to reconcile with the Palestinians. On a scale of 1 to 7 (1 = do not agree, 7 = strongly agree), the participants could choose between statements such as "I think we should work to promote reconciliation between Israelis and Palestinians," "I think the Palestinians are just like us," "I would like to learn more about the culture of the Palestinians." The Cronbach Alpha index for this index changed from .84 before the intervention to .90 after the intervention.

## 3.4 Data Processing Was Carried Out in Two Ways

The first test analyzed how each indicator changed as a result of the intervention and whether the change was significant. For this purpose, we used the Repeated Measures ANOVA test separately for each of the dependent variables. The setting is mixed 2 * 2 with a measurement variable (before intervention/after intervention) as a variable within-subject and the type of group (intra-group/inter-group) as a variable between subjects.

The second test examined how the correlations between the different variables changed after the intervention. This test was designed to examine how each of the interventions affected the general map of the conflict perception beyond the question of how each of the individual variables changed. Strengthening the correlations between the various variables means a more coherent conception of the conflict, which attests to a more consolidated approach to the conflict. The weakening of the variables, on the other hand, means a more confused perception, which indicates a lack of clarity and understanding of the positions regarding the conflict. For this test, we calculated Pearson correlations for all the variables before and after each intervention for each group and examined whether the differences in the correlations between the pre-intervention and post-intervention measurements were significant by using Pearson and Filon's Z (1898) test.

## 4. Findings

### 4.1 Descriptive Statistics

Table 1 presents averages, standard deviations, and various analyzes of the variables before and after the interventions by comparing the intra-group and the inter-group. Despite the small sample, significant effects of change (before and after) were found in both groups for the following variables: fear of Palestinians ($F_{(1,24)} = 13.66$, $p < .01$) and anger towards Palestinians ($F_{(1,24)} = 5.45$, $p < .05$). Marginal significant effects of change (before and after) were found in both groups for the following variables: legitimacy of the Palestinian narrative ($F_{(1,24)}=3.52$, $p=.07$), hatred towards Palestinians ($F_{(1,24)} = 3.54$, $p =.07$), and trust in Palestinians ($F_{(1.24)} = 3.11$, $p =.09$). Interaction effects (before/after) X group (intra-group/inter-group) were found for the following variables: fear of Palestinians ($F_{(1.24)} = 4.62$, $p < .05$) and shame towards Palestinians ($F_{(1,24)}=5.33$, $p<.05$). We found no significant effects in the variable of the willingness to reconcile.

Table 1 Averages, standard deviations, and various analyzes of the variables before and after the interventions

| | | Intra-Group | | Inter-Group | | F value | |
|---|---|---|---|---|---|---|---|
| | | Before | After | Before | After | Within subject | Interaction |
| Legitimacy | Israeli narrative | 3.72 (±.65) | 3.72(±.68) | 3.30(±.35) | 3.52 (±.61) | 1.69 | 1.69 |
| Empathy | Israeli narrative | 3.20(±.73) | 3.34(±.54) | 3.11(±.33) | 3.21(±.29) | 1.07 | 0.31 |
| Anger | Israeli narrative | 2.05(±.59) | 2.26(±.47) | 1.98(±.54) | 2.08(±.63) | 1.49 | 0.21 |
| Knowledge | Israeli narrative | 3.80(±.73) | 3.96(±.71) | 4.14(±.65) | 4.05(±.61) | 0.49 | 0.77 |
| Legitimacy | Palestinian narrative | 3.19(±.66) | 3.47(±.63) | 3.21(±.48) | 3.37 (±.54) | 3.52 | 0.26 |
| Empathy | Palestinian narrative | 2.85(±.75) | 2.96(±.82) | 2.91(±.61) | 2.92(±.51) | 0.32 | 0.18 |
| Anger | Palestinian narrative | 2.36(±.71) | 2.35(±.62) | 1.91(±.58) | 1.91(±.44) | 0.00 | 0.00 |
| Knowledge | Palestinian narrative | 3.69(±.79) | 3.77(±.76) | 3.75(±.65) | 3.95(±.53) | 0.71 | 0.13 |
| Hatred | | 2.82(±1.29) | 2.53(±1.13) | 2.22(±.83) | 1.78(±.83) | 3.54* | 0.15 |
| Fear | | 4.53(±1.01) | 4.24(±1.20) | 4(±1.26) | 2.89(±1.17) | 13.66** | 4.62** |
| Anger | | 3.94(±1.25) | 3.53(±1.63) | 2.78(±1.20) | 2.11(±.78) | 5.45* | 0.31 |
| Shame | | 2.29(±1.31) | 3.29(±1.76) | 1.89(±1.27) | 1.67(±.87) | 2.16 | 5.35* |
| Trust | | 4.33(±1.52) | 4.77(±1.2) | 5.04(±1.12) | 5.33(±.94) | 3.11 | 0.11 |
| Willingness to reconcile | | 5.93(±.73) | 5.86(±.89) | 6.41(±.39) | 6.37(±.47) | 1.38 | 0.01 |

* p<.05   ** p<.01

Table 2 The correlations matrix between the variables in the intra-group before (upper triangle) and after (lower triangle)

Correlations

(up=before)

| | reconcile | trust | shame | anger | fear | harte | know P | anger P | empathy P | leg P | know l | anger l | empathy l | leg l |
|---|---|---|---|---|---|---|---|---|---|---|---|---|---|---|
| leg l | 0,08 | -.614** | -.504* | 0,45 | .714** | .503* | 0,04 | 0,17 | -0,36 | -0,18 | 0,12 | -.604* | 0,35 | — |
| empathy l | -0,07 | -0,19 | -0,32 | 0,00 | 0,21 | -0,13 | -0,09 | 0,21 | -0,44 | 0,05 | -0,05 | -0,27 | — | .757** |
| anger l | 0,19 | .713** | .648** | -0,31 | -.483* | -0,40 | -0,04 | -0,21 | .497* | 0,36 | -0,03 | — | -.544* | -.572* |
| know l | -0,07 | 0,13 | 0,13 | 0,23 | 0,35 | 0,15 | .916** | -.533* | 0,25 | 0,18 | — | -0,27 | 0,15 | 0,13 |
| leg P | 0,36 | .539* | 0,35 | -0,19 | 0,01 | -0,33 | 0,24 | -.509* | .510* | — | 0,07 | -0,01 | 0,17 | 0,35 |
| empathy P | 0,30 | .526* | 0,31 | -0,22 | -0,15 | -0,37 | 0,26 | -.660** | — | .492* | 0,06 | 0,45 | -0,10 | -0,32 |
| anger P | -0,08 | -.495* | -0,13 | 0,30 | -0,05 | 0,21 | -.568* | — | -0,34 | -0,45 | -0,36 | 0,17 | 0,23 | 0,12 |
| know P | 0,03 | 0,22 | 0,15 | 0,22 | 0,34 | 0,07 | — | -0,451 | 0,09 | 0,10 | .961** | -0,27 | 0,16 | 0,12 |
| hatred | -0,11 | -.661** | 0,00 | .772** | .607** | — | 0,26 | 0,35 | -.534* | -0,46 | 0,23 | -0,04 | 0,10 | 0,11 |
| fear | 0,29 | -.654** | -0,17 | .772** | — | .735** | 0,31 | 0,43 | -0,25 | -0,30 | 0,38 | -0,11 | 0,29 | 0,21 |
| anger | 0,07 | -.659** | -0,03 | — | 0,48 | .829** | -0,06 | .483* | -.723** | -.548* | -0,05 | -0,16 | 0,10 | 0,10 |
| shame | 0,23 | 0,38 | — | -0,3 | 0,02 | -0,24 | -0,11 | 0,27 | .619** | 0,15 | -0,08 | 0,47 | -0,01 | -0,23 |
| trust | -0,01 | — | 0,22 | -.509* | -.523* | -.550* | 0,13 | -0,20 | 0,43 | 0,15 | 0,18 | 0,22 | -0,17 | -0,28 |
| reconcile | — | .593* | .631** | -.549* | -0,43 | -.601* | 0,13 | -0,05 | .573* | .494* | 0,12 | 0,20 | 0,14 | -0,04 |

Table 3  The correlation matrix between the variables in the inter-group before (upper triangle) and after (lower triangle)

Correlations

| reconcile | trust | shame | anger | fear | hatred | know P | anger P | empathy P | leg P | know I | anger I | empathy I | leg I | up=before |
|---|---|---|---|---|---|---|---|---|---|---|---|---|---|---|
| -0,58 | 0,04 | -0,19 | 0,05 | 0,33 | 0,53 | -0,01 | 0,15 | -.815** | -.669* | 0,00 | -0,33 | 0,46 | _ | leg I |
| -0,70 | -0,11 | -.811** | 0,47 | 0,35 | 0,22 | 0,30 | 0,05 | -0,27 | -.720* | -0,13 | -0,27 | _ | 0,22 | empathy I |
| 0,56 | 0,62 | -0,16 | 0,21 | -0,21 | -0,34 | -0,49 | 0,54 | 0,11 | 0,45 | -0,39 | _ | -0,36 | -.937** | anger I |
| -0,46 | -0,36 | 0,02 | -0,14 | -0,07 | 0,07 | 0,66 | -0,38 | 0,06 | 0,03 | _ | -0,04 | 0,22 | 0,03 | know I |
| .728* | 0,46 | 0,57 | -0,38 | -0,15 | -0,40 | -0,41 | -0,16 | 0,64 | _ | 0,42 | -0,43 | -0,20 | 0,36 | leg P |
| 0,33 | 0,14 | 0,26 | -0,35 | -0,40 | -.721* | 0,13 | -0,58 | _ | 0,44 | -0,09 | 0,40 | -0,50 | -0,42 | empathy P |
| 0,16 | 0,14 | -0,36 | .760* | 0,43 | 0,53 | -0,30 | _ | 0,16 | -0,33 | 0,05 | .796* | -0,50 | -.717* | anger P |
| -.754* | -0,48 | -0,30 | 0,24 | -0,05 | 0,05 | _ | 0,02 | -.723* | -0,05 | 0,59 | -0,30 | 0,54 | 0,24 | know P |
| -0,35 | -0,19 | -0,09 | 0,55 | .857** | _ | -0,15 | 0,42 | 0,12 | 0,16 | -0,33 | 0,17 | -0,59 | -0,23 | hatred |
| -0,28 | 0,12 | -0,16 | 0,59 | _ | 0,36 | -0,13 | -0,41 | 0,16 | .753* | -0,02 | -0,66 | -0,39 | 0,61 | fear |
| -0,31 | -0,05 | -.674* | _ | 0,56 | 0,62 | 0,23 | 0,24 | -0,29 | 0,15 | -0,01 | -0,20 | -0,58 | 0,27 | anger |
| 0,51 | 0,12 | _ | -0,49 | -0,04 | 0,06 | -0,16 | 0,05 | 0,58 | 0,29 | -0,10 | 0,12 | 0,16 | -0,30 | shame |
| 0,24 | _ | 0,10 | 0,23 | 0,15 | 0,00 | 0,50 | 0,00 | 0,05 | 0,48 | 0,66 | -0,06 | 0,04 | 0,07 | trust |
| _ | 0,42 | 0,45 | -0,28 | -0,10 | -0,22 | -0,21 | -0,17 | 0,46 | 0,03 | -0,14 | 0,16 | 0,04 | -0,19 | reconcile |

In accordance with the second hypothesis, the correlations between the various variables increased in the intra-group. However, in the inter-group, the correlations between the variables weakened or remained similar to the initial correlations. To examine whether the differences in the correlations between pre-intervention and post-intervention measurements were significant, we performed a series of Pearson and Filon's Z tests (1898) to examine whether the differences in the correlations between pre-intervention and post-intervention measurements were significant.

## 4.2    Findings for the Intra-Group

Some of the results are noteworthy. We could find significant changes ($z = -2.10$, $p < .05$) between trust in Palestinians and the willingness to reconcile before ($r = -.01$) versus after intervention ($r = .59^*$) in the intra-group. Moreover, while the correlation between the variables was negative before, it became significantly positive after the intervention. Other significant differences in the correlation between the stages (before and after) were found in the relationship between the willingness to reconcile and the measures of feelings: anger toward Palestinians ($z = 2.10$, $p < .05$) before intervention ($r = .07$) versus after ($r = -.55^*$) and the fear of Palestinians ($z = 2.44$, $p < .05$) before intervention ($r = .30$) versus after ($r = -.43$). Marginal significance ($z = 1.74$, $p = .08$) was found between the willingness to reconcile and hatred towards Palestinians before intervention ($r = -.11$) versus after ($r = -.60^*$).

## 4.3    Findings for the Inter-Group

The difference in the correlation between the legitimacy of the Palestinian narrative and the willingness to reconcile before the intervention ($r = .73^*$) versus after ($r = .03$) was marginally significant ($z = 1.90$, $p = .06$).

## 5.    Discussion

In this study, we examined two types of dialogue groups intending to advance the acknowledgment of the collective narrative of the other and advocating for a greater willingness to reconcile. The first type of dialogue group was an inter-group, which brought together representatives of two groups in conflict. The second type was an intra-group in which the other was represented through its collective narratives. The questions for comparative research were: How does the type of dialogue group (inter- or intra-group) affect the achievement of the objectives of interventions? Is there an advantage to interpersonal contact, or does the contact block processes of recognizing the other? For this purpose, we examined indices of the results of the various interventions: the perception of the collective narrative of the in-group and the out-group, different feelings towards the other, the degree of trust in the other, and the willingness to reconcile.

As expected, both interventions increased the willingness to legitimize the Palestinian narrative, and thereby, they partially achieved their stated purpose. However, contrary to the research hypothesis, other measures of collective narrative perceptions (empathy, anger, and knowledge) did not change in both groups. Sagy et al. (2011) found similar results in a study that examined changes in the perceptions of narratives of the other over time in the context of the political situation. The long-term study revealed that the Israelis' recognition of the Palestinian narrative increased during periods of peace talks, but Israelis expressed this recognition instead by legitimizing than by empathizing with the narrative. Legitimizing the narrative of the other is easier to attain than empathy.

The knowledge index on the Palestinian narrative did not increase due to the interventions. This is a surprising finding since the groups obtained a great deal of knowledge during the interventions. The participants may have reflected the information about their lack of knowledge of the Palestinian narrative in their response. The findings of this study indicate partial recognition of the collective narrative of the other as a result of both types of interventions.

We suggest two possible explanations for these findings. The first explanation is substantive, and the second is related to the index. The essential explanation is that a change in the perception of the collective narratives is a deep and thorough process that requires an extensive period of time. A short intervention, however successful, may not be enough to recognize the narrative of the other entirely. The additional explanation for the findings is that the narrative index is a complex measure. It includes eight questions on seven different events, while the emotion index, for example, asks only one straightforward question. It may be that the emotion index that asks a single question expresses immediate and short-term change after intervention because this reflects what is expected of the participants, whereas the more complex narrative index does not express an immediate and spontaneous reaction but a rather complex one.

Moreover, the results showed that, contrary to the research hypotheses, the perception of Israeli collective narratives did not change in any of the indices in either group. These findings differ from the results of Ben David et al. (2017), who examined an intra-group of Jewish Israeli students, where legitimacy and empathy for the Israeli narrative also increased. However, it is essential to emphasize that although the perception of the Israeli narratives did not strengthen, it also did not decrease, as reported in several studies (Ron and Maoz 2013).

According to the research hypotheses, a change was indicated in most of the emotional measures as a result of the two interventions. Among Jewish participants in both groups, there was a decrease in the level of hatred, fear, and anger toward Palestinians. The fear of Palestinians decreased more significantly in the inter-group

Learning the Narrative of the Other | **197**

than in the intra-group. This difference can be explained by the direct contact with the Arab participants. The change in the emotional parameters after the dialogue groups took place is significant considering the important role of feelings towards the other in situations of conflict between groups (Bar Tal and Halperin 2009; Cohen Chen et al. 2014; Halperin and Gross 2011; Horovitz 1985; Petersen 2002) and indicates that the intra-group has as much influence as the inter-group. It is possible that the influence of the dialogue groups on feelings towards the other was direct and immediate, matching what was expected of the group participants. The changes examined in the other indices require more complex emotional and cognitive processing of a change in the perception of narratives.

According to the research hypotheses, Jewish participants in both groups showed a marginally significant increase in their level of trust in Palestinians. The importance of the trust index and its frequency in studies of group conflict (Gaertner and Dovidio 2000; Maoz and Ellis 2008) reveals the similar effectiveness of both types of groups. Contrary to the research hypothesis, none of the interventions showed a change in the degree of willingness to reconcile. A possible explanation for these results is the "ceiling effect" (Wang et al. 2008), which stated that the initial scores in this index were high and difficult to cross, especially in the inter-group.

Concurrently with the various analyses that revealed similarities in the results between the two groups, the analysis of correlations revealed that the correlations between the various variables were strengthened in the intra-group, whereas no change occurred in the inter-group. Strengthening the connections between the various variables indicates the formulation of a more coherent and less "confused" approach to the Israeli-Palestinian conflict and, in effect, a more precise position on the conflict based on the recognition and understanding of each other's narratives. The primary influence of intra-group meetings is the consolidation of a more coherent and clearer stance regarding the conflict, as opposed to the inter-group, which left its participants lacking clarity and understanding of positions concerning the conflict.

## 5.1 Contribution of the Study

This study compared two types of dialogue groups, aiming at acknowledging the collective narrative of the other and increasing the participants' willingness to reconcile. The first group, an inter-group, has received extensive research attention and is usually found to be an effective intervention in achieving its goals. On the other hand, there is little research on the second type, the intra-group. The findings of this comparative study, which supported the effectiveness of the intra-group in achieving its goals, allows further development of new tools and methods of intervention to reduce inter-group conflicts and understand the conflict and its sources. This opportunity is particularly important since it is not always possible for members in conflict to meet in person.

## 5.2    Limitations of the Study

A significant limitation of the study was the small number of subjects, which made it difficult to find significant results. In addition, we cannot exclude the possibility that the replies to the questionnaires contained a particular element of social willingness because the students received a grade for their participation in the course. To separate the course from the study, we sent the link to the questionnaires via personal email instead of via the facilitators who led course sessions.

### Conclusions and Recommendations

The findings of the comparative study support the latest research findings (Ben David et al. 2017) on the effectiveness of the intra-group. The present study found that the intra-group not only achieved its goals similarly to the inter-group it also had an advantage in formulating a more coherent approach to the conflict.

This study provides a basis for further studies. First, the intra-group has been studied by members of the majority group and not by members of the Arab minority group within Israel. Due to the different needs of the majority and minority groups that we described throughout this paper; it would be interesting to conduct a similar study that compares an intra-group to an inter-group among minority groups. Second, an interesting and meaningful research approach could consist of a longitudinal study that combines quantitative and qualitative tools to compare the process and results of the intra-group work over the years and examine to what extent they are affected by changes in external reality. A similar study was conducted by Sagy (2006) among inter-groups. Finally, in light of the difficulties in the existence of dialogue groups with direct contact during conflict situations (Sagy 2017), this study indicated the effectiveness of familiarity with the collective narrative of the other. It raised the need to further explore this approach with various types of interventions.

### References

Allport, G.W. 1954, *The Nature of Prejudice*, Addison Wesley, Cambridge, MA.
Bar, H., Bar Gal, D. 1995, *Living with Conflict,* The Jerusalem Institute for Israel Studies. Jerusalem [in Hebrew].
Bar Tal, D. 2013, Intractable Conflicts. Socio-Psychological Foundations and Dynamics, Cambridge University Press, Cambridge, UK.
Bar Tal, D. 2007, *Living with the Conflict. Social Psychological Analysis of Jewish Society in Israel*, Carmel, Jerusalem [in Hebrew].

Bar Tal, D. 2002, 'The Elusive Nature of Peace Education', in *Peace Education. The Concept, Principles and Practice in the World*, eds G. Salomon, B. Nevo, Lawrence Erlbaum, Mahwah, NJ, pp. 27–36.

Bar Tal, D., Halperin, E. 2009, 'Overcoming Psychological Barriers to Peace Making. The Influence of Mediating Beliefs about Losses', in *Prosocial Motives, Emotions and Behavior*, eds. M. Mikulincer, P.R. Shaver, American Psychological Association Press, Washington, DC, pp. 431–448.

Ben David, Y., Hameiri, B., Benheim, S., Leshem, B., Sarid, A., Sternberg, M,. Nadler, A., Sagy, S. 2017, 'Exploring Ourselves within Inter-Group Conflict. The Role of Intra-Group Dialogue in Promoting Acceptance of Collective Narratives and Willingness Towards Reconciliation', *Peace and Conflict. Journal of Peace Psychology*, vol. 23, pp. 269–277.

Bohm, D. 1990, *On Dialogue*, Routledge, London.

Cohen Chen, S., Halperin, E., Porat, R., Bar Tal, D. 2014, 'The Differential Effects of Hope and Fear on Information Processing in Intractable Conflict', *Journal of Social and Political Psychology*, vol. 2, no. 1, pp. 11–30.

Falach-Galil, R., Kawshinsky, F., Bargal, D. 2002, 'We and Them - Before We Are All Together. The Importance of the Process in Separate Groups Before an Intergroup Meeting', in R. Lev-Weisel, L. Kassen (eds), *Group Work in a Multicultural Society*, Chrykover, Tel Aviv [in Hebrew], pp. 23–40.

Ford, K.A. 2012, 'Shifting White Ideological Scripts. The Educational Benefits of Inter- and Intra-Racial Curricular Dialogues on the Experiences of White College Students', *Journal of Diversity in Higher Education*, vol. 5, no. 3, p. 138.

Foulkes, H. 2017, 'Education and Employment among Young Arabs', in *State of Israel Report 2017*, Taub Center for Social Policy Studies in Israel, Jerusalem [in Hebrew].

Gaertner, S.L., Dovidio, J.F. 2000, *Reducing Intergroup Bias. The Common Ingroup Identity Model*, Taylor and Francis, Philadelphia, PA.

Halperin, E. 2011, 'Emotional Barriers to Peace. Emotions and Public Opinion of Jewish Israelis about the Peace Process in the Middle East', *Peace and Conflict*, vol. 17, no. 1, pp. 22–45.

Halperin, E., Gross, J. 2011, 'Emotion Regulation in Violent Conflict. Reappraisal, Hope and Support for Humanitarian Aid to the Opponent in Wartime', *Cognition and Emotion*, vol. 25, no. 7, pp. 1228–1236.

Hameiri, B., Nadler, A. 2017, 'Looking Backward to Move Forward. Effects of Acknowledgment of Victimhood on Readiness to Compromise for Peace in the Protracted Israeli–Palestinian Conflict', *Personality and Social Psychology Bulletin*, vol. 43, pp. 555–569.

Hewtone, M., Brown, R. 1986, 'Contact Is not Enough. An Intergroup Perspective on the 'Contact Hypothesis'', in *Contact and Conflict in Intergroup Encounters*, eds M. Hewstone, R. Brown, Blackwell, Oxford, pp. 1–44.

Horowitz, D.L. 1985, *Ethnic Groups in Conflict*, University of California Press, Berkeley, CA.

Kelman, H.C. 1998, 'Social-Psychological Contributions to Peacemaking and Peacebuilding in the Middle East', *Applied Psychology*, vol. 47, no. 1, pp. 5–28.

Lev-Weisel, R., Kassen, L. 2002, 'Introduction. Israel as a Multicultural Society', in *Group Work in a Multicultural Society*, eds R. Lev-Weisel, L. Kassen, Chrykover, Tel Aviv [in Hebrew], pp. 15–20.

Liu J., Hilton D. 2005, 'How the Past Weighs on the Present. Social Representations of History and Their Rule in Identity Politics', *British Journal of Social Psychology*, vol. 44, pp. 1–21.

Mana, A., Sagy, S., Srour, S., Mjally-Knani, S. 2015, 'On Both Sides of the Fence. Perceptions of Collective Narratives and Identity Strategies among Palestinians in Israel and in the West Bank', *Mind and Society*, vol. 14, pp. 57–83.

Maoz, I. 2011, 'Does Contact Work in Protracted Asymmetrical Conflict? Appraising 20 Years of Reconciliation-Aimed Encounters Between Israeli Jews and Palestinians', *Journal of Peace Research*, vol. 48, no. 1, pp. 115–125.

Maoz, I., Ellis, D.G. 2008, 'Intergroup Communication as a Predictor of Jewish-Israeli Agreement With Integrative Solutions to the Israeli-Palestinian Conflict. The Mediating Effects of Out-Group Trust and Guilt', *Journal of Communication*, vol. 58, no. 3, pp. 490–507.

Nadler, A. 2000, 'Inter-Group Conflict and its Reduction. A Perspective of the Social Psychology', in *Dialogue between Identities. Jews and Arabs Encounters in Neve Shalom*, ed. R. Halabi, Hakibbutz Hameuchad Publishing, Tel Aviv [in Hebrew], pp. 28–46.

Nadler, A., Liviatan, I. 2006, 'Intergroup Reconciliation. Effecte of Adversary's Expressions of Empathy, Responsibility and Recipient's Trust', *Personality and Social Psychology Bulletin*, vol. 32, pp. 459–470.

Nadler, A., Shnabel, N. 2006, 'Instrumental and Socio-Emotional Paths to Intergroup Reconciliation and the Need-Based Model of Socio-Emotional Reconciliation', in *Social Psychology of Intergroup Reconciliation*, eds A. Nadler, T. Malloy, J.D. Fisher, Oxford University Press, New York, pp. 37–56.

Pearson K., Filon, L.N.G. 1898, 'Mathematical Contributions to Theory of Evolution. IV. On the Probable Errors of Frequency Constants and on the Influence of Random Selection and Correlation'. *Proceedings of the Royal Society of London*, vol. 62, pp. 173–176.

Petersen, R.D. 2002, *Understanding Ethnic Violence. Fear, Hatred, and Resentment in Twentieth-Century Eastern Europe*, Cambridge University Press, Cambridge.

Pettigrew, T.F., Tropp, L.R. 2011, *When Groups Meet. The Dynamics of Intergroup Contact*, Psychology Press, New York.

Ron, Y., Maoz, I. 2013, 'Dangerous Stories. Encountering Narratives of the Other in the Israeli-Palestinian Conflict', *Peace and Conflict. Journal of Peace Psychology*, vol. 19, no. 3, pp. 281–294.

Saguy, T., Dovidio, J.F., Pratto, F. 2008, 'Beyond Contact. Intergroup Contact in the Context of Power Relations', *Personality and Social Psychology Bulletin*, vol. 34, no. 3, pp. 432–445.

Sagy, S. 2017, 'Can We Emphatize with the Narrative of Our Enemy? A Personal Odyssey in Studying Peace Education', *Intercultural Education,* vol. 28, pp. 1–11.

Sagy, S. 2006, 'The Impact of the Political Context on Discourse Characteristics in Jewish-Arab Encounters in Israel. Between Peace Talks and Violent Events', Lecture Presented in 29 Annual Scientific Meeting of the International Society of Political Psychology, July 12–15, 2006.

Sagy, S., Ayalon, A., Diab, K. 2011, 'Perceptions of the Narrative of the 'Other' among Arab and Jewish Adolescents in Israeli. Between Peace Talks and Violent Events', *Intercultural Education*, vol. 22, pp. 191–206.

Sagy, S., Adwan, S., Kaplan, A. 2002, 'Interpretations of the Past and Expectations for the Future among Israeli and Palestinian Youth', *American Journal of Orthopsychiatry*, vol. 72, no.1, pp. 26–38.

Sagy, S., Steinberg, S., Fachiraldin, M. 2002, 'The Personal Self and Collective Self in the Intergroup Encounter of Jews and Arabs in Israel. Discussion of Two Intervention Strategies', *Megamot*, vol. 4 [in Hebrew], pp. 534–556.

Salomon, G. 2002, 'The Nature of Peace Education. Not All Programs Are Created Equal', in *Peace Education. The Concept, Principles, and Practices Around the World*, eds G. Salomon, B. Nevo, Lawrence Erlbaum, Mahawah, NJ, pp. 3–14.

Shnabel, N., Nadler, A., Ullrich, J., Dovidio, J.F., Carmi, D. 2009, 'Promoting Reconciliation through the Satisfaction of the Emotional Needs of Victimized and Perpetrating Group Members. The Needs-Based Model of Reconciliation', *Personality and Social Psychology Bulletin*, vol. 35, no. 8, pp. 1021–1030.

Sidanius, J., Pratto, F. 1999, *Social Dominance. An Intergroup Theory of Social Hierarchy and Oppression*, Cambridge University Press, New York.

Smooha, S. 2001, 'Arab-Jewish Relations in Israel as a Jewish and Democratic State', in *Trends in Israeli Society*, eds E. Yaar, Z. Shavit, The Open University, Tel Aviv, pp. 231–365 [in Hebrew].

Sonnenschein, N., Hijazi, A. 2000, 'The Home Group. The One-National Framework in the Jewish-Arab Encounter', in *Dialogue Between Identities. Jews and Arabs Encounters in Neve Shalom*, ed R, Halabi, Hakibbutz Hameuchad Publishing, Tel Aviv, pp. 131–150 [in Hebrew].

Srour, A., Mana, A., Sagy, S. 2016, 'Perceptions of Collective Narratives among Arab and Jewish Adolescents in Israel. A Decade of Intractable Conflict', in *A Social Psychology Perspective on the Israeli-Palestinian Conflict*, eds K. Sharvit, E. Halperin, Springer International Publishing, Cham, pp. 77–96.

Srour, A., Sagy, S., Mana, A., Mjally-Knani, S. 2013, 'Collective Narratives as Indicators of Examining Intergroup Relations. The Case of Palestinian Muslims and Christians in Israel', *International Journal of Conflict Management*, vol. 24, no. 3, pp. 231–244.

Stephan, W.G., Stephan, C.W. 2001, *Improving Intergroup Relations*, Sage, Thousand Oaks, CA.

Sternberg, M., Litvak Hirsch, T., Sagy, S. 2018, 'Nobody Ever Told Us. The Contribution of Intragroup Dialogue to Reflexive Learning about Violent Conflict', *Peace and Conflict. Journal of Peace Psychology*, vol. 24, no. 2, pp. 127–138.

Suleiman, R. 2000, 'The Planned Encounter as a Microcosm. Psychological and Social Aspects", in *Dialogue Between Identities. Jews and Arabs Encounters in Neve Shalom*, ed R. Halabi, Hakibbutz Hameuchad Publishing, Tel Aviv, pp. 47–66 [in Hebrew].

Wang, L., Zhang, Z., Mcarde, J.J., Salthouse, T.A. 2008, 'Investigating Ceiling Effects in Longitudinal Data Analysis', *Multivariate Behavioral Research*, vol. 43, no. 4, pp. 476–496.

Becky Leshem, Shifra Sagy

# Legitimization of the Other Narrative as a Mediator of the Relationships Between National Honor, Dignity Perceptions, and the Willingness to Reconcile

## The Case of the Israeli-Palestinian Conflict

### Abstract

Becky Leshem and Shifra Sagy's paper on the *Legitimization of the Other Narrative as a Mediator of the Relationships Between National Honor and Dignity Perceptions and Willingness to Reconcile: The Case of the Israeli-Palestinian Conflict* examines the role played by the perception of dignity and national honor – identified as basic elements in national conflict cultures – to promote or obstacle willingness to reconcile among a sample of 343 Israeli Jewish university students. More precisely, legitimization of the Palestinian narratives has been tested here as a mediator of the relationship between personal dignity, perceptions of national honor, and the willingness to reconcile. The findings indicate that perceptions of personal dignity are positively connected with the willingness to reconcile, whereas perceptions of national honor are negatively related. The paper also presents direct and indirect positive relationships between legitimizing the narratives of the other and the willingness to reconcile by discussing practical implications for conflict resolution endeavors and future research.

### 1. Introduction

Studies of national conflicts and reconciliation have identified that both sides of conflict suffer from restrictions on their basic needs for appreciation, honor, and human dignity. In intractable conflicts, these feelings become part of the "conflict-culture" (Bar Tal and Nahhas 2012), affecting conflict resolution and, particularly, the reconciliation processes (Kelman 2008). Considering the importance of willingness to reconcile to conflict resolution, we examined the relationships between these concepts to better understand the potential capacity of human dignity and national honor perceptions to promote and facilitate this willingness. Moreover, studies of barriers to reconciliation in conflict areas have identified harm to the sense of respect (Baumeister, Stillwell and Heatherton 1994; Scheff 1994) and the need to restore the sense of dignity of the conflicted groups (Foster and Rusbult

1999), whereas perception of others as humans (Staub 2006), as well as recognizing and providing legitimization for their narratives (Aurbach 2010) could promote willingness to reconcile.

## 2. Human Dignity and National Honor

The concepts of human dignity and national honor evolved in parallel during the Age of Enlightenment, a period characterized by philosophical, political, and social revolutions. Enlightenment philosophical conceptions of dignity emphasized the equality of human beings. Simultaneously, anti-Enlightenment concepts developed, focusing on values that divide individuals by placing them into different national or social groups (Sternhell 2010). The constant interaction between the two concepts is often dialectical. This study examined the interplay of these concepts in the intractable Israeli-Palestinian conflict.

The contemporaneous concept of dignity evolved at the end of World War II. It refers to the innate and indisputable right of all human beings to be recognized, valued, and treated humanely – a right arising by virtue of being a human being (Taylor 1994). The perception of dignity derives from universal human values, enabling one to perceive the other as a human being with whom they can have dialogue and social interactions in order to understand their ideas and concepts. Dignity views the other as a human being in a way that is detached from the conflict and may even enable a more objective perception of the conflict and reduce the influence of conflict-related collective content.

On the other hand, national honor is based on collective values and nourished and sustained by collective narratives, whose importance overcomes personal values in a collective society. A significant difference between dignity and honor derives from their different reference points, such as human/personal vs. group/collective. The reference point for dignity determines the threshold for interpersonal behavior: "All human beings are born free and equal in dignity and human rights" (UN 1948). While the perception of human dignity stems from universal human values, it also relates to social values supported by collective narratives. Recognizing the dignity of the other promotes treating others as human beings. Listening to and trying to understand them could increase the willingness to reconcile (Ericson 2001).

Furthermore, the perception of human dignity examines the other through values that equate and unite people, whereas perceptions of national honor focus on the values that distinguish and separate national groups. Focusing on unifying values could make it possible to perceive the other as equal and worthy of equality. Moreover, such a perception can promote the willingness to reconcile with the adversary, whereas focusing on separating values stigmatizes the other as different, inferior, not worthy of equal treatment, and thus not a suitable partner for reconciliation. While honor promotes competition and frequently relates to fear of humiliation and shame, dignity calls for consideration and constraint, accompanied by empathy, solidarity, and humanistic obligation (Kamir 2002). Thus, the universal perception of human dignity could undermine the ethnic and national boundaries that form the basis of perceptions of national honor.

While the reference point for dignity is personal and anchored in universal values, the reference point for national honor is collective since it reflects mutual values embedded in collective narratives related to the national group (Olick 1999). The term "national honor" refers to a cultural code of honor derived from social hierarchies that shape a person's identity and values within the group. Self-esteem and social status are achieved by compliance with norms of behavior and socio-cultural values of the group to which the individual belongs. In contrast, the failure to comply with group norms harms a person's self-esteem and social status (Mosquera, Manstead and Fischer 2002a, 2002b). The perception of national honor relates to individuals who identify with the same national group. This concept includes loyalty and identification with national symbols and narratives and a notion of responsibility for the national group members. Another aspect may also be the idea of "loyalty to loyalty," i. e., loyalty to the concept of loyalty to the group (Perla 1918, p. 56). The perception of national honor gains importance during national conflicts. Each side recognizes and supports its national narrative, accepts its national norms, remembers the injuries that the other caused to their national honor, and understands the required response in retaliation for future injuries (Hamilton, Sherman and Castelli 2002; Von Borries 1997; Pennebaker and Banasik 1997). Conflicts with national honor components are difficult to settle because they originate from national group acts, behaviors, and symbolic interactions that address emotional needs. Thus, such conflicts rarely emerge from carrying out transactions or by receiving concessions from the other (O'Neill 2003). People driven by strong national honor examine and respond to the way members of other national groups perceive their national honor (O'Neill 2001). Therefore, any injury to national honor during conflict requires healing as a precondition for conflict resolution (Huth 2009). Restoring damaged honor can be formally achieved by asking for forgiveness (Cohen 2004; Gonzalez, Manzi and Noor 2011). Maintaining national honor and dealing with feelings of injured national honor play an essential part in conflict culture. This culture forms a social-psychological infrastructure of negative feelings, negative beliefs, and attitudes towards the other, intensifying the conflict and serving as a significant obstacle to reconciliation (Bar Tal 2007). The differences between personal dignity and perceptions of national honor could imply a negative relationship between the two, especially in conflict areas.

## 3. The Role of Perceptions of National Honor and Dignity in Intractable Conflicts

Perceptions of both national honor and human dignity can be remarkably significant during intractable national conflicts as they are prominently involved in the themes which constitute the social-psychological repertoire that defines the conflict ethos (Bar Tal 2007; Bar Tal, Halperin and Oren 2010). The denial of the enemy's human dignity is a key element of the opponent's de-legitimization theme, while national honor is associated with a positive self-image, victimization, patriotism, and group goals. The conflict ethos provides the ideological foundation for the conflict culture, fulfilling the basic individual needs that arise during violent national conflicts: the need to understand the present reality and to have a predictable future; the need for personal safety and security; the need for a positive national image, the need for a defined collective identity, the need for a justice motive, and the need to belong to a group identity in order to differentiate from other groups (Bar Tal 2007). While the conflict ethos provides individuals with functional tools for coping with the conflict, it could serve as a barrier to conflict resolution and help group leadership sustain and reinforce the conflict culture (Bar Tal and Nahhas 2012). Thus, providing the other with a sense of dignity seems essential for reconciliation, whereas denial of dignity could harm the reconciliation process (Hicks 2009 2011; Kelman 2004; Van der Merwe and Chapman 2008).

On the other hand, accepting the enemy's right to be treated with dignity challenges various elements of the conflict ethos. It provides a complex experience by masking moral differences, undermining the justification for violence, challenging the groups' asymmetric power relations, and recognizing the other as a possible partner for dialogue – a dialogue that could expose one to the narrative of the other and promote one's own willingness to reconcile (Hicks 2009, 2011; Kelman 2004; Van der Merwe and Chapman 2008). There is a clear correlation between the basic principles of the conflict ethos and perceptions of national honor, indicating that conflict ethos could serve as a barrier to intractable conflict resolution (Bar Tal 2007) by promoting the hypothesis that individuals with perceptions of strong national honor will be less willing to reconcile.

## 4. Perceptions towards the Narrative of the Other

Intractable conflicts are characterized by delegitimization of the other, embedded in collective conflict supporting narratives (Bar Tal 2007; Bar Tal, Oren and Nets Zehngut 2014). Delegitimization nourishes the conflict culture by impairing the ability to recognize the value of the other, which is perceived as an enemy who is inferior in human and ethnic terms (Oren and Bar Tal 2007; Tileaga 2007).

Delegitimization does not allow treatment of the other as a human being worthy of personal dignity. Moreover, delegitimization does not provide recognition for both parties as a precondition for reconciliation (Shnabel et al. 2009). Delegitimizing the narrative of the other is an important feature of conflict culture (Bar Tal 2007).

In most cases, it is based on negative attitudes and emotions toward the other and conflict-related national narratives without actual familiarity with the other's narratives. Examining the attitudes toward the narratives of the other can provide insights into the relationship between the groups in intractable conflicts (Sagy, Adwan and Kaplan 2002). Previous studies have found that acknowledgement or legitimization of the other's narratives enables a person to see the conflict from the perspective of the other and reduces aggression. This strategy even encourages pro-social actions and caring for the other (Batson 1991; Batson and Ahmad 2009; White 1998). As a result, acknowledging of the other's narratives could moderate the conflict and promote reconciliation (Pettigrew and Tropp 2006).

Honor and dignity are essential components of any national narrative, particularly among collectivist societies (Sagy, Orr and Bar-on 1999). This study focuses on the Israeli and Palestinian societies' intractable national conflict (Bar-Tal 2007). In collectivist groups, the needs and aspirations of the group have priority over the needs and aspirations of the individual. In "honor societies," honor has the utmost cultural importance and exerts a significant impact on self-esteem, social status, and the emotional well-being of the individuals and the group (Kamir 2004; Triandis et al. 1988).

In the context of this study, Israeli society reveals collectivist and individualistic indicators (Sagy et al. 2001). Moreover, Shafir and Peled (2002) identified diverse areas of discourse in Israeli society. Two of them relate to perceptions of national honor and dignity. The national-honor-based discourse links civil status to the level of identifying with state goals and contributing to their fulfillment, while the dignity-based discourse emphasizes individuality and eliminates grouping. It seems that the protection of national honor and dealing with feelings of an injured national honor could play an essential role in the lives of individuals in Israeli society and feed their attitudes towards the other and the conflict (Bar Tal 2007).

## 5.    Mediation Model

In this study, we suggest a mediation model that links national honor and personal dignity perceptions to the willingness to reconcile. Legitimization of the narrative of the other serves as a mediator (see Figure 1).

We hypothesized that higher levels of dignity-based perceptions would promote the willingness to reconcile. On the other hand, the adverse contribution of perceptions of national honor to the conflict culture led us to expect that higher levels

Figure 1: Suggested Model: The Relationships between Perceptions of Dignity, Perceptions of National Honor, Legitimization of the Narrative of the Other, and Willingness to Reconcile

of perceptions of national honor would be linked to lower levels of the willingness to reconcile. We expected that the legitimization of the narratives of the other would be connected to the willingness to reconcile and serve as a mediator of the relationships between personal dignity and perceptions of national honor. The proposed model incorporates these hypothesized relationships as three links: 1. a positive direct link between perceptions of personal dignity and the willingness to reconcile; 2. a direct negative link between perceptions of national honor and the willingness to reconcile; 3. a positive direct link between the legitimization of the other's narrative and the willingness to reconcile. I also assumed a positive link between perceptions of dignity and narrative legitimization as well as a negative link between perceptions of national honor and narrative legitimization.

The willingness to reconcile is linked with national honor and perceptions of personal dignity, both directly and indirectly. The indirect links take effect through legitimizing the narratives of the other, suggesting that legitimization of the narratives of the other mediates the relationships between perceptions of national honor and dignity and the willingness to reconcile.

## 6. Method

Our sample consisted of 343 (104 males, 239 females), first degree (92.6%), and second degree (7.4%) Israeli Jewish students from Ben-Gurion University of the Negev, aged 18–68 (M = 24.75, SD = 5.24). The participants' places of residence varied: 11.7% came from the northern part of Israel, 44.6% from the center, and 43.7% from the south. A computerized data collection platform was used to administer the questionnaires. The data was collected in the first semester of the academic year.

## 7. Measures

1. *Sociodemographic Information.* The questionnaire included questions about the participants' age, gender, religion, place of residence, and the levels of education of their parents.

2. *Dignity Perceptions (DP).* The participants rated their degree of agreement with two statements relating to the Palestinians' right to dignity on a 7-point Likert scale (1 = fully disagree, 7 = fully agree). Both statements were positive, i. e. "The Palestinians are entitled to be valued and respected" and "The Palestinians are entitled to have equal opportunities," producing a scale (with Cronbach's alpha = .82), range = 11–77, M = 5.04, SD = 1.64 ($\alpha$ = .84). Higher scores indicate higher perceptions that the Palestinians are entitled to be treated with dignity.

3. *Perceptions of National Honor* (PNH). Respondents were asked to rate their degree of agreement with statements regarding national honor concepts on a 7-point Likert scale (1 = fully disagree, 7 = fully agree). The tool included two positive statements, i. e., "Our people must protect our national honor at any cost," and two negative statements, such as "protecting our national honor is not worth significant loss of human lives on both sides," producing a scale with Cronbach's alpha = .77, range = 11–76.75, M = 53.0810, SD = 1.3530 ($\alpha$ = .76). Higher scores indicate higher perceptions of national honor.

4. *Legitimization of the Palestinian Narratives.* The Perceptions of Collective Narratives Questionnaire (Sagy, Adwan and Kaplan 2002) used in the current study has been validated in past studies (Ayalon and Sagy 2011; Srour et al. 2013). In these studies, the measure of reliability varied with sample age, nationality, and religion ($\alpha$= .70 - .92). The measure includes seven national historical experiences associated with core issues of the Israeli-Palestinian conflict, such as the Holocaust, the 1948 war, and the Palestinian refugees. The events were presented to the participants from the perspective of the mainstream collective narrative of the other." The perceptions were measured by 5-point Likert responses (1= very untrue, 5= very true) to positive and negative statements for the perception of the narrative of each experience, i. e. "This narrative is legitimate," "I feel empathy toward the narrative," and "I feel anger toward the narrative." The final scale was calculated by averaging the responses for all events (range = 1–5, M = 2.60, SD = .87, $\alpha$= .86). Higher scores indicate higher legitimization of the Palestinian narrative, i. e., accepting that the Palestinians are entitled to have their own narrative and are entitled to support the narrative that they perceive as the truth.

5. *Willingness to Reconcile* (WTR). The Willingness to Reconcile questionnaire (Shnabel et al. 2009) was used. The participants were presented with six statements, such as "I feel I can forgive the Palestinians for their terror attacks against Israeli civilians," "It is the responsibility of Israelis to do more in order to reduce the tension between Israelis and Palestinians," "I support the idea that Israelis should apologize to the Palestinians for the suffering they endure as refugees and as people living under military occupation." They were asked to rate their levels of support for the statements on a 7-point Likert scale (1 = I totally reject the statement, 7 = I totally support the statement). The WTR scale score was provided by the average of scores for all six items (range = 1–7, $M$ = 3.73, $SD$ = 1.45, α= .89).

## 8. Results

1. *Preliminary Analysis.* Among Israeli Jews, the univariate analysis revealed no significant demographic-based differences in the levels of perceptions of dignity, perceptions of national honor, perceptions of the Palestinian narrative, and the willingness to reconcile (see table I).

Table 1  Statistics of Research Variables

| Measure | M | SE | SD | N |
|---|---|---|---|---|
| Perception of Dignity | 5.04 | .10 | 1.64 | 267 |
| Perception of National Honor | 3.08 | .08 | 1.30 | 267 |
| Legitimizing the Palestinian Narrative | 2.6 | .05 | .87 | 284 |
| Willingness to Reconcile | 2.93 | .09 | 1.45 | 269 |

M = Mean; SE = Standard Error; SD = Standard Deviation; N = Valid Cases
Note: No significant gender-based differences were observed for any variable.

2. Bivariate Analyses. Testing the full sample (N = 343) for correlations between the willingness to reconcile and other study variables revealed significant Pearson-r correlations for all tested variables. The willingness to reconcile was positively correlated with legitimizing the Palestinian narrative ($r$ = .716, p < .01) and perceptions of dignity towards the Palestinians ($r$ = .588, p < .01). Moreover, the willingness to reconcile was negatively correlated with perceptions of national honor ($r$ = -.578, p < .01), and perceptions of dignity were also negatively correlated with perceptions of national honor ($r$ = .541, p < .01) but positively correlated with all other research variables (see table II for details). The test results were similar for female and male participants.

Table 2  Correlation coefficient matrix of study variables

| Measure | M | SE | SD | N |
|---|---|---|---|---|
| Perceptions of Dignity | 5.04 | .10 | 1.64 | 267 |
| Perceptions of National Honor | 3.08 | .08 | 1.30 | 267 |
| Legitimizing the Palestinian Narrative | 2.6 | .05 | .87 | 284 |
| Willingness to Reconcile | 2.93 | .09 | 1.45 | 269 |

$\alpha$ Denotes the criterion (outcome) variable; ** = p<.01

3. Predictors of Willingness to Reconcile. The regression analysis indicated that the willingness to reconcile could be predicted (F = 82.72, p < .001, R2 = .60) by legitimizing the Palestinian narrative ($\beta$ = .493, p < .000), perceptions of national honor ($\beta$ = -.218, p < .000), and perceptions of dignity ($\beta$ = .203, p < .000). The tested factors accounted for 60% of the variance of WTR (see table III).

4. Path Model Validation. A structural equation analysis was used to test the suggested path model. The proposed model presents a set of relationships between the research variables, suggesting that legitimization of the Palestinian narrative mediates the relationship between perceptions of dignity, perceptions of national honor, and the willingness to reconcile. Testing the model by using SEM (see figure 2) showed a reasonable model fit between the empirical data and theoretical model ($\chi^2$ = 77.91, df = 1, p < .001, $CFI^1$ = .824).

Table 3  Regression Analysis: Dignity, National Honor, and Feelings towards the Palestinian Narrative as Predictors of Willingness to Reconcile

| Model | Unstandardized Coefficients | | Standardized Coefficients | | | |
|---|---|---|---|---|---|---|
| | B | Std. Error | Beta | t | Sig. | $R^2$ |
| 1  (constant) | 1.472 | .443 | | 3.319 | .001 | |
| Gender | .006 | .125 | -.002 | -.045 | .964 | |
| Dignity | .182 | .044 | .203 | 4.108 | .000 | |
| National Honor | -.243 | .054 | -.219 | -4.484 | .000 | .60 |
| Legitimizing the Palestinian Narrative | .810 | .083 | .493 | 9.801 | .000 | |
| Dependent variable: **Willingness to reconcile** | | | | | | |

Figure two shows the direct and indirect effects between the predictive variables that were introduced into the model and the predicted variable of the WTR. Perceptions of national honor, on the contrary, have a negative contribution to the WTR

---

1  CFI: Comparative Fit Index, A value close to 1 indicates a good fit

through a negative connection with the legitimization of the Palestinian narrative. A standardized regression coefficients review shows that perceptions of dignity and national honor have significant, direct, and indirect roles in predicting WTR. Perception of Dignity was found to have a significant positive direct contribution to WTR. Furthermore, perception of dignity also had a significant indirect effect on WTR through the increase in the legitimization of the Palestinian narrative, which was positively connected to WTR. While the perception of dignity had a positive effect on the WTR, the perceptions of national honor had a significant negative direct effect on the WTR and a significant indirect effect on the WTR through the decrease in the legitimization of the Palestinian narrative. Analysis coefficient matrixes reveal that legitimizing the narrative of the other had the most substantial effect on the WTR ($\beta = .403^2$, $p < .001$), followed by the perception that the other should be treated with dignity ($\beta t^3 = .400$, $\beta d = .154$, $\beta i = .246$, $p < .01$) and perceptions of national honor ($\beta t = -.381$, $\beta d = -.177$, $\beta i = -.204$, $p < .001$).

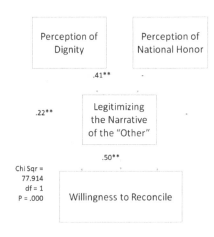

Figure 2 Path Model: Dignity, National Honor, and Legitimization of the Palestinian Narrative as Predictors of Willingness to Reconcile (standardized coefficients)

All effects are significant at $p < .001$.

The indirect effects of perceptions of dignity and national honor on the willingness to reconcile were stronger than the direct effects. This outcome supports the hypothesis that the legitimization of the narratives mediated the effects.

---

2 A standard coefficient of $\beta=.403$ indicates that a 1 standard deviation change of the independent variable will results in an .403 standard deviations change of the dependent variable.
3 $\beta t$: standardized total effect; $\beta d$: standardized direct effect; $\beta i$: standardized indirect effect

## 9. Discussion

We sought to examine the effects of perceptions of national honor and perceptions of personal dignity on the willingness to reconcile and test the legitimization of the narratives of the other as a possible mediator of the effects by using a model with direct and indirect relationships between the research factors. According to the proposed model, we found contradicting effects and directions between perceptions of national honor and perceptions of dignity. Stronger personal perceptions of dignity significantly predicted a higher willingness to reconcile and a higher legitimization of the narratives of the other. In comparison a stronger perception of national honor significantly predicted a lower willingness to reconcile and lower legitimization of the narratives of the other. The model also verified previous findings and directly linked the legitimization of narratives to the willingness to reconcile.

Furthermore, we have found significant indirect links, more robust than the direct ones, and verified that the legitimization of narratives could mediate the relationships between the perceptions of dignity, of national honor, and the willingness to reconcile. Higher levels of perception of personal dignity were connected to higher levels of narrative legitimization, which were linked with a higher willingness to reconcile, whereas higher levels of perceptions of national honor were connected to lower levels of narrative legitimization and further linked with a lower willingness to reconcile (see figure 1).

Perceptions of national honor and human dignity are embedded in cultural content domains and social networks. Thus, their realization defines the sense of belonging and the individual's worth in society (Kleinman 2006). However, while perceptions of dignity use a personal reference point and involve universal values, perceptions of national honor are embedded in collective narratives and serve the individual dynamically (Bynum, Hunt and Biernacki 1999) by reflecting how one perceives the other. The dramatic differences between the effects of the two concepts can be explained by the differences between the personal reference point that defines human dignity as opposed to the collective reference point that characterizes national honor.

The contradictory relationship can be explained by social identity theory (Tajfel and Turner 1986), which identifies one's self-image as including both a personal identity component and a group identity component. In contrast, social behavior is embedded on a scale between interpersonal and intergroup behavior. On one end, one's self-image is only based on belonging to interpersonal relationships, and on the other, it relates only to social and group affiliations. The concept of human dignity is linked to personal identity and interpersonal behavior, whereas the concept of national honor is related to group identity and intergroup behavior. Thus, in the course of a national conflict, the individual's reference point makes it hard to simultaneously maintain a strong sense of national honor and recognize the enemy's human right to be treated with dignity.

In the context of this study, the negative correlation between perception of dignity and the perception of national honor among the Israeli participants could be explained by the opposing discourses on national honor and dignity within the Israeli society (Shafir and Peled 2002). Different groups within Israeli society adopt different discourses and the different intellectual paradigms resulting from them (Mizrahi 2011). The variance in the perceptions of honor and dignity between groups in the Israeli population affects the perception of the conflict. Groups that base the civil discourse on the interpersonal paradigm and human dignity might see Palestinians as potential partners for dialogue and conflict resolution. In contrast, groups that focus on the national discourse and the inter-social paradigm consider Palestinians as a threat to national identity and safety as well as inconceivable partners for reconciliation.

Legitimizing the Palestinian narrative correlated positively with perceptions of human dignity and negatively correlated with perceptions of national honor. In other words, participants who accept the right of others to be treated with dignity were more likely to legitimize the narratives of the other. In contrast, participants with stronger national honor were less likely to legitimize the narrative. Although legitimizing the narrative of the other was not tested as a primary factor in this study, we found that it had the most substantial direct effect on the participants' willingness to reconcile. Our findings support previous studies that identified narrative legitimization as a major factor in enabling the willingness to reconcile (Aurbach 2010; Ben David et al. 2017; Sagy, Adwan and Kaplan 2002), suggesting its importance as part of the path to reconciliation. Future studies should explore diverse education and intervention programs that provide conflicting parties with the knowledge and tools to acknowledge and legitimize the narrative of the other.

## 10. Conclusion

The relationship between the perception of national honor and human dignity can be described as a kind of contest in which personal and social preferences affect to what extent a person identifies with the national conflict ethos and human perception of the other. During intractable violent national conflicts, the conflict ethos satisfies the individual's basic psychological and emotional needs. Those with higher perceptions of national honor embrace the conflict ethos. By doing so, their basic needs are satisfied, and they are less likely to forfeit the emotional security offered by the national narratives. Does this predict no prospects for a positive change for a society trapped in an intractable national conflict? We argue otherwise. Findings suggest a possible path toward reconciliation by pushing the point of balance between the two perceptions in the direction of human dignity and away from national honor. Achieving such a change in a society of honor is challenging as basic needs of individuals with strong perceptions of national honor are satisfied by the conflict ethos. Our findings also support the hypothesis that legitimizing the narratives of the other could mediate the effects of national honor and the perceptions of dignity by highlighting the importance of narrative acknowledgment. Some peace education interventions have reported successful change by learning the narrative of the other (Ben David et al. 2017; Sternberg, Litvak Hirsch and Sagy, 2018). Future studies should better understand how individuals who commit to national honor cope with personal emotional needs that arise during intractable conflicts. Longitudinal studies should examine peace education interventions that could bridge the gap between the opposing discourses and encourage the legitimization of the narratives of the other to promote the willingness to reconcile through this process.

## 11. Limitations

The study was carried out only among a group of Israeli Jewish participants. Thus, we cannot generalize the findings to their Palestinian counterparts or other populations. We used a convenience sample that is not sufficiently demographically diverse and should not be considered a representative sample of the population. In order to produce generalized results, further studies should use a multi-population representative sample with demographic and geographic diversity and with additional population groups involved in other national conflicts. The construction of the study is cross-sectional and provides a snapshot of the situation that only enables the examination of relationships between the variables.

Further testing of processes and causality would require longitudinal studies. Regardless of its limitations, these findings shed light on the relationships between dignity and the perceptions of national honor and the willingness to reconcile. This study has provided significant results regarding the important and complex role of legitimizing the narratives of the other. This outcome can lead to the development and evaluation of meaningful peace education programs and applications to increase willingness to reconcile.

## References

Aurbach, Y. 2010, 'National Narratives in a Conflict of Identity', in *From Conflict Resolution to Reconciliation*, ed Y. Bar Siman Tov, The Jerusalem Institute for Israel Studies, Jerusalem [in Hebrew].

Ayalon, A., Sagy, S, 2011, 'Acculturation Attitudes and Perceptions of Collective Narratives. The Case of Israeli-Arab Youth', *Youth and Society,* vol. 43, no. 3, pp. 819–844.

Bar Tal, D. 2007, *Living with the Conflict. Socio-Psychological Analysis of the Jewish Society,* Carmel Press, Jerusalem.

Bar Tal, D., Nahhas, E. 2012, 'Foundations of Culture of Conflict, in *Diversity, Intercultural Encounters and Education,* eds S. Goncalves, M. Carpenter, Routledge, New York, pp. 91–112.

Bar Tal, D., Halperin, E., Oren, N. 2010, 'Socio–Psychological Barriers to Peace Making. The Case of the Israeli Jewish Society', *Social Issues and Policy Review,* vol. 4, no. 1, pp. 63–109.

Bar Tal, D., Oren, N., Nets Zehngut, R. 2014, 'Sociopsychological Analysis of Conflict-Supporting Narratives. A General Framework', *Journal of Peace Research,* vol. 51, no. 5, pp. 662–675.

Batson, C.D. 1991, *The Altruism Question. Toward a Social-Psychological Answer,* Lawrence Erlbaum Associates, Hillsdale, NJ.

Batson, C.D., Ahmad, N.Y. 2009, 'Using Empathy to Improve Intergroup Attitudes and Relations', *Social Issues and Policy Review,* vol. 3, no. 1, pp. 141–177.

Baumeister, R.F., Stillwell, A.M., Heatherton, T.F. 1994, 'Guilt. An Interpersonal Approach', *Psychological Bulletin,* vol. 115, no. 2, pp. 243–267.

Ben David, Y., Hameiri, B., Benheim, S., Leshem, B., Sarid, A., Sternberg, M,. Nadler, A., Sagy, S. 2017, 'Exploring Ourselves within Inter-Group Conflict. The Role of Intra-Group Dialogue in Promoting Acceptance of Collective Narratives and Willingness Towards Reconciliation', *Peace and Conflict. Journal of Peace Psychology,* vol. 23, pp. 269–277.

Cohen, R. 2004, 'Apology and Reconciliation in International Relations', in *From Conflict Resolution to Reconciliation,* ed Y. Bar Siman Tov, Oxford University Press, Oxford, pp. 177–196.

Ericson, M. 2001, *Reconciliation and the Search for a Shared Moral Landscape. An Exploration Based upon a Study of Northern Ireland and South Africa,* Peter Lang Publishing, New York, NY.

Foster, C.A., Rusbult, C.E. 1999, 'Injustice and Power Seeking', *Personality and Social Psychology Bulletin,* vol. 25, no. 7, pp. 834–849.

Gonzalez, R., Manzi, J., Noor, M. 2011, 'Intergroup Forgiveness and Reparation in Chile. The Role of Identity and Intergroup Emotion', in *Beyond Prejudice Reduction. Pathways to Positive Intergroup Relations,* eds L.R. Tropp, R. Mallett, Psychology Press, Washington DC, pp. 221–240.

Hamilton, D.L., Sherman, S.J., Castelli, L. 2002, 'A Group by any Other Name. The Role of Entitativity in Group Perception', *European Review of Social Psychology,* vol. 12, no. 1, pp. 139–166.

Hicks, D 2011, *Dignity. The Essential Role it Plays in Resolving Conflict,* Yale University Press, New Haven, CT.

Hicks, D. 2009, 'Dignity for All', in *No Enemy to Conquer. Forgiveness in an Unforgiving World*, ed M. Henderson, Baylor University Press, Waco, TX, pp. 35–78.

Huth, P.K. 2009, *Standing Your Ground. Territorial Disputes and International Conflict*, University of Michigan Press, Ann Arbor, MI.

Kamir, O. 2004, *Israeli Honor and Dignity. Social Norms, Gender Politics and the Law*, Carmel Press, Jerusalem.

Kamir, O. 2002, 'Honor and Dignity Cultures. The Case of Kavod and Kvod Ha-Adam in Israeli Society and Law', in *The Concept of Human Dignity in Human Rights Discourse*, eds D. Kretzmer, E. Klein, Kluwer, Amsterdam, pp. 231–262.

Kelman, H.C. 2008, 'A Social-Psychological Approach to Conflict Analysis and Resolution', in *Handbook of Conflict Analysis and Resolution*, eds D.J. Sandole, S. Byrne, I. Sandole-Staroste, J. Senehi, Routledge, London, pp. 170–183.

Kelman, H.C. 2004, 'Reconciliation as Identity Change. A Social-Psychological Perspective', in *From Conflict Resolution to Reconciliation*, ed Y. Bar Siman Tov, Oxford University Press, Oxford, pp. 111–124.

Kleinman, A. 2006, *What Really Matters. Living a Moral Life amidst Uncertainty and Danger*, Oxford University Press, Oxford.

Mizrachi, N. 2011, 'Beyond the Garden and the Jungle. On the Social Boundaries of the Human Rights Discourse in Israel', *Ma'asei Mishpat*, vol. 4, pp. 51–74 [in Hebrew].

Mosquera, P.M.R, Manstead, A.S., Fischer, A.H. 2002a, 'Honor in the Mediterranean and Northern Europe', *Journal of Cross-Cultural Psychology*, vol. 33, no. 1, pp. 16–36.

Mosquera, P.M.R, Manstead, A.S., Fischer, A.H. 2002b, 'The Role of Honor Concerns in Emotional Reactions to Offences', *Cognition and Emotion*, vol. 16, no. 1, pp. 143–163.

Olick, J.K. 1999, 'Collective Memory. The Two Cultures', *Sociological Theory*, vol. 17, no. 3, pp. 333–348.

O'Neill, B. 2003, 'Mediating National Honour. Lessons from the Era of Dueling', *Journal of Institutional and Theoretical Economics*, vol. 159, no. 1, pp. 229–247.

O'Neill, B. 2001, *Honor, Symbols, and War*, University of Michigan Press, Ann Arbor, MI.

Oren, N., Bar Tal, D. 2007, 'The Detrimental Dynamics of Delegitimization in Intractable Conflicts. The Israeli-Palestinian Case', *International Journal of Intercultural Relations*, vol. 31, no. 1, pp. 111–126.

Pennebaker, J.W., Banasik, B.L. 1997, 'On the Creation and Maintenance of Collective Memories. History as Social Psychology', in *Collective Memory of Political Events. Social Psychological Perspectives*, eds J.W. Pennebaker, D. Paez, B. Rimé, Lawrence Erlbaum Associates, Hillsdale, NJ, pp. 3–19.

Perla, L. 1918, *What is "National Honor"? The Challenge of the Reconstruction*, The Macmillan Company, New York.

Pettigrew, T.F., Tropp, L.R. 2006, 'A Meta-Analytic Test of Intergroup Contact Theory', *Journal of Personality and Social Psychology*, vol. 90, no. 5, pp. 751–783.

Sagy S., Adwan, S., Kaplan, A. 2002, 'Interpretations of the Past and Expectations for the Future among Israeli and Palestinians Youth', *American Journal of Orthopsychiatry*, vol. 72, no. 1, pp. 26–38.

Sagy, S, Orr, E., Bar-On, D., Awwad, E. 2001, 'Individualism and Collectivism in Two Conflicted Societies. Comparing Israeli-Jewish and Palestinian-Arab High School Students', *Youth and Society*, vol. 33, no. 1, pp. 3–30.

Sagy, S., Orr, E., Bar-On, D. 1999, 'Individualism and Collectivism in Israeli Society. Comparing Religious and Secular High-School Students', *Human Relations*, vol. 52, no. 3, pp. 327–348.

Scheff, T.J. 1994, *Bloody Revenge. Emotions, Nationalism, and War*, Westview Press, Boulder, CO.

Shafir, G., Peled, Y. 2002, *Being Israeli. The Dynamics of Multiple Citizenship*, Cambridge University Press, Cambridge.

Shnabel, N., Nadler, A., Ullrich, J., Dovidio, J.F., Carmi, D. 2009, 'Promoting Reconciliation through the Satisfaction of the Emotional Needs of Victimized and Perpetrating Group Members. The Needs-Based Model of Reconciliation', *Personality and Social Psychology Bulletin*, vol. 35, no. 8, pp. 1021–1030.

Srour, A., Sagy, S., Mana, A., Mjally-Knani, S. 2013, 'Collective Narratives as Indicators of Examining Intergroup Relations. The Case of Palestinian Muslims and Christians in Israel', *International Journal of Conflict Management*, vol. 24, no. 3, pp. 231–244.

Staub, E. 2006, 'Reconciliation after Genocide, Mass Killing, or Intractable Conflict. Understanding the Roots of Violence, Psychological Recovery, and Steps Toward a General Theory', *Political Psychology*, vol 27, no. 6, pp. 867–894.

Sternberg, M., Litvak Hirsch, T., Sagy, S. 2018, 'Nobody Ever Told Us. The Contribution of Intragroup Dialogue to Reflexive Learning about Violent Conflict', *Peace and Conflict. Journal of Peace Psychology*, vol. 24, no. 2, pp. 127–138.

Sternhell, Z. 2010, *The Anti-Enlightenment Tradition*, Yale University Press, New Haven, CT.

Tajfel, H., Turner, J.C. 1986, 'The Social Identity Theory of Intergroup Behavior', in *Psychology of Intergroup Relations*, eds S. Worchel, W.G. Austin, Nelson-Hall, Chicago, IL, pp. 7–24.

Taylor, C. 1994, 'The Politics of Recognition', in *Multiculturalism*, ed A. Gutman, Princeton University Press, Princeton, NJ, pp. 25–73.

Tileaga, C. 2007, 'Ideologies of Moral Exclusion. A Critical Discursive Reframing of Depersonalization, Delegitimization and Dehumanization', *British Journal of Social Psychology*, vol. 46, no. 4, pp. 717–737.

Triandis, H.C., Bontempo, R., Villareal, M.J., Asai, M., Lucca, N. 1988, 'Individualism and Collectivism. Cross-Cultural Perspectives on Self-Ingroup Relationships', *Journal of Personality and Social Psychology*, vol. 54, no. 2, pp. 323–338.

UN General Assembly 1948, *The Universal Declaration of Human Rights*, (General Assembly resolution 217 A, https://www.un.org/en/universal-declaration-human-rights/

Van der Merwe, H., Chapman, A.R. (eds). 2008, *Truth and Reconciliation in South Africa. Did the TRC Deliver?* University of Pennsylvania Press, Philadelphia, PA.

Von Borries, B. 1997, 'Political Attitudes and Decisions Based on Historical Experiences and Analyses', in *Youth and history*, eds M. Angvik, B. Von Borries, Körber Stiftung Edition, Hamburg, pp. 153–176.

White, R.K. 1998, 'American Acts of Force', *Peace and Conflict. Journal of Peace Psychology,* vol. 4, no 2, pp. 93–12.

Manar Faraj

# Palestinian Students introduced to the historical narrative of the other

The role the intragroup Dialogue Encounters [Play] in Reconciliation

## Abstract

In May and October of 2017, the Jena Center of Reconciliation, as part of the "Hearts of Flesh–Not Stone" project, invited Palestinian students for a trip to Germany to learn about the history of Germany and the narrative of the "other" by visiting the Buchenwald Concentration Camp. Manar Faraj's paper, Palestinian Students Encountering the Suffering of the Other: *The Role, the Intergroup and Intragroup Dialogue Encounters Play in Reconciliation*, compares two groups of Palestinian students, the intergroup who had intergroup dialogue meetings with the other before the trip and the intragroup that never had this experience before the trip. The measurements of her research focus on three scales: positive attitude, more understanding, and more readiness for reconciliation. The findings show significant differences between the intergroup and intragroup. Moreover, in the focus groups, the discussion of both groups was more in-depth and explored more of the measurements, which had more positivity and more willingness to work on reconciliation.

## 1. Introduction

### 1.1 The Background of the Palestinian-Israeli Conflict Since 1948

The Israeli occupation of Palestine dates back to before 1948. The year 1948[1] is a significant milestone as it marks the time the state of Israel was established after what the Israelis call the *War of Independence* and what the Palestinians call the *Nakba*, Arabic for the "catastrophe." The Nakba resulted in around 80 percent of the Palestinians who had resided in the land now part of Israel becoming refugees. They fled their lands during the attack. Thus, the *Nakba* came to represent "the loss of the homeland, the disintegration of society, the frustration of national aspirations,

---

1 https://www.un.org/unispal/history/

and the beginning of a hasty process of destruction of their culture" to Palestinians (Saʿdi 2002, p. 175).

In his book *The Ethnic Cleansing of Palestine*, Jewish historian Ilan Pappé has covered the gaps in history, using archives as proof of what has been done to the Palestinians. He found that long before the 1948 Palestinian *Nakba*, Zionist organizations had planned the ethnic cleansing of the Palestinians and geared up for the war. With the destruction of the Arab leadership, there was no threat to the Zionist plan to ethnically cleanse Palestine because the Palestinians had no military or support (Pappé 2014, p. 11).

The situation of the Palestinians further deteriorated in 1967 after the Six-Day War, in which Israel, in a kind of preventive strike, attacked Egypt, Jordan, and Syria and won in only six days. The war yielded significant gains for Israel. It had seized and occupied the West Bank from Jordan, the Golan Heights from Syria, the Gaza Strip, and the Sinai Peninsula from Egypt, causing once again a mass exodus of hundreds of thousands of refugees. Except for the Sinai, which was returned to Egypt in 1982, Israel continues to occupy the other territories militarily. About 3 million Palestinians still live in the West Bank and Gaza under Israeli occupation, despite United Nations Resolution 242, passed in November of 1967, which calls for Israeli withdrawal from the territories[2] .

The first Palestinian Intifada or uprising against the Israeli occupation began in late 1987 and intensified in 1988, 40 years after the birth of Israel. Intifada, translated from Arabic, means "a tremor, a shudder or a shiver," the root of the word, *nafada*, meaning "to shake off, to rid oneself of something, to refuse to have anything to do with something" (. The Intifada began as a youth movement resulting from long-standing economic, social, and political aggravations felt by the Palestinians living in the occupied territories. It was mainly a period of civil disobedience during which the Palestinians boycotted Israeli goods and jobs and refused to pay taxes. Violence was kept in check and was limited to the throwing of stones by children and young people at Israeli soldiers.

Various attempts were made to establish peace between the Israelis and Palestinians through the Oslo Accords in 1993, and their follow-up, Oslo II, was signed in 1995. In 2000, President Bill Clinton hosted former Israeli Prime Minister Ehud Barak and Palestinian Authority leader Yasser Arafat at Camp David to further the peace process. However, Arafat walked out, unsatisfied with Barak's concessions.

In June 2002, the Israeli government decided to begin building a physical barrier between Israel and the Palestinian territories, which known as the "security fence." While most of the barrier is an electronic fence fortified by barbed wire and 60-meter-wide trenches dug on either side, it is a concrete wall built between six to

---

2  https://peacemaker.un.org/sites/peacemaker.un.org/files/SCRes242%281967%29.pdf

eight meters high in more populated areas. For this reason, it is called the Separation Wall, or the Apartheid Wall, by Palestinians and Israeli Human Rights organizations such as B'Tselem.

## 1.2 Theoretical Background: Israeli occupation of Palestine as Identity-Conflict

This paper does not aim to provide a historical narrative but to look at the current Israeli occupation of Palestine in the present and the peacebuilding initiatives. The perspective of the current paper is that the Israeli occupation of Palestine is described as a conflict of identity between two populations who claim the same territory as their homeland. This means that the conflict is not just about land; instead, the land is a central part of the identity of both people. The land is even so important that it is religiously highly significant. For religious Jews, it is the land promised by God. Muslims and Christians believe possessing the "Holy Land" is religiously important. Land claims made by the other side mean that not only interests or possessions but also identity is threatened. (Kelman 2007, p. 288). "The other's identity and its associated narrative challenge the group's claims to ownership – at least to exclusive ownership – of the land and its resources" (Kelman 2001, p. 192). Even if identity plays a vital role in almost all political conflicts in the Israeli occupation of Palestine, every compromise on land implies a kind of betrayal of an essential part of one's identity. This is one of the reasons why negotiated conflict resolution is difficult to achieve. Preparation and backing through social processes are needed. The majority of these processes have been organized on the grassroots level, aiming at building coexistence, cooperation, and reconciliation among Palestinians and Israelis. More than 100 organizations are working on that grassroots level for peace between Israel-Palestine [3].

## 2. Theories of Change Used by Previous Initiatives and Researches

This paragraph attempts to give a sketch of previous approaches to change in the attitude of Israelis and Palestinians. Those theories are important for the experiences described in the Hearts of Flesh–Not Stone Project. The not fully satisfying results of empirical applications of the previous theories explain why to move on towards a new model. The approach used in the Hearts of Flesh experience can be characterized as the "reconciliation-oriented way of separate and individual

---

3 For a not complete list see the members of Alliance for Middle East Peace: http://www.allmep.org/members

learning." This approach and the consequence of this experience will be described later. First, we resume the classical contact hypothesis (according to Allport), narrative model and dialogue encounter model (according to Bar-On), the circle of forgiveness (according to Nadler), and intragroup approach (according to Sagy) in order to discuss achievements and limits very briefly.

## 2.1 The Classical Contact Hypothesis

A prevalent social-psychological approach is based on the contact hypothesis presented by the American social psychologist Gordon Allport (1954). Social psychologist Yehuda Amir (1969) developed this theory in the Israeli context. Contact theory states that there will be less prejudice if people involved in the conflict meet under certain conditions (Allport 1954). According to contact theory, many intergroup encounters have been organized between Israelis and Palestinians. Just a short time ago, football matches between Israeli and Palestinian youth were organized and presented in newspapers as a step toward understanding and peace[4]. Such short-time encounters have none, almost no positive and often even negative effects. Gordon Allport already described this: "Where segregation is the custom contacts are casual, or else firmly frozen into superordinate-subordinate relationships. Such evidence indicated that such contacts do not dispel prejudice; it seems more likely to increase it" (Allport 1954, p. 263). Allport describes mistrust and suspicion as factors to activate prejudice in casual encounters.

However, if there are more intensive and long-term experiences of contact that respect both parties' status as equal (while making sure of differentiate between the occupier and the occupied) and create cooperation for common objectives, it should be more likely that there will be less prejudice and more solidarity, according to Allport. He asserts that the "nub of the matter seems to be that contact must reach below the surface in order to be effective in altering prejudice." (Allport 1954, p. 276).

Relatively closely to this approach comes the activities of NGOs, which brought together adolescent Israelis and Palestinians and others from conflict areas to a camp stay with leadership training, learning about the conflict, conflict resolution, other joint activities, and encounters during the following year. Although Allport noted that the type of contact, as established by the contact hypothesis, is what leads people to do things together and is likely to result in changed attitudes (Allport 1954, p. 276), the limits of such initiatives, in this case, include the difficulty in

---

4  cf. for a match in 2014: https://www.spiegel.de/consent-?targetUrl=https%3A%2F%2Fwww.spiegel. de%2Flebenundlernen%2Fschule%2Fvoelkerverstaendigung-israelis-und-palaestinenser-spielen-fussball-a-989366.html&ref=https%3A%2F%2Fwww.google.com%2F

building long-term relationships between Israeli and Palestinian participants with the increasing difficulties for Palestinians from the Westbank and Gaza to meet with Israelis. A general criticism of encounter and cooperation projects is that it is challenging to address trauma and almost daily conflict incidents in such groups. If the conflict is identity-based conflict, more profound experiences are needed to change the identities and construct a new identity. In addition to that, the presentation of the Israeli occupation of Palestine provoked discussions and criticism from the Palestinian side.[5] An approach not built on a single story but the two narratives of the two people and individual narratives of every person seemed to be more promising.

## 2.2 The Narrative Model/Storytelling Model with Dialogue Encounters

The focus on dialogue encounters is very strong in the conflict resolution and peacebuilding field. Sometimes those encounters follow communication rules and try to create empathic listening. The target is to understand each other, creating a common culture in the intergroup dialogue encounters that can be taken back to mobilize the community positively and peacefully (Schwartz 1989). However, Abu Nimer (1995) argues that some of the dialogue group encounters can weaken political development because of the power relations among the participants.

It seems to be particularly promising to combine the encounter with listening to and acknowledging the other's narrative. This narrative model was developed by the late Israeli psychologist Dan Bar-On, first with dialogues between Jewish survivors of the Holocaust and German children of perpetrators, then in encounters between Israelis and Palestinians (Bar-On 2006). This model uses a narrative approach where participants from different groups—in this case, Palestinians and Israelis—share stories about their lives in the conflict and how the conflict affects their identity (Bar-On 2000, 2006, 2008; Maoz 2004). Dealing with emotions of anger and hate, the Narrative Model digs deep into the very sensitive issues of the conflict (Maoz and Bar-On 2002). It aims to help participants see the other as a human being and to understand and listen to the other as a human being without all the negative emotions (Kassem 2004). Different narratives can be accepted and stand side by side. At least a few deep and sustainable friendships could be built through those dialogues, such as between Sami Adwan and Dan Bar-On. Even issues of confession of guilt and forgiveness could be addressed in those intensive groups.

Increasing difficulties for Israelis and Palestinians to meet and daily politics often interfered with scheduled meetings. Today, after the separation wall Aparthied Wall as Palestinian call it and Dan Bar-On's death in 2008, only special groups of

---

5 cf. https://electronicintifada.net/content/can-we-talk-dle-east-peace-industry/8402

personally concerned victims of the conflict, such as the Parents'Circle or Combatants for Peace, represent this type of approach with deep listening to each other's narrative, going into emotions and building friendships across the conflict lines. Those groups are critical and can one day become models for these societies. The limits of such groups lie in the necessarily small number of participants. Attempts to make an educational approach out of the narrative encounter groups did not find the needed reception in classrooms and cannot lead to any progress in the Israeli-Palestinian peace process as long as both populations are so fundamentally separated (cf. PRIME et al. 2009). The presentation of a parallel history, one as the Israeli and the other as the Palestinian narrative, even if there are lines in the middle to write one's narrative, can even foster the fixation of two irreconcilable versions of the history of the conflict.

## 2.3 The Apology-Forgiveness Circle (Arie Nadler)

According to Arie Nadler an even more profound but still very challenging approach is socio-emotional reconciliation. Nadler distinguishes between instrumental forms of reconciliation, which are more or less built on contact and socio-emotional reconciliation with apologies, and forgiveness. Even storytelling is built on contact and meetings. The stories can lead to understanding, sympathy, and less hurtful interpretations of suffering and adversities inflicted by the other side. A more profound way is taken if somebody in the perpetrator position presents a sincere and believable apology to the victims, and the victim forgives them, the other. This dynamic means that the different needs of victims and perpetrators are to be respected. Victims need empowerment, security ("never again"), and agency. Perpetrators need to be accepted in the moral community again. Like in an exchange, apology and forgiveness provide both parties what they need (cf. Nadler et al. 2008). This approach, however, presupposes those persons are willing to apologize and forgive. In the Israeli occupation of Palestine, such persons are not easily found. The apology-forgiveness-circle requires at least certain contact between conflicting parties, but what can be done if no contact is possible? And the occupation continues?

## 2.4 Intragroup Approach

The trilateral Heart of Flesh project was built as a completely new start, because intergroup experiences are challenging to achieve, and *separate* educational experiences can prepare for reconciliation. The trilateral project, Hearts of Flesh–Not Stone, funded by DFG, the German Research Foundation, is a cooperation between the Jena Center for Reconciliation Studies, Tel Aviv University, Ben-Gurion University of the Negev, and Wasatia Institute in East Jerusalem. The project comprises different research, one being the intragroup dialogue in separate groups conducted at Ben-Gurion University. Previous research literature does not present the intra-group approach as much as the intergroup approach in the context of conflict and the other. Dan Bar-On's disciple and successor at Ben-Gurion University, Shifra Sagy and team describe how their research team conducted qualitative and quanti-tative research on a year-long course with Israeli students (Ben David et al.2017). The research mainly focused on Identity of oneself and the other, emotions and feelings toward the other. Presenting a new approach to the intragroup dialogue method, the team at Ben-Gurion University fills in some of the gaps in the literature. The results of that project are in this volume. They show how reflective processes within groups can lead to different views on the conflict. My research is about Palestinians in the same project having a different experience of encountering the suffering of Jewish people without directly meeting Jews or Israelis.

## 3. Background

The Hearts of Flesh–Not Stone project included three travel experiences of groups of Palestinians going to Concentration camps in Europe where Jewish people were suffering: The first one, in April 2014, was to Auschwitz-Birkenau Concentration Camp was a journey where participants met with Israeli researchers and witnesses; on the second and third trips, in May and October of 2017, students came to Germany and visited several historical places, including a visit to the Buchenwald Concentration Camp. In experiences 2 and 3, no Israeli participant was present, and no Israeli was encountered.

For this paper, I will only present the two trips in 2017. The participants who went on the trips were independent and did not represent any university; they agreed to come on these trips voluntarily. However, the groups who had separate experiences (without meeting of Israelis on the trip) were quite different regarding their previous experiences and habits of contact with Israelis. Some of them were members of peace groups and had experience with talking about the conflict, reconciliation, and meeting with Israelis. I call those participants the intergroup participants or intergroup students, using the word "students" not because they are enrolled in a university but because it was an educational experience. For other trip participants of the trips, I name intragroup participants or intragroup students. They are really and deeply "intragroup" because they have no contact with Israelis apart from soldiers, no usual dialogue with them, and do not participate in peace initiatives.

### 3.1 Hypothesis of this Paper

The participants experienced in intergroup dialogue meetings would have more positive attitudes toward the other, a deeper understating of the other's narrative, and were more willing to act toward reconciliation than the intragroup participants. The latter would have less positive attitudes toward the other, a more shallow understanding of the other's narrative, and less willingness to act toward reconciliation.

## 3.2 Method

A questionnaire was collected from the students who went on the second and third trips to Germany as part of the trilateral project.

The questionnaire has 15 questions that deal with three concepts: the attitude toward the other, a better understanding of the other, and the readiness to act toward reconciliation. The research analyzed the questionnaires by selecting cases from the data downloaded to SPSS by the researcher. The researcher chose the two groups: the intergroup and the intragroup. The research did the following tests to analyze the data: the descriptive statistics and the mean differences between the two groups.

The questionnaire had the 5-point Likert Scale ranging from 1 (I strongly disagree) to 5 (I strongly agree).

Focus groups: the researcher conducted focus groups with the intragroup and the intergroup students as individual groups and then together.

Personal observations: the researcher joined the students for the first trip to Auschwitz and was one of the main coordinators for the second trip to Germany. The researcher also followed the intergroup students' experience by meeting with Israelis two years before the trip to Germany.

## 3.3 Sample

Twenty students, ten females and ten males, all from the West Bank in Palestine, participated in this questionnaire. Ten of them participated in an intergroup model dialogue with a group of Israelis in different peacebuilding projects before the trip to Germany. The other 10, in the intragroup, were presented the other's narrative for the first time through visiting the Buchwald concentration camp during the HoF project's trip.

Table 1 Sample Group

|       |        | Frequency | Percent | Valid Percent | Cumulative Percent |
|-------|--------|-----------|---------|---------------|--------------------|
| Valid | Male   | 10        | 50.0    | 50.0          | 50.0               |
|       | Female | 10        | 50.0    | 50.0          | 100.0              |
|       | Total  | 20        | 100.0   | 100.0         |                    |

Table 2  Participation in dialogue meetings before the trip

|  |  | Frequency | Percent | Valid Percent | Cumulative Percent |
|---|---|---|---|---|---|
| Valid | Yes | 10 | 50.0 | 50.0 | 50.0 |
|  | No | 10 | 50.0 | 50.0 | 100.0 |
|  | Total | 20 | 100.0 | 100.0 |  |

## 3.4  Measurements

The first measurements are of the positive attitudes toward the other with three questions concerning belief in the other's willingness to work on building peace and reconciliation. The second measurements are about a better understanding of the other with eight questions that deal with understanding of the others' suffering and narratives. The third measurement is about the readiness to act toward reconciliation; three questions ask the participants if, after this trip, they are more willing to work on peacebuilding and reconciliation.

## 3.5  Results

The intergroup dialogue meetings were conducted in different peacebuilding organizations that focus on the narrative model and its role in reconciliation. For the intragroup students, it was their first time going through the experience of the narrative of the other.

Table 3  The Mean of the Axes

| I was involved with intergroup dialogue encounters before the trip |  | Positive attitudes toward the other | Better understanding | Readiness to Act |
|---|---|---|---|---|
| Yes | Mean | 3.4000 | 3.8333 | 1.1333 |
|  | N | 10 | 10 | 10 |
|  | Std. Deviation | 1.03994 | .56314 | .32203 |
| No | Mean | 1.6333 | 2.9250 | 1.6000 |
|  | N | 10 | 10 | 10 |
|  | Std. Deviation | 1.20134 | .72217 | .43885 |
| Total | Mean | 2.5167 | 3.3792 | 1.3667 |
|  | N | 20 | 20 | 20 |
|  | Std. Deviation | 1.42030 | .78383 | .44459 |

According to the tests of the questionnaire, the results showed for the axes are as follows:

The intergroup students had a more positive attitude toward the other (N=3.6) than the intragroup students (N=1.6), which strongly disagrees.

A majority of the intergroup students agreed with the claim that they view the other side more positively; it was the opposite for the intragroup.

The average of the second axis for the intergroup is (n=3.8), which is in "agreement"; the intragroup is (n=2.92), which is "I don't know."

A clear majority of the intergroup students had a better understanding of the other's viewpoint, the suffering, and even a better understanding of the roots of the conflict and their positions on it. The intergroup students agreed with the saying that the trips allowed them to discover and better understand the roots of the Israeli occupation of Palestine, while the intragroup did not know how much this trip benefited them in understanding the other.

Despite these statistical differences, it is worth mentioning the similarity of both groups' responses to the second statement of the axis, "the other can not really understand my pain and show solidarity, "in which both groups showed a strong agreement with this statement—4.3 by the intergroup students and 4.8 by the intragroup students.

Both groups also agreed with the fifth statement, "I know very well the narrative of the other."

The mean of the third axis (readiness to act toward Reconciliation) for the intergroup is (n=1.13), which is a yes, and the intragroup results show a not readiness to act toward reconciliation. The quantitative results show that a majority of intergroup students were interested in working together to promote joint causes and advance a solution to the Israeli occupation of Palestine.

## 4.    The Discussion

The researcher believes that the gap in the answers between the intergroup students and the intragroup students stems from the fact that, for the Palestinian intragroup students, this was their first encounter with the suffering of the other. Palestinian's usual everyday experiences with the occupation lead them to solely recall images of active-duty Israeli soldiers or Israeli fanatic groups. From their previous experiences and encounters with the other, some of the intergroup students had formed personal connections, which included, among other things, telephone contact or social media, and, in some cases, visits and personal meetings.

The lower result in the intragroup may indicate a lower understanding of the complexity of the conflict and the difficulty some of them feel in letting go of what they see as the one "right" narrative. On the other hand, the intergroup were "more positive". Palestinian intergroup students in the focus group were asked whether the understanding they gained changed their attitude towards the Israelis for the better. Most answered that it did, but only slightly, since they had arrived to the encounter with a positive attitude. In the student intragroup, a student who described herself as someone who had experienced great turmoil said, "With me, instead of bringing down the wall, they were being built...I realized that it is very complicated." Another participant from the intragroup claimed that she came on the trip with heavy feelings and left it with heavier feelings: "Not from their side. What discouraged me most was the historical narrative and what humans can do to each other." These two students allow the researcher to a better understanding of the processes the participants undergo.

As mentioned by researchers in the past, changing known thought patterns toward the other is no simple matter, particularly in the midst of a protracted conflict, as under the current circumstances which encourage the exclusion of the other, blurring the variety in each group. The fact that the intragroup students made an effort to attend the focus group after the trip to Germany is an optimistic sign.

According to *Contact Theory*, the meeting of groups in a conflict contributes to creating positive mutual viewpoints. The *Narrative Model* of the meetings focuses on recognizing the narrative of the others and attempting to understand them, even while disagreeing with them. This behaviour denotes recognition of the other's existence, suffering, and ambitions. According to the model, this recognition promotes the aspiration to live in peace (Bar-On 2002).

The findings indicate different trends, which might explain the gaps between different schools (e. g., private or governmental) between intergroup and intragroup. In governmental schools in Israel and the Palestinian Authority, the government does not encourage open discourse, questions, or critical analysis of the state of affairs; there is an increasing silencing of and concern among educators, limiting their capability for action. There are, nonetheless, schools in which action is possible, in which the standing of male teachers is more robust, thus allowing them more freedom.

One of the intragroup student participants testified that he "took the initiative and spoke about his participation in the classroom, arguing with those who disagreed with him. Afterward, he spoke about the subject on Facebook, the social media site."[6] The meaningful reasoning for his actions relies on his belief that by working together, it is possible to influence reality, mitigate Palestinian suffering under the occupation, and perhaps also influence Israeli public opinion and Israeli decision-makers to end the occupation. An intergroup student emphasized the importance of joint action so long as it remains political: "Our conflict is political. With all due respect to humanitarian efforts, that is not what will bring us closer to a solution to the conflict."

The quantitative data is supported by the words of the participants of the German trip: "I joined because I felt the need to do something so there will be peace." "The

---

6 Focus group, 28.11.2017.

program of the trip is built perfectly,"[7] but "what comes of it? That is a different question." Shortly after completing the trip, the intragroup students initiated a meeting: "We held a meeting on Saturday initiated by the intragroup, and discussions were raised, and we'll see how to continue."[8] An intergroup participant from the focus group described how the trip moved him to action: "The subject of narrative, and the visits to the German historical sites, from there I decided to continue to act and participate in dialogue meetings so I can let the world know about the suffering of the Palestinians and about the need for peace."[9]

In order to enable the inter-and intragroup students to contribute to conflict transformation and reconciliation, the researcher recommends including more content beyond the models of human relations from the school of psychology and content from the Conflictual Model, which hinges on the field of conflict resolution, to enable readiness for action towards resolving the conflict. For example, workshops that include tools and capacity building in conflict analysis, strategy building for dealing with conflicts and their transformation, simulation games, and tools for directing negotiations could better lead the groups to another level of understanding the other and working on peace and reconciliation.

## 4.1  Medium-Long-Term Results, Impact and Sustainability

Despite Israeli soldiers' attacks on and the ongoing killing Palestinians between May and October of 2017, participants generally serve as agents of change in society, working within a framework supporting action that provides them with a relatively easy transition from attitude changes to acting towards change. The intergroup students, who initiated meetings with the intragroup students to motivate them to action, were also invited to meet with different peacebuilding organizations.

Most of the participants of these trips joined a social media network, where they created a Facebook group to talk about issues regarding the trip to Germany and what to do next. A participant from the intragroup has left the Facebook group. After a discussion with her in the focus group, she said, "I cannot continue with this because I always remember my brother who was burnt to death from the Israeli settlers after they put gas in his mouth and was burnt alive."[10] An intergroup participant said he does not "see the Israelis understanding the suffering that Palestinians go through every day,"[11] while he does understand the suffering the Jews and others faced during the Holocaust. Another intergroup participant said that due to her

---

7  Focus group, 28.11.2017.
8  Focus group, 28.11.2017.
9  Focus group, 28.11.2017.
10  Focus group, 28.11.2017.
11  Focus group, 28.11.2017.

participation in the trip, "I have hope that understanding is possible and that an agreement can be reached so we can avoid another event like this, meaning the Holocaust."[12]

## 4.2 Horizontal Impact

To find out the trips' indirect circles of impact, the groups were asked whether they shared their experiences in the program with family and friends, and what reactions they received. Surprisingly, a clear majority of the participants from both groups shared their experiences and insights with additional circles. The program thus influenced other circles through the participants' sharing of their experiences with family and acquaintances. This can be considered a preliminary outcome of meetings. However, it might be leveraged by developing a strategy and methodical action.

Sixty percent of the intragroup students answered that they shared their experiences with friends and/or family, and 90% of the intergroup students answered that they shared their experiences of the trip with friends and or family.

Table 4   Are you going to talk about the trip to family and friends Intergroup

|       |       | Frequency | Percent | Valid Percent | Cumulative Percent |
|-------|-------|-----------|---------|---------------|--------------------|
| Valid | Yes   | 9         | 90.0    | 90.0          | 90.0               |
|       | No    | 1         | 10.0    | 10.0          | 100.0              |
|       | Total | 10        | 100.0   | 100.0         |                    |

Table 5   Are you going to talk about the trip to family and friends Intragroup

|       |       | Frequency | Percent | Valid Percent | Cumulative Percent |
|-------|-------|-----------|---------|---------------|--------------------|
| Valid | Yes   | 6         | 60.0    | 60.0          | 60.0               |
|       | No    | 4         | 40.0    | 40.0          | 100.0              |
|       | Total | 10        | 100.0   | 100.0         |                    |

This result is surprisingly positive in light of the context, particularly concerning the intragroup students and the lack of public support for dialogue meetings. The researcher carefully suggests viewing this as faith in the Jena Center for Reconciliation Studies' effective contribution to promoting a solution. An intragroup participant said, "I shared my experience from the trip with some of my friends;

---

12  Focus group, 28.11.2017.

mostly they were interested to know more, and one of them stopped being friends with me and called me a collaborator with the enemy."[13]

One of the intergroup students interviewed claimed that he stopped sharing his experiences with family and acquaintances because he has no patience for cynical remarks. Another participant said that although she shared her experience, it was "without success." However, another participant added that she bought some books by Dan Bar-On and Sami Adwan and she forced family members and friends to read them.

## 5. The Contribution of the Trip Program's Components to Reconciliation and Peacebuilding

The participants of both focus groups emphasized specific components as having a significant impact on them. First and foremost were the visit to the Berlin Wall and the visit to the Buchenwald Concentration camp; then comes the underlying approach of the program, various activities, and their combination – the format and the team. There was a complete agreement regarding the power of the visit to the Berlin Wall, and the lecture that followed by Professor Martin Leiner about the wall and the connection between the Apartheid wall that Israel built and the Berlin wall.

There was disagreement in the focus groups about two topics. First, the program objectives; should the goal be to promote reconciliation to develop support and a willingness to accept peace processes, or should it be to end the occupation? An argument arose during the discussion about whether the conflict should be discussed directly. Second, is it right to create equality as a directing value of the process, when, in reality, there is no equality? "I don't understand what it means to be reconciled; why do we need to put the conflict on the table?"[14] Another participant responded: "I can meet a German without talking about the Holocaust, but the occupation is happening here and now, it is too early. Israelis need to understand what it is about, and it needs to be processed. Outside, hate reigns. But I agree that in the group, we need to determine the agenda together if we ever meet with Israelis in dialogue groups." A participant from the intragroup caused animated discussion after raising the question of the apparent equality in the dialogue intergroup encounters, feeling it was important to convey his message: "I

---

13 Focus group, 28.11.2017.
14 Focus group, 28.11.2017.

object to the false presentation of symmetry in these groups, meaning the intergroup dialogue meetings."[15]

As for the program's structure, an intragroup student said to the focus group, "It was a powerful experience, taught me a lot about myself and about them. I listen to people differently now. That sometimes you just need to be silent and listen and not think constantly about how to respond...the formal structure."[16] Another intragroup participant said she felt that the participants of the trip, in general, were examined, at first, through the prejudices some of the leaders of the group had about them—especially the internationals. "Although it wasn't callous, I felt the pressure."[17] She added that it was important to her to "make the knowledge they lacked approachable."[18]

There was agreement in the focus groups about the trip to the Buchenwald Concentration Camp being a significant component of the program. "The trip to the concentration camp was one of the most important to the understanding of the narrative and the roots of the conflict,"[19] said one of the participants from the intergroup.

There was complete agreement about the impact of the lecture at the Jena Center for Reconciliation Studies by Professor Leiner about reconciliation and examples of different conflicts around the world, and the discussion that irrupted afterward. However, some said that the presentations of different topics by the students were not processed appropriately: "excellent idea, but the activity needs to be processed."[20]

Most of the participants in the group indicated the need for more processing time regarding, activities, discussions, and implementation programs of the next steps.

## 6.    Summary

This research examines the second and third trips to Germany, which began in May 2017 and ended in October 2017, with intergroup students who had participated in dialogue narrative encounters with Israelis before the trip and intragroup students who had never participated in dialogue meetings with Israelis and were, for the first time, encountering the narrative of the "other." The two groups had different experiences and responses to the measurements of the trips' impacts in terms of

---

15  Focus group, 28.11.2017.
16  Focus group, 28.11.2017.
17  Focus group, 28.11.2017.
18  Focus group, 28.11.2017.
19  Focus group, 28.11.2017.
20  Focus group, 28.11.2017.

a positive attitude toward the other, more understanding of the other, and the readiness to act for reconciliation. Overall, participants from the focus groups expressed their appreciation for this opportunity to learn about the other. This experience led them to learn more about themselves and their identity in this conflict. In addition, the program components influenced both groups' knowledge.

### References

Abu Nimer, M. 1995, *Conflict Resolution and Dialogue in Arab-Jewish Relations in Israel: A Case of Change and Control*, Paper Presented at the American Sociology Association annual meeting. Toronto. August 19–23, 1995

Allport, G.W. 1954, *The Nature of Prejudice*, Addison-Wesley, Reading, Mass.

Amir, Y. 1969, 'Contact hypothesis in ethnic relations', *Psychological Bulletin, 71/5*, pp. 319–342.

Bar-On, D. (2008). *The Others within us: Constructing Jewish-Israeli identity*. (N. Canin, Trans.). Cambridge University Press.

Bar-On, D. 2006, *Tell your Life Story. Creating Dialogue between Jews and Germans, Israelis and Palestinians*. Budapest/New York: Central European University Press.

Bar-On, D. 2002, Conciliation through storytelling: Beyond victimhood. In G. Salomon & B. Nevo (eds.), *Peace Education: The concept, principles, and practices around the world*. Mahwah, NJ: Lawrence Erlbaum. (pp. 109–116).

Bar-On, R. (2000). Emotional and social intelligence: Insights from the Emotional Quotient Inventory. In R. Bar-On & J. D. A. Parker (Eds.), *The handbook of emotional intelligence: Theory, development, assessment, and application at home, school, and in the workplace* (pp. 363–388). Jossey-Bass.

Ben David, Y., Hameiri, B., Benheim, S., Leshem, B., Sarid, A., Sternberg, M, Nadler, A., Sagy, S. 2017, 'Exploring Ourselves within Inter-Group Conflict. The Role of Intra-Group Dialogue in Promoting Acceptance of Collective Narratives and Willingness Towards Reconciliation', *Peace, and Conflict. Journal of Peace Psychology*, vol. 23, pp. 269–277.

Btselem.org 2011, *The Separation Barrier | B'Tselem*. [online] Available at: http://www.bt-selem.org/English/Separation_Barrier/ [Accessed: 20 June 2019] Storytelling as a Way to Work Through Intractable Conflicts: The German-Jewish Experience and Its Relevance to the Palestinian-Israeli Context June 2004 Journal of Social Issues 60(2):289 – 306 DOI:10.1111/j.0022-4537.2004.00112.x

Kelman HC. Preconditions in Mideast negotiations. The Boston Globe. 2007: A17.Abstract Preconditions_in_Mideast_negotiations_2007.pdf.

Kelman HC. How to renew the Israeli-Palestinian peace process. The Boston Globe. 2001: A11. how_to_renew_the_i-p_peace_process_2001.pdf

Maoz, I. 2004, Does contact work in protracted asymmetrical conflict? Appraising 20 years of reconciliation-aimed encounters between Israeli Jews and Palestinians. *Journal of Peace Research* , 115–125

Maoz, I., & Bar-On, D. (2002). From working through the Holocaust to current ethnic conflicts: Evaluating the TRT group workshop in Hamburg. *Group, 26*(1), 29–48. https://doi.org/10.1023/A:1015595027902

Nadler,A., Malloy, T., Fisher, J.D. 2008,*The Social Psychology of Intergroup* Reconciliation, Oxford University Press, New York.

Pappé, I. 2014,*The Ethnic Cleansing of Palestine*. Oneworld Publications, Oxford.

PRIME (2009) (= Peace Research Institute in the Middle East), Adwan, S.; Bar-On, D., Naveh, E. (Eds.) =, *Limid et HaNarrativ HA HistorischelHa'Acher/Ta'allumAr-riwaya At-tarihhiya li-t-taraf al-ahar,* Bethlehem.

Sa'di, Ahmad. (2002). Catastrophe, Memory and Identity: Al-Nakbah as a Component of Palestinian Identity. Israel Studies. 7. pp. 175–198. 10.1353/is.2002.0016.

Schwartz, R.D. 1989, 'Arab Jewish Dialogue in the United States', in *Intractable Conflicts and Their Transformations*, eds L. Kriesberg, L. Kriesberg, T. Northrup, S. Thorson, Syracuse University Press, Syracuse, pp. 180–209.

## Appendix: Tables

Table 1   Participants

|  |  | Frequency | Percent | Valid Percent | Cumulative Percent |
|---|---|---|---|---|---|
| Valid | Male | 10 | 50.0 | 50.0 | 50.0 |
|  | F | 10 | 50.0 | 50.0 | 100.0 |
|  | Total | 20 | 100.0 | 100.0 |  |

Table 2   Participation in intergroup dialogue encounters

|  |  | Frequency | Percent | Valid Percent | Cumulative Percent |
|---|---|---|---|---|---|
| Valid | Yes | 10 | 50.0 | 50.0 | 50.0 |
|  | No | 10 | 50.0 | 50.0 | 100.0 |
|  | Total | 20 | 100.0 | 100.0 |  |

## Manar Faraj

Table 3  Participation in intergroup dialogue encounters

| I Participated in intergroup Dialogue encounters before the Trip to Germany | | Positive attitudes toward the other | Better understanding | Readiness to Act |
|---|---|---|---|---|
| Yes | Mean | 3.4000 | 3.8333 | 1.1333 |
| | N | 10 | 10 | 10 |
| | Std. Deviation | 1.03994 | .56314 | .32203 |
| No | Mean | 1.6333 | 2.9250 | 1.6000 |
| | N | 10 | 10 | 10 |
| | Std. Deviation | 1.20134 | .72217 | .43885 |
| Total | Mean | 2.5167 | 3.3792 | 1.3667 |
| | N | 20 | 20 | 20 |
| | Std. Deviation | 1.42030 | .78383 | .44459 |

Table 4A  Intergroup. I know the story of the other very well

| | | Frequency | Percent | Valid Percent | Cumulative Percent |
|---|---|---|---|---|---|
| Valid | Disagree | 2 | 20.0 | 22.2 | 22.2 |
| | Don't know | 1 | 10.0 | 11.1 | 33.3 |
| | Agree | 1 | 10.0 | 11.1 | 44.4 |
| | Strongly Agree | 5 | 50.0 | 55.6 | 100.0 |
| | Total | 9 | 90.0 | 100.0 | |
| Missing | System | 1 | 10.0 | | |
| Total | | 10 | 100.0 | | |

Table 4B  Intragroup. I know the story of the other very well

| | | Frequency | Percent | Valid Percent | Cumulative Percent |
|---|---|---|---|---|---|
| Valid | Disagree Strongly | 2 | 20.0 | 20.0 | 20.0 |
| | Agree | 1 | 10.0 | 10.0 | 30.0 |
| | Agree Strongly | 7 | 70.0 | 70.0 | 100.0 |
| | Total | 10 | 100.0 | 100.0 | |

## Table 5A Intergroup. The other cannot understand my Pain

|       |                | Frequency | Percent | Valid Percent | Cumulative Percent |
|-------|----------------|-----------|---------|---------------|--------------------|
| Valid | Disagree       | 1         | 10.0    | 10.0          | 10.0               |
|       | Agree          | 4         | 40.0    | 40.0          | 50.0               |
|       | Agree Strongly | 5         | 50.0    | 50.0          | 100.0              |
|       | Total          | 10        | 100.0   | 100.0         |                    |

## Table 5B Intragroup. The other cannot understand my Pain

|       |                | Frequency | Percent | Valid Percent | Cumulative Percent |
|-------|----------------|-----------|---------|---------------|--------------------|
| Valid | Agree          | 2         | 20.0    | 20.0          | 20.0               |
|       | Agree Strongly | 8         | 80.0    | 80.0          | 100.0              |
|       | Total          | 10        | 100.0   | 100.0         |                    |

## Table 6A Intergroup. Will you share this experience with Family and Friends

|       |       | Frequency | Percent | Valid Percent | Cumulative Percent |
|-------|-------|-----------|---------|---------------|--------------------|
| Valid | Yes   | 9         | 90.0    | 90.0          | 90.0               |
|       | No    | 1         | 10.0    | 10.0          | 100.0              |
|       | Total | 10        | 100.0   | 100.0         |                    |

## Table 6B Intragroup. Will you share this experience with Family and Friends

|       |       | Frequency | Percent | Valid Percent | Cumulative Percent |
|-------|-------|-----------|---------|---------------|--------------------|
| Valid | Yes   | 6         | 60.0    | 60.0          | 60.0               |
|       | No    | 4         | 40.0    | 40.0          | 100.0              |
|       | Total | 10        | 100.0   | 100.0         |                    |

Sharón Benheim

# The Impact of Encountering the Other

## A Long-Term Study of Jordanian, Palestinian, and Israeli Participants in a Multicultural Program at the Arava Institute for Environmental Studies

### Abstract

Despite a large body of research about programs that bring together Palestinians and Israelis, little has been written about long-term full-time residential programs where participants from social groups in conflict live, study, and participate in full-time activities together. Sharón Benheim's paper presents initial results of interviews conducted with alumni of the Arava Institute for Environmental Studies who completed their participation between five and twenty-five years ago. The voices of the alumni – not yet heard – enable us to understand the impact of learning to understand the other in conflict. The alumni interviewed described their belief in the possibility of a shared peaceful existence in a healthy environment – made so by working cooperatively on environmental challenges. They describe a lack of faith in the world around them – in their own government as well as the others. And yet, in spite of that despair, they continue in small or larger ways to promote the possibility. The paper describes how the alumni highly value the experience they have had at the Arava Institute, expressing, therefore, an underlying hope and a conviction to continue to in spite of everything.

### 1.    Introduction

What happens when students from conflicted parties meet in the framework of an international group of students interested in the environment and want to learn more about that conflict? This chapter presents initial results from a study of the impact of participation in the Arava Institute for Environmental Studies (AIES) on Middle Eastern participants, five to twenty-five years after completing the program – based on research conducted as part of the Hearts of Flesh–Not Stone project. This DFG-funded project, "Hearts of Flesh–Not Stone," is a reconciliation-oriented project that aims to explore the effects of encountering the suffering of the other on one's level of empathy and understanding in the Israeli-Palestinian context.

During the Arava Institute program, Israeli and Palestinian participants, together with those from around the region and the world, encounter the suffering of the other, the collective narratives of the groups in the "immediate" Middle East, and the historical and current events that comprise the Palestinian-Israeli conflict. While participants share interests in environmental issues, in deepening their education, and in practical applications, they generally report that their interest in the rare opportunity to encounter the other was a driving factor in choosing to apply for the program. Reconciliation may be seen as describing a process, as in Leiner's definition, "the overarching approach to conflicts with [a] focus on processes of rebuilding relationships. Its goal is to create 'normal,' 'trustful,' and if possible 'good' and 'peaceful' relationships (Leiner 2018, 179)." The model of the Arava Institute is to use cooperation on important environmental issues as a base upon which to build this trust.

In her work, From Heart of Stone to Heart of Flesh, Barakat (2017) describes the ability of people to make a shift from extremism and inflexibility (the heart of stone) to moderation and reconciliation (the heart of flesh); she describes how the role of family, religion, education, and ethics cannot be underestimated in causing transformation. Barakat's From Heart of Stone to Heart of Flesh (2017) describes how events can play a significant role in shaping the individual and collective consciousness and allowing reconciliation to blossom through mutual empathy, building trust, and showing compassion. The Arava Institute program seeks to help participants explore all of these while living together during a semester or year and experiencing a structured framework interspersed with unstructured time to help create the basis for this kind of shift.

In this pilot study, I sought to develop an in-depth understanding of the long-term impact participation in the Arava program had on its alumni by learning about the alumni perspectives years afterwards. Moreover, I include interpretations based on qualitative methods to understand the experience more thoroughly (Denzin and Lincoln 2018; Snape and Spencer 2003). I asked alumni about the impact of the AIES experience on their attitudes, perceptions, willingness to reconcile, understanding, empathy, and/or acknowledgment of the other over time. The alumni have a shared experience that is unique to Arava alumni. In the interviews, I sought to learn of the identity, narratives, and systems of meanings that they created. (Leiblich, Tuval-Mashiach and Zilber 1998, p. 9)

A review of the existing literature on programs that bring together Arabs and Jews in Israel or Palestinians and Israelis reveals little research on a semester or yearlong full-time residential programs where participants from social groups in conflict live, study, and participate in full-time activities together. A few scholars had conducted research on the Arava Institute, looking at how the Institute succeeded in times when many other programs failed (Zohar et al. 2010), considering environmental peacebuilding and empathy in the context of "the geography of peace" (Schoenfeld et al. 2015), and examining the role of education activities in the context of environmental peacebuilding (Ide and Tubi 2019). The current study contributes to this research with a focus on the perceptions, attitudes, and experiences of the participants a long time after they completed the program with a focus on themes relevant to the "Hearts of Flesh–Not Stone" project, studying the effects of encountering the suffering of the other on one's level of empathy and understanding in the Israeli-Palestinian context.

Maddy-Weitzman (2005) and Lazarus (2011) researched alumni of Seeds of Peace, a three-week summer camp in the USA, who participated in alumni activities in the region afterward. Sonnenschein (2019) recently wrote about the personal stories of Middle Eastern graduates of the courses at the School for Peace in Wahat Al-Salaam/Neve Shalom. None of these examples is a semester or yearlong full-time residential program experience, though, like this study, they conducted interviews with participants years after they enrolled in the original program.

My research attempts to add to the body of knowledge about the impact of participation in peacebuilding programs by conducting in-depth interviews with participants who spent one or two semesters in a full-time residential international program with a shared focus on environmental issues and the Palestinian–Israeli conflict. Alumni also participated in some of the alumni activities offered by the Institute's Arava Alumni Environmental and Peace Network (AAPEN). This chapter presents results from interviews with seven alumni who were raised and remained as adults in the Middle East – in Israel, West Bank, or Jordan. I conducted these in-depth interviews with alumni between ten and twenty years after participating in the program. These interviews address questions such as their intentions to participate in the program, what they remember most, the impact of encountering the narratives of the others in the immediate Middle East, what had happened since they completed the program, and the impact on their willingness to reconcile, and whether they changed their perceptions, positions, and/or narratives from those held before they participated in the program. I explored both the stories the alumni told me and specific activities, attitudes, and behaviors they described, which might reflect the impact of the program experience.


## 2.    Theoretical Background

The Arava Institute was founded to teach about the shared environment as a bridge to cooperation and peacebuilding in the Middle East. Since 1996, the Arava Institute has worked to bring Jewish Israeli, Palestinian, and Jordanian participants together with their international peers to learn about each other's identity, culture, and collective narratives. Generally, institutions, such as schools, houses of worship (synagogue, church, mosque), and community groups that are involved in a conflict pass on collective narratives in ways that simplify the situation and build solidarity for the message that "we are right" and "they (the other group) are wrong" (Bar Tal 1998 2000). This message often reflects the belief that "our group is good, moral, and caring" and "they are evil, dangerous, blood-thirsty, immoral" (Bar Tal 2013). Groups build up solidarity among their members via victimhood stories (Adwan and Bar-On 2001; Bar Tal et al. 2009; Noor et al. 2012).

In the context of the Palestinian-Israeli conflict, dialogues and encounters are well established and have been studied by researchers (Abu Nimer and Lazarus 2007; Bar-On and Kassem 2004; Maoz 2012; Sonnenschein, Halabi and Friedman 1998; Steinberg 2004). General programs use approaches based on contact theory (Allport 1954), conflict models (Maoz 2012; Halabi 2000; Sonnenschein 2019), and/or the interactionist approach (Sagy 2002).

Many programs use facilitated dialogue based on the contact theory (Allport 1954) to build the empathy needed to end violence and foster cooperation between groups in conflict. Some programs bring young people from groups in conflict together to meet each other and break down stereotypes into a more realistic understanding of the other (Allport 1954; Salomon 2006; Schoenfeld et al. 2015). There is a large collection of studies on peace education with members of the "two sides" of the conflict or dialogue processes between the two groups (Maoz 2000, 2012; Salomon 2004, 2006; Steinberg 2004; Abu Nimer and Lazarus 2007).

By bringing groups together under appropriate conditions, contact theory allows interpersonal contact to reduce the prejudice and discrimination between members of the minority and majority groups (Allport 1954; Brewer 2000). Since Allport published his theory, social science researchers have applied and expanded the theory to go beyond racism by applying the method to many different relationships between social groups in conflict (Pettigrew and Tropp 2006). Despite the advantages of the contact approach and the research support for its effectiveness in reducing group conflict, research has found limitations of this approach in recent years. One limitation, for instance, is that interpersonal experiences do not necessarily affect attitudes toward the whole group (Forbes 1997; Rothbart and John 1985; Hewstone and Brown 1986). Another limitation is the difference between the needs of the majority and minority groups and their expectations of the process.

Sidanius and Pratto (1999) argue that people from dominant groups have an interest in preserving the status quo as an advantage, while the minority group has an invested interest in change. Accordingly, studies have shown that in joint meetings, members of the minority group preferred to talk about the inequality of power between groups, whereas the majority group tried to blur the inequalities and draw attention to the similarities between the groups and lead the dialogue to a more personal discourse (Suleiman 2000; Maoz 2000; Saguy, Dovidio and Pratto 2008). Despite its limitations, the contact approach is still the main approach on which dialogue groups are based, both within and between societies in conflict.

Dialogue encounters between Palestinians and Israelis face a tension that has developed between different approaches based on contact theory (Allport 1954). These approaches focus on interpersonal relationships, those based on intergroup relationships, and those based on the social identity theory (Tajfel and Turner 1979). Research on the different types of intergroup dialogue encounters sheds light on the challenge of working in the context of an ongoing violent conflict with asymmetry of power between the sides (Maoz 2011, 2012; Rouhana 2004; Sonnenschein 2019). Some methods use intragroup work as a supportive framework within an overall intergroup encounter (Halabi 2000; Lazarus 2011; Rothman 2014). Usually, this intragroup setting provides a time and space to speak in one's native tongue and to process the intergroup experience within the ingroup (Halabi 2000; Lazarus 2011; Sonnenschein 2019). Recent studies have begun to explore the role of work on conflict in intragroup dialogue to promote the willingness to reconcile and accept the other (Ben David et al. 2017; Sternberg, Litvak Hirsch and Sagy 2018; Rothman and Alberstein 2013).

An interactionist approach to dialogue, proposed by Sagy (2002), buildsintegration between the focus on the interpersonal and collective dimensions of conflict dialogue. Using this approach, the focus of the dialogue can adapt to the goals and specific context of the dialogue encounter and allows for interdependence between the interpersonal and intergroup or intragroup processes (Sagy 2002; Sternberg, Litvak Hirsch and Sagy, 2018). The ability to recognize the inherent complexity of conflict relations and acknowledge the other's narrative has the potential to promote readiness to reconcile (Adwan and Bar-On 2004; Sagy, Ayalon and Diab 2011; Sagy, Adwan and Kaplan, 2002; Sagy 2017). The Arava Institute created a unique approach to teaching about the environment in which all share as a bridge to cooperation and peacebuilding in the Middle East (Benheim 2011).

## 3.    Background on the Arava Institute

Since 1996, the Arava Institute for Environmental Studies has used academic coursework to bring together students from around the world while keeping an emphasis on students from the region of Israel, Palestine, and Jordan (Benheim 2011; Zwirn 2001). The participants live at the Arava Institute for one or two semesters and participate in full-time activities while living in dormitories, eating in a communal dining room, taking classes and field trips, and attending other student activities together. This is a very intense level of contact between participants over a relatively long period of time. With a focus on the shared concern for the environment and a framework of accredited university-level coursework on environmental issues, the program also included a required seminar that was not for credit (in this chapter, I call it the Seminar).

The Seminar evolved over time, and the "institute has, through design and trial-and-error, developed a group culture that cultivates empathy. As students participate in this culture, they go through processes that are aimed at cultivating peaceful interpersonal relationships" (Schoenfeld et al. 2015, p.171). The Arava Institute was founded without a specific theoretical basis about facilitating the meetings between the participants but with a deep hope that the shared interest in the environment would bring the people together (Tal, personal communications 2018). The Seminar was centered on regular weekly dialogue sessions facilitated by staff. Most sessions were held in English in the mixed multicultural group and some in small native language/national-based groups. Facilitators brought their training into the process, including the Wahat Al-Salaam/Neve Shalom approach, Non-Violent Communication, and the Compassionate Listening model. The Seminar enabled participants to learn about the basic concepts of identity, the complexity of collective narratives, empathy, deep and active listening techniques, and each other's personal stories. The activities were designed to help participants challenge themselves to simultaneously contain more than one narrative for each group in the conflict while also building skills, such as compassionate listening, nonviolent communication, mediation, consensus building skills, and other leadership abilities. The Seminar was constructed as a safe space in which questions could be raised without necessarily finding answers to them. The imbalance of power and situations outside the program were explored, confronted, and acknowledged during Seminar sessions.

The Seminar focused on the Palestinian-Israeli conflict. For many participants of the Seminar, it was the first time in their life they had met the other, the "first Israeli Jew" or "first Palestinian," since it was their first experience as equal participants in a program with someone from the other national group. Ice-breakers and campus life activities allowed students to meet the other from the start. They then lived together in shared dormitories for four to ten months in a kind of "bubble" in the desert. Inevitably, the students learned about the other (or several others) in part from the personal stories and experiences of their colleagues. Regular course interactions allowed participants to develop respect and empathy for each other. Campus council meetings evolved as a forum for dealing with issues related to life on campus and gave students equal access to setting rules and solving their problems.

During the program, students met guest lecturers and took trips to meet with organizations that work within the conflict, either in single group projects or cooperative projects in the region, which enriched the Seminar experience. Participants were asked to reflect critically on the projects. As part of the program, students underwent a process of developing their knowledge, confronting their assumptions, increasing and expressing empathy to others, learning about leadership abilities, communication skills, and problem-solving tools, as well as developing friendships that last past the end of the program according to their self-reports. "The experience of study at the Arava Institute is only partly about developing shared knowledge and exploring shared solutions. It is also about transforming adversarial relationships into empathic ones." (Schoenfeld et al. 2015, p. 173)

## 4. Study Population

The current pilot study focuses on Palestinian, Israeli, and Jordanian alumni of the Arava Institute for Environmental Studies who grew up in that region and still permanently live there. Initial contact with the alumni was via a presentation and private conversations at Alumni Conferences, followed by emails and phone calls. Alumni have shown an eager willingness to participate. The pilot study included four men and three women ages between twenty-five and forty-three.

## 5. Methodology

I used semi-structured interviews and observations, asking alumni to share their understanding of the world and the meaning they attach to their experience. The phenomenological approach was appropriate for this pilot study as it focuses on uncovering meanings from within people's conversations or texts (Snape and Spencer 2003). My goal was to collect the reflections of participants on the experiences they had during their time at the Arava Institute, the significance of those experiences, and the role the experiences play in their life today – years post-program. The paradigm for analysing the interviews was interpretive, using the phenomenological approach (Schwandt and Gates 2018). For this pilot study, I traveled to Jordan, the West Bank and within Israel to conduct interviews in English, which is the language of study in the Arava Institute program. Since I am fluent in Hebrew, I agreed if alumni requested to be interviewed in Hebrew. All interviews were transcribed, and the Hebrew interviews were translated into English.

In addition to the interviews, I collected notes from several annual alumni conferences and activities of the past and several informal gatherings of alumni in the Middle East. I am a member of a closed Facebook group of alumni, where members have often discussed conflict-related topics, environmental issues, and current events. When it seemed relevant, I asked alumni for permission to use this information for my research, capturing what they wrote and saving it as a document. In addition, some alumni wrote stories and articles published in a magazine several times, and I kept files from those projects. In more recent years, an online blog replaced this forum.

Schwandt and Gates (2018) suggest that interpretive case studies can be conducted by using phenomenological attention to the lived experience and can also include ethnographic methods based on contextualizing of the group contents within a specific social reality. I conducted a phenomenological analysis of my data by clustering concepts and creating a story within which the reader can vicariously experience what the alumni have experienced and reach similar conclusions (Starks and Brown Trinidad 2007). I used phenomenological components, asking for the alumni's comprehension of the experience to capture the meaning or essence of the experience of getting to know the other in a multicultural group.

Finlay (2014) talks about breaking away from what we already know. I "know" quite a bit about the community I am studying as someone who had worked in the Institute for more than fifteen years. I worked explicitly with alumni, including creating the alumni network. I used the phenomenological approach that Finlay (2014) describes to put my existing "knowledge" aside and submerge myself in the data collected in these interviews to learn from them. Before asking about the issues that seemed essential to me, I have made an effort to focus on what the alumni considered important topics to discuss. I aimed to understand the alumni in the context of their culture and social world as it is today.

## 6. Results

In this chapter, I focus on the process the alumni experience – from their motivation to attend the program and perceptions of the other before coming to the experience they have gained throughout the program and their current attitude towards the program. Here, I included four of the themes found in the analysis of the pilot interviews:

- How the alumni valued the chance to meet and learn about the other as they perceived themselves as equals in the program
- Valuable skills and knowledge they received at the Institute – perception of themselves as privileged over others for having received these skills and tools through academic and extracurricular experiences
- Environmental action – continuing the tasks they learned at the Institute and how they implemented those behaviors in their everyday life or at work
- Disillusionment about the chance for peace the alumni have felt as time has passed – the almost euphoric hopefulness or belief that they could achieve peace together began to crumble over time in the face of harsh reality when back home

## 6.1 First Time to Meet the Other – Treated as Equals

All the alumni I interviewed were enthusiastic about how much they gained from the program in meeting and learning about the other. This experience was a common theme in alumni blogs and newsletters. For many, it had been their first chance to truly meet and talk with someone from the other group. Many Arabic-speaking students came from West Bank or Jordan with great trepidation about living with the enemy or being normalizing (*tatbi'a* in Arabic). Many alumni described the pressure of the *tatbi'a* when they arrived or talked about the experience afterward. For many participants, being at Arava was the first opportunity where they felt like equals regarding their status, which sort of neutralized the conflict reality outside the program.

Saqer,[1] a man from West Bank who studied at the Institute in the early 2000s, explained that attending the AIES was a step towards preparing himself for the Palestinian state he believed was imminent. He felt this was a legitimate way to gain additional education and meet the Israelis he would need to deal with as neighbors, not as soldiers. He said:

> So that was the first thing that the Arava Institute gave me; a chance to meet Israelis as civilians, rather than soldiers, occupiers in the West Bank […] to meet Israelis in the Arava Institute, it's this bubble in the middle of nowhere […] We can meet them, talk to them, eat together, sometimes share rooms […] it was a life-changing experience for me. It was very hard to deal with this situation at the beginning, for the first two or three weeks. Really hard, it wasn't an easy thing to deal with. It's like there is a wall that you need to break. I do remember the first three weeks; they were really hard.

While describing the experience as hard, Saqer highly values the experience for his current situation. He told story after story about how constant contact during the program broke down barriers between the students during the program and on campus. He was surprised to find how much they had in common and how he could get along with individual students regardless of their group of belonging.

Many alumni found that they had not articulated their personal identity until they began to explain it to the others in the program. Aseel, a male Palestinian citizen of Israel who studied in the late 2000s, for example, shared his experience and explained how the opportunity to feel like an equal participant changed his attitude to his identity within Israeli society. He said:

---

1 All names are pseudonyms chosen from within similar cultural names (Arabic, Hebrew, etc.)

Overall, the Institute is one of the only places in Israel that I think is really based on equality [...] not one hundred percent, but I felt equality, and they were trying as much as they could to create equality between all the participants. [...] For example, it's the only place that recognized that I'm Palestinian. At a [major Israeli] University and wherever I went, I'm not even considered that. [...] I'm considered the other. In the state of Israel, because I'm half Ukrainian and half Palestinian, I'm not even considered Arab.

Aseel found that at the Institute, his fellow participants affirmed for him his choice of personal identity in the discussions at the beginning of the Seminar.

Dahlia, an Israeli Jewish woman who studied in the early 2000s, explained that one of the things which drew her to the program was the chance to meet Palestinians in person.

And the reason I wanted to go initially was because I had a very strong feeling about [...] we're not being told what's actually happening and that I needed to talk to Palestinians as civilians. [...] Anyway, so when I went there to the *Machon* (Institute), I was like ok, first of all, I need to talk to actual people and not the news, and I need to understand what's really happening, what they're experiencing. I had no idea, and I'm living in a bubble, and I don't know anything.

Dahlia valued her experience at Arava as one that granted her direct access to the Palestinian other. All interviewed participants described interacting playfully during leisure time and straightforward discussions during the Seminar as well as privately afterward. In the interviews, nearly every participant described late or all-night discussions about identity and politics near the dorm rooms.

Ephraim and Rania, a Jewish Israeli man and a Muslim Palestinian woman who studied at the Institute in the early 2000s, submitted their story to the Alumni Magazine. They felt it was emblematic of the difference in their perceptions of the other, when, before the program, they were opposed to the equality and openness they found within the program. Together, Efraim and Rania tell an interesting story. When Efraim came to the Institute, it was the first time he ever seen a woman wearing a *hijab* up close and personal. He was not sure what to think, and he was a little in shock that someone "that religious" could come to study at a place like the Arava Institute. He was not sure how to handle it. Little by little, he got to know Rania and stopped noticing the *hijab*. He developed a strong respect for her knowledge and opinions. He grew to be her friend and stopped seeing the *hijab* – seeing Rania instead. A few weeks later, Rania was coming out of her room. She saw an Israeli soldier walking onto the campus. Out of fear and dread, she closed the door and hid inside. All of her contact with soldiers had been at checkpoints and had been unpleasant – humiliating, and she could not take it. Later she realized it was Efraim, having returned from his reserve duty. He heard that she had been frightened of him and came to speak with her. She realized that inside the uniform was her friend Efraim whom she could respect and talk openly with. They laughed together and remarked how concrete and convincing their experience was; how they learned not to judge by how someone looks; how one could have, along with the identity of an Israeli soldier or an observant Muslim woman, a personality and opinions and a whole world inside the costume.

Rania and Ephraim reported that their understanding was not an automatic result of being together in the program. Instead, it was a result of the deep interactions throughout the entire semester that integrated interaction as equals with learning and facilitated dialogue to address the issues of the conflict. This pair of students argued fiercely about whether Ephraim should have reported when called to reserves. Ephraim said he felt he must defend his country, and Rania felt he would be serving as an oppressor for her and her family and her people. What they felt was precious to them, and what they tried to share in this story was that they felt comfortable arguing about these perspectives – from their own intimate viewpoint. Each had to trust the other to contain each other's fear and anger.

## 6.2    The Arava Institute as a Source of Valuable Skills and Tools

The alumni spoke appreciatively of the skills and knowledge they gained from the Arava Institute program, feeling that these helped them in their work and/or lives today. Although perhaps one would expect a student in an academic program would gain these skills, the alumni emphasized that skills and knowledge gained from the Seminar or the multicultural aspect of the residential program, not only academic content, were highly valuable. Some alumni gained university credits for their undergraduate degree; some completed a master's degree partially based on course work or fieldwork done at the Institute, while others continued at different universities to gain a master's and/or Ph.D. degree.

In Saqer's case, coming as a student with his first degree, the program served as a graduate study springboard.

> Through the Arava Institute, I managed to go on to study at [a major Israeli] University. I did my master's degree and my Ph.D there. Without coming here to the Arava, I wouldn't have had that chance to study in Israel. This is the second way the Arava Institute changed my life.

Saqer felt that having participated in a facilitated dialogue with a diverse group of students, he could manage to continue to study within Israel despite the political situation. He and other Palestinian and Jordanian participants explained how limited the opportunity for advanced degrees is at home and expressed great appreciation for the opening of doors that the Arava Institute provides them. Sometimes, the chance to prove their ability to study well in English was enough to help them get accepted to programs in Europe or North America. In other cases, the ties of Arava with specific faculties opened doors for participants.

Those who continued to study in Israel said that the alumni network of the Arava formed an informal support group for one another in which the acknowledgment of the complexity of their situation continued, and they encouraged each student to do their best. Sometimes, the alumni helped each other practically by translating materials, editing English work, and so on. They described alumni gatherings as a chance to reconnect with what they referred to as the Arava family – a place to be "oneself" and be accepted as part of a complex and challenging network.

Ahlam, a Christian Jordanian woman who attended Arava in the early 2000s, described how her experience of studying at the Institute allowed her to be more open about things that she did not know about before she joined the program, which she considers a skill that helped her succeed in her work today. She explained that homosexuality and/or sexual preferences are topics nobody talked about in her culture and are not socially acceptable, including issues, such as the existence and needs of the members of the LGBTQ community (Pew Report 2013; Movahedi 2017). She also described her experience at the Institute as the first time she left the comfort of her community as a Christian minority. Ahlam explained that it was the first time she had lived in a diverse community and learned about diversity regarding religion, people's looks, sexual preferences, or ethnicity.

She considers herself a "flexible" person but credits the Arava experience with opening her mind to issues of acceptance and diversity. Part of the Seminar dealt with personal identity questions, including sexual preference and gender identity, and it was the subject of informal discussions on campus. In her current position in an organization that hosts international students (predominantly from Western countries), she considered this knowledge and her ability to be open and accepting as something that helped her excel and gain promotion within the organization. Ahlam described her experience:

> Because when I first met a gay person, it was more a friend than a gay student or a gay person. […] So now when I encounter – because I have to deal with LGBTQ students all the time – it's usually very well. First there's the acceptance, but it's also professional because I'm here to help them and support them. So basically, it has affected my role as a person who's helping those students in their cross-cultural experience.

Ahlam said that even today, the subject is taboo, and no one else in her area in Jordan speaks about it. She felt that if it were not for her, the organization she works

The Impact of Encountering the Other | **253**

for would ignore it as they did before and possibly lose international students or have more severe problems. Ahlam explained how her experience also enriched her ability to relate specifically to the Jewish students in the organization where she works:

> When a student comes and tells me, you know, I need to go – I'm going to go to Israel […] to celebrate Pesach with my family. I mean, if I wasn't *there*, I wouldn't understand what he is even talking about […] or also what challenges they might have been being Jews in a Muslim country. I know how to support them, I know how to talk to them in a way that is not – I mean, I would say in a way that is politically correct […] being able to accept someone who's not the same.

"There" refers to Israel and the Arava Institute. Ahlam emphasized how she feels connected to Israel and the places in Israel where she has been, as well as the people she met – some of whom are still good friends. She emphasized that her ability to relate well to their experience comes from her own experience, first as a Christian in a Muslim majority country and then as a Jordanian who studied in Israel. She felt her ability to relate to being a stranger in a strange land, such as Jewish students in Jordan or Palestine in a Muslim country, was gained through her experience at the Arava Institute.

Dahlia described the skills she learned in workshops for Non-Violent Communication (NVC) and Compassionate Listening (CL), held at the Institute in the Seminar framework, as valuable in her current professional work and in nearly every interaction that she has. She said:

> In terms of the NVC, in terms of really CL, the way that I can listen to someone after the Institute is something different that I don't think that a lot of people I meet have. It's actually a very important tool. I think everyone should learn those skills. […] It would change the world. […] [laughs] And I think all of my knowledge has only grown since that and since going to visit friends there, and since being more involved. It's like […] waking up.

Dahlia valued her abilities with these listening techniques very highly as a benefit of her experience. She described how gaining knowledge of the Palestinian experience, her visits to the West Bank with other alumni, and the places visited during the program formed her ability to plan trips during her undergraduate studies at an Israeli academic institution.

> Like, I'll give you an example, after the institute, I went to finish my degree in [an Israeli] College, and I was in a Jewish-Arab dialogue group and it was run by two women […] and

they wanted to create a field trip. So, I basically organized all of the content for the field trip. […] I organized the content. We went to grassroots Al-Quds where we weren't allowed to speak Hebrew […] and in Sheik Jarah[2]. […] We went to all these different places that I wouldn't have known of without the Arava Institute, and all of these experiences that I wanted the students that are usually sitting comfortably in a classroom, I wanted them to experience what it's like when you can't feel confident or safe enough to speak your language. What is it like when your language is taboo? To really understand things […] deeply. […] So many different things.

For these Israeli college students, Dahlia wanted to recreate some of the discoveries and the understanding the other she experienced with Arava. When the facilitators of a Jewish-Arab dialogue group wanted to take a field trip, she wanted to share some of the experiences she had and focused on disrupting their comfortable "normal life" within the reality of the conflict by sharing her knowledge of places and issues.

## 6.3 Acting Environmentally

In many interviews, the alumni explained that they came to the program because of their interest in the environment. While some were already environmental activists and/or had studied a related subject at university, some adopted activist attitudes and behaviors during the program. When Dahlia came to the institute, she described her interest in the environment as "burning," but her knowledge as lacking. She stated that what she learned is still part of her life today. Indeed, her list of practices reflects a model environmentalist.

I continued doing permaculture and being in the environmental scene here – so I think the classes were important for that aspect. My awareness of how important it all is started at the Machon – and I got really good at it […]. Conserving water, recycling, composting, not buying new things if there is a way around it, not printing unless I have to, joining rides with other people, not using disposable stuff, and buying organic […] and of course going on and on, again and again, to everyone around me on these subjects […].

In addition to practicing environmental behaviors in her own life in northern Israel and teaching environmental education in a few part-time frameworks, Dahlia declared that she tries to influence everyone around her, especially in her workplace, to adopt these behaviors.

---

2  An East Jerusalem neighborhood with controversial issues of Jews forcefully taking over property from Palestinian families.

Ahlam listed examples of environmental behaviors that she acquired at the Institute and still practices today, such as recycling, reusing, and reducing. She said she was determined to promote environmental ideals in her workplace in Jordan:

> Like in the office, for example, I always make sure we don't bring disposables. Uh, I do reuse the paper, so I use them as a draft paper. I make sure I put paper in the recycling. I'm always watching out for those who print out a lot, and I talk to them, like [laughs] what are you doing, why are you printing all that, why do you need this? Um, and again, it's not because of the – of the, you know, I'm not trying to save money for paper, but I'm also – I'm trying to save paper […] and this I have learned in the Institute. Because I didn't know there was recycling before I came because it was not something that we do here.

One example of reframing behavior was Ahlam's explanation about reusing glass bottles and jars. She explained that her family had always done this, but after she learned the environmental aspect related to reusing things, she became very proud of their behavior:

> The thing that I'm doing while I'm aware why I'm doing it is the reuse. I grew up in a house where we reused *everything*. You know, the bottles, glass bottles, the jars, the coffee jars. So now I know why we do this, and I'm very happy we're doing it in the house. While it might seem for some people that it's oh, you don't – you know, it's a social status thing. So, when you consume more and you buy more things. So oh, you don't have money to buy, like, the matching jars, for example. But I don't want matching jars. I want – I want *those jars*. [Laughs] Um, so I became, like, more aware and I had more – now I have more pride in doing this, other than trying to, you know, buy matching things.

Aseel described the same attitude to reuse and recycling as Ahlam, mentioning that he is a kind of teacher/missionary about this in every place he works. Saqer described himself as an activist trying to get more Palestinians in the West Bank involved with issues around wildlife and water issues. At alumni conferences, the alumni presented how they shared valuable knowledge about renewable energy, reuse, and various small low-tech solutions. Some have worked in New Zealand and Africa to help implement techniques in areas that are off-grid, without most services, while others presented the implementations at homes and workplaces in the region.

## 6.4  Losing the Belief that Peace Is Possible

The interviewees seemed sad or resigned that they did not see peace around the corner; perhaps it was not even possible. They firmly maintained that their relationships with other students across the conflict lines were intact and good friendships would mean that the friends could work together to create peace. Several years after returning to Jordan, Ahlam worked on joint regional programming at an NGO, hoping to make a difference. Now, she feels disillusioned by politics, religion, and others. With a loud sigh and sad face, she said:

> I don't think it's possible now, from what I see. [shakes her head sadly] Because at the Institute it was basically a bubble. And we have been always talking about this when we were there. Like oh, we live in a bubble now. Which was very nice. Uh, and as I told you life was pink, you know, peace, love and all of that [...] but now I don't – [pause] I mean, I don't think – I don't believe there's going to be peace [...] well first because there is a big political game. So, I mean, that's – that's a side [...] religion is another factor. And then the fact that people [sigh] don't want peace.

Ahlam explained how she saw "real life" as standing in the way of peace-building measures. She spoke about the troubles in nearby countries, such as Syria, and also about *Daesh* (ISIS/ISIL).

Similarly, Dahlia was also sad about what she described as not "changing things." She acknowledged being disheartened at the lack of change at the country level.

> It's a lot to do with my personal connection to the oppression of the Palestinians. That's where it began, at the *Machon* – that's where it closed the loop for me, [pause] and yet today, I don't see anything changing. I don't see how we can change things – even though we want to – all of us from the *Machon* want to change the situation. We trust each other and know we can live together – but like, we haven't made the countries change or other people change except maybe the few friends we get to go to the *Machon* [...].

Dahlia is convinced that studying at Arava has some impact on the students, but she does not believe that alumni have the power to change things at the country level. She describes the experience at the Institute as one that builds trust and develops an understanding of possible ways of living together but also acknowledges the difficulties in spreading that message across the region.

Saqer described his loss of faith in the possibility of peace. He also sighed and looked sad as he told me:

It's hard. I lost hope of having a Palestinian state. [sigh] But the lives are still there. Plants are still there, birds are still there, and we need to take care of the nature. So that's why I'm still working on this subject in the West Bank. And maybe I might not be correct about there not being a Palestinian state, still in the back of my brain I have this little hope that things might change, so we have to have information about the wildlife around us. So, we need to do conservation projects, we need to do research, we need to do the survey in order to know about the species that we have, which ones are threatened, which ones we need to conserve [...] I know these ideas contradict each other, losing hope of having a Palestinian state but still working on nature conservation and research, but nature will always be there, and someone needs to take care of it.

Despite these comments, the alumni continued to contribute their time to the alumni network, AAPEN, teach courses at the Institute, and work in Arava research programs. They expressed hope that maybe things will change, and their connections will be able to contribute to building peace.

## 7.  Discussion

The alumni reported that during the Arava Institute program, they constantly revised their understanding and worldview as Jewish Israelis, Arab Israelis, Palestinian citizens of Israel, Jordanians of Palestinian origin, Jordanians of Bedouin origin, Palestinians, overseas students – often referred to as internationals. Their assumptions or perceptions regarding Judaism, Islam, Christianity, and other religions acquired new layers as various traditions were explored, and holidays and holy days were celebrated together. The complexity they faced while living together challenged the narratives they held before, which were usually much simpler. The process continued throughout the semester, which meant their ideas and perceptions changed constantly. The alumni often described the Seminar sessions as unpleasant, bringing up controversial subjects and deep emotions. They described discussions that ended in shouting or crying. Some alumni even reported leaving a session because they felt they were not being heard and understood. Facilitators met with individuals between the sessions to ensure that all participants were heard.

This research is unique in following up with participants between five and twenty-five years after they finished the program. While nearly every dialogue program includes an evaluation immediately after the program, such as feedback from the participants by using questionnaires and interviews, these are mostly for donor reporting. The critical literature hardly provides any report of evaluation studies years later. Therefore, this research can be considered a "case study" in the sense that these alumni form a kind of community of people with a unique experience (Schwandt and Gates 2018).

Reading about the alumni's disillusionment, I find myself sifting through the transcript to explore why, almost without exception, they said they were glad about their experience. For example, Dahlia emphatically stated: "All in all I still think that with all the triggers, and with all the complexity and with everything, it was an amazing experience and I would never take it back, ever." Similar statements were shared in my interviews and were found to be nearly universal in previous research about alumni (Schoenfeld et al. 2015).

For me, a significant discovery in these pilot interviews was the fact of how much "daily life" wore down the energies of these impressive participants and how that reality led to their resignation. The alumni describe a compelling force to behave inconspicuously to settle down, earn a living, raise children, and care for their parents and how that feels concerning the dream of changing the world, particularly in societies that have difficulties to accepting differences. In these interviews, the alumni expressed their belief in the people they worked with at Arava, their empathy for the other (Palestinian, Jordanian, or Israeli), and their frustrations with the behavior of their own and neighbouring country. The alumni also expressed pragmatic decisions that they have made. They sadly describe how they participate less in organized alumni activities as their children or work responsibilities require more of their focus. They described a reduction in their participation in activities with the Arava alumni over time, but they remain "in the network" and are ready to help when possible. Some alumni described that they participate in activities once in a while as a kind of "booster" to keep their spirit alive.

All of the alumni I spoke with have described a lack of faith in the world around them, in their government, and others. They feel despair towards the idea of a peaceful solution in the area. However, despite the feeling of despair and the lack of faith, they continue in small or large ways to promote the possibility of peace. For instance, some alumni sent a nephew or younger sibling to study at the Arava Institute. Others suggested working on a cooperative project with the Institute despite the anti-normalization movement. Some attended protests, some promoted environmental action, and some continued collecting data, hoping their country would use that data for favourable decisions. Nearly all alumni encouraged each other via social media to "keep it up." They not only value being part of a network but also the experience they had. There is underlying hope and conviction to continue their aims despite the obstacles.

## References

Abu Nimer, M., Lazarus, N. 2007, 'The Peacebuilder's Paradox and the Dynamics of Dialogue. A Psychosocial Portrait of Israeli/Palestinian Encounters', in *Beyond Bullets and Bombs. Grassroots Peacebuilding Between Israelis and Palestinians,* ed J. Kuriansky, Greenwood Press, Westport, CT, pp. 19–32.

Adwan, S., Bar-On. D. 2004, 'Shared History Project. A PRIME Example of Peace Building Under Fire', *International Journal of Politics, Culture and Society,* vol. 17, no. 3, pp. 513–521.

Adwan, S., Bar-On, D. (eds) 2001, *Victimhood and Beyond,* TRT and PRIME, Newton Centre, MA.

Allport, G.W. 1954, *The Nature of Prejudice,* Perseus Books, Cambridge, MA.

Barakat, Z.M. 2017, *From Heart of Stone to Heart of Flesh. Evolutionary Journey from Extremism to Moderation,* Herbert UTZ Verlag, Munich.

Bar-On, D., Kassem, F. 2004, 'Storytelling as a Way to Work through Intractable Conflicts. The German-Jewish Experience and its Relevance to the Palestinian-Israeli Context', *Journal of Social Issues,* vol. 60, no. 2, pp. 289–306.

Bar Tal, D. 2013, *Intractable Conflicts. Socio-Psychological Foundations and Dynamics,* Cambridge University Press, Cambridge, UK.

Bar Tal, D. 2000, *Shared Beliefs in a Society. Social Psychological Analysis,* Sage, Thousand Oaks, CA.

Bar Tal, D. 1998, 'Social Beliefs in Times of Intractable Conflict. The Israel Case', *International Journal of Conflict Management,* vol. 9, pp. 22–50.

Bar Tal, D, Chernyak-Hai, L., Schori, N., Gundar, A. 2009, 'A Sense of Self-Perceived Collective Victimhood in Intractable Conflicts', *International Review of the Red Cross,* vol. 91, no. 874, pp. 229–258.

Ben David, Y., Hameiri, B., Benheim, S., Leshem, B., Sarid, A., Sternberg, M,. Nadler, A., Sagy, S. 2017, 'Exploring Ourselves within Inter-Group Conflict. The Role of Intra-Group Dialogue in Promoting Acceptance of Collective Narratives and Willingness Towards Reconciliation', *Peace and Conflict. Journal of Peace Psychology,* vol. 23, pp. 269–277.

Benheim, S. 2011, 'Arava Institute for Environmental Studies. Teaching Environment as a Bridge to Peace and Understanding in the Middle East', *Middle East Environment. New Approaches and New Actors,* vol. 2, Middle East Institute, Washington D.C.

Brewer, M. 2000, 'Reducing Prejudice through Cross-Categorization. Effects of Multiple Social Identities', in *Reducing Prejudice and Discrimination,* ed S. Oskamp, Erlbaum, Hillsdale, NJ, pp. 165–183.

Denzin, N.K., Lincoln, Y.S. 2018, 'The Discipline and Practice of Qualitative Research', in *Handbook of Qualitative Research,* eds N.K. Denzin, Y.S. Lincoln, Sage, London, pp. 1–26.

Finlay, L. 2014, 'Engaging Phenomenological Analysis', *Qualitative Research in Psychology,* vol. 11, no. 2, pp. 121–141.

Forbes, H.D. 1997, *Ethnic Conflict. Commerce, Culture, and the Contact Hypothesis,* Yale University Press, New Haven, CT.

Halabi, R. (ed) 2000, *Israeli and Palestinian Identities in Dialogue. The School for Peace Approach*, Rutgers University Press, New Brunswick, NJ.

Hewstone, M., Brown, R. 1986, 'Contact Is not Enough. An Intergroup Perspective on the 'Contact Hypothesis'', in *Contact and Conflict in Intergroup Encounters*, eds M. Hewstone, R. Brown, Blackwell, Oxford, pp. 1–44.

Ide, T., Tubi, A. 2019, 'Education and Environmental Peacebuilding. Insights from Three Projects in Israel and Palestine', *Annals of the American Association of Geographers*. Retrieved from: https://www.tandfonline.com/doi/full/10.1080/24694452.2019.1613954

Lazarus, N. 2011, *Evaluating Peace Education in the Oslo-Intifada Generation. A Long-Term Impact Study of Seeds of Peace 1993–2010*, (Unpublished doctoral dissertation) American University, Washington DC.

Leiblich, A., Tuval-Mashiach, R., Zilber, T. (eds) 1998, *Narrative Research. Reading, Analysis, and Interpretation*, Sage, Thousand Oaks, CA.

Leiner, M. 2018, 'From Conflict Resolution to Reconciliation', in Alternative Approaches in Conflict Resolution, eds M. Leiner, C. Schliesser, Palgrave Macmillan, London/New York, pp. 175–186.

Maddy-Weitzman, E. 2005, *Waging Peace in the Holy Land. A Qualitative Study of Seeds of Peace 1993–2004*, (Unpublished doctoral dissertation) Boston University, Boston, MA.

Maoz, I. 2012, 'Contact and Social Change in an Ongoing Asymmetrical Conflict: Four Social-Psychological Models of Reconciliation-Aimed Planned Encounters between Israeli Jews and Palestinians', in *Beyond Prejudice Extending the Social Psychology of Conflict, Inequality and Social Change,* eds J. Dixon, M. Levine, Cambridge University Press, Cambridge, UK, pp. 269–285.

Maoz, I. 2011, 'Does Contact Work in Protracted Asymmetrical Conflict? Appraising 20 Years of Reconciliation-Aimed Encounters between Israeli Jews and Palestinians', *Journal of Peace Research,* vol. 48, no. 1, pp. 115–125.

Maoz, I. 2000, 'An Experiment in Peace. Reconciliation-Aimed Workshops of Jewish-Israeli and Palestinian Youth', *Journal of Peace Research,* vol. 37, no. 6, pp. 721–736.

Maoz, I. 2000, 'Power Relations in Intergroup Encounters. A Case Study of Jewish-Arab Encounters in Israel', *International Journal of Intercultural Relations*, vol. 24, no. 4, pp. 259–277.

Movahedi, M.J. 2017, 'Gay-Bashing in Jordan – by the Government', *The New Arab*. Retrieved from https://www.hrw.org/news/2017/08/30/gay-bashing-jordan-government

Noor, M., Shnabel, N., Halabi, S., Nadler, A. 2012, 'When Suffering Begets Suffering. The Psychology of Competitive Victimhood between Adversarial Groups in Violent Conflicts', *Personality and Social Psychlogy Review,* vol. 16, no. 4, pp. 351–374.

Pettigrew, T.F., Tropp, L.R. 2006, 'A Meta-Analytic Test of Intergroup Contact Theory', *Journal of Personality and Social Psychology*, vol. 90, no. 5, pp. 751–783.

Pew Report 2013. Retrieved from https://www.pewresearch.org/global/2013/06/04/the-global-divide-on-homosexuality/

Rothman, J. 2014, 'From Intragroup Conflict to Intergroup Cooperation', *Research in Social Movements, Conflicts and Change*, vol. 37, pp. 107–123.

Rothman, J., Alberstein, A. 2013, 'Individuals, Groups and Intergroups. Understanding the Role of Identity in Conflict and its Creative Engagement', *The Ohio State Journal on Dispute Resolution*, vol. 28, no. 3, pp. 1–30.

Rothbart, M., John, O.P. 1985, 'Social Categorization and Behavioral Episodes. A Cognitive Analysis of the Effects of Intergroup Contact', *Journal of Social Issues*, vol. 41, no. 3, pp. 81–104.

Rouhana, N.N. 2004, 'Group Identity and Power Asymmetry in Reconciliation Processes. The Israeli Palestinian Case', *Peace and Conflict. Journal of Peace Psychology*, vol. 10, no. 1, pp. 33–52.

Saguy, T., Dovidio, J.F., Pratto, F. 2008, 'Beyond Contact. Intergroup Contact in the Context of Power Relations', *Personality and Social Psychology Bulletin*, vol. 34, no. 3, pp. 432–445.

Sagy, S. 2017, 'Can we Empathize with the Narrative of Our Enemy? A Personal Odyssey in Studying Peace Education', *Intercultural Education*, vol. 28, no. 6, pp. 1–11.

Sagy, S. 2002, 'Intergroup Encounters between Jewish and Arab Students in Israel. Towards an Interactionist Approach. Intercultural Education', vol. 13, no. 3, pp. 259–274.

Sagy, S., Ayalon, A., Diab, K. 2011, 'Perceptions of the Narrative of the 'Other' among Arab and Jewish Adolescents in Israel. Between Peace Talks and Violent Events', *Intercultural Education*, vol. 22, no. 2, pp. 191–206.

Sagy, S., Adwan, S., Kaplan, A. 2002, 'Interpretations of the Past and Expectations for the Future of Israeli and Palestinian Youth', *American Journal of Orthopsychiatry*, vol. 72, pp. 26–38.

Salomon, G. 2006, 'Does Peace Education Really Make a Difference?', *Peace and Conflict. Journal of Peace Psychology*, vol. 12, no. 1, pp. 37–48.

Salomon, G. 2004, 'A Narrative-Based View of Coexistence Education', *Journal of Social Issues*, vol. 60, no. 2, pp. 273–287.

Schoenfeld, S., Zohar, A., Alleson, I., Suleiman, O., Sipos-Randor, G. 2015, 'A Place of Empathy in a Fragile Contentious Landscape. Environmental Peacebuilding in the Eastern Mediterranean', in *Geographies of Peace*, eds F. McConnell, N. Megoran, P. Williams, I.B. Tauris, London, pp. 171–193.

Schwandt, T.A., Gates, E.F. 2018, 'Case Study Methodology', in *Handbook of Qualitative Research*, eds N.K. Denzin, Y.S. Lincoln, Sage, London, pp. 341–358.

Sidanius, J., Pratto, F. 1999, *Social Dominance. An Intergroup Theory of Social Hierarchy and Oppression*, Cambridge University Press, New York, NY.

Snape, D., Spencer, L. 2003, 'The Foundations of Qualitative Research', in *Qualitative Research Practice*, eds J. Ritchie, J. Lewis, Sage, London, pp. 2–23.

Sonnenschein, N. 2019, *The Power of Dialogue Between Israelis and Palestinians. Stories of Change from the School for Peace*, Rutgers University Press, New Brunswick, NJ.

Sonnenschein, N., Halabi, R., Friedman, A. 1998, 'Legitimization of National Identity and the Change in Power Relationships in Workshops Dealing with the Israeli/Palestinian

Conflict', in *The Handbook of Interethnic Coexistence*, ed E. Weiner, Continuum, New York, pp. 600–614.

Starks, H., Brown Trinidad, S. 2007, 'Choose Your Method. A Comparison of Phenomenology, Discourse Analysis, and Grounded Theory', *Qualitative Health Research*, vol. 17, no. 10, pp. 1372–1380.

Steinberg, S. 2004, 'Discourse Categories in Encounters between Palestinians and Israelis', *International Journal of Politics, Culture and Society*, vol. 17, no. 3, pp. 471–489.

Sternberg, M., Litvak Hirsch, T., Sagy, S. 2018, 'Nobody Ever Told Us. The Contribution of Intragroup Dialogue to Reflexive Learning about Violent Conflict', *Peace and Conflict. Journal of Peace Psychology*, vol. 24, no. 2, pp. 127–138.

Suleiman, R. 2000, 'The Planned Encounter as a Microcosm. Psychological and Social Aspects', in *Dialogue between Identities. Jewish and Arab Encounters in Neve Shalom*, ed R. Halabi, Hakibbutz Hameuchad Publishing, Tel Aviv [in Hebrew], pp. 47–66.

Tajfel, H., Turner, J.C. 1979, 'An Integrative Theory of Intergroup Conflict', in *The Social Psychology of Intergroup Relations*, eds W.G. Austin, S. Worchel, Brooks/Cole, Monterey, CA, pp. 33–47.

Zohar, A., Schoenfeld, S., Alleson, I. 2010, 'Environmental Peacebuilding Strategies in the Middle East. The Case of the Arava Institute for Environmental Studies', *Peace and Conflict Review*, vol. 5, no.1, pp. 1–14.

Zwirn, M. 2001, 'Promise and Failure. Environmental NGOs and Palestinian-Israeli Cooperation', *Middle East Review of International Affairs*, vol. 5, no. 4, pp. 116–126.

Yael Ben David, Orly Idan

# Talking Politics

## The Delimitation of the "Political" as a Gendered Disciplinary. Mechanism in Intragroup Dialogue among Young Israelis

### Abstract

Yael Ben David and Orly Idan's essay on *Talking Politics* concentrates on the discursive mechanisms that construct the way young Israeli women and men talk about politics. *The Delimitation of the 'Political' as a Gendered Disciplinary Mechanism in Intra-group Dialogue among Young Israelis* demonstrates how the gendered patriarchal mechanisms that exclude women from the political sphere are produced re-produced, and challenged in interpersonal, political conversations. Their research is based on a year-long intra-group dialogue process. The group they explored met for weekly sessions during two semesters, during which the members discussed and expressed their thoughts and feelings regarding the Israeli–Palestinian conflict. Critical discourse analysis demonstrates how the political space is marked, defined, and delimited through gendered discursive practices throughout the paper. The authors present the different roles participants take in the group, focusing on the strategies women use in the face of discursive disciplinary mechanisms. In particular, the authors underline that women deploy emotionality as a tool of resistance to challenge gender binaries and masculine dominance.

### 1. Introduction

The current research results from a collaboration between two researchers and is based on a recently published paper (Ben David and Idan 2018). It addresses how discursive power mechanisms that exclude women from the political arena come into play in inter-personal political discussions held among a group of undergraduate Jewish-Israeli students. This group included women and men who met regularly and discussed political issues as part of an academic course that dealt with the Israeli-Palestinian conflict. Observing inter-personal interaction, they reveal how mechanisms that operate at the societal level are being initiated, re-created, challenged, and resisted. The authors aim to use the dynamic and developmental nature of inter-personal interaction to avoid stereotyping and replicating gender differences and address the various practices of resistance to discursive power mechanisms, particularly the use of emotionality to reclaim the link between women and political talk.

In continuation of various feminist works that use an ethnographic and narrative methodology to challenge gender binaries by revealing multiple voices of both women and men in this context (e. g., Harel-Shalev and Dafhna-Tekoah 2016; Sasson-Levy 2003), the authors chose to concentrate on the micro-level of interpersonal interactions in order to assess the complexity and multiplicities of gendered power mechanisms. They seek to assess how they are being produced and re-produced and how they are being challenged and transformed. In order to do so, we rely on Foucault's (1978) and Butler's (1990; 1993) perspectives on power and resistance and methodological frameworks of critical discourse analysis (Lakoff 2003; Van Dijk 1993).

In this paper, the authors aim to show how the same disciplinary mechanisms that separate public from private manners of speech may serve as a fertile ground for initiating resistance and carry the potential for transforming the political discourse, resulting in greater acknowledgment of the suffering of the other.

## 2. Literature Review

Ongoing conflicts are based on and maintained by a mutual influence of cultures, structures, and actions. To understand why conflicts are maintained, we need to look at the deep cultural assumptions and structural contexts in which they occur (Bar Tal 2013; Sagy, Adwan and Kaplan 2002; Rubel-Lifschitz et al. present volume; Webel and Galtung 2007). Regarding structures, social hierarchies based on race, class, and gender serve as fertile ground for the naturalization of conflicts as they legitimize hierarchies between people (Eisler 1994). This process, in turn, is co-enforced by cultural assumptions and discursive mechanisms that are inherited in the constitution of the modern state as androcentric and on the knowing subject as a white man (Peterson 1999; Yuval-Davis 1997).

In Israel, that is constituted by the protracted Israeli-Palestinian conflict and the fact that the voice of women is almost absent from the centers of national decision-making, in general, and decision-making in security matters, in particular (Steinberg 2013; Tzameret-Kertcher et al. 2016). This limited presence of women in politics in Israel is due to various discursive mechanisms that are grounded in a deep cultural assumption that Israel is facing a constant existential threat (Herzog and Shamir 1994). In this regard, feminist authors point out that the way "security" is being framed and defined determines the status of women (Aharoni 2014; Berkovitch 1997; Herzog 1998, 2004; Sa'ar et al. 2011). Security is being conceived solely at the national level, excluding other aspects from the discourse, such as nutritional and personal security, which are identified with the private sphere and women, who are (together with children) the primary sufferers of the lack of these kinds of securities during violent conflicts (Francis 2010).

The security discourse not only dichotomizes between the public and the private but also dictates differentiated manners of speech within each sphere. In her analysis of the discourse in Israeli secondary school history books, Peled-Elhanan (2010) demonstrates how utilitarian and instrumental discourses serve as effective tools for dealing with massacres conducted by the Israeli state and preparing Israeli youth for military service and taking part in an ongoing occupation. In this way, the patriarchal social order preserves the ongoing violent conflict by splitting rationality and emotionality.

Though women in Israel are secondary to the political arena, and their allocation to the private sphere is highly prioritized by society (Berkovitch 1997), they are still entering the political sphere through military service, compulsory for both women and men. In her study, Sasson-Levy (2003) shows how women who serve in "masculine" roles adopt various discursive and bodily masculine practices. The author points to the twofold interpretation of their performance since, on the one hand, these practices are perceived as a subversion of gender dichotomy (Butler 1990), yet on the other hand, as adherence to an androcentric social order. While in the army, women are welcome to serve in roles traditionally occupied by men as long as they keep with the masculine ground rules, research has shown that attempts to participate in the political sphere in ways that challenge the patriarchal order are not tolerated, and women who dare to cross this line have to expect severe punishment. Helman and Rapoport (1997), for example, describe how women who participated in public demonstrations against the occupation as part of their activity for "Women in Black," who used to conduct regular weekly demonstrations in central junctions in various parts of the country. These women were constantly exposed to harassment that delivered the message to women that their place is at home and not in the public sphere and that they belong to their husbands and children as dependent members of their families.

The constant standing of these women reflects another practice of reclaiming the public space. That is the use of feminine markers of identity as tools for political change and disruption of gender dichotomies between public and private spheres and the common social order within Israeli society (Butler 1993). "Women in Black" were followed by additional Israeli women organizations, such as "Machsom Watch", "Women Coalition for Peace," and "Women Wage Peace". Although these movements are different in their views, strategies, and feminist consciousness, they all use their identity as women strategically to reclaim their position in the public sphere. Women's participation in the Israeli public sphere portrays two practices of resistance. First, through mimicry of traditional masculine roles within the public sphere, women subvert the masculine regime (Butler 1990). However, by doing so, women also collaborate with the androcentric norms (Sasson-Levy 2003).

The second and perhaps the more radical practice is reclaiming the public sphere through which women strategically use markers of feminine identity within the public sphere, which challenges gender dichotomies (Butler 1993).

Our research explores how participation in the political sphere is embodied through interpersonal interactions. We aim to address the limitations and opportunities of both women and men who participate in political discussions within the context of a hyper-masculine society. Within the constantly changing nature of interpersonal interactions of group dynamics, we attempt to address the complex positioning of women and men as well as various forms of participation that may not only reiterate but also transform patriarchal discourse. We focus particularly on different practices in which resistance is enacted, the forms it takes, and the reactions it provokes.

In our study, we adopt a critical discourse analysis (CDA) to analyze the practices in which masculine dominance appears to be natural and legitimate and the practices by which speakers resist dominance (Van Dijk 1993; 2009). Observing the dialectical relations between context, linguistic style, and topics (Van Dijk 1993; 2009) in dynamic yearlong group discussions enables us not only to detect the structural characteristics of power mechanisms that preserve masculine dominance in political discourse but also to see how these mechanisms form and develop. Three essential questions guided us in the inquiry: (1) what characterizes political discourse within the group? This question referred to the primary assumptions, definitions, and boundaries of the political arena that were prominent and accepted by the group members; (2) what are the positioning strategies each member adopts concerning the political arena? This question focuses on the cognitive and emotional aspects as well as choices that different group members made within the discussion; and (3) in what ways do gendered power mechanisms work in order to discipline group members in the discussion, and what kinds of practices of resistance are being used in the face of these mechanisms?

## 3. Methodology

### 3.1 Participants and Procedure

Sixteen group meetings between twenty-four Jewish-Israeli undergraduate students at the Department of Education at the Ben-Gurion University of the Negev are the source of the research data (see: Ben David et al. 2017; for a detailed description of the group, Sternberg, present volume).

## 3.2 Analysis

Data analysis was based on transcriptions (of the group meetings and tours) made by two research assistants, who observed the group through a one-sided mirror. Additionally, the researchers analyzed insights from the debriefing meetings held in the facilitation unit following every session.

We conducted CDA by following Van Dijk's (1993) parameters of analysis, integrated with initial categories derived from our three primary research questions. The categories were divided according to context and text. In terms of context, we addressed (1) the broad societal context of masculine discourse regarding the Israeli-Palestinian conflict; (2) the specific group context, referring to the setting, group developmental stage, and events that occurred during the process, and (3) specific individual context, referencing to social identities and background. The text was divided into three sub-categories as follows: (1) content, linked to primary assumptions regarding the political and topics that were raised during the discussion; (2) argumentation – how participants build their arguments and how they legitimate and validate their talk; and (3) rhetoric, referring to linguistic style, the use of specific words and metaphors. Our analysis revealed the dialectical relations between context and text: how the discussion was monitored and by whom, what topics were raised and by whom, what was considered valid information, what practices were used to preserve and resist discourse limits, and how transgression from discourse norms influenced the group dynamics. We analyzed the data using ATLAS TI version 7.

## 4. Results

We identified three main turning points in the group discourse by analyzing the group process according to our three research questions. We present the results accordingly and address their significance in the political context.

## 4.1 Rationality and Reason. Baseline Assumptions and Positioning in Relation to the Political

The group's first meeting was dedicated to a general introduction to the subject and a personal introduction among the participants. In terms of context, discourse boundaries were set after androcentric cultural assumptions according to which men are considered authoritative in the political arena (Peterson 1999; Yuval-Davis 1997). The discussions in these meetings were primarily led by the male participants of the group, who dominated the conversation and thus replicated previous findings (Spender 1980). The group dynamics at this stage reflected the assumption (held by most of the group members) that political discourse should be rational and analytical without any expression of emotions.

Throughout the opening meeting, the participants were asked why they chose to participate in the course. Their responses revealed similar underlying assumptions regarding what is considered "political." However, we traced a variation regarding the positioning of women and men concerning these assumptions. The political and the personal sphere were perceived as distinct, and a line was drawn between the two. For example, Erez, one of the male participants, replied:

> It is clear why this seminar was chosen. Everything that has to do with politics interests me. I saw a program on Jews and Palestinians on television, and this is exactly what this course is about. I find it interesting [...]; what is less interesting is that I am already on the other side of the political map. I know a bit about the others' suffering, but it is interesting to see whether this will give me something more [...]. I place myself on the left side of the political map and, of course, this workshop has a political context because it is not only about the other's suffering but an attempt to create a platform for some action [...].

In terms of content, Erez perceives the political as a collective action that occurs on the societal level and not as a personal or an interpersonal issue. This idea is also reflected in his argumentation, in which he confidently positions the encounter with the other as a means for political action and not as an end in itself. Hadas, one of the female participants, presents a similar definition of the political sphere:

> I was afraid that the subject (of the course) would be superficial [and that it would contain] political contexts [...]. After I saw the syllabus, I understood that an encounter (with Palestinians) was planned, indicating that there was another layer in the course. It was meaningful to know that there was a Palestinian group and that there was a deeper thought [given into the course design] [...]. It is important for me to meet and not just to have an opinion rather than seeing it in the news or reading it in the newspaper.

In terms of content, Hadas identifies two distinct layers of the political and the personal: content provided by the media as opposed to face-to-face interaction. Her definition reflects a split between the cognitive and the emotional. Whereas the cognitive (attitudes and opinions) is associated with the political, the personal is associated with the interpersonal encounter. While both participants share similar assumptions regarding the political, Erez and Hadas rhetorically position themselves differently in relation to the political. Erez starts his talk with a confident statement that he knows the aim of this course, whereas Hadas uses reserved rhetoric ("I am afraid"). Erez is confident in the political and expresses his political ideology with certainty and knowledge, whereas Hadas perceives the political as superficial and prefers not to be concerned with politics. Further demonstration of the distinct positioning between women and men is also detected among the other participants, demonstrating how the public-private split (Nicholson 1992; Pateman 2014) is reflected and reproduced in the distinct rhetorical positioning of the male and female participants, demonstrating gender differences in discursive style (Lakoff 2003; Tannen 2003). We also see how the discursive mechanisms that define the political arena as belonging to the public sphere are reflected in the way all participants construct the topic.

## 4.2 Resistance within the Ground Rules of Political Discourse

At the sixth meeting, disagreements between group members started to evolve, and a few women began to take an active and leading role in the discussion. However, group discussions stayed within the initial ground rules of reason and rationality. An example of this pattern occurred in a group discussion held on a day when a famous cultural icon passed away. The group discussed his significant impact and expressed their sorrow over his loss. Meirav, one of the female participants, challenged the mainstream point of view in the group and claimed that he only had such a massive impact because he belonged to an elite group in society and pointed at the way power constructed feelings and respect for someone. She mentioned the name of a great religious figure who did not receive the respect he deserved due to the disadvantaged groups he represented. An argumentative discussion started, in which pros and cons were presented by using strategies of reason and validation regarding the mentioned controversial issue.

> Meirav: "[…] when I went to study in Beit Midrash and sat there for a very long time, I was exposed to the Rabbi Ovadia Yossef as a hero of a generation in which no one else reached his greatness. And the dissonance between what he truly was, his great religious creation, to how he was represented in the media, it was very painful for me. And then when he died, I was in shock that they put sad songs (on the radio) and that people were even sad because of it […]; it was so strange […]."
> Male participant 1: "Wait a minute. If we believe everything we read […] there are things he said that can't be ignored."
> Male participant 2: "I don't know who Rabbi Ovadia Yossef is for me; he didn't have any part in my belief. I acknowledge that he was a significant man for three or ten million people, but I don't see myself as part of this ten million […]."
> Male participant 3 (Lior): "I had a dissonance too but maybe from the other side. I know him as a man, and he really is a great symbol for religious people, but I heard him calling for racism between Ashkenazim and Mizrachim."
> Merav: "Great, that is what they (the media) choose to show you."

Lior: "I really want to understand why he was so great for so many people, and excuse me for saying 'these people'[…]."

Merav: "But Lior, maybe you don't know why he is so important."

Lior: "I know that I don't understand."

Merav: "So go and learn why he is so important, what do you want me to say to you?"

In terms of the group context, this discussion presents the first conflict encountered in the process. Interestingly, Meirav, as a Mizrachi woman who comes from a religious background, is the focus of this conflict. For many participants in the group, she represents the other in the room. This discussion reflects an intersecting power dynamic between a Mizrachi religious woman and Ashkenazi secular males. In other words, Meirav is being disciplined by three male participants and indirectly accused of racism for supporting the supposedly racist Mizrahi Rabbi Ovadia Yossef. In terms of argumentation, Meirav uses masculine ground rules of rationalization to make a stand and make her clear statement legitimate. Rhetorically, she begins by declaring her knowledge and personal experience rather than directly expressing her anger and pain. In doing so, she complies with the common assumption held by the group about how to talk politics. As a woman who claims to be knowledgeable and credible in the political arena, she undermines the assumption that men own political knowledge and thus triggering male participants in the group to demonstrate the disciplinary reaction women face when they position themselves as independent and knowledgeable (Lakoff 2003; Solnit 2014). The male responses object to her claim of the "truth" in an attempt to weaken her validation. The men use various rhetoric styles in order to discipline Meirav. Male participant 1 uses the plural "we," suggesting an authoritative approach and thus maintaining masculine dominance. Male participants 2 and 3 create a distinction between "us" and "them" in order to establish domination (Van Dijk 1993). The three male speakers mark themselves as belonging to a particular group that embodies the "we" as opposed to "these people," who are the others that represent the Mizrachi, a religious and less sophisticated sector of society. Their tone is arrogant and derogative.

When Meirav was facing attempts to discipline her, she resisted by pulling the ground rules of knowledge against Lior, claiming that he was the one lacking the knowledge, and suggested to him to "go and learn." In this sense, her positioning in the discussion reflects the twofold mechanism of resistance and compliance to masculine social order (Sasson-Levy 2003). In sum, the discussion demonstrates the power struggle over truth in which the speakers (both women and men) attempted to establish their position through rationality and knowledge.

Talking Politics | **271**

## 4.3    Conflict and Split between the Rational and the Emotional

Towards the middle of the course, another turning point in the group discourse was detected as emotions began to surface, particularly by a "pioneer" female participant. In this particular discussion, the group debated the deeds of the Israeli army in the West Bank. The atmosphere was tense, and participants were active throughout the discussion. One of the male participants, Avner, provoked the group by stating that he would have joined Hamas if he had been Palestinian. Paralleling between the Israel Defense Force (IDF) and the Palestinian resistance forces, Avner led the group into a loud discussion. Being a male combat soldier, Avner is perceived as an authority with much freedom to say his opinions in terms of this context. Even when challenging the group with his provocative statements, Avner easily gained respect from the group, which was shocked by his provocative statements on the Israeli army and accepted his authority as someone who served on the front line and had first-hand experience (Van-Dijk 1993).

Dina, a female participant, appalled by this comparison, entered the discussion. She directly contradicted Avner by claiming that the deeds of the IDF were justified and that Hamas (the Islamic Resistance Movement) were terrorists. Other male participants joined the discussion and tried to prove her wrong by providing first-hand accounts that the IDF was carrying out horrible and immoral acts, but Dina insisted on her argument:

> Dina: "I am not saying that I don't understand them. I do, but I do not think that killing people and carrying out terror attacks is the way. I really understand their pain and what they are going through, but I would never have become like that."
> Male participant: "The thing is that you don't see the acts that we do there as murder […]."
> Dina: "I see it as a response."
> Male participant : "We need to understand the objective picture. There is a need to see that these things happen and we are stronger than them and are doing crazy things all the time […]. It is like the Big Brother, cameras everywhere. When an Arab raises his head, two soldiers jump on him."
> Dina: "But it is out of fear."
> Male participant: "The question is not just out of what it is, but what is behind it."
> Facilitator: "Dina, I want to understand more. You started to say something and Avner interrupted you. Please tell us where this fear is coming from."
> Dina: "I look at my fear and remember the first time I arrived to [sic] Beer Sheva, and there were sirens. Who even heard about sirens? Today every time a motorbike passes by, I am frightened to death. This is for me a siren."

Dina expressed a clear voice that departed from the representative of the masculine authority, stressing that the IDF's actions were justified and even moral. Moreover, she validated her stance with the rhetorical use of emotional language, directly expressing her feelings of fear. Unlike Meirav, who chose to challenge the group within the ground rules by using knowledge-based arguments, Dina's example reveals a much more radical resistance to the discourse, which uses emotionality instead of facts to justify and establish a political stand. The group reacted strongly to Dina. No less than three male participants questioned her stand. At a certain point in the group discussion in which Dina was often interrupted, one of the group facilitators felt the need to use her authority to make room for Dina to express her feelings that otherwise would not have been heard. The male participants, who reacted to Dina, tried to bring her (and the group) back to reason. They asked her to "consider the objective picture" and to "pay attention to the dry facts," using rational arguments in order to legitimize their speech (Van Leeuwen 2007). In terms of content, they communicated at length about their own experience as soldiers, demonstrating first-hand expertise but dismissed her pain and fear as illegitimate and childish. In terms of rhetoric, we recognised the recurring use of "we." Similar to the previous example, the use of "we" serves both as a practice of establishing authority (as in "we need to see the objective picture") but also as emotional distancing from the deeds of the IDF, which were done by some of them personally (as some of the male participants disclosed). This instance exemplifies how the practice of rational talk and depersonalization go hand in hand by avoiding to perceiving oneself as a perpetrator (Bandura 1999; Nadler and Shnabel 2008) and creating legitimation in the face of doubts expressed toward the masculine authority (Van Leeuwen 1997).

## 4.4 From Emotional Distancing to Emotional Engagement in Face of the Other's Suffering

In the subsequent meeting, the group visited Ramle and Lida, two Palestinian cities from which most inhabitants had been evacuated during the war in 1948. The Palestinian tour guide, Hassan, exposed the students to difficult events, including a massacre in a mosque during the conquest of Lida. For most of the students, Hassan's Palestinian narrative was new. They had never heard this side of the story from a Palestinian with strong political awareness in a non-filtered way. In terms of context, the story addressed transgressions executed by Israelis toward Palestinians, positioning the participants as perpetrators. During the first part of the discussion, which followed the tour, participants expressed anger towards Hassan and accused him of presenting an inaccurate narrative. The group attempted to delegitimize the factual basis on which he based his stance and instead turned to a discussion on the non-national state solution he proposed. In this stage, the group discussion demonstrated an attempt to create an emotional distance from the suffering of the other (Bandura 1999; Shnabel and Nadler 2008). Rhetorically, the discourse was highly argumentative, and the participants initially focused on facts instead of emotions. At a certain point, the facilitators conveyed to the group that some female participants were not talking. Although the silent women did not respond to the invitation to participate, an apparent change in the discourse was detected. Female participants took a more active part in the discussion and expressed emotional voices that had not been heard before. In this sense, the facilitators' authority enhanced female participants' access to the discussion (Van Dijk 1993).

> Gali (female participant): "I feel that from the beginning of the discussion, the discourse is a little bit distant because it is difficult for us to accept what Hassan said during the tour. For example, the massacre at the mosque is hard to contain, so we translate this discourse into identity and the non-national state solution."
> Avner: "What do you want to say about the massacre?"
> Gali: "It is horrible. I do not have anything to say about it, but this was the guts of the tour."
> Avner: "It is not. It was a gimmick the way that Hassan presented it."
> Gali: "When I heard that the Jews, who are supposed to have a value for life bombed the mosque with 250 in it, I asked myself – who does such a thing?"
> Avner: "I think he succeeded in what he was trying to do – to turn a particular event into a generalized one. In each complicated situation, there are irregular events. Had there been a legal procedure for such irregular events, the problem would have been solved."

At this point, several female participants joined the discussion and expressed their emotions, emphasizing their pain, shame, and fear regarding the events that underlie the political solutions to the Israeli-Palestinian conflict and the rational discussion about it. For example, one of the female participants noted that "[…] the fact that they want a non-national state deters me for I fear that they want to kill us and expel us. That really scares me. The fact that they want shared living calms me."

It is interesting to note that in the same session, a significant shift in the discussion was detected from a reactive stance of emotional distancing and delegitimizing the Palestinian guide's argument through rational talk to a transformative stance of emotional engagement. An additional transformation in the gendered positioning was evident at this point since several other female and male participants joined in and expressed the emotions that override the rational and controlled political discourse. In this sense, emotionality is not only used by women as a practice in which they reclaim their voice in the discussion, but it serves as a transformative tool that allows both women and men to acknowledge the pain experienced by the group as a result of their encounter.

## 4.5 Towards an Integrated and Inclusive Political Discourse

In the last two course meetings, the group started to directly address the role of emotions in political discourse and their initial assumptions regarding what was political and its effect on the group dynamic. In the context of the course ending, the content raised in the group related to the discourse boundaries within the group. Who were the dominant speakers? Who did not have a place to speak? What were the rules and regulations of group discourse? The power balance changed as soon as the emotional and female voices grew stronger, and female participants insisted on talking about emotions even though resistance was conveyed:

> Male participant: "I do not think that we are not talking about emotions. I just think that the emotion is not explicit but rather is expressed through the things that we say. We don't have to (explicitly) talk about how I feel."
> Female participant: "Why?"
> Male participant: "Because the other's suffering is complex."
> Female participant: "Why can't you say how you will feel?"
> Another female participant: "I sat in the tour and felt awful. I listened and felt as if I was in a Holocaust memorial ceremony."
> Another male participant: "For me, every day I was in the army, especially in the West Bank, was a negative emotional burden. I could not live with it, and I do not know whether I can go to reserve again. When I get called to the army, I feel a weight […]."

The latter discussion among the male and female participants demonstrates an implicit struggle regarding the place of emotional talk in political matters. The first male participant emphasizes the negation of explicit emotions in terms of content. Emotions are inherent and do not require direct attention. His rhetoric reflects this attitude: "We don't have to talk about how I feel." Here, the participant is distancing between the collective and public levels of speech and the individual, private and emotional speech. This male participant attempts to mark the boundaries between the political and the private, by stating that emotions are private and do not belong within political discourse. Following his words, some women insisted on talking about emotions and confronted him. They persistently asked him about his inability to express his emotions.

The dialogue reflects a power shift in which women interrogate men. At this point, another male participant joined the discussion and provided the answer to that question. He shared his emotional experience in the army by focusing on how he felt rather than what he did. This example contrasted previous talks about the army in which men primarily shared the actual actions and not the emotional experience that underlies them. His words reflected the necessity of emotional distancing in order to collaborate with a situation of ongoing violence. According to Peled-Elhanan (2010), emotional distancing is precisely what facilitates and enables soldiers to take part in violent military actions.

There were two intertwined processes in these last sessions. First, the discussion turned from factual rhetoric, judgment, and blame (self and other) to the reflexive observation of the emotions and thoughts provoked by facing the "other." Second, the gendered dynamics in the discussion shifted. Female participants took it upon themselves to speak up, reclaiming their place in the political discourse; then, both male and female participants shared their emotional experiences concerning the political experiences that were not accepted in previous discussions. Even though silent women were still present, there was an openness to other voices. Simultaneously, these two processes unfolded since inclusivity supported participation, which led to a broadening of the political discourse within the group.

## 5.  General Discussion

The current research demonstrates to what extent interpersonal and political conversations are a space for reflecting deep cultural assumptions of a society in conflict. Moreover, the research highlights the importance of interpersonal space in sustaining and challenging cultural assumptions that preserve conflict. Notably, we show how gendered power mechanisms that are fundamental in societies in conflict (Peterson 1999) manifest, but also how resistance to these mechanisms emerges and promotes change in the balance of power. The dialectics among topics, rhetoric, and linguistic style, which participants used to position themselves within the discussion and the context in which ideas were expressed, provide an added value to understanding gendered interpersonal dynamics'multi-layered nature. Additionally, the participants used forms of agency and the reciprocal relationship between the personal and the social. The analysis reveals that political space is primarily perceived as a public space based on knowledge and facts instead of emotions and subjective experience. The analysis also reveals how the practices of women's exclusion, which occur in the public sphere (Aharoni 2014; Helman and Rapoport 1997; Herzog 1998; Sa'ar et al. 2011), are embodied within the group dynamic. This creates a hierarchy of knowledge between those on the "battlefront" with first-hand experience and those on the "home front" with less knowledge and experience. In this context of hierarchized discourse, both women and men were limited in participation. Particularly in their inability to express their emotions regarding politics. While men dominated the discussions with confident and factual rhetoric, women in the group were estranged and required to use masculine discursive practices to participate.

The process revealed that the development in the group discussion was strongly intertwined with practices of resistance to the masculine discourse that was reflected in the way female participants chose to position themselves. The first form of resistance observed conveyed female dominance in the political use of masculine ground rules. This form of mimicry of traditional masculine roles within the discussion subverts the masculine regime but, at the same time, collaborates with the androcentric norms (Butler 1990; Sasson-Levy 2003). However, as the course unfolded, a more radical form of resistance emerged as pioneer female participants expressed emotions. Specifically, at the meeting where this turning point took place, one of the female participants chose an emotional language to legitimize her political opinion and thus reclaimed emotions within the public sphere (Butler 1993). In the latter sense, an emotionality is a political tool of resistance that challenges masculine dominance and ground rules. This incident eventually led to a change in the group discussion that consisted of more emotional voices leading to a more integrated and inclusive discussion.

We detected two simultaneous processes of engagement and inclusion in the group dynamics. Participants expressed greater emotional engagement and acknowledgement of the other's suffering throughout the course. This development was accompanied by greater participation and a broader scope of discussion, allowing both women and men to speak up and express their voices and feelings regarding the issues at hand. The latter supports the theoretical argument, which claims that emotional presence, as opposed to instrumental talk (Peled-Elhanan 2010) and psychological distancing (Bandura 1999; Daphna-Tekoah and Harel Shalev 2014), fosters a greater acceptance of the other and their suffering (Nadler and Shnabel 2008). In this context, women served as agents of change and had a crucial role in this transformation, utilizing their social accessibility to emotional talk (Lakoff 2003).

Interestingly, the latter argument gained support and was highlighted by a male participant who used the word "we" regarding feelings. The use of "we" was repeated on several occasions by various male participants. We propose that this use indicates men's position in society as both gatekeepers and front-liners. As gatekeepers, they express dominance by using the collective form of speech; and as front-liners, they emotionally distance themselves from the emotional consequences of inflicting pain on others in the context of violent conflict.

In sum, this research highlights the importance of daily interpersonal interactions in creating, sustaining, and changing the political discourse of a society in conflict. Specifically, our study sheds light on the multiple forms and constant evolvement of resistance to disciplinary mechanisms. It highlights the importance of considering the role of gender in political discussions. Moreover, the research emphasizes the need for women to perceive themselves as political actors who can lead and influence political change within the communities to which they belong. One does not have to be a public figure, a politician, or a parliament member, to be an agent in transforming the ethos of conflict (Bar Tal 2013), which is present in everyone's daily life — whether in societies in a conflict in general or particularly in Israel.

## References

Aharoni, S.B. 2014, 'Internal Variation in Norm Localization. Implementing Security Council Resolution 1325 in Israel', *Social Politics*, vol. 21, no. 1, pp. 1–25.

Bandura, A. 1999, 'Moral disengagement in the Perpetration of Inhumanities', *Personality and Social Psychology Review* 3, no. 3, pp. 193–209.

Bar Tal, D. 2013, *Intractable Conflicts. Socio-Psychological Foundations and Dynamics*, Cambridge University Press, Cambridge, UK.

Ben David, Y., Idan, O. 2018, 'We Don't Have to Talk about How I Feel. Practices of Power and Resistance in Political Discourse Among Israeli Students. A Gendered Socio-Linguistic Perspective', *International Feminist Journal of Politics*, vol. 21, no. 2, pp. 271–294.

Ben David, Y., Hameiri, B., Benheim, S., Leshem, B., Sarid, A, Sternberg, M., Nadler, A., Sagy, S. 2017, 'Exploring Ourselves within Intergroup Conflict. The Role of Intragroup Dialogue in Promoting Acceptance of Collective Narratives and Willingness Toward Reconciliation', Peace and Conflict. Journal of Peace Psychology, vol. 23, no. 3, pp. 269–277.

Berkovitch, N. 1997, 'Motherhood as a National Mission. The Construction of Womanhood in the Legal Discourse in Israel', *Women's Studies International Forum*, vol. 20, no. 5–6, pp. 605–619.

Butler, J. 1993, 'Critically Queer', *GLQ. A Journal of Lesbian and Gay Studies*, vol. 1, no. 1, pp. 17–32.

Butler, J. 1990, *Gender Trouble. Feminism and the Subversion of Identity*, New York and London, Routledge.

Daphna-Tekoah, S., Harel-Shalev, A. 2014, 'Living in a Movie. Israeli Women Combatants in Conflict Zones', *Women's Studies International Forum*, vol. 44, pp. 26–34.

Eisler, R. 1994, 'From Domination to Partnership. The Hidden Subtext for Sustainable Change', *Journal of Organizational Change Management*, vol. 7, no. 4, pp. 32–46.

Foucault, M. 1978, *The History of Sexuality*, volume I, New York, Vintage.

Francis, D. 2010, *From Pacification to Peacebuilding. A Call to Global Transformation*, London and New York, Pluto.

Harel-Shalev, A., Daphna-Tekoah, S. 2016, 'Bringing Women's Voices Back in Conducting Narrative Analysis in IR', *International Studies Review*, vol. 18, no. 2, pp. 171–194.

Helman, S., Rapoport, T. 1997, 'Women in Black. Challenging Israel's Gender and Socio-Political Order', *The British Journal of Sociology*, vol. 48, no. 4, pp. 681–700.

Herzog, H. 2004, 'Family-Military Relations in Israel as a Genderizing Social Mechanism', *Armed Forces and Society* vol. 31, no. 1, pp. 5–30.

Herzog, H. 1998, 'Homefront and Battlefront. The Status of Jewish and Palestinian Women in Israel', *Israel Studies*, vol. 3, no. 1, pp. 61–84.

Herzog, H., Shamir, R. 1994, 'Negotiated Society? Media Discourse on Israeli Jewish Arab Relations', *Israel Social Science Research*, vol. 9, pp. 55–88.

Lakoff, R. 2003, 'Language, Gender, and Politics. Putting 'Women' and 'Power' in the Same Sentence', in *The Handbook of Language and Gender*, eds J. Holmes, M. Meyerhoff, Blackwell, Oxford, pp. 161–179.

Nicholson, L.J. 1992, 'Feminist Theory. The Private and the Public', in *Defining Women. Social Institutions and Gender Divisions*, eds L. McDowell, R. Pringle, Polity Press, Cambridge, pp. 36–45.

Pateman, C. 2014, *Sexual Contract*, John Wiley and Sons, New Jersey.

Peled-Elhanan, N. 2010, 'Legitimation of Massacres in Israeli School History Books', *Discourse and Society*, vol. 21, no. 4, pp. 377–404.

Peterson, V.S. 1999, 'Political Identities/Nationalism as Heterosexism', *International Feminist Journal of Politics*, vol. 1, no. 1, pp. 34–65.

Sa'ar, A., Sachs D., Aharoni, S. 2011, 'Between a Gender and a Feminist Analysis. The Case of Security Studies in Israel', *International Sociology*, vol. 26, no. 1, pp. 50–73.

Sagy, S., Adwan S., Kaplan A. 2002, 'Interpretations of the Past and Expectations for the Future in Two Conflicted Societies. The Case of Israeli and Palestinian Youth', *American Journal of Orthopsychiatry*, vol. 72, no. 1, pp. 26–38.

Sasson-Levy, O. 2003, 'Feminism and Military Gender Practices. Israeli Women Soldiers in 'Masculine' Roles', *Sociological Inquiry*, vol. 73, no. 3, pp. 440–465.

Shnabel, N., Nadler, A. 2008, 'A Needs-Based Model of Reconciliation. Satisfying the Differential Emotional Needs of Victim and Perpetrator as a Key to Promoting Reconciliation', *Journal of Personality and Social Psychology*, vol. 94, no. 1, pp. 116–132.

Steinberg, P. 2013, *Women's Representation in Security Decision Making 2013–2014*, Jerusalem, The Van-Leer Jerusalem Institute [in Hebrew].

Sternberg, M. 2022, 'When Israeli Students Encounter Palestinian Narratives', present volume.

Tannen, D. 2003, 'Gender and Family Interaction', in *The Handbook of Language and Gender*, eds J. Holmes, M. Meyerhoff, Blackwell, Oxford, pp. 179–202.

Tzameret-Kertcher, H., Herzog, H., Chazan, N., Basin, Y., Brayer-Garb, R., Ben Eliyahu, H. 2016, *The Gender Index. Gender Inequality in Israel*, Jerusalem, The Van-Leer Jerusalem Institute [in Hebrew].

Van Dijk, T.A. 2009, 'Critical Discourse Studies. A Sociocognitive Approach', in *Methods for Critical Discourse Analysis*, eds R. Wodak, M. Meyer, Sage, London, pp. 1–33.

Van Dijk, T.A. 1993, 'Principles of Critical Discourse Analysis', *Discourse and Society*, vol. 4, no. 2, pp. 249–283.

Webel, C., Galtung, J. (eds) 2007, *Handbook of Peace and Conflict Studies*, Routledge, Oxford.

Yuval-Davis, N. 1997, 'Women, Citizenship and Difference', *Feminist Review*, vol. 57, no. 1, pp. 4–27.

Shiri Levinas

# Women in Conflict, Narratives from the Periphery

## Stories of Women Living in the Southern Periphery of Israel

### Abstract

Gender roles are charged with new meanings and significance in societies involved in violent conflicts. Shiri Levinas' contribution to *Women in Conflict. Narratives from the Periphery. Stories of Women Living in the Southern Periphery of Israel* presents how women that live in such areas narrate their lives and make sense of them. Through in-depth semi-structured interviews, the author analyzes the narratives of forty Jewish women of various social classes and ethnic origin living in a small town near the Israeli border with the Gaza strip. The motherhood issue in a situation of conflict often lies at the core of their narratives. The paper shows that motherly worries motivate many women in conflict to concrete action and how it is the role of saviors and warriors, particularly in life-threatening situations, that mothers took upon themselves. The author, therefore, challenges the widespread representation of passivity and victimhood of women and mothers prevalent in the literature on violent conflict, giving voice to agency, resourcefulness, and courage.

\*\*\*

This paper is based on my Ph.D. research project and presents initial findings from the analysis of the first round of interviews which provide a glimpse into the broad question of women's experience in violent conflict.

Bruria, an elderly woman in her seventies, was born in Morocco and arrived at the periphery town of Ofakim with her family when she was around ten years old. The town of Ofakim is situated in the geographic, social, economic, and cultural periphery of Israel. It sits close to the border of the Gaza Strip. We asked Buria what she does during the interview when she hears the siren, which indicates that a rocket is about to hit her town in forty-five seconds.

Bruria: "I sit here crying and shaking but not getting up."
Interviewer: "Did you try to request or demand that a shelter be placed nearby for you?"
Bruria: "So many times we asked, and yet they did nothing."
Interviewer: "Whom did you ask?"
Bruria: "I don't know from who they requested it, I think from the army, or... I don't know, I don't know... And all the time, I bless the creator of the universe [...] I have no safe room, those who have one are not willing for us to come in with them, what can I tell you?"

Interviewer: "So when there is a siren, what do you do?"
Bruria: "I sit here."
Interviewer: "And what do you feel?"
Bruria: "What do I feel? Fear, fear..."

In this short dialogue, Bruria's words provide an insight into how security is connected to her social and economic status. Bruria cannot afford to build a safe room in her house and is also not invited to the safe room of her neighbor's home. Feeling alone and neglected, she only sits at home and prays to G-d. Bruria also describes her fear and feeling that "there is nothing she can do" about the situation, leaving her with the only possibility to "pray to G-d." On the other hand, when we asked the same question to Bruria's granddaughter, Shlomit, who is in her early twenties, she stated that:

"When there was more of a war and there were sirens, we would go from bomb shelter to bomb shelter."
Interviewer, "So when you heard... when you hear a siren actually what do you do?"
Shlomit, "If I am on the street, I simply get very close to a wall and lay on the ground with my hands on my head. If I am inside a bomb shelter, I simply go in and calm people down.... it wasn't so hard for me in truth, because it's something I have gotten used to, to get up and do – to get up and help – so it flows with the whole issue..."
Interviewer, "So your way of coping with the situation of the war is?"
Shlomit, "To go and help others."

In contrast to her grandmother's, Bruria, Shlomit's words tell a story of agency and capability. Shlomit expresses that acting is what helps her to feel safe. Shlomit described a terrifying situation as if there is nothing unique about it and if it were normal to expect rockets in the middle of the day. She feels in control. Moreover, the situation of a violent conflict that involves civilians, which is an integral part of the "new wars," is what provides her with the opportunity to act. Helping others also helps her cope with this abnormal situation and gain a sense of worthiness. Shlomit's story directs the attention to the possibility that situations of violent conflict may also increase the perception of worthiness among women and strengthens their agency. These two examples help to shed light on the complexity and diversity of women's experiences in violent conflict and support feminist researchers from around the world who argue that women's roles, experiences, and needs are much more diverse in comparison to the limited and biased description of women in the mainstream literature of conflict studies (Sjoberg and Via 2010).

Most of the mainstream scholarship about violent conflicts focuses on the causes, the characteristics, and the effects on various aspects of social and personal lives, yet they do not consider the aspect of gender (Harders 2011). Most of the critical literature about Israel (Yuval-Davis 1997; Bar Yosef and Padan-Eisenstark 1977) and elsewhere fails to comprehend the complexities involved in societies in conflict as well as to offer viable solutions (Lundy and McGorern 2008). The widespread of "new wars" toward the end of the twentieth century and their dramatic impact on civil society in general and women, in particular, led to an increase in feminist research, in particular, the approach that deals with documenting women's experience in conflict zones (Bennett at al. 1995). Such research revealed that changes in the fabric of society affect the variety of women's roles by emphasizing the increased burden on women and recognizing the agency and possibilities of change that such a crisis may enable (Cockburn 2010). This approach also provided evidence to the feminist theories which claim that gender categories are not homogeneous. By including intersectionality theory in conflict and security studies, scholars promote the claim that how violent conflict shapes women's experiences and daily lives are the main effects of the intersections of the various social positions' women occupy in the hierarchies of race, class, ethnicity, and nationality (El Bushra 2003).

In my research, I follow this path and focus on the narratives of women who live in a small town located on Israel's geographical and social periphery, next to the Gaza strip. The ongoing conflict is a permanent and integral part of their daily lives. More specifically, the research explores how living in such a reality shapes their narrative regarding gender roles and security. The analysis uses in-depth semi-structured interviews with forty women (in the case of this article it focuses on the first seven interviews) of different ages and different stages in their lives. In this research, I focus on how social categories, such as class, gender, and ethnicity affect their experience in violent conflict.

## 1. Feminist Theory in the Study of Conflict

Scholars with a different approach to conflict research agree that violent conflicts have a dramatic influence on states and populations. The reality of living in a violent conflict includes long-term exposure to physical and psychological threats, coping with high levels of uncertainty, and loss of both symbolic and material resources, among others (Barnett and Adger 2007). Despite the growing recognition of the dramatic impact of violent conflicts on the life of women and men, the literature review provides little to no reference to gender perspectives (Tickner 1992; Anderlini, 2006, 2011). Besides, in the last decade, there has been an expansion of literature that investigating the phenomenon of "new wars." The writings on the subject include various approaches that examine and argue the cause that leads to the outbreak of these conflicts (Ben Eliezer 2009).

Nevertheless, there is a widespread consensus that this phenomenon includes conflicts characterized by the low intensity, which persist over a long period, accompanied by extremely violent outbreaks. This violence is mainly targeted at civilians and leads to a severe increase in victims, refugees, and displaced populations (Munkler 2005; Kaldor 2013). While the literature on new wars includes the growing attention to civil society, only a little attention was drawn to the particular influences of these wars on women. For instance, they do not examine significant phenomena, such as the expansion of political violence, including sexual terror, which increases the number of female victims disproportionally (Kinsella 2007).

According to feminist scholars, gender as a category of analysis transforms the study of war. In order to approach war adequately, conflict studies need to correctly understand what those involved in war are "doing and saying" (Dufort 2013). As such, feminist research encourages the use of personal narrative that documents the daily life of women and men in conflict, considering a feminist theory of intersectionality. This attempt enables research to shed light on women's unique experiences in conflict emphasizing women from marginalized groups. Verwimp and Van Bavel (2013), for instance, conducted research in Burundi and found that, as a result of the violent conflict, the education gap between boys and girls grew mainly among girls that came from low-income families. Ronney's (2005) research in Northern Ireland also indicates that the lack of attention to the needs of women from marginalized group hinder the implementation of the peace process.

Feminist research focuses on several issues, of which the most prominent are (a) the study of narratives of security, which raises questions of what security is, whose security counts, when do women feel secure, what happens when state security and personal security conflict, and what is violence? (Sylvester, 2002; Tickner 1992, 2004), and (b)studies concerning the way gender roles affect conflict and are affected by it. This theme developed at first as a critique of the mainstream narrative that presents women either as inherently more peaceful or merely as victims (Coulter 2015). Now, this theme focuses on questions of how gender roles, gender perceptions, and gender identities influence the process of the conflict. Do gender relationships change in conflict? How is gender inequality influenced by and influencing the conflict (Hyndman 2008)? This body of literature exposes how changes and breakdowns in the fabric of communities and society influence the role women take by emphasizing the increasing burden on women and recognizing the agency and possibilities that these breakdowns sometimes enable (Cockburn 2001).

The findings of leading researchers like El Bushra (2003, 2005), Anderlini (2006, 2011), and El Jack (2003) challenge the mainstream perceptions by shedding light on the diverse role women play in conflict, such as terrorist, peace activist, guerila fighter, and community leader, among others (Cohn 2013). An extensive field research study by Judi El Bushra and Ibrahim Shal (El Bushra and Shal 2005) in five countries in Africa involved in conflict demonstrated that gender roles change, but these changes were explained using conservative gender ideology. Therefore, the increased burden on women was perceived as a part of the ideology of women as the central pillar of the home.

Another example is presented in the research of Chris Coulter (2015) on Bush wives – young women and girls who were abducted from their homes and families by the rebel fighters and were unofficially married to one of the soldiers to receive protection – and girl soldiers in Sierra Leone in which she found that women's experience was diverse and context-specific. Her research reveals how international efforts to end protracted conflicts in Sierra Leone, including sustained investments in the "Disarmament, Demobilization, and Reintegration" (DDR) of combatant's process, failed women and girls. The DDR policy and process are aimed at combatants, providing them with new possibilities, such as education, allowance, and training to reintegrate into their society. However, despite their fighting roles, many of the young women were only classified as "dependents," although their real experiences were not acknowledged, and they were precluded from receiving the benefits provided to "combatants."

Another impact of gender was revealed when the women returned to their homes from the "bushes." They were then accused of being traitors, feared, and not trusted by their own families. While men who suffer from the same attitude could live by themselves and build a new life somewhere else, a woman on her own depended entirely on her family, that, in many cases, had rejected her. These examples indicate that civilians who deal with violent conflict are mediated by social position and power relations, mainly gender, class, and ethnicity. The process of reacting to a conflict situation is interwoven with the complexity of resources and responsibility, and these aspects significantly differ between men and women, rich and poor, members of major or minor groups and other categories (Sylvester 2012). Feminist researchers aim to seek stories situated far from the center of power. They attempt to display that there is always more than one story to tell and how the choice to present one perspective instead of another is neither innocent nor obvious but always a political choice (Wibben 2011).

## 2. Personal Narrative and Feminist Theory in the Study of Conflict in Israel

Feminist researchers in Israel add gender perspective to the vast body of literature concerning the Israeli-Palestinian conflict (e. g., Chazan 1991; Golan 1997; Herzog 2003). They shed light on how the conflict and the dominant discourse of security and militarism create social priorities and resource allocation that split rigid gender roles and promote gender inequalities (Mazali 2003; Ben David and Orlan, present volume). Given the military's dominance in Israel, the prominent research done by feminists in Israel focuses on the relationship between gender, nationality, and the military (Klein 2002). Their findings indicate that, similar to other militarized countries, women in Israel endure lower status compared to men and that the militaristic discourse leads to the construction of the Jewish women identity and role as "mother of the nation" (Herzog 2003). This research significantly contributed to the understanding of how the issue of national security affects gender relations, (Lieblich 1989; Sharoni 1992), how the military shapes and organizes gender perceptions and practices (Robbins and Ben Eliezer 2000), and how the national discourse in Israel shapes the identity of women and dictate their citizenship (Herzog 2004; Berkovitch 1997; Lubin 2002). However, the critical literature also points to research still missing in the feminist project. These include the experience of Palestinian women who hold Israeli citizenship and research on the differences between social groups in Israeli society and the deferential influence of the conflict in their daily lives. During the last decade, this gap has started to close since feminist research from the Feminist Security Studies started to investigate the particular experience of different groups of women. By learning personal narratives of young Israeli women who served in combat roles in the IDF, Harel-Shlev, and Shir-Tekoa (2015), for instance, reveal different types of agencies, resistance, and coping strategies of these soldiers with traumatic experiences. Additional significant findings evolve from recent research done by Sachs, Sa'ar, and Ahroni (2017), who tested if the common hypothesis about women's increased tendency to experience high anxiety levels by responding to political violence was accurate. Their findings indicated that not all women in Israel shared such symptoms. They depend on three factors: exposure to sexual and domestic violence, economic hardships, and ethnic discrimination, mainly from marginalized groups, such as Palestinians, *mezrachiot* (descended from Jews from Arab countries), and immigrants. This research follows this path and examines the differential influence of the Israeli-Palestinian conflict on different groups of women, primarily women from marginalized groups located at the intersection of multiple oppressions. For that reason, this research is performed in the small city of Ofakim, which is located in proximity to the border with Gaza and the social and cultural periphery of Israeli society.

## 3.    Method

I used a qualitative narrative analysis methodology to grasp the daily experience of the women in Ofakim. The use of narratives is anchored in an interpretative perspective that claims no objective truth exists. Instead, there is a value to the subjective meaning that people attach to the so-called "objective" events. The narrative approach follows the action of telling a life story an action of creating meaning

(Clandinin 2006; Lieblich and Josselson 1997). All the women I asked to interview (and have interviewed so far) have lived in the city of Ofakim for at least the last ten years. During this time, there had been an escalation in the violent eruption between Israel and Gaza. However, they differ in age, family status, class, and religious affiliation. Although most of the women we interviewed come from an ethnic origin of North Africa and Asia, the interviews will also include women who emigrated from the former Soviet Union, the US, and Ethiopia.

As a research tool, I conducted forty in-depth semi-structured interviews among women who live in Ofakim. A semi-structured interview allows a look into issues and perspectives that shed light on the subjective definition of the reality of the interviewee. Together with the interviewer, the interviewed woman can proactively perform the content of the questions, the type of answers, and the level of willingness on issues of her choosing (Galletta 2013.(

### 4. Ofakim

According to the Central Bureau for Statistics (CBS), the following represents statistical data for Ofakim:

> Ofakim was established in 1955 as an urban center for rural communities in the area. Until the early 1990s, the population of the town consisted mainly of Jewish immigrants from North Africa and East Asia, such as Morocco, Tunisia, Iran, Egypt, and India. In the 1990s, a large population from the former Soviet Union was sent to Ofakim, and since 2000, ultra-Orthodox people have settled in the city in large numbers. Today, according to the 2016 Central Bureau of Statistics, the population of the city is 29,312, and its grade on the socioeconomic scale is three out of ten. The percentage of the population that earns less than the average salary is 40%, and almost one-third of the household is supported by welfare services.

Like other developed cities in Israel, Ofakim suffers from a secondary employment market based on total dependence on the state due to poor planning and neglect of social, and economic aspects in the state policy. Such a reality results in a lack of employment stability, low payments, unemployment, lack of promotions, a weak education system and a low level of services (Cohan 2007).

Although the entire Israeli population is exposed to security threats, some areas are more endangered than others, and Ofakim is among them. Situated in proximity to the Gaza Strip, Ofakim has begun to suffer from an ongoing threat of rockets attacks, whether sporadic or in time of active military operations, since 2006. The city's geographic location suggests that when rockets are launched from Gaza, it takes up to forty-five seconds before they reach the area of the city. Most of the houses in the city do not have a safe room, and the number of public shelters is low and not suitable to provide safety to the population in daily life. The sporadic rocket attacks are not regarded as a situation of war by the Israeli government. These circumstances result in a lack of financial support for the population and a lack of adequate resource allocation, such as compensation for missing workdays, mental help by psychologists and social workers, and the spread of temporary shelter structures around the city. According to the literature on trauma in violent conflict, such threats do not have equal influence on the population, and among the more vulnerable population are women and people with low income (Mashich 2008).

## 5.    Results

This part focuses on several examples from the interviews conducted so far (seven interviews). The questions that were asked revolve around how the reality of the conflict affects the women's daily lives, their actions, and how they perceive their role in the situation of conflict. Alongside the talk about the danger, the devastating constant fears and worries tightly connected to their motherhood, they also downplay the effects the violent conflict has on their lives by comparing Ofakim to other places, by normalizing the worries, or by stating that they decide that the fears will not affect their lives.

The prominent themes that emerge from the interviews: are (1) the perception of security and (2) motherhood in conflict. By reading through the interviews, we found various definitions of the term "security." None of them used the language of mainstream literature or government policy. Motherhood was the central reference point of the women we interviewed concerning their gender role, actions, and perception of the situation. Interestingly, besides the worry and care for their families, motherhood was represented as the role of the breadwinner, the protector of the family, and as a concept that shapes the women's political perspective in their stories. This chapter provides an overview of the findings by providing one example for each topic.

### 5.1    What is Security?

When Ilana, a mother of three in her forties, was asked about the security situation, she connected her sense of security with her economic condition. When we asked what security means to her, she replied, "having a home." Ilana continued and tied her lack of security to the employment situation in Ofakim and matters of social security, such as education:

"Our security is also not adequate, but also our personal security as Ofakim is not wonderful. I... It's not acceptable to me that the director of Weitzman Institute (prestigious –such as NIH) has to worry about a physics teacher, like a physics teacher, simply in the school, in the Amirim school, which is thought of as a school for excellence, you don't have a physics teacher, you will have the charity of the director of the Weitzman Institute, it's... but... Tel Aviv, there is no such thing as they have no teacher, it's true the teachers do not want to come teach in the periphery."

Every time security is brought up during the interview, Ilana adds the perception of economic and social position.

"The one who has money was really able to add a safe room and the one who does not have money or who lives in a rented apartment... and even if it is his own private home and he has no money... or he is still without a safe room and he is still running to the protective shelter on the street... but the country says, like, they don't have... yet if there were even a few drops of what we have happening here, happening in Tel Aviv – the war would have arrived already, the war would have already arrived a long while ago. The division of Israel between the periphery and the center is extremely meaningful in everything. In work, in salary, and in security... Yes, in security you can see that there is something here."

Ilana's words not only reflect an awareness of the social and economic gap between the periphery and the center but also accompany the recognition of her life as worthless. Ilana's story reveals how her social position of class and ethnicity affect her sense of security and exposes what she needs to feel safe in a situation of conflict.

## 5.2    Mothers and Motherhood in a Conflict Zone

Although the interviewers never asked about or mentioned the aspect of motherhood, it turned out to be a dominant theme that frequently appeared during the interviews, shaping the experiences and perceptions of the participants' lives.

### 5.2.1   Talking about their "Lion" Mothers

The participants talked in length about their mothers. When Ilana and Yael, aged forty and sixty and both mothers themselves, talked about their own (origin) families and childhood, they hardly mentioned their fathers, and if they did, it had a negative connotation. In contrast, they spoke in-depth about their mothers as powerful women who served as role models and influenced their lives. Yael's following explanation exemplifies this circumstance.

"He [the father] says all the time that I'm sick and in pain, my mother not, my mother [pause] my mother says I'm the healthiest person in the world and the strongest in the world and my mother is very sick. Very sick. She has very severe heart problems and my mother is after the cancer that she coped with, she says I'm strong, I'm healthy no need to worry about me, I'm stronger than all of you. My mother, her personality is different to his. Really. My mother is an amazing, amazing, amazing person, she can't hear that things are bad for someone or that someone has it tough or that someone's lacking, none of it, she can't [bear to] hear it."

### 5.2.2 Motherhood as a Source of Worries

Motherhood is not only a source of admiration, but it is also a source of constant worries. As motherhood is central in our interviewees' narratives, so are the worries. Caring for children and worrying about children shapes the entire narrative of our participants to the point that worrying about children defines motherhood and vice-versa. In addition to a sense of all-consuming worries, the participants expressed more specific worries concerning children's future. In their stories, both grandmothers, Bruria and Pnina, feared that they might become criminals, if they did not provide enough for their children and grandchildren. Pnina, who is in an economically stable position, says:

"We always supported them; we always gave them everything. Because we didn't know how to say no. Like at home they didn't say to us no, we didn't say no to the kids and this, I don't know whether it was good or not. Even now I don't say no to them…let me tell you we were scared of the [pause] scared they may be going off the rails [end up in a bad place]."

Such worries may seem familiar to mothers everywhere, but when put in the context of violent conflict, these worries are amplified and become extremely dramatic. When they talk about the danger and fears of the wars and rocket attacks, their children suffered physically and emotionally from fears and anxieties. Yael told about her experience during the last war when her daughter suffered from a severe traumatic response.

"During [the] Cast Lead Operation it was so hard for me because of Orit [her daughter]. Orit's reactions were very extreme, she was so frightened. During every siren she would pee on herself without even feeling it…"

She adds:

"That last siren, boy oh boy, I won't forget that day. I worked the night shift and my husband worked the night shift and Noa [her daughter-in-law] was at her husband's jail and Orit sat here at home with the two little ones [the grandchildren, the children of her imprisoned son], I said to him [her son], 'Yair I don't know why, I have a feeling that today will be something, please don't leave Orit alone'…and afterwards at 1 am when there were sirens, there was a shelling of six, seven, I started shaking and shouting that she didn't answer the phone and I got stressed out. A friend at work said to me, take my car and go. I said to her how can I drive with all of this shelling? How will I go outside? I said to her I'm not scared about Orit; I'm scared about her reaction with two small kids at home."

### 5.2.3 Motherhood as a Motivation for Action

Above, I discussed motherhood as a source of various worries. This classification is only part of the story as these motherly worries also motivate action. If worries are an integral part of the stereotypical perception of motherhood, the actions to which they motivate are not. Both the grandmothers and mothers employ motherhood to explain why they enter the labour market, as Yael explains:

"I have four kids and I have a sick girl at home, you have to bankroll them, take care of them, you have to go out to work. You don't have a choice. And then I thought about working in a retirement home, I began working as a cleaner, and the head nurse said to me…Yael, the girls tell me that you pick up [things] and you know how to change and know this, come and do a carer's course, it will be easier for you, your salary will be higher, there are nights [night shifts], there's this, it will help you in life and she really pushed me."

Throughout all the narratives, the mothers roll up their sleeves and realize almost impossible things to save their children during rough economic times, while the fathers, if mentioned, seem to tag along. Thus, the mothers expanded their traditional role to include, what used to be considered, and to a large degree, still is, the traditional role of the fathers – providing for the family.

From the women's stories, we also learn that in their role as mothers, the women were motivated to act and impact on the public sphere. For example, Ilana began volunteering for the "Community Resilience Center" in Ofakim following her experience with her two daughters during the war. The "Community Resilience Center" is an NGO that trains people to offer first aid to trauma victims and promote community work, particularly during political violence. Ilana drew connections between her perceptions of motherhood and her volunteer work in the center.

"I do not think a woman gets more stressed, I think that a woman has the maternal thing, and even if she is not a mother, there is a kind of a lioness thing, a maternal thing when now there's a siren so I have to check that my children, everything's alright, to make calls to check that my mother and this one and that one to check everyone is ok and ... That doesn't mean I'm stressed. It's I'm like starting to work outside the box when [there's] a siren now. I have to worry to take care of my list – this one, that one, and the other, to check that everyone is okay and I'm stronger. What does a man do? It's nothing, what are you all afraid of? Well. Daddy, well I'll stand with you all… it's not that he really isn't afraid, it's just to show off [being macho]."

By establishing a connection between volunteering in her community, especially in an organization that provides aid in violent times, and her role as a mother, Ilana extended her motherly role by including the protection of her community. She, therefore, challenged the dominant perception of mothers being only in charge of their homes and families.

## 6. Discussion and Summary

By addressing the lacuna of security studies, which failed to look into the gendered effects of violent conflicts and the new wars, I delved into the question of how these wars shape the daily life of women in this paper. How do women with varied backgrounds and who live in Israel's geographical and social periphery near a conflict zone experience and make sense of their daily lives? In the first chapter of the finding, I presented the different manifestations of "security" in the women's stories. While some of them tied their state of security to their economic status, other women connected their state of security to the well-being of their children. However, their perception of security and safety was linked to their extended responsibility for their families and communities in all stories. As the second section of the result chapter reveals, the interviewees are talking in length about the all-consuming state of constantly worrying. Although the worries were of various kinds, they were all connected to motherhood in one way or the other. Many mothers experience the feeling of carrying a heavy burden of worries in times of conflict. The critical literature well supports this feeling. The Women's Security Index (2014) research found that the worries about their loved ones are one of the major causes of stress and anxiety among women during a war period. The majority of women (55%) who live with their children experience high levels of fear and worries compared with 10% among women who do not live with their children. Regarding women who feared losing their lives, the result was almost double compared of women without children.

These motherly worries do not lead to passivity or inaction. In contrast, motherhood served as a motivation for action for our participants. I illustrated how the perception of motherhood in a life of uncertainty and danger leads the women (both mother and mother-to-be) to expand their role and take actions in spaces and arenas that traditionally are not associated with motherhood. These actions include mainly breadwinning and protection. Those mothers felt their duty to provide for their families and protect them. The protection role is not limited to their own family but includes their entire community. In doing so, they offer a different and extended model of motherhood. This new image still contains grave concerns but can transform them into actions that challenge motherhood's traditional and limited perceptions.

These findings contrast the literature on security scholarship discussion, which usually refers to women as passive victims in need of protection. When referring to mothers and motherhood, it is usually the traditional role of caretakers of their family members or as the "mothers of the nation." Present findings suggest that along with the worries connected to living in a conflict zone, there are also concerns related to living in the periphery, the margin of society, such as the fear that their children may become involved in crime. Such concerns reflect the situation in Ofakim, a town with high rates of unemployment and poverty that only provides limited options for young people. Therefore, the mothers have to work much harder and be in full control if they want to secure the safety of their children. Perhaps the most explicit reference to the unique situation of living in both the periphery and a violent conflict area is expressed in the women's stories about the missing safe room. All the interviewees emphasize that they cannot afford to build a safe room, and the state does not allocate reasonable resource shelters for the people of Ofakim. It is evident that the periphery is not merely a matter of geography, as often argued in the literature, but of class and social orders (Yiftachel 2006). Moreover, the daily experience of women is shaped by their social position (McCall 2005), and in our case, by living on the periphery. The authorities neglect both their economic situation and their security.

Looking at the findings, it became clear that motherhood shaped the women's perceptions and how they experienced their lives, hopes, and fears. At the same time, the model of motherhood presented by the participants is more complex than it is usually discussed in the literature, as it challenges the traditional presentation of women and mothers. Mothers take the role of savers and warriors, especially in life-threatening situations. These actions represent motherhood not as passive victimhood but as a position of agency, resourcefulness, and courage. By emphasizing this aspect of motherhood, this research contributes to an understanding of how women cope with situations of violent conflict and to what extent this is shaped by social forces and positions, such as class, age, and gender. This understanding enables us to explore these women's interpretations of dramatic events and exposes what resources are available to them, what kind of negotiation they choose regarding their role in the society, and what risks and opportunities they have. This new knowledge is relevant to conflict resolution since it reveals the complexity and the relevance of gender to the understanding of conflict dynamics, enabling the development of alternative narratives to the hegemonic discourse about the conflict.

## References

Anderlini, S.N. 2011, 'WDR Gender Background Paper', *World Development Report Background Papers*, World Bank, Washington, DC. Retrieved: http://documents.worldbank.org/curated/en/619611468164986180/WDR-gender-background-paper.

Anderlini, S.N. 2006, 'Mainstreaming Gender in Conflict Analysis. Issues and Recommendations', *Social Development Papers*, 33.

Barnett, J., Adger, W.N. 2007, 'Climate Change, Human Security and Violent Conflict', *Political Geography*, vol. 26, no. 6, pp. 639–655.

Bar Yosef, R., Padan-Eisenstark, D. 1977, 'Role System under Stress. Sex Roles in War', *Social Problems*, vol. 25, pp. 135–145.

Ben David, Y., Idan, O. 2022, 'Talking Politics. The Delimitation of the "Political" as a Gendered Disciplinary Mechanism in Intragroup Dialogue among Young Israelis', present volume.

Ben Eliezer, A. 2009, 'Old Conflict, New War. The Changing Institutional Context of Activating Power in Israel Wars', *Israeli Sociology*, vol. 10, no. 2, pp. 403–436. [in Hebrew]

Bennett, O., Bexley, J., Warnock, K. 1995, *Arms to Fight Arms to Protect. Women Speak Out about Conflict*, Panos, London.

Berkovitch, N. 1997, 'Motherhood as a National Mission. The Construction of Womanhood in the Legal Discourse in Israel', *Women's Studies International Forum*, vol. 20, no. 5–6, pp. 605–619.

Chazan, N. 1991, 'Israeli Women and Peace Activism', in *Calling the Equality Bluff. Women in Israel*, eds B. Swirski, M. Safir, Pergamon Press, New York, pp. 152–161.

Clandinin, D.J. 2006, 'Narrative Inquiry. A Methodology for Studying Lived Experience', *Research Studies in Music Education*, vol. 27, no. 1, pp. 44–54.

Cockburn, C. 2010, 'Gender Relations as Causal in Militarization and War. A Feminist Standpoint', *International Feminist Journal of Politics*, vol. 12, no. 2, pp. 139–157.

Cockburn, C. 2001, 'The Gendered Dynamics of Armed Conflict and Political Violence', in *Victims, Perpetrators or Actors. Gendered Armed Conflict and Political Violence*, eds C.O.N. Moser, F. Clark, Zed Books, London, pp 13–29.

Cohen, A. 2007, *The Development of the Development towns: Sderot, Netivot, and Ofakim (1951–1965)*, Ben-Gurion University of the Negev, Beer Sheva.

Cohn, C. (ed) 2013, *Women and Wars. Contested Histories, Uncertain Futures*. John Wiley, New York.

Coulter, C. 2015, *Bush Wives and Girl Soldiers. Women's Lives through War and Peace in Sierra Leone,* Cornell University Press, Ithaca, NY.

Dufort, P. 2013, 'Introduction. Experiences and Knowledge of War', Cambridge Review of International Affairs, vol. 26, no. 4, pp. 611–614.

El Bushra, J., Sahl, I.M.G. 2005, *Cycles of Violence. Gender Relations and Armed Conflict,* Acord, Nairobi.

El Bushra, J. 2003, 'Fused in Combat. Gender Relations and Armed Conflict', *Development in Practice,* vol. 13, no. 2–3, pp. 252–265.

El Jack, A. 2003, *Gender and Armed Conflict. Overview Report,* BRIDGE, Institute of Development Studies, University of Sussex Brighton, UK.

Galletta, A. 2013, *Mastering the Semi-Structured Interview and Beyond. From Research Design to Analysis and Publication,* NYU Press, New York.

Golan, G. 1997, 'Militarization and Gender. The Israeli Experience', *Women Studies International Forum,* vol. 20, pp. 581–586.

Harders, C 2011, 'Gender Relations, Violence and Conflict Transformation', in *Advancing Conflict Transformation. The Berghof Handbook II,* eds B. Austin, M. Fischer, H.J. Giessmann, Barbara Budrich Publishers, Opladen/Farmington Hills, pp. 132–151.

Harel-Shalev, A., Daphna-Tekoah, S. 2015, 'Gendering Conflict Analysis. Analysing Israeli Female Combatants' Experiences', in *Female Combatants in Conflict and Peace,* ed S. Shekhawat, Palgrave Macmillan, London, pp. 69–83.

Herzog, H. 2004, 'Both an Arab and a Woman. Gendered, Racialized Experiences of Female Palestinian Citizens of Israel', *Social Identities,* vol. 10, no. 1, pp. 53–82.

Herzog, H. 2003, 'The Fighting Family. The Impact of the Arab-Israeli Conflict on the Status of Women in Israel', in *In the Name of Security. The Sociology of Peace and War in Israel in Changing Times,* eds M. Al Haj, U. Ben Eliezer, University of Haifa, Haifa, pp. 401–419. [in Hebrew]

Hyndman, J. 2008, 'Feminism, Conflict, and Disasters in Post-Tsunami Sri Lanka', *Gender, Technology, and Development,* vol. 12, no. 1, pp. 101–121.

Kaldor, M. 2013, 'In Defense of New Wars', *Stability. International Journal of Security and Development,* vol. 2, no.1, pp. 1–16.

Kinsella, H.M. 2007, 'Understanding a War That Is not a War. A Review Essay', *Signs. Journal of Women in Culture and Society,* no. 33, vol. 1, pp. 209–231.

Klein, U. 2002, 'The Gender Perspective of Civil-Military Relations in Israeli Society', Current Sociology, vol. 50, no. 5, pp. 669–686.

Lieblich, A. 1989, *Transition to Adulthood during Military Service. The Israeli Case,* State University of New York Press, Albany, NY.

Lieblich, A., Josselson, R. 1997, *The Narrative Study of Lives,* Sage, Thousand Oaks, CA.

Lubin, O. 2002, 'Gone to Soldiers. Feminism and the Military in Israel', *The Journal of Israeli History,* vol. 21, no. 1–2, pp. 164–192.

Lundy, P., McGovern, M. 2008, 'Whose Justice? Rethinking Transitional Justice from the Bottom Up', *Journal of Law and Society,* vol. 35, no. 2, pp. 265–292.

Mashiach, R.T. 2008, 'The Impact of Continued Terror. Distress and Resilience among the Israeli Population', *Social Issues in Israel*, vol. 6, pp. 6–28. [in Hebrew]

Mazali, R 2003, "And What About the Girls? What a Culture of War Genders Out of View", *Nashim. A Journal of Jewish Women's Studies and Gender Issues*, vol. 6, no. 1, pp. 39–50.

McCall, L. 2005, 'The Complexity of Intersectionality', *Signs. Journal of Women in Culture and Society*, vol. 30, no. 3, pp. 1771–1800.

Munkler, H. 2005, *The New Wars*, Polity Press, Cambridge, UK.

National Insurance Institute of Israel, Report for 2016. Retrieved: https://www.btl.gov.il/mediniyut/situation/statistics/btlstatistics.aspx?type=1andid=31

Robbins, J., Ben-Eliezer, U. 2000, 'New Roles or 'New Times'? Gender Inequality and Militarism in Israel's Nation-In-Arms', *Social Politics. International Studies in Gender, State and Society*, vol. 7, no. 3, pp. 309–342.

Rooney, E. 2005, 'Women's Equality in Northern Ireland's Transition. Intersectionality in Theory and Place', *Feminist Legal Studies*, vol. 14, no. 3, pp. 353–375.

Sachs, D, Sa'ar, A., Aharoni, S. 2007, 'How can I Feel for Others When I Myself Am Beaten? The Impact of the Armed Conflict on Women in Israel', *Sex Roles*, vol. 57, no. 7–8, pp. 593–606.

Sharoni, S. 1992, 'Every Woman is an Occupied Territory. The Politics of Militarism and Sexism and the Israeli-Palestinian Conflict', *Journal of Gender Studies*, vol. 1, no. 4, pp. 447–462.

Sjoberg, L., Via, S. 2010, 'Conclusion. The Interrelationship between Gender, War, and Militarism', in *Gender, War, and Militarism. Feminist Perspectives*, eds L. Sjoberg, S. Via, ABC-CLIO, Santa Barbara, CA, pp. 231–239.

Sylvester, C. 2012, 'War Experiences. War Practices. War Theory', *Millennium Journal of International Studies*, vol. 40, no. 3, pp. 483–503.

Sylvester, C. 2002, *Feminist International Relation. An Unfinished Journey*, Cambridge University Press, Cambridge.

Tickner, J.A. 2004, 'Feminist Responses to International Security Studies', *Peace Review*, vol. 16, no. 1, pp. 43–48.

Tickner, J.A. 1992, *Gender in International Relations. Feminist Perspectives on Achieving Global Security*, Columbia University Press, New York.

Verwimp, P., Van Bavel, J. 2013, 'Schooling, Violent Conflict, and Gender in Burundi', *The World Bank Economic Review*, vol. 28, no. 2, pp. 384–411.

Wibben, A. 2011, *Feminist Security Studies. A Narrative Approach*, Routledge, Abingdon.

Women's security Index-Report for 2014, eds A. Istoshina, I. Zamir. Retrieved: http://women-security-index.org/

Yiftachel, O. 2006, *Ethnocracy. Land and Identity Politics in Israel/Palestine,* University of Pennsylvania Press, Philadelphia, PA.

Yuval-Davis, N. 1997, *Gender and Nation*, Sage, London.

Iyad Muhsen Al Dajani

# Applied Ethics in Digital Humanities for Reconciliation Processes

## Abstract

Iyad Muhsen Al Dajani's article *Applied Ethics in Digital Humanities for Reconciliation Processes* describes a method known as Phronesis – an Aristotelian concept defined as "Prudence" – to illustrate a driven way for best practice, known as "Applied Phronesis." Using Internet Communication Technologies (ICT), Dajani introduces Applied Phronesis to reconciliation processes in the middle of a conflict (a concept denoted in the Hölderlin Perspective). The author provides a philosophical and theoretical framework that impacts social change by applying digital humanities to online social media (such as Facebook, Twitter, and YouTube) in the middle of the conflict toward the reconciliation process within societies. The article illustrates challenging, innovative methods for applying theory to practice within the reconciliation process. These concurrent research components will provide essential context and meaning for what is identified as digital research in the reconciliation process to be recognized as "Inclusive Reconciliation." This cohabitating reconciliation process in digital research, applied in digital platforms, can reach inclusivity in the reconciliation process in the middle of conflicts in different layers and construct a method of multi-inter-trans-disciplinary research and impact social change.

## 1.    Introduction

Reconciliation processes have a long history, beginning formally at the end of World War II (WWII). It is worth reminding the reader of events that have characterized the historical reconciliation process in the middle of the conflict and affected the world after wars and atrocities. Nations were, at the time, responsible for heinous crimes in history but then dealt with reconciliation processes and developed good relationships with their former enemies, perpetrators, and victims. These processes changed the minorities that wanted reconciliation into majorities, even in the middle of conflict (Leiner, 2016). What was missing was continuity, validity, and sustainability for such processes. Reconciliation was mentioned as part of a settlement agreement or peace agreement after atrocities or wars.

The context of reconciliation in digital research is proposed as a process with a broad meaning for understanding the word. It conjugates many different aspects in different domains to construct peaceful relations.Reconciliation is defined as the "restoration of relationships between individuals, groups, states after violence, war, genocide, civil war, gross human rights violations like segregation (Apartheid), enslavement, or similar activities. Reconciliation as policy requires a long term strategy with many practices with multiple levels" (Leiner, 2016, p. 183). Later, the process for developing reconciliation in the middle of conflicts was identified as the "Holderlin Perspective."

Reconciliation processes are altered within digital research platforms, focusing on alternative conflict transformation and transitional shifts. These platforms research peacebuilding, conflict transformation, transitional shifts toward peace, and reconciliation processes in the middle of the conflict. In addition, they aim to analyze conflicts to develop a common future between enemies, including researching reconciliation processes in various locations and through multiple disciplines; as a result, making an in-depth, thorough investigation into its processes, achievements, and its impact. This research on the past and future of conflicts, and the development of understanding of the deep divide between enemies in the middle of a conflict, has led to the term "*Inclusive Reconciliation Process*" and is now held as best practice.

Digital research of the reconciliation process would lead to tangible experiences of peaceful cohabitation, opportunities to stabilize and enhance non-violent conflict resolution and develop thorough practice methods and strategies. It can implement prevention strategies, mechanisms, and processes for advancing frozen, progressive, protracted, or what is known as intractable conflicts through a more dynamic change. For example, it could affect change in frozen peace processes between enemies within the conflict or elements of division or start to develop economic trade toward prosperous acknowledgment between both entities in conflict.

Digital research for reconciliation processes is considered a transdisciplinary, interdisciplinary, and multidisciplinary approach and research method. It adheres to the theoretical and methodological framework within the cohabitations of various disciplines that develop intercultural transformation and integrate knowledge about different strategies, methods, concepts, theories, and online practices. The use of internet communication technologies (ICT) necessary for digital research is considered part of an alternative method of conflict transformation and transitional shifts in conflicts in our present time.

This approach exposes human rights policies and introduces analytical and practical skills in effective conflict management for peacebuilding, peacemaking, peacekeeping, and violence prevention, including international relations cooperation between entities or enemies in conflict. It also integrates philosophical, ethical, psychological, sociological, and anthropological components with information and internet communication technologies for the purpose altered above. It can adhere to governments' social, cultural, economic, and political policies, develop shared policy decisions, and make social changes in its cultural, economic, and political capitals.

Digital research in the reconciliation process can become a method that evaluates political strategies and ongoing projects in security, international law, violence prevention, reconciliation studies, and human rights. It would evolve alternative methods of conflict transformation and develop transitional shifts such as reconciliation methods and peacebuilding. Introducing the best practices in researching and understanding the cause of conflicts impacting a wide range of stakeholders will assist in making the transition needed in the middle of conflicts towards the reconciliation process.

There are many variations of reconciliation processes in digital domains using different approaches and theories. Digital research embraces a developing new era of interdisciplinary and transdisciplinary methods of practice in conflict research that inflicted influence reconciliation processes, conflict transformation, and transitional shifts into different social science research disciplines. These new methods are therefore advancing reconciliation processes into more inter-trans-multi-disciplines research.

Digital research in the reconciliation process can cohabitate within groups that conflict in many aspects, such as in cultural, political, and economic environments. Both groups can unite in their political-economical cultural systems and develop a single political entity in the inner or outer states resulting from digital platforms. Nevertheless, in conflicts between nations, a relationship between two entities must be created to have the acceptance and the recognition of the other, apologize to each other for past adversaries and atrocities, restore good relations with good intentions, and develop a political restructuring of former relations. With the assistance of ICT, the divide between enemies in conflicts, whether in nations or communities in intractable conflicts, can be bridged.

## 2.    Concepts

In our present time, reconciliation processes cohabitating with ICTs have been researched as an alternative academic study towards developing an interactive communication of knowledge about theories and methods of peacebuilding, conflict transformation, and transitional shifts toward reconciliation processes and practices. Digital Research in reconciliation processes alters social, economic, and political capital in conflicts. It develops a bridge in the digital divide between enemies and influences intractable conflicts or conflict divisions that have persisted for an extended period.

The Jena Center for Reconciliation Studies at Friedrich-Schiller University adopted the concept of the *"Hölderlin Perspective"* for reconciliation during conflicts, as Leiner (2016) explained in his book *Latin America between Conflict and Reconciliation*. The book explains the *"Hölderlin Perspective" coming* from the German poet Friedrich Hölderlin (1770–1843), who wrote in his novel *Hyperion "Versohnung ist mitten in Streit und all Getrennte find sich wider"* (Leiner and Flamig 2012, pp. 8–18). In English, it is translated as "reconciliation is in the middle of the strife and all that was separated finds each other again" (Hölderlin 2004, p. 169).

The *Hölderlin Perspective* introduces the concept that reconciliation can develop conflict transformation by inducing a transitional shift towards peaceful relations within the conflict and transforming the minority who wants reconciliation into the majority. In the book *From Conflict Resolution to Reconciliation* by Yacov Bar-Simon-Tov (year?), many scholars state that it is always required that the majority of society support reconciliation for it to be possible or that reconciliation can happen only through a political agreement or peaceful settlement. However, from the *Hölderlin Perspective,* reconciliation must be in the middle of the conflict. It can work even within the minority to become a majority who accepts the reconciliation process. Reconciliation is holistic as an outcome and as a process; both are combined in a recurrent action to establish an effect on both parties in conflict.

By applying an Aristotelian philosophy, *Phronesis,* to reach a high level of knowledge of wisdom, accredited to the research of *Applied Phronesis in Social Science* (Flybjerg et al. 2013), ICT platforms become tools for t developing processes from theory to practice methods toward peacebuilding and reconciliation, as proposed originally by Al Dajani (2020). These new innovative methods in applying digital humanities for the reconciliation process and peacebuilding are referenced as a concept of applied Phronesis for digital research in the reconciliation process, identifying it as *Inclusive Reconciliation.*

The philosophical and theoretical framework proposed is to apply the *"Holderlin Perspective"* with its methods and strategies to compel societies in protracted or intractable conflict toward peacebuilding and reconciliation processes using ICT as a tool in the applied Phronesis philosophical framework. When used on digital platforms, a prudent level of wisdom in the middle of the conflict as part of the reconciliation process can be reached. Figure 1 below illustrates the theoretical framework foundation for digital research in the reconciliation process.

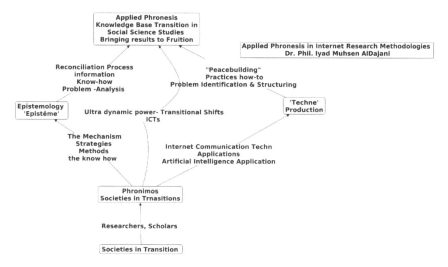

Figure 1  Applied Ethics in Digital humanities philosophical framework
Note: The Figure illustrates the Theoretical Framework Foundation for the phenomenology of Applied Phronesis for Digital Research in the Reconciliation Process.

To explore this phenomenology, Flyvbjerg (2001) calls for the "*Phronimos*," agents that orchestrate the development of change and introduce the interaction between the two elements to develop change within an ultra-dynamic power relation. The first element is '*Episteme*,' and The second element is '*Techne*.' Flyvbjerg also introduces the existence of the power relation with knowledge; "*knowledge leads to power, and power leads to knowledge* (Flyvbjerg 2001, p.89)". This develops and references it as an ultra-dynamic relation between both elements of power and knowledge to develop a new relation of change.

According to Al Dajani, Figure 1 illustrates two evolving elements that influence conflict transformation and transitional shifts towards societies' reconciliation processes in the middle of conflicts, such as conflict resolution and intractable conflicts. The participants who initiate the ultra-dynamic force for change apply these power relations to advance conflict transformation, both know-how and the how-to towards the reconciliation process. In this context, the ultra-dynamic powers are the element of internet communication technologies evolving with the *Phronimos*, the agent that introduces the change.

Figure 1 identifies knowledge of the reconciliation process as "Episteme" and ICT in the cohabitation process as "Techne." Combined and integrated, they reach the path to the reconciliation process and evolve into prudency in conflict resolution and conflict transformation. It is the evolution of different participants to develop knowledge (know-how) of reconciliation, methods, strategies, practices, and the strategies (how-to) such as reconciliation towards peacebuilding using internet communication technologies. The whole procedure develops a knowledge base in the society that thrives in a reconciliation process toward peacebuilding, conflict transformation, and transitional shifts toward a shared good common future (Al Dajani 2020). The Applied Phronesis in internet communication technologies for the reconciliation process develops a spiral mode of ultra-dynamic power exchange towards the reconciliation process. The next section explains the how-to method and describes the power ultra-dynamics for such a procedure.

### 3.  From Theory to Practice

Digital research methods and practices can enforce reconciliation methods, strategies, and practices as part of digital research integration, and they are introduced in the following, according to Al Dajani (2020, pp. 85–88):

1. Digital research endorses apology in the middle of a conflict within ICT platforms. Apology illustrates confrontation with the past and taking responsibility for the actions done during, after, and even prior to the conflict. If this type is not dealt with, reconciliation is impossible because each party portrays themselves as the victims, harbouring negative feelings; those negative feelings might instigate new conflict. As Bar-Tal and Bennink (2004, p. 29) stated, an "apology is a formal acceptance of responsibility for misdeeds carried out during the conflict and appeals to forgiveness victims. It implies pursuing justice and truth". Digital research can contribute to developing apologies through online social networks such as online forms, YouTube channels, videos, and other ICT applications. For example, it can be a unilateral apology using different ICT platforms, where entities in conflict can express sorrow about what happened during the conflict and in the past, recognize apologies and empathize with the other. These apologies can occur in online media and other means of ICTs. It is a means to express forgiveness by accepting online social media apologies between the perpetrators and victims.

2. A digital platform can reveal the truth and endorse reconciliation practices such as the Truth and Reconciliation Commissions (TRCs) created in the reconciliation process. TRCs can exist on online platforms such as Facebook, Twitter, and YouTube channels. The TRC method in online platforms can develop a way to deal with the atrocities done in the past, reveal the truth about what happened in the past, and represent it in the present time; it can be considered a mechanism to serve justice for victims of past atrocities and bridge the divide. It can reveal acts of violence, discrimination, violations of human rights, and other racist deeds in the conflict. Some of the truth and reconciliation commission aims involve establishing a comprehensive record of the cause of the brutal acts, their nature, and the extent of the violation of human rights. TRCs usually

give amnesty to perpetrators, as it transforms them into becoming part of the solution to disclose violent acts in a political context.

3. On the other hand, TRCs restore the victims' dignity by recounting their experiences and shared future. It includes preventing human rights violations and recommending that reparations as digital platforms can significantly impact the exploitation of TRCs in the reconciliation process. Digital research can help find experts in TRCs using online search engines and find other case studies, including witnesses, perpetrators, and victims, by locating them online. ICTs can spread information about TRCs occurring to millions of viewers. It can be a means of developing acknowledgment and recognition for the perpetrators' atrocities and recognizing regrets for the other's suffering.

4. Digital research can affect and publish public trials distinguishing them from online public trials. The public trials are a significant part of the reconciliation process, bringing a perpetrator to justice who committed human rights violations and crimes against humanity. Digital research using online platforms aims to expose, acknowledge, and reveal the victim's suffering and recognize the perpetrator's violent acts. When trials are carried out, it can be online, where victims can see that perpetrators are brought to justice for the deeds and atrocities committed under their jurisdictions in the past. A type of retribution occurs for the victim; therefore, justice was carried out in front of a live audience using online platforms. However, those trials are subject to only the perpetrator and not the group, which allows them to be a part of the reconciliation process. ICT exposes trails by making them public, introducing what happens in the conflict, and developing archives to store memories and histories of atrocities. They can also store peace agreements or conduct peacebuilding and reconciliation processes to learn from them to develop best practices.

5. The digital platform can also be used for reparations given within online platforms. This method is most appealing in the reconciliation process. It requests parties to take responsibility for wrongdoing and compensate the victims of the atrocity committed by entities in the conflict. This method indicates the admission of guilt and the recognition of the other's suffering, where the victim is willing to forgive his or her perpetrator. ICT platforms and applications can develop a medium for donations to support reconciliation processes, such as endorsing victims of conflict.

6. Digital platforms can be used for writing a shared common history for parties in conflict. It calls for recreating past history, as agreed on by the parties who conflicted. The past can be learned from its atrocities and the idea of "Never Again." It takes historians from both sides to agree on a shared history and negotiate an agreed past of both parties' memories that may contradict. It also provides a basis for a new collective memory, which leads toward reconciliation. It can document archives of each group's history and memories using online

media and online video archives or online research hubs. ICT can also develop a shared history of those in conflict by building a blog or other database with documents, photos, and videos. Both parties can store their memories and histories online, which develops an understanding of the other's narrative and moves society closer to empathy.

7. Digital platforms can support the education endorsing reconciliation process. It can introduce change within the past's psychological barriers, thereby promoting reconciliation education involving peace studies and reconciliation studies and influencing society's students and members to think about change. Education constructs the students' ways of thinking, such as their values, beliefs, attitudes, motivations, skills, and behaviors. Through education, reconciliation processes are endorsed, preparing them to live in an era of peace and conflict transformation. It can expose reconciliation theories, such as online courses, to teach peacebuilding and the reconciliation processes in various cases.

8. Digital Platforms are an innovative way to cross borders and bridge ideas between entities for peacebuilding and reconciliation on online social platforms such as Facebook, Twitter, YouTube, LinkedIn, etc. Online platforms can bridge communication between nations in conflict, as they can help expose their views across the globe. Today, digital research depending on online platforms has become part of daily human life as it is part of people's mobility, social, communicative, and political habits. As such, it can spread information about new reconciliation strategies that can influence nations in conflict. Most importantly, digital research can serve as a channel for communication to send messages for peace and reconciliation to different rivals in conflict.

9. Digital research can develop online publications such as encyclopaedias and book series exposing worldwide research on the varieties of the reconciliation process to be identified all over the internet.

10. Exposing non-governmental organizations (NGOs) empirical work in the reconciliation processes using digital research platforms. Non-governmental organizations (NGOs) that are either part of the society or from an international community can contribute to reconciliation. NGOs can illustrate that peace relations can benefit societies in conflict by spreading messages about the importance of the reconciliation process, the prosperity of reconciliation, and the benefits of having peaceful relations with past enemies. The digital platform can help connect NGOs against the conflict to develop communication and build peacebuilding and reconciliation processes knowledge.

11. Online joint reconciliation workshops and projects are significant, as these can bridge and break barriers between enemies who conflict. It can facilitate and research psychological reconciliation. It can connect members of two groups from different levels of society in the same project. Online digital platforms allow different members from different parties in conflict to have personal

Applied Ethics in Digital Humanities for Reconciliation Processes | **303**

encounters and group encounters to work together towards a reconciliation process, compelling the minority that is for reconciliation into becoming a majority.

12. Culture exchange in digital research can help those in conflict to exchange cultures through online videos and other interactive chat applications. This exchange can help each opponent in conflict learn about the other through translating books, visiting artists, and learning from academics from different conferences, exhibitions, festivals, games, and other online documentaries to help expose other cultures to those in conflict.

13. Enhancing empathy in conflict using virtual reality as part of digital research exposes different perspectives on what is happening in the conflict. It might develop empathy towards the other, understanding one's own enemies' narrative, and develop indirect empathy with one's enemy.

## 4.    Summary

Digital research in the reconciliation process calls for restructuring social, cultural, economic, and political spheres in the middle of conflicts. This restructured system can be implemented in both outer and inner groups to develop conflict transformation and transitional shifts toward the reconciliation process in the middle of conflicts. The reconciliation process is always illustrated between enemies or within the inner-groups, reconciliation within entities in conflict. Digital research in the reconciliation process links a means to investigate the cause of violence, violence prevention, and the paths towards transforming protracted and intractable conflicts by inducing a shared common future. This type of reconciliation mechanism method, such as the applied Phronesis in the reconciliation process using internet communication technologies, develops inclusivity, validity, and sustainability and can be referenced as the "Inclusive Reconciliation Process."

Digital research is the means and ends for advancing peacebuilding, peacekeeping, and peacemaking into reconciliation in the middle of conflicts. It develops strategies and methods to overcome the impasse in social, political, or regional conflicts by analyzing and interpreting their causes and researching different conflict transformation approaches. Digital research then facilitates transitional shifts into developing an "Inclusive Reconciliation Process" that adheres to conflict resolution and can then build a common shared future between adversaries.

One of the important aspects of developing digital research in the reconciliation process is reaching validity and lasting sustainability. Then, a better-shared future between enemies who acknowledge the other's narrative in different conflict dilemmas such as social, cultural, and political spheres can emerge. Also, it introduces a mutual recognition and knowledge of the other's narrative and bridging relations of cohabitation for former enemies. Also, it recognizes the interests and goals of both entities in conflict, providing the environment for mutual trust, mutual recognition, development of cultural, economic, and political relations, and respecting the sensitivity and consideration of the other parties' needs in bridging the conflict divide.

The concept for the theory of Applied Phronesis in Internet Communication Technologies can be adopted to explore the reconciliation process's ramifications and other social science disciplines. Usually, such research investigating the influence of change in research studies for reconciliation using internet communication technologies is referred to as digital research in reconciliation studies. For example, applying ICT in Phronetic social science, such as the phenomenology of ICT for social change toward reconciliation processes (AlDajani, 2020), can be part of the digital research on the reconciliation process. Phronesis is prudent and often taken from Habermas' *The Abstract of the Force for a Better Argument* (Flyvbjerg, 2001, p. 96).

The theoretical framework for digital research is the collaboration of knowledge and technology as one part of the philosophical and theoretical framework integrating different methods such as the *Hölderlin Perspective,* the episteme part, and applied Phronesis in Internet communication technologies. Inputting this theoretical framework into the reconciliation process as a techne part to reach Phronesis in the reconciliation process using any digital platform will create a new method of addressing conflict. The concept would develop a communicative knowledge of the relationship between two parts, epistemology and Techne, and apply the Habermas appeal for the force of a better argument Phronesis.

This application of reconciliation terminology, philosophy, and techniques will lead to a social change toward a reconciliation action process inhabiting digital platforms. The article illustrated how to develop digital research on the reconciliation process from the abstract view into practice and how transitional shifts and conflict transformation can evolve from conducting such research.

Table 1  Digital Research in the Reconciliation Process for conflict transformation for online digital online participants behaviour (hermeneutics).

| Methods for the Reconciliation process | Netnography | Conflict Transformation Practice | Examples of ICTs |
|---|---|---|---|
| Apology<br>Education<br>Published meetings<br>Truth and reconciliation commissions<br>Public Trials<br>Reparations Payments<br>The Work of NGOs<br>Joint Projects | Introspection<br>Investigation<br>Information<br>Interview inspection<br>interaction<br>immersion<br>indexing<br>interpretation<br>iteration<br>instantiation<br>integration | Provide Information | Internet Connectivity<br>Mobile Phone and personal<br>Data assistant.<br>Geographic Information systems.<br>Forums<br>Radio<br>Chat<br>Videos |
| Writing a common history<br>Published meetings<br>Truth and reconciliation commissions<br>Public Trials<br>Reparations Payments<br>The Work of NGOs<br>Joint Projects | As the Above | Help People Process Information | Social Network sites, and portals.<br>Data Visualization Tools.<br>Online dispute resolution tools. |
| Education<br>Public Trials<br>The Work of NGOs<br>Joint Projects | As the Above | Improve decision making | Virtual Command Center.<br>Games and Simulations<br>Online dispute resolution tools. |
| Education<br>The Work of NGOs<br>Joint Projects | As the Above | Reduce Scarcity | Mobile Phones.<br>The hand-Held portable devices, such as iPad, Tablets. |
| Apology<br>Published meetings.<br>Truth and reconciliation commissions<br>Public Trials<br>Reparations Payments<br>The Work of NGOs<br>Joint Projects | As the Above | Support Relationship | Social Network Tools<br>Online Collaboration Tools<br>Mobile Phones<br>Virtual Reality<br>Telecenters. |
| Apology<br>Truth and reconciliation commissions<br>Public Trials<br>Reparations Payments<br>Joint Projects<br>The Work of NGOs | As the Above | Help People Understand Each other | Translation Software Blogs.<br>Social Network Tools.<br>Multimedia |

Finally, the table describes digital research in the reconciliation process and its impact on social change towards the reconciliation process within cultural, political, and economic capitals. As a result, one can understand that digital research can be an instrument one may use to influence conflict transformation and transitional shifts toward peacebuilding and reconciliation processes. It can develop methods and strategies for dialogue in conflicts, recognition of the narrative of the other, negotiations, coexistence, and peace towards a democratic society (Aldajani,2020).

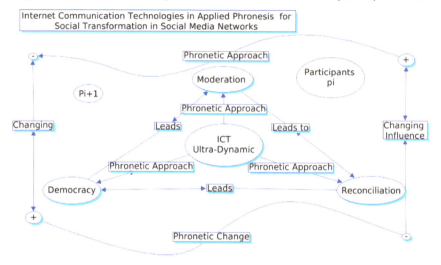

Figure 2   The Figures illustrated the procedure of applied ethics in digital humanities for the reconciliation process. Introducing in practice the conflict transformation and transitional shifts toward the reconciliation process in the middle of conflict using Internet communication technologies.

The article is derived from a monograph published as a book by Springer ltd International; the book title is *Internet Communication Technologies for Reconciliation: Applied Phronesis Netnography in Internet Research Methodologies.*

## References

AlDajani I. M. (2020) Internet Communication Technologies for Reconciliation: Applied Phronesis Netnography in Internet Research Methodologies, Springer. https://doi.org/10.1007/978-3-030-41203-6

Al-Dajani, I, Leiner (2019) Reconciliation In The Middle Of The Israelis Palestinian Conflict, In Palestinian Israel Journal, Jerusalem, pp. 119–125.

Bar-Siman-Tov, Y. (2004). From Conflict to Reconciliation. Oxford: University Press.

Charlamobs Vrasidas, Michalinos Zembylas, Gene V Glass. (2009). ICT for Education, Development, and social justice. Charlotte: Information Age.

Creswel, J. W. (2014), Research Design Qualitative, Quantitative, and Mixed Method. California: SAGE.

Creswell J., Vicki L, Clark P. (2018). Designing and Conducting Mixed Method Research. California: SAGE Publication.

Dietrich, W. (2014). "A Brief Introduction to Transrational Peace Research and Elicitive Conflict Transformation" [online article]. Journal of Conflictology. Vol. 5, Iss. 2, pp. 48–57. Campus for Peace, UOC. [Consulted: 09/09/20].

Dietrich W. (2012), *Interpretations of Peace in History and Culture.* Translated by Norbert Koppensteiner, Many Peaces, Vol. 1. London: Palgrave Macmillan.

Dietrich W. (2013), *Elicitive Conflict Transformation and the Transrational Turn in Peace Politics.* Translated by Wolfgang Sützl and Victoria Hindley, Many Peaces, Vol. 2. London: Palgrave Macmillan.

Dietrich W., Echavarría J., Esteva G., Ingruber D. & Koppensteiner N. (eds.). 2011. *The Palgrave International Handbook of Peace Studies: A Cultural Perspective.* London: Palgrave Macmillan.

Flyvbjerg, B. (2001). Making Social Science Matter. Cambridge: Cambridge University Press.

Flyvbjerg, B., Landman, T., & Schram, S. (Eds.). (2012). Real Social Science: Applied Phronesis.Cambridge: Cambridge University Press. doi:10.1017/CBO9780511719912

Kevin Hill R. (2017) The Will to Power (Penguin Classics) Paperback – March 28, 2017, by Friedrich Nietzsche, Kindle edition.

Kozinets, R. (2015). Netnography Redefined. London: SAGE Publication Ltd.

Krippendorff, K. (2013). Content Analysis, An Introduction to its methodology. California: SAGA Publication Ltd.

Leiner, M. (2016). Thinking differently about identity and harmony - The Potential of Asian thinking for reconciliation. In Asia-Pacific between Conflict and Reconciliation (p. 293). Gottingen: Vandenhoeck & Ruprecht GmbH & Co. KG.

Leiner M. Flamig S. (2012), Latin America between Conflict and Reconciliation. Bristol: Vandenhoeck & Ruprecht LLC.

Leiner M. (2016) Thinking differently about Identity and Harmony - The Potential of Asian thinking for reconciliation. Is reconciliation a topic for East Asia? In: Phillip Tolliday/ Maria Palme/Dong-Choon Kim /ed.), Asia-Pacific between Conflict and Reconciliation, Göttingen: Vandenhoeck & Ruprecht, pp. 185, 186.

Leiner M., Palme M., & Stöckner P. (eds), Societies in Transition. Sub-Saharan Africa between Conflict and Reconciliation, Vandenhoeck & Ruprecht, Göttingen, 2014.

Leiner M. & Flämig S. (eds), Latin America between Conflict and Reconciliation, Vandenhoeck & Ruprecht, Göttingen, 2012.

Leiner M. & Schliesser C. (eds), Alternative Approaches in Conflict Resolution, Palgrave, London 2018.

Newman. (2010). Networks. Oxford: Oxford University Press.

Rehrmann C., Biermann R., Tolliday P. (eds) (2020), Societies in Transition. The Balkans and South Caucasus between Conflict and Reconciliation, Vandenhoeck & Ruprecht, Göttingen, 2020.

Tolliday P., Kim D.C.& Palme M. (eds), (2015), East Asia and Australia between Conflict and Reconciliation, Vandenhoeck & Ruprecht, Göttingen.

## About the Editors

Francesco Ferrari, Ph.D., is a post-doc researcher and lecturer at the Friedrich-Schiller University Jena and Goethe University Frankfurt; he collaborates with the Academy of Sciences and Literature of Mainz (project "Buber Korrespondenzen Digital"); he is the coordinator of the Jena Center for Reconciliation Studies (JCRS) and its doctoral school Religion Conflict Reconciliation. He wrote three monographs dedicated to Martin Buber's thought, served as editor of volume 11 of Martin Buber's Werkausgabe (*Schriften zur politischen Philosophie und zur Sozialphilosophie*), and is also the author of several essays and translations regarding authors from the Jewish philosophy and culture of the XX century (among which Arendt, Buber, Derrida, Landauer, S. Zweig). His current research deals with the concept of reconciliation after Auschwitz.

Martin Leiner is director of the Jena Center for Reconciliation Studies (JCRS) at Friedrich Schiller University Jena and professor of Systematic Theology and Ethics. He is the leader of the DFG-project "Hearts of Flesh–Not Stone." He received his Ph.D. in Heidelberg University with Prof. Theißen on "Psychologie und Exegese" (published by Gütersloh 1995) about the introduction of psychological concepts, methods, and results of research to understand better the New Testament. His habilitation was in Mainz on Martin Buber and his reception in protestant theology. Published as *Gottes Gegenwart*, Gütersloh 2000. He published a manual with methods for systematic theology and philosophy of religion (*Methodischer Leitfaden Systematische Theologie und Religionsphilosophie*, Göttingen 2008). Since 2008, Professor Leiner has been working on transdisciplinary Reconciliation Studies from a global perspective. In 2013, Prof. Leiner founded the Jena Center for Reconciliation Studies (JCRS).

Dr. Zeina M. Barakat is a Jerusalem-born Palestinian scholar who holds a doctorate from Friedrich-Schiller University in Jena, Germany. Since 2019 she is a Research Associate fellow at the Von Hügel Institute, University of Cambridge, and undertaking postdoctoral research. She taught at al-Quds University in Jerusalem, Europa-Universität Flensburg, and Friedrich-Schiller University in Jena. She is the author of many academic books and articles including, *Sexual Harassment* (2012), one of the few books in Arabic dealing with this taboo topic in Arab society. She is a co-author of *Holocaust: Human Agony: Is there a Way out of Violence* (2012) and co-editor of *Teaching Empathy and Reconciliation in the Midst of Conflict* (2016). She is also a contributing author of *Jerusalem from the Lens of Wasatia* (2010),

*The Future of Jerusalem* (2012), and *Israelis and Palestinians: Contested Narratives* (2013). Her book, *From Heart of Stone to Heart of Flesh: Evolutionary journey from Extremism to Moderation*, (2017), and co-editor of *Islam and Democracy: Law, Gender and the West* (2022), and co-editor *Reconciliation and Refugees: The Academic Alliance for Reconciliation Studies in the Middle East and North Africa I*, (2022). Her most recent book, *Envisioning Reconciliation: Signs of Hope for the Middle East*, was published in (2022). Her current position is the Executive Director of the European Graduate School for Peace and Conflict Resolution at Europa-Universität Flensburg, Germany.

Michael Sternberg is a postdoctoral fellow at the Martin Springer Center for Conflict Studies at the Ben-Gurion University of the Negev. His studies focus on the contribution of dialogue, community-based strategies, and action research to conflict transformation. He is interested in the interrelation between intergroup and ingroup conflict in the context of intractable conflicts and in potential strategies and interventions that may contribute to socio-political discourse attuned to openness towards the other and readiness for reconciliation. He received a Ph.D. in conflict management and resolution from Ben-Gurion University. Michael holds an MA in applied conflict transformation studies from Novi Sad University (Serbia) and sociology and social anthropology from the Hebrew University of Jerusalem.

Boaz Hameiri is a Senior Lecturer in the Program in Mediation and Conflict Management at Tel Aviv University. He received his Ph.D. in social psychology at Tel Aviv University in 2019. Between 2018 and 2020, he was a Postdoctoral Fellow in the Peace and Conflict Neuroscience Lab at the University of Pennsylvania. His research program consists of examining different psychological barriers to attitude change and conflict resolution and the development of psychological interventions to address these barriers and promote better intergroup relations and conflict resolution.

# About the Authors

Dr. Iyad Al-Dajani's research areas are in Applied Computer Science and Digital Humanities for reconciliation and peace education. He holds a doctorate from Friedrich-Schiller University, Jena, Germany, and is an ICT application reconciliation studies, educational scholar. He who earned a Bachelor's in Computer Sciences and was awarded a Certificate of Completion for the Executive Education Program in Cybersecurity: The Intersection of Policy and Technology Program at John F. Kennedy School of Government at Harvard University & Awarded a certificate of completion for the Leading in Artificial Intelligence: Exploring Technology and Policy Program from Harvard Kennedy School of Government at Harvard University, Executive Education and awarded a certificate from Oxford Artificial Intelligence program from Saïd Business School, the University of Oxford and a Reference Class Forecasting practitioner for the Oxford Global Projects Academy School, University of Oxford, a Master's in Regional and American Studies from the Al-Quds University. He then became a webmaster and obtained a Master's in web-development certificate from HackerU in Tel-Aviv.

Dr. Zeina M. Barakat is a Jerusalem-born Palestinian scholar who holds a doctorate from Friedrich-Schiller University in Jena, Germany. Since 2019 she is a Research Associate fellow at the Von Hügel Institute, University of Cambridge, and undertaking postdoctoral research. She taught at al-Quds University in Jerusalem, Europa-Universität Flensburg, and Friedrich-Schiller University in Jena. She is the author of many academic books and articles including, *Sexual Harassment* (2012), one of the few books in Arabic dealing with this taboo topic in Arab society. She is a co-author of *Holocaust: Human Agony: Is there a Way out of Violence* (2012) and co-editor of *Teaching Empathy and Reconciliation in the Midst of Conflict* (2016). She is also a contributing author of *Jerusalem from the Lens of Wasatia* (2010), *The Future of Jerusalem* (2012), and *Israelis and Palestinians: Contested Narratives* (2013). Her book, *From Heart of Stone to Heart of Flesh: Evolutionary journey from Extremism to Moderation*, (2017), and co-editor of *Islam and Democracy: Law, Gender and the West* (2022), and co-editor *Reconciliation and Refugees: The Academic Alliance for Reconciliation Studies in the Middle East and North Africa I*, (2022). Her most recent book, *Envisioning Reconciliation: Signs of Hope for the Middle East*, was published in (2022). Her current position is the Executive Director of the European Graduate School for Peace and Conflict Resolution at Europa-Universität Flensburg, Germany.

Dr. Yael Ben David is a social and organizational psychologist and a faculty member at the Baruch Ivcher School of Psychology at Reichman University. Her work focuses on small group dynamics and the role of social power hierarchies in group discourse. She also explores the implications of virtuality and hybridity on group work and teams. Her research contains an active dialogue with the social and organizational field. Dr. Ben David has a MA in Social Psychology from Tel Aviv University and a Ph.D. in sociology from Ben-Gurion University. She was a research fellow and a post-doc at Truman Institute, the Hebrew University of Jerusalem.

Sharón Benheim is currently a doctoral student in the conflict management and resolution program at the Ben-Gurion University of the Negev. She holds a B.Sc in psychology from the University of Maryland, attended the Hebrew University of Jerusalem graduate program in clinical/medical psychology, and in 2008 she completed an MA in public policy: mediation and conflict resolution at Tel Aviv University. Sharón currently serves as the Martin Springer Center for Conflict Studies coordinator at the Ben-Gurion University of the Negev. Sharón is interested in peace education, the long-term impact of participation in environmental peacebuilding programs, and intergroup processes, relationships, and conflicts.

Dr. Dina Dajani Daoudi was born in Amman, Jordan, and raised in Jerusalem. She holds a Ph.D. in Reconciliation Studies from the Friedrich-Schiller University of Jena, where she also instructed in the Political Science Department. She received her Bachelor of Arts in political studies from the American University of Beirut and a Master of Arts in European Studies from Heinrich Heine University Düsseldorf. Dr. Dajani Daoudi coordinated the JAS/ Empower Global School Learning Solutions Pilot for Supporting Adolescent Girls in Palestine. She worked as a researcher with the Georg Eckert Institute for International Textbook Research. She was a senior educator on the Israeli-Palestinian conflict with Abraham's Vision, Center for Transformative Education. She also coordinated the International/Academic Summer Project at the Issam Sartawi Center, worked as a senior researcher and editor at Wasatia and was the Head of the International Relations Unit at the Palestinian Agricultural Disaster Risk Reduction and Insurance Fund (PADRRIF).

Dr. Manar Faraj is from Dheisheh Refugee Camp in Bethlehem, Palestine. She got her Ph.D. at the Friedrich-Schiller University Jena. Faraj focuses on women, refugees, reconciliation, and conflict. She holds a bachelor's degree in Global Trade from High Point University in the United States and a master's degree in Peace and Reconciliation from Coventry University in the United Kingdom. She has studied peace methods and conflict transformation in a number of international settings, including Rwanda, and she also obtained a Conflict Transformation Certificate from the School of International Training in Vermont. Throughout her career, she has lectured, managed programs, and implemented projects related to conflict in several different countries, also working as a facilitator, project manager, and consultant in peace and conflict initiatives in countries such as Libya and Lebanon.

Francesco Ferrari, Ph.D., is a post-doc researcher and lecturer at the Friedrich-Schiller University Jena and Goethe University Frankfurt; he collaborates with the Academy of Sciences and Literature of Mainz (project "Buber Korrespondenzen Digital"); he is the coordinator of the Jena Center for Reconciliation Studies (JCRS) and its doctoral school Religion Conflict Reconciliation. He wrote three monographs dedicated to Martin Buber's thought, served as editor of volume 11 of Martin Buber's Werkausgabe (*Schriften zur politischen Philosophie und zur Sozialphilosophie*), and is also the author of several essays and translations regarding authors from the Jewish philosophy and culture of the XX century (among which Arendt, Buber, Derrida, Landauer, S. Zweig). His current research deals with the concept of reconciliation after Auschwitz.

Rahav Gabay is a Ph.D. student at Tel Aviv University. She is interested in conflicts in interpersonal relationships and, more specifically, the tendency for interpersonal victimhood and its effects within relationships. In her research, she built an empirical tool to measure the personality tendency for victimhood and investigated its cognitive biases and behavioral effects. Rahav is also interested in personal development and people's ability to overcome feelings of victimization to create a sense of internal locus of control. She applies insights from her research to therapy by using tools such as mindfulness and guided imagination.

Boaz Hameiri is a Senior Lecturer in the Program in Conflict Management and Mediation at Tel Aviv University. He received his Ph.D. in social psychology at Tel Aviv University in 2019. Between 2018 and 2020, he was a Postdoctoral Fellow in the Peace and Conflict Neuroscience Lab at the University of Pennsylvania. His research program consists of examining different psychological barriers to attitude change and conflict resolution and the development of psychological interventions to address these barriers and promote better intergroup relations and conflict resolution.

Orly Idan is a lecturer in psycholinguistics, language in the context of conflict, and academic research at Reichman University (Interdisciplinary Center, Herzliya), and a senior associate researcher at the Psychology of Intergroup Conflict and Reconciliation Lab, The Hebrew University of Jerusalem. She was a postdoctoral associate at the Salutogenic Research Center and the Conflict Management Program at the Ben-Gurion University of the Negev, focusing on salutogenic interventions in conflictual settings. Her Ph.D. dissertation from Tel Aviv University focused on resilience sources, socio-emotional self-perceptions, family climate, and hopeful thinking among students. She completed her MA degree in psycholinguistics at Tel Aviv University. Her current research interests and teaching domains focus on the role of linguistic cues in inducing emotions, in particular within the context of intractable conflicts and negotiations; discourse and narrative analysis in the context of conflict and health; a comparison of native and foreign language use relating to conflict, in particular, Hebrew and Arabic; and, attitude change in the context of intractable conflicts.

Yoav Kapshuk is a Lecturer at Kinneret College on the Sea of Galilee, Israel, and Head of the Israel Studies Unit at the Department of Multidisciplinary Studies. Visiting Fellow in the Summer of 2018 and 2019 at the LSE Middle East Center and 2017 at the Peace Research Institute Frankfurt. Dr. Kapshuk's research focuses on the Israeli-Palestinian conflict, transitional justice, and conflict resolution. He received his Ph.D. in Political Science and International Relations from Tel-Aviv University (2017).

Martin Leiner is director of the Jena Center for Reconciliation Studies (JCRS) at Friedrich Schiller University Jena and professor of Systematic Theology and Ethics. He is the leader of the DFG-project "Hearts of Flesh–Not Stone." He received his Ph.D. in Heidelberg University with Prof. Theißen on "Psychologie und Exegese" (published by Gütersloh 1995) about the introduction of psychological concepts, methods, and results of research to understand better the New Testament. His habilitation was in Mainz on Martin Buber and his reception in protestant theology. Published as *Gottes Gegenwart*, Gütersloh 2000. He published a manual with methods for systematic theology and philosophy of religion (*Methodischer Leitfaden Systematische Theologie und Religionsphilosophie*, Göttingen 2008). Since 2008, Professor Leiner has been working on transdisciplinary Reconciliation Studies from a global perspective. In 2013, Prof. Leiner founded the Jena Center for Reconciliation Studies (JCRS).

Becky Leshem wrote her dissertation on the subject of "Exposure to community violence and its impact on adolescents in Israel: Can parent and teacher support moderate the impact of exposure?" at the Hebrew University of Jerusalem. Her study mapped the characteristics of exposure to community violence among Jewish adolescents in Israel by testing the psychological, behavioral, cognitive, and somatic effects of exposure to community violence. She examines the ability of family and teacher support to moderate the impact of exposure to violence. Continuing her research on the effects of community violence and related factors in various populations, she focused more and more on the effects of political violence and conflict resolution.

Shiri Levinas is an expert in conflict transformation. Specializing in gender and conflict, she combines fieldwork with academic research. In the last fifteen years, Shiri has devoted her time and effort to promoting reconciliation among social groups who face conflict by developing and facilitating programs that train women in peace politics. Other projects of hers promote dialog and reconciliation among social groups in Israel and work with the education system on CRE (Conflict Resolution Education). She is one of the founders of Women Wage Peace and is currently a Ph.D. candidate at the Ben-Gurion University of the Negev. Shiri holds an MA in conflict resolution from the IDC University in Herzliya.

Arie Nadler, Ph.D. (1976, Psychology, Purdue University, USA) is a Professor Emeritus of Psychology at Tel Aviv University (1988). He served as the Head of the Psychology Department (1984–1988) and Dean of the Faculty of Social Sciences at Tel Aviv University (1993–1998). He co-founded the Tami Steinmetz Center for Peace Research and served as the first head of its academic committee (1992–2002), and established and was the first head of the Institute for Diplomacy and Regional Cooperation at Tel Aviv University (1999–2003). Prof. Nadler was the incumbent of the Argentina Chair of the Psychology of Conflict and Cooperation (2000–2014), established by the Argentinean Friends of Tel Aviv University. Professor Nadler served as the Chairperson of the Israeli Trustees Foundation (formerly the Ford Foundation, Israel) to support research in Israel's social sciences and education. His publications include over 150 scientific papers, many of which are in top journals in his field, and edited and written books published by reputable publishers (e. g., Academic Press, Oxford University Press, Wiley). His major research interests are: (a) Psychological processes of interpersonal and intergroup reconciliation and (b) Interpersonal and intergroup helping as hierarchical and solidarity-based social relationships. Professor Nadler also served as the chairperson of NGOs in Israel (e. g., "the council for the child in placement") and consulted in his areas of expertise in non-profit and for-profit organizations (e. g., Intel Electronics, Israeli Ministry of Finance).

Martin J. O'Malley is a research scholar and instructor at the Center for Applied Ethics (Ethikzentrum) at the Friedrich-Schiller University, Jena where he has been since 2007. He is chair of the university's Ethics Commission/Internal Review Board and is associated with the Jena Center for Reconciliation Studies (JCRS), having worked as FSU coordinator of the "Hearts of Flesh–Not Stone" project from 2013 until 2018. He teaches in the MA program "Applied Ethics and Conflict Management" on topics of negotiation theory and contemporary philosophical ethics. Research areas include reconciliation, value ethics, conceptual analysis, ethics of emerging sciences, and pragmatism. A graduate of Hamilton College (BA 1988), he received an MA in Philosophy at St. Louis University (1993). He holds advanced degrees from Weston Jesuit School of Theology in Cambridge, USA (MDiv 1998, Licentiate-STL 2008). O'Malley holds a Ph.D. from Boston College in theological ethics (2007). He held teaching fellowships at Harvard University (1996, 1998) and Boston College (2004, 2005) and was an instructor at LeMoyne College (1993–1995) and Loyola College, Maryland (2004–2006).

Tammy Rubel-Lifschitz is an academic faculty member at the Department of Sociology and Anthropology at the Hebrew University of Jerusalem and head of the MA program in Organizational Studies. She received her Ph.D. in organizational behavior from the Hebrew University in 2016, where she also graduated with an MA in social psychology in 2005. Her work focuses on organizational development and research. She is particularly interested in interpersonal relations, including collaboration, conflict, and power dynamics, as well as the interplay between personality traits, such as a tendency for interpersonal victimhood, and organizational or social power positions. Her research was published in leading academic journals, such as the Journal of Personality and Social Psychology, Organizational Analysis, and Peace and Conflict.

Shifra Sagy is professor emerita of psychology in the Department of Education at the Ben-Gurion University of the Negev in Israel. She is a former chair of the Department of Education and founding director of the multidisciplinary graduate program of conflict management and resolution. She is the head of the Martin Springer Center of Conflict Studies at BGU. Sagy's major research interests are salutogenesis, coping, and adjustment to stressors, both normative and non-normative. She is also involved in studies in political psychology concerning the historical and political consciousness of Israelis and Palestinians. She has published both empirical and theoretical articles extensively in a variety of professional journals in the USA, Europe, and Israel. During the past three decades, Sagy has been involved in peace education in the Palestinian-Israeli context: teaching, lecturing, writing, researching, participating and initiating dialogue workshops.

Anat Sarid is a doctoral student in the conflict management and resolution program at Ben-Gurion University. She finished her MA in social psychology at Tel Aviv University in 2001 and has worked as an evaluator in several educational organizations. Her research is about the effect that a sense of national coherence has on the willingness to end the conflict in peaceful ways in the context of the Israeli-Palestinian conflict.

Anan Srour received his doctoral degree upon completing the conflict management and conflict resolution program at Ben-Gurion University in the Negev. The title of his dissertation is "Sense of community coherence, collective narrative perceptions, and openness to the 'other' group: The case of Muslim-Christian relationships in Israel." His interests include studying the perception of collective narratives as a method to understand intergroup relations in various conflictual contexts. Anan works as a professional supervisor in educational psychology, and he is the director of the psychological team in the center for psychological services in East Jerusalem. He has also worked as a team supervisor for several psychosocial organizations in the West Bank. He is co-editor of the book *Israeli and Palestinian Collective Narratives in Conflict: A Tribute to Shifra Sagy and Her Work* (2020).

Michael Sternberg is a postdoctoral fellow at the Martin Springer Center for Conflict Studies at the Ben-Gurion University of the Negev. His studies focus on the contribution of dialogue, community-based strategies, and action research to conflict transformation. He is interested in the interrelation between intergroup and ingroup conflict in the context of intractable conflicts and in potential strategies and interventions that may contribute to socio-political discourse attuned to openness towards the other and readiness for reconciliation. He received a Ph.D. in conflict management and resolution from Ben-Gurion University. Michael holds an MA in applied conflict transformation studies from Novi Sad University (Serbia) and sociology and social anthropology from the Hebrew University of Jerusalem.

André Zempelburg holds a Ph.D in religious studies from the Friedrich-Schiller University Jena. He is associated with the Jena Center for Reconciliation Studies (JCRS). His research interests are philosophy of religion, biblical, rabbinic and qur'anic studies. André mainly focuses on the concept of reconciliation in religions, religious myths and the relation of religion and AI.

Efrat Zigenlaub, Ph.D., is a socio-organizational psychologist, a candidate at the Israeli Institute for Group Analysis, and a group facilitator and advisor in various public and commercial organizations. Her research deals with relationships and dynamics between groups in conflict. She teaches group facilitation and conflict resolution courses at the Netanya Academic College of Arts and Society, the Haifa University School of Social Work (the Bnei-Brak branch), and the Tel Aviv University two-year Group Facilitation Program.